FileMaker® 8
FUNCTIONS
and Scripts
DESK
REFERENCE

Scott Love
Steve Lane
Bob Bowers

QUE®

800 East 96th Street, Indianapolis, Indiana 46240 USA

FileMaker 8 Functions and Scripts Desk Reference

International Standard Book Number: 0-7897-3511-3

Library of Congress Catalog Card Number: 2005938385

Printed in the United States of America

First Printing: February 2006

09   08   07   06   4   3   2   1

Trademarks

Warning and Disclaimer

Bulk Sales

Que offers excellent discounts on this book when ordered in quantity for bulk purchases or special sales. For more information, please contact

U.S. Corporate and Government Sales
1-800-382-3419
corpsales@pearsontechgroup.com

For sales outside of the U.S., please contact

International Sales
international@pearsoned.com

Associate Publisher
Greg Wiegand

Acquisitions Editor
Stephanie J. McComb

Development Editor
Laura Norman

Managing Editor
Charlotte Clapp

Senior Project Editor
Matthew Purcell

Indexer
Erika Millen

Proofreader
Jessica McCarty

Technical Editor
Jay Welshofer

Publishing Coordinator
Sharry Lee Gregory

Book Designer
Anne Jones

Page Layout
Susan Geiselman

Contents at a Glance

Table of Contents

About the Authors

Scott Love has been working with FileMaker for over a decade. He is one of four founding partners at Soliant Consulting, a company dedicated to custom software development, is a speaker at the FileMaker Developer's Conference, and an Authorized FileMaker Trainer. He served at *MacUser/MacWEEK* as an online Managing Editor, at Apple Computer as its Web Publishing Technology Evangelist, followed by directing the Technical Marketing team at Macromedia. He has written dozens of feature and review articles on FileMaker and Internet/web topics, and co-authored *Special Edition Using FileMaker Pro 7* and *Special Edition Using FileMaker 8*.

Steve Lane has worked with relational databases for 16 years. He has written for *FileMaker Advisor* magazine, and co-authored two other books, *Advanced FileMaker Pro 6 Web Development* and *Special Edition Using FileMaker 7*, as well as the forthcoming *Special Edition Using FileMaker 8*. He is a founding partner with Soliant Consulting and has led training classes in FileMaker technologies all over the country, both in open sessions and in onsite client engagements. He regularly speaks at the annual FileMaker Developer's Conference, where in 2003 he was awarded the FileMaker Fellowship Award for "pushing the boundaries of FileMaker Pro."

Bob Bowers, CEO of Soliant Consulting, is a columnist and contributing editor for FileMaker Advisor magazine and has co-authored three other books: *Advanced FileMaker Pro 5.5 Techniques for Developers*, *Advanced FileMaker Pro 6 Web Development*, and *Special Edition Using FileMaker Pro 7*. At the 2002 FileMaker Developer's Conference, where he is a perennial speaker, he was awarded the FileMaker Fellowship Award for "developing outstanding technical and educational resources for FileMaker."

Dedications

To my crew out in the Wild West…without all of you, each of you (even the curmudgeons!), I'd be lost. You're an amazing group of colleagues and I'm grateful we're here building a company together.
> —Scott Love

To Signe, Erlend, and Rona: I guess this doesn't quite count as "never again"?
> —Steve Lane

To Eleanor, my new project management challenge.
> —Bob Bowers

Acknowledgments

This book could not exist were it not for the hard work and support of our colleagues and friends. Writing it would have been impossible otherwise and we'd like to share our gratitude with those who have toiled with us.

First off, Stephanie McComb at Que Publishing gave us an impossible task some months ago: She asked that we update *Special Edition Using FileMaker 7* for the upcoming release of FileMaker 8—*and* that we cut its length by 10%. Full of pluck, we suggested an alternative: Allow us to add 50% and create two books instead. Her vision and championship of the idea has led to the book you now have in your hands. We believe this to be the reference we want on our own desks as we work and we're deeply grateful to Stephanie for making what started as a longshot into reality.

The rest of the team at Que Publishing is no less deserving of thanks. It's our deep pleasure to work with development editor Laura Norman again; her good humor and steady wisdom provides a strength of support that cannot be overstated. Matt Purcell, our project editor, and Jessica McCarty, our proofreader, have worked through our dense material diligently, and contributed countless improvements to our work. It's a relief that they've been by our side through this whole process.

Taking a page from our own work in software development, Mickey Burns joined our team as a project manager who found a perfect blend between bullying and babying as he helped us through (and at times past) each deadline. Liz Kinsella put in tireless hours pulling together demo files, screenshots, facts, and figures. Jan Jung lent her tremendous design skills. Carlos Ramirez, Thomas Andrews, Brent Durland, and David Simerly made significant contributions of code and examples.

No acknowledgement would be complete without mentioning all the work our friends at FileMaker, Inc. do to make everything in our careers possible. FileMaker 8 is a remarkable suite of products and we're terrifically excited by the future promise the FileMaker platform shows.

Last, we'd like to thank Jay Welshofer, our technical editor, for his dedication and friendship: The impact your work has on our lives, in all its facets, is inexpressible.

We Want to Hear from You!

As the reader of this book, *you* are our most important critic and commentator. We value your opinion and want to know what we're doing right, what we could do better, what areas you'd like to see us publish in, and any other words of wisdom you're willing to pass our way.

As an associate publisher for Que Publishing, I welcome your comments. You can email or write me directly to let me know what you did or didn't like about this book—as well as what we can do to make our books better.

Please note that I cannot help you with technical problems related to the topic of this book. We do have a User Services group, however, where I will forward specific technical questions related to the book.

When you write, please be sure to include this book's title and author as well as your name, email address, and phone number. I will carefully review your comments and share them with the author and editors who worked on the book.

Email: feedback@quepublishing.com

Mail: Greg Wiegand
            Associate Publisher
            Que Publishing
            800 East 96th Street
            Indianapolis, IN 46240 USA

For more information about this book or another Que Publishing title, visit our website at www.quepublishing.com. Type the ISBN (excluding hyphens) or the title of a book in the Search field to find the page you're looking for.

Introduction

Welcome to the FileMaker 8 Desk Reference

Just the Facts, 8 to the Point

This is the book we want on our desks—even after writing it. Just as a writer always needs a dictionary nearby, we've found over the years that it would be great to have a quick set of reminders within reach. It's impossible to recall each function's syntax, or every script step's attributes. Although we use the Let() function every day, the exact output of RelationInfo() can be a little less fresh in our minds. This desk reference contains notes on all the script steps and calculation functions in FileMaker, and provides lists of other facts like error codes, port numbers, XML grammar, and more. This book will provide invaluable assistance to like-addle-minded developers everywhere, regardless of one's experience with FileMaker.

Help Is a Function Key Away

Before going any further, we'd like to congratulate the tech writers, engineers, and product managers at FileMaker, Inc. for an excellent help system and set of both printed and electronic documentation. If you've never used FileMaker's help resources or website, you're missing a wealth of information. Both are fantastic places to learn, refresh your memory, or uncover areas of FileMaker you had no idea were there.

Sometimes, however, it's nice to leave what's on your screen unchanged, keep your work and your reference material separate, and be able to turn to actual paper. (It's hard to take notes in the help system, for example!)

Some of this book may overlap a bit with the help system, especially in cases where there's really nothing more to add: for example, as in the Abs() function. Where we hope this book will prove useful is in the additional information and examples we're able to provide, the fact that it's collected all here on paper, and that it's a bit more accessible during those times when you may not be in front of FileMaker or a laptop.

Hopefully, Some of This Is Familiar

For those of you paying attention, you may note that we've made use of material presented in our 2004 *Special Edition Using FileMaker 7* book (Que Publishing,

ISBN 0-7897-3028-6). We discovered that the prior book, aside from qualifying for its own ZIP Code, was struggling to serve two audiences: developers looking to find quick reference information and people trying to learn or understand the concepts behind developing systems in FileMaker Pro.

This desk reference is intended to be just that—a reference. It should serve beginners and experts alike and isn't intended to be read from cover to cover. Rather, the intent is that you'll look up functions you've forgotten, dog-ear useful pages, take notes, and find it a handy tool for building solutions quickly in FileMaker.

If you'd like to learn more about developing solutions in FileMaker, digest in-depth techniques, or get more background information, we hope you will find our companion volume, *Special Edition Using FileMaker 8,* helpful. In applicable locations, we've provided cross-references between the two books.

How This Book Is Organized

FileMaker 8 Functions and Scripts Desk Reference is divided into six parts, each of which can stand on its own.

Part I: FileMaker Specifications

This first part covers the nuts and bolts of FileMaker's product family.

- Chapter 1, "FileMaker 8 Product Line," provides an overview of all the FileMaker products and what purposes and audiences they serve.
- Chapter 2, "Specifications and Storage Limits," details the various hardware and software specifications of each product and other pertinent load statistics.
- Chapter 3, "Field Types and Import/Export Formats," reviews field data types and import/export formats supported.

Part II: Calculation Functions

Part II details all FileMaker calculation functions, syntax, and usage.

- Chapter 4, "Working with Calculations Primer," reviews the layout and functionality of calculation dialogs.
- Chapter 5, "Calculation Signatures," lists the syntax and the output type for each calculation function.
- Chapter 6, "Calculation Functions," provides a complete description of each calculation function, lists examples, and in many cases offers additional comments on usage.

Part III: Custom Functions

Part III offers real-world examples of custom functions.

- Chapter 7, "Custom Functions Primer," introduces the mechanics of creating custom functions, including how to build functions that use recursive logic.

- Chapter 8, "Useful Custom Functions," presents a collection of functions the authors have found useful or representative.

Part IV: Script Steps

Part IV reviews FileMaker's script steps and their options in detail.

- Chapter 9, "Scripting Primer," provides an overview of the mechanics of ScriptMaker and of working with script parameters, script results, and script variables.
- Chapter 10, "Script Step Reference," lists in alphabetical order all script steps in FileMaker, their options, and notes on usage.

Part V: Quick Reference

Part V provides quick reference to commonly needed FileMaker facts.

- Chapter 11, "FileMaker Error Codes," provides a complete list of all error codes.
- Chapter 12, "FileMaker Keyboard Shortcuts," lists shortcuts for both Mac and Windows.
- Chapter 13, "FileMaker Network Ports," lists information useful for IT/infrastructure support.
- Chapter 14, "FileMaker Server Command Line Reference," lists common commands used with fmsadmin.
- Chapter 15, "FileMaker XML Reference," details FileMaker's XML grammars and provides a Custom Web Publishing command reference.

Part VI: Other Resources

Part VI will help you discover other ways to learn about FileMaker.

- Chapter 16, "Where to Go for More Information," presents a list of additional resources we have found helpful in FileMaker development.

Special Features

This book includes the following special features:

- **NEW** **The new version icon**—This icon will identify things that are new in FileMaker 8. We've used it to call out areas that are particularly new and noteworthy in 8, or things that are particularly different from the way things would have been done in earlier versions.
- **Cross-references**—Many topics are connected to other topics in various ways. Cross-references help you link related information together, no matter where that information appears in the book. When another section is related to one you are reading, a cross-reference directs you to a specific page in the book on which you will find the related information. We have also added cross-references to relevant sections of *Special Edition Using FileMaker 8*, where appropriate.

Typographic Conventions Used in This Book

This book uses a few different typesetting styles, primarily to distinguish among explanatory text, code, and special terms.

Key Combinations and Menu Choices

Key (and possibly mouse) combinations that you use to perform FileMaker operations from the keyboard are indicated by presenting the Mac command first in parentheses followed by the Windows command in brackets: (⌘-click) for Mac and [Ctrl+click] for Windows, for example.

Submenu choices are separated from the main menu name by a comma: File, Define, Value Lists.

Typographic Conventions Used for FileMaker Scripts

Monospace type is used for all examples of FileMaker scripting. FileMaker scripts are not edited as text, but are instead edited through FileMaker's graphical script design tool called ScriptMaker. As a result, scripting options that are presented visually in ScriptMaker need to be turned into text when written out. We follow FileMaker's own conventions for printing scripts as text: The name of the script step comes first, and any options to the step are placed after the step name, in square brackets, with semicolons delimiting multiple script step options, as in the following example:

```
Show All Records
Go to Record/Request/Page [ First ]
Show Custom Dialog [Title: "Message window"; Message; "Hello, world!"; Buttons: "OK"]
```

Who Should Use This Book

We hope that anyone who develops FileMaker systems will find many aspects of this book useful. It's a book we, the authors, will use in our day-to-day work, but that doesn't mean it is limited to experts. The reference material is meant to be convenient and accessible to everyone.

Again, we'd like to plug our companion work, *Special Edition Using FileMaker 8,* as a good place to turn if you'd like to learn how to use FileMaker, explore more deeply the functionality and features within its suite of tools, and get information on data modeling, programming concepts, and how to approach building and deploying a FileMaker solution.

PART 1

FileMaker Specifications

## CHAPTER 1

FileMaker 8 Product Line

Overview of FileMaker Products

The FileMaker product line is composed of a number of distinct pieces. Understanding their different strengths, capabilities, and requirements is an important part of your FileMaker knowledge base. In this chapter we give a quick overview of the purpose and profile of each piece of the FileMaker software suite, along with relevant operating system requirements.

FileMaker Pro 8

FileMaker Pro is the original, all-in-one database design, development, deployment, and access tool. Users of FileMaker Pro have access to a full suite of database design tools and can create their own databases from scratch, with full authoring privileges. FileMaker Pro can host databases, sharing them across very small groups of users, via FileMaker network sharing or Instant Web Publishing (IWP). A copy of FileMaker Pro is required in order to open and use FileMaker databases created by others, unless you're using IWP.

If you are an advanced developer or working to build a complex system, we recommend FileMaker Pro Advanced. If you wish to share your databases with more than a few FileMaker users at a time, you'll need FileMaker Server. If you need to share your databases with similar numbers of users via the Web or ODBC/JDBC, you'll need FileMaker Server Advanced.

Operating system requirements are as follows:

Mac: Mac OS X 10.3.9 or greater

Windows: Windows 2000 (Service Pack 4), Windows XP (Service Pack 2)

FileMaker Pro 8 Advanced

FileMaker Pro Advanced is the successor to FileMaker Developer. FileMaker Pro Advanced includes all of the features and functionality present in the regular FileMaker Pro software, but has a series of additional features aimed at application developers. These include tools for debugging scripts; the capability to design custom functions, custom menus, and tooltips; the capability to perform file maintenance; a Database Design Report that can help document a system; and a set of tools that let you create a variety of "run-time" executable solutions. Pro 8 Advanced also includes many new features that speed development, such as the capability to copy and paste fields, tables and script steps.

We strongly recommend FileMaker Pro Advanced for any FileMaker developer who is serious about designing high-quality database systems. The extra tools are well worth the additional cost and, by using Advanced, developers can extend the functionality of their systems to end users by utilizing tool tips and custom menus.

Operating system requirements are as follows:

Mac: Mac OS X 10.3.9 or greater

Windows: Windows 2000 (Service Pack 4), Windows XP (Service Pack 2)

FileMaker Server 8

FileMaker Server is the tool of choice for sharing FileMaker files with more than a handful of concurrent FileMaker users. Whereas the peer-to-peer file hosting available in FileMaker Pro and Pro Advanced can host no more than 10 files for no more than 5 users, FileMaker Server can host as many as 125 files for as many as 250 concurrent FileMaker users. FileMaker Server can also perform regular, automated backups of database files, handle automatic distribution of plug-ins to FileMaker clients, and log various usage statistics.

If you want to share your databases with more than a few users, you'll want to invest in FileMaker Server.

Operating system requirements are as follows:

Mac: Mac OS X or Mac OS X Server 10.3.9 or greater

Windows: Windows 2000 Server (Service Pack 4), Windows XP (Service Pack 2), Windows 2003 Server Standard Edition (Service Pack 1)

FileMaker Server 8 Advanced

FileMaker Server Advanced is required in order to host databases via Instant Web Publishing (IWP) or ODBC/JDBC to more than a few clients at once. It's also necessary in order to take advantage of FileMaker's XML-based Custom Web Publishing (CWP). FileMaker Pro and Pro Advanced can perform hosting for IWP or ODBC/JDBC for a small number of clients, but CWP is available only via Server Advanced. Server Advanced can host up to 250 combined FileMaker and ODBC/JDBC connections, and up to 100 IWP connections. The number of CWP connections is generally limited only by the underlying server operating system and hardware and web server capabilities.

Operating system requirements are as follows:

Mac: Mac OS X or Mac OS X Server 10.3.9 or greater; Apache 1.3 Web Server

Windows: Windows 2000 Server (Service Pack 4), Windows XP (Service Pack 2), Windows 2003 Server Standard Edition (Service Pack 1); Internet Information Server (IIS) 5.0 on Windows 200 Server, or IIS 6.0 on Windows Server 2003

FileMaker Mobile 8

FileMaker Mobile is software that enables you to download FileMaker databases (or subsets thereof) to a PocketPC or PalmOS device. Databases downloaded to a handheld may be used in an "offline" fashion and later synchronized with the master database via the handheld device's synchronization software, in combination with FileMaker Mobile.

Up to 50 tables may be installed on a single handheld device. There are limitations on the size of downloaded data sets: Field length limitations are stricter than in the regular FileMaker Pro client, and only 50 fields per table can be shared with the handheld device.

NEW Previous versions of FileMaker Mobile could only synchronize with local (non-hosted) FileMaker databases. FileMaker Mobile 8 adds the very significant capability of synchronizing a handheld database with a FileMaker database hosted elsewhere than on the FileMaker Mobile computer (for example, by FileMaker Server, or by another FileMaker Pro client hosting the files in peer-to-peer mode).

Operating system requirements are as follows:

Mac: Mac OS X 10.3.9 or greater; Palm Desktop 4.2 with Hotsync Manager for PalmOS devices

Windows: Windows 2000 (Service Pack 4), Windows XP (Service Pack 2); Palm Desktop 4.1 with Hotsync Manager for PalmOS devices; ActiveSync 3.8 for PocketPC devices

## CHAPTER 2

Specifications and Storage Limits

Knowing Your Limits

Whenever you work with a piece of software, it's a good idea to be aware of the software's limits, both practical and theoretical. Important design considerations can hinge on a correct appraisal of the capabilities of your tools. If you need to build a system that can correctly work with dates prior to those in the AD era, it's a good idea to be aware of the storage capabilities of FileMaker's date field type, for example.

Some of these limits are more theoretical than practical, and you're better off observing the practical limits. We don't recommend you build systems with a million tables, for example, or write calculations containing 30K of text. If you feel you need to push these upper limits, you may want to recheck your assumptions and, if necessary, rethink your approach.

Table 2.1 provides the limits of some of the most important measurable capacities of the FileMaker product line.

Table 2.1   FileMaker Limits

Characteristic	Capacity
Maximum file size	8 terabytes
Maximum tables per file	1,000,0000
Maximum fields per table	256 million over the life of the file
Maximum number of fields in a handheld database (FileMaker Mobile)	50
Maximum records per file	64 quadrillion over the life of the file
Maximum records in a handheld database (FileMaker Mobile)	5,000
Maximum field name length	100 characters
Maximum table name length	100 characters
Maximum field comment length	30,000 characters
Maximum calculation text length	30,000 characters
Maximum custom function text length	30,000 characters

Table 2.1 FileMaker Limits (continued)

Characteristic	Capacity
Maximum amount of data in a text field	2 gigabytes (about a billion Unicode characters)
Maximum amount of data in a text field in FileMaker Mobile	2,000 characters
Range of a number field	-10^{400} to -10^{-400} and 10^{-400} to 10^{400} (and 0 as well)
Precision of a number field	Up to 400 significant digits
Maximum amount of data in a number field in FileMaker Mobile	255 characters
Range of a date field	1/1/0001 – 12/31/4000
Range of a time field	1 – 2,147,483,647
Range of a timestamp field	1/1/0001 12:00:00 AM – 12/31/4000 11:59:59.999999 PM
Size of data in a container field	4 gigabytes
Maximum size of data used for indexing	Up to 100 characters of data per word
Maximum files open in FileMaker client	Limited only by memory on the client computer
Maximum number of databases on a handheld device (FileMaker Mobile)	50
Maximum database files hosted by Filemaker client, peer-to-peer	10
Maximum connected FileMaker, Instant Web, or ODBC/JDBC clients, peer-to-peer	5
Maximum files hosted by FileMaker Server	125
Maximum connected FileMaker clients using FileMaker Server	250
Maximum Instant Web Publishing clients using FileMaker Server Advanced	100
Maximum ODBC/JDBC clients using FileMaker Server Advanced	50
Maximum RAM addressable by FileMaker Server	4 gigabytes
Maximum cache setting for FileMaker Server	800 megabytes
Maximum number of records in IWP table view	50
Maximum number of records in IWP list view	25
Maximum dimensions of a FileMaker layout	121 inches×121 inches

Notes:

- Unicode characters take up a variable number of bits, dependent on the character, so it's not possible to define a precise upper limit to the size of a text field.
- FileMaker Pro clients and ODBC/JDBC clients draw from the same pool of available connections on FileMaker Server/Server Advanced, so the upper limit is a *total* of 250 connected users of both types together. Of these, no more than 50 may be ODBC/JDBC users.

## CHAPTER 3

Field Types and Import/Export Formats

Knowing Your Data

Besides just knowing the raw statistics and capacities of your software tools ("speeds and feeds," as the machinists like to say), it's wise to understand the basic data formats with which your database software can work. In this chapter we give a brief overview of each of the underlying FileMaker field data types, and we also discuss the various data formats available for import and export.

First, a word about data types in FileMaker: Unlike certain other database engines, FileMaker is somewhat forgiving about data types. You can add text characters to a number field, for example, without being stopped by FileMaker. The price you pay for this flexibility is the possibility that you'll make a mistake or permit something undesirable to happen. So it's necessary to have a firm grasp of FileMaker's data types, and how each of them works and relates to the others.

FileMaker Field Types

In the previous chapter, on FileMaker specifications, we called out a number of the raw capacities of FileMaker's field types, in the briefest possible format. Here we dwell on each data type and its characteristics in a bit more detail.

→ *For more information on FileMaker fields and field types,* **see** *Special Edition Using FileMaker 8, Chapter 3, "Defining and Working with Fields.*

Text

FileMaker's text field type is able to hold up to 2 gigabytes of character data per text field. FileMaker 8 stores text internally as Unicode, which requires about 2 bytes per character (the exact number varies by the specific character and encoding). So a single FileMaker text field can hold about a billion characters of data (nearly half a million regular pages of text).

There's no need to specify the "size" of the text field in advance; FileMaker will automatically accommodate any text you enter, up to the field size maximum.

FileMaker's text field can be indexed on a word-by-word basis, so it's possible to search quickly for one or more words anywhere within a text field.

In other database systems, such as those based on SQL, it is often necessary to specify the maximum size of a text field in advance. Many SQL databases do go beyond the SQL standard in offering a text data type of flexible size.

Number

The number field type is FileMaker's only numeric data type. Unlike some other tools, FileMaker does not have separate data types for integers and floating point numbers. All numbers are capable of being treated as floating point.

FileMaker 8's numeric data type can store numbers in the range 10^{-400} through 10^{400}, and -10^{400} through -10^{-400}, as well as the value 0. The data type can account for 400 digits of precision. By default, though, numeric values will only account for 16 digits of precision. To achieve higher precision, you'll need to use the SetPrecision() function.

Numeric fields can accept character data entry, though the character data will be ignored. If the field's validation is also set to Strict Data Type: Numeric Only, even the entry of character data will be disallowed.

In other database systems, such as those based on SQL, integers and floating point numbers tend to be considered as two different data types, and it's often necessary to choose in advance between lower-precision and higher-precision floating point numbers, though SQL does also offer arbitrary-precision numbers as well.

Date

FileMaker's date type can store dates from 1/1/0001 to 12/31/4000. Internally, these dates are stored as integer values between 1 and 1,460,970, indicating the number of days elapsed between 1/1/0001 and the date in question. This is significant in that it means that integer math can be performed on dates: 12/31/2001 + 1 = 1/1/2002, and 12/21/2001 – 365 = 12/21/2000.

FileMaker will correctly interpret oddly formed dates, as long as they're within its overall date range. For example, 4/31/2005 will be interpreted as 5/1/2005, whereas 12/32/2005 will be interpreted as 1/1/2006. But 12/31/5000 will be rejected outright.

FileMaker's date type is stricter than the text and number types, and will reject any date outside the range just mentioned, including those containing textual data. Field validation options can also be configured to force entry of a full four-digit year.

Though the date type is stored as an integer, it can be entered and displayed in a wide variety of well-known or local date display formats. By default it will use settings it inherits from the current user's operating system, but the date display format can be over-ridden on a field-by-field basis on each individual layout.

By comparison, SQL-based database systems also offer a date data type, measured in days.

Time

Like the date type, FileMaker's time data type stores its information in an underlying integer representation. In the case of the time field type, what's being stored is the number of seconds since midnight of the previous day, yielding a range of possible values from 1 to 86,400. As with the date type, it's possible to perform integer math with time values: So Get(CurrentTime) + 3600 will return a time an hour ahead of the current time. And 15:30:00 – 11:00:00 returns 4:30:00, so "time math" can be used to compute time intervals correctly as well.

Also like the date type, the time data type can accept entry and display of time data in a variety of formats. "Overlapping" times work in the same way as overlapping dates: FileMaker will interpret the value 25:15:00 as representing 1:15 a.m. on the following day. (This is exactly what happens when you store a value greater than 86,400 in a time field, which FileMaker will certainly allow.)

By comparison, SQL-based database systems generally offer a time data type, sometimes with the capability to track a time zone as well.

Timestamp

FileMaker's timestamp data type is like a combination of the date and time types. A timestamp will be displayed as something like "11/20/2005 12:30:00." Internally, like both dates and times, it is stored as an integer. In this case the internally stored number represents the number of seconds since 1/1/0001. The timestamp can represent date/time combinations ranging from 1/1/0001 00:00:00 to 12/31/4000 11:59:59.999999 (a range of over a hundred billion seconds).

As with the related date and time field types, timestamps can be displayed and entered in a variety of formats. It's also possible to perform math with timestamps as with dates and times, but since timestamps can measure time in days but are stored in seconds, the math may get a bit unwieldy.

The timestamp data type is commonplace in the database world. Some flavors of timestamp offer the capability to track a time zone as well.

Container

The container data type is FileMaker's field type for binary data (meaning data that, unlike text and numbers, does not have an accepted plain-text representation). Binary data generally represents an electronic file of some sort, such as a picture, a movie, a sound file, or a file produced by some other software application such as a word processor or page layout program.

A single container field can store a single binary object up to 4 gigabytes in size. Though any type of electronic file can be stored in a container field (one file per field), FileMaker has specialized knowledge of a few types of binary data, and can play or display such objects directly by calling on operating system services. Specifically, FileMaker can play or display pictures, sounds, and movies (and in fact any "movie-like" file supported by QuickTime, if QuickTime is installed). Additionally, on Windows, a container field can store and display Object Linking and Embedding (OLE) objects.

When working with container fields, it's important to understand the distinction between storing the data directly (embedding the entire file in the FileMaker database and increasing its file size by tens or hundreds of K or indeed by megabytes) and storing it by reference (storing just the path to the specified file). The former leads to larger database files; the latter relies on the binary files being stored in a fixed location and not moving relative to the database.

Many other database systems are able to handle binary data, but there's little in the way of an agreed-upon standard for doing so. In general, each database tool has its own means for dealing with binary data.

Calculation

From the point of view of data types, calculations are not a data type at all. They are instead a *field* type, and can be constructed to return their results as any of the six fundamental data types: text, number, date, time, timestamp, or container.

Summary

Summary fields are another example of a field type rather than a data type. Summary fields perform summary operations on sets of grouped records, and always return a numeric result.

Importing Data

FileMaker can import data from one or more static, external files on the hard drive of the FileMaker client machine or on a shared network volume. FileMaker can also import data from remote data services. The following sections outline the various sources for importing data and the specific requirements and limitations of each.

→ *For more information on importing data in FileMaker,* **see** Special Edition Using FileMaker 8, Chapter 19 "Importing Data into FileMaker."

File-Based Data Sources

FileMaker can import data from individual files, available on a local hard drive or networked volume, in any of the following formats:

- Tab-separated text
- Comma-separated text
- SYLK
- DIF
- WKS
- BASIC
- Merge files
- DBase files

In addition to importing from these common text file formats, FileMaker can also perform more specialized imports from files created in Excel, or in FileMaker itself.

Importing from Excel

When importing data from an Excel file, FileMaker can detect multiple worksheets within the source Excel file. FileMaker can also detect the existence of any *named ranges* in the source document. When importing, if named ranges or multiple worksheets are detected, FileMaker will give you a choice as to whether to import from a worksheet or named range, and allow you to select the specific worksheet or range from which to import.

When importing from Excel, as with all imports, FileMaker brings in only the raw data it finds in the source file. Formulas, macros, and other programming logic are not imported.

FileMaker Pro assigns an appropriate field type (text, number, date, or time) if all rows in the column hold the same Excel data type. Otherwise, a column becomes a text field when imported into FileMaker.

Importing from FileMaker

FileMaker can also import data from other FileMaker files. These may be files that are present on the local client machine, or files that are hosted on another machine.

Much as an Excel file can contain multiple worksheets, a FileMaker database can contain multiple tables. It's necessary to choose a single table as your data source when importing from a FileMaker file.

Importing from FileMaker can be particularly convenient if the source file has a structure that matches that of the target file. In this case, rather than manually configuring the import mapping on a field-by-field basis, it's possible to choose the Arrange by Matching Field Names option. When you do so, fields of the same name in the source and target tables will be paired in the import mapping.

Importing Multiple Files at Once

It's also possible to import data from multiple files at a time. You can import data from either text or image files. You can import both the raw data in the file, and also extra data about each source file's name and location.

In each case, the files being imported must all be grouped in or underneath a single folder. You can specify whether to look simply inside the one folder, or whether to search all the way down through any subfolders.

Importing from Multiple Text Files

When importing from a batch of text files, you may import up to three pieces of data from each text file:

- Filename
- Full path to file
- Text contents

You may choose to import any or all of these.

Unlike with a regular import from a text file, the internal structure of the text file is disregarded. The entire contents, whether containing tabs, carriage returns, commas, or other potential delimiters, is imported into a single target field.

Importing from Multiple Image Files

Importing from multiple image files is quite similar to importing from multiple text files. When importing a batch of images, you may import any or all of the following data fields:

- Filename
- Full path to file
- Image
- Image thumbnail

In addition to filename, file path, and file contents (an image, in this case), FileMaker allows you to import an image thumbnail, either in addition to or instead of the full image. You may wish to do this to save file space or screen space. FileMaker creates these thumbnails via its own algorithms, so you have no control over the exact details of thumbnail size or quality.

When importing images, you have the choice (as you always do when working with data in container fields) of importing the full image into the database, or merely storing a reference. Importing full images will take up more space in the database (probably much more), whereas importing only the references will mean that you'll need to make the original files continuously available from a hard drive or network volume that all users of the database can access.

Importing Digital Photos (Mac OS)

On the Mac OS, FileMaker can also import images directly from a digital camera, or from any device capable of storing digital photos. This process is quite similar to a batch import of images from a single folder with only a few differences.

FileMaker will allow you to specify which images to import. You may choose them individually, or via a range such as "last 12 images." FileMaker will also handle transferring the files from the storage device to a download location of your choice. And, as with other imports, you can choose whether to import the full image into FileMaker, or simply store a reference.

Whereas the regular batch import of images brings in only four pieces of data about each image, a digital image import may have access to much more data about each image. If the selected images contain EXIF data (a standard for embedding extra data into an image file), FileMaker can also detect and import many additional pieces of data about the image such as shutter speed, ISO setting, and the like.

Importing from an ODBC Data Source

FileMaker can import data from a data source accessed via ODBC. Many types of data can be accessed via ODBC, but it's most commonly used to retrieve data from a remote database, often one running some flavor of the SQL language.

Working with OBDC data sources requires three things:

- **A data source able to provide data via ODBC**—Again, this is most often a remote database server of some kind. The administrators of the data source may need to perform specific configuration of the data source before it can accept ODBC connections.

- **An ODBC driver, installed on the local computer that's running FileMaker, that's able to talk to the specific ODBC data source in question**—ODBC drivers need to be installed on each computer that will access a data source. So, much like a FileMaker plug-in, ODBC drivers generally need to be installed on the computer of each FileMaker user who will be using ODBC access. ODBC drivers are specific to a particular data source (the PostgreSQL or Sybase databases, for example), and also specific to a particular platform (Mac or PC). In order to connect to an ODBC data source, you must have a driver specific to both your data source and platform (Sybase 12 driver for Mac OS, for example).

- **A DSN (Data Source Name) that specifies the details of how to connect to a specific data source**—DSNs are configured differently on each platform, and generally contain information about a specific data source (server name, user name, password, database name, and the like).

→ *For more information on configuring ODBC access in FileMaker,* **see** *Special Edition Using FileMaker 8, Chapter 19, "Importing Data into FileMaker," and Chapter 20, "Exporting Data from FileMaker."*

Once you have successfully configured and connected to an ODBC data source, the process for selecting data to import is a bit different than for regular imports. Before proceeding to the field mapping dialog, you'll need to build a SQL query that selects the fields and records you want. (For example, your SQL query might read SELECT name_last, name_first, city, state, zip FROM customer). Once you've done this, you'll be able to map the resulting fields to those in your FileMaker database.

Importing from an XML Data Source

FileMaker can import data from XML-based data sources. The source can either be a physical file, stored on a locally accessible volume, or a remote XML data stream accessed over HTTP.

In order to import data from an XML source, the XML data must be presented in the correct format, which FileMaker calls a *grammar*. FileMaker can only import data from XML sources that use the FMPXMLRESULT grammar. If the XML data is not in the FMPXMLRESULT grammar, you will need to specify an XSLT stylesheet at the time of import; that stylesheet needs to be written in such a way as to transform the inbound XML into the FMPXMLRESULT grammar.

→ *For more information on FileMaker's XML import capabilities,* **see** *Special Edition Using FileMaker 8, Chapter 22, "FileMaker and Web Services."*

Creating New Tables on Import

NEW FileMaker 8 has a nice new capability. When importing data, you can now specify that the inbound data should be placed in a new table rather than adding to or updating an existing table. The new table will take its field names from those present in the data source.

Exporting Data

FileMaker can export its data to a variety of data types, as follows:

- Tab-separated text
- Comma-separated text
- SYLK
- DIF
- WKS
- BASIC
- Merge
- HTML table
- FileMaker Pro
- Excel

Most of these are straightforward: The records in the found set will be exported to a file of the specified format.

A few of these formats deserve special mention and are detailed in the sections that follow.

→ *For more information on exporting data in FileMaker,* **see** *Special Edition Using FileMaker 8, Chapter 20, "Exporting Data from FileMaker."*

Exporting to HTML

When exporting to "HTML Table," the resulting file will be a complete HTML document consisting of an HTML table that displays the chosen data, somewhat like FileMaker's Table View.

Exporting to FileMaker Pro

The result of this export choice will be a new FileMaker Pro 7/8 file, with fields and field types that generally match those of exported fields. But note that the logic underlying calculation and summary fields will not be preserved. Those fields will be re-created based on their underlying data type: A calculation field returning a text result will be inserted into a Text field, whereas summary field data, if exported, will be inserted into a Number field. Only the raw data from the original file will be exported; none of the calculation or scripting logic will carry over.

Exporting to Excel

When exporting records to Excel, you have the option to create a header row where the database field names will appear as column names. You can also specify a worksheet name, document title, document subject, and document author.

NEW Exporting records to Excel is similar to, but a bit more flexible than, FileMaker 8's new Save Records As Excel feature. Save Records As Excel will only export fields from the current layout, and will not export fields on tab panels other than the active one.

Automatically Opening or Emailing Exported Files

NEW New in FileMaker 8 is the capability to automatically open and/or email an exported file. These choices are selected via two checkboxes in the Export dialog.

Automatically opening a file is a convenience for the user: A newly created Excel file would open right away in Excel. Automatic email is an even more powerful tool. When this choice is selected, a new email will be created in the user's default email client with the exported file as an attachment. (The user will still need to specify the email recipients manually.)

PART 2

Calculation Functions

## CHAPTER 4

Working with Calculations Primer

The calculation dialog in FileMaker serves as a fundamental element in nearly all development activities. Beyond simply defining calculation fields, you will also work with the dialog within scripts, for setting some auto-enter field options, for field validation, and even within a file's security settings. We encourage all developers to become deeply familiar with calculation functions and to that end have assembled here a concise reference to how the dialog works.

The Calculation Function Interface

The Calculation dialog allows developers easy access to the data fields in their solutions and to a complete function list (see Figure 4.1).

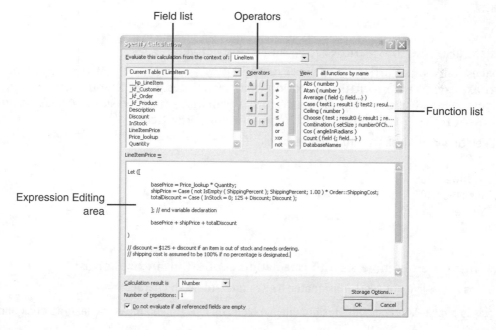

Figure 4.1

Both field names and calculation templates can be double-clicked to insert them into the expression editing area.

➔ *If you'd like more detail on calculations including complete examples of how they work,* **see** *Chapter 6, "Calculation Functions."*

➔ *For more detail and explanation on calculations, including in-depth discussion of beginning and advanced uses, please* **see** *Chapter 8, "Getting Started with Calculations," and Chapter 14, "Advanced Calculation Techniques," in our companion book,* Special Edition Using FileMaker 8.

Calculations: Things to Remember

When working with calculation fields and the various places within FileMaker that make use of calculation functions, there are some common issues to keep in mind:

- The four special operators in FileMaker are:

  & Concatenates the result of two expressions. 1 & 2 will result in "12".

  "" Designates literal text.

  ¶ Carriage return.

  () Designates a function's parameter list and controls the order of operations for math expressions.

- Entering a less-than character followed by a greater-than character (<>) equates to the "not equal to" operator (≠) within an expression. The following expressions are functionally identical:

  1 <> 2

  1 ≠ 2

  This is also true for >= and <= for ≥ and ≤, respectively.

- Spaces, tabs, and carriage returns (¶ or "pilcrows") are ignored within the calculation syntax, except when within quotation marks (that designate literal text). This allows developers to use these characters to format calculation expressions for easy reading. So the following two expressions are functionally identical:

  ```
  If ( fieldOne < 10; "less than 10"; "not less than 10" )
  If(
      fieldOne < 10;
      "less than 10";
      "not less than 10"
  )
  ```

- You may insert comments into calculation expressions in two forms:

  ```
  // this is a one-line comment, designated by two forward-slash characters

  /* this is a multi-line comment designated in a block by a beginning forward-slash-asterisk and

  closed by an ending asterisk-forward-slash.

  */
  ```

- To enter a tab character into an expression (either as literal text or simply to help with formatting), use Ctrl-Tab on Windows, and Opt-Tab on the Mac.
- FileMaker allows for a shorthand approach to entering conditional Boolean tests for non-null, non-zero field contents. The following two expressions are functionally identical.

```
Case ( fieldOne; "true"; "false" )
```

```
Case ( (IsEmpty (text) or text = 0); "false"; "true" )
```

Please note that the authors do not recommend this shortcut as a best practice. We tend to believe one should write explicit (and, yes, more verbose) code, leaving no room for ambiguity.

- FileMaker allows for optional negative or default values in both the Case() and If() conditional functions. The following are all syntactically valid:

```
Case ( fieldOne; "true" )
```

```
Case (
    fieldOne = 1; "one";
    fieldOne = 2; "two"
)
```

```
Case (
    fieldOne = 1; "one";
    fieldOne = 2; "two";
    "default"
)
```

We strongly recommend you always provide a default condition at the end of your Case statements, even if that condition should "never" occur. The next time your field shows a value of "never happens", you'll be glad you did.

- The Case() function features a "short circuiting" functionality whereby it only evaluates conditional tests until it reaches the first true test. In the following example, the third test will never be evaluated, thus improving system performance.

```
Case (
    1 = 2; "one is false";
    1 = 1; "one is true";
    2 = 2; "two is true"
)
```

- Functions inserted from the function list in the upper right will at times use brackets to denote either optional or repeating elements.
- Fields with repeating values can either be accessed using the GetRepetition() function or via a shorthand of placing an integer value between two brackets. The following are functionally identical:

```
Quantity[2]
```

```
GetRepetition ( Quantity; 2 )
```

- While the default menu in the function list says "All functions by name", it does not actually display all FileMaker functions (to the general bemusement of the community). The Get, Design, and External functions are excluded from those listed (and are arguably less commonly used or more advanced than the other functions). In order to view these functions, you'll need to choose to view the desired function group specifically by choosing Get, Design, or External from the menu of function groups.

- Make careful note of the context option at the top of the Calculation dialog. In cases where the calculation's source table is represented by more than one table occurrence on the Relationships Graph, this menu will become active. Calculation field and expression results can vary depending on the perspective and relationships from which a calculation is evaluated.

- Note also the data type returned menu at the lower portion of the dialog. It is a common source of bugs when developers forget to choose the correct data type for calculation results. (Returning a result as a number instead of a text type is a common and bewildering bug, at least when you see it the first time.)

- Turning off the Do Not Evaluate If All Referenced Fields Are Empty option will ensure that no matter the condition of referenced fields at least *some* value will be returned. This is useful for cases involving, for example, financial data where it's often helpful to see an explicit zero listed in a field.

- Calculation fields that reference related data, summary fields, other un-indexed calculation fields, or globally stored fields cannot be indexed; otherwise, even though by definition a calculation field returns different results based on different input values, a calculation field can be indexed.

- FileMaker Pro client computers typically are where calculations are evaluated; however, certain unstored calculations are evaluated on the host or server computer. In cases where certain information relies on a client computer but is evaluated on the server, the server will essentially cache this information when an account logs in and can, at times, be out of sync with conditions on the client. The following functions may be subject to this:

Get(ApplicationLanguage)

Get(DesktopPath)

Get(DocumentsPath)

Get(FileMakerPath)

Get(PreferencesPath)

Get(PrinterName)

Get(SystemDrive)

Get(SystemIPAddress)

Get(SystemLanguage)

Get(SystemNICAddress)

Get(UserName)

## CHAPTER 5

Calculation Signatures

Aggregate Functions

Aggregate functions apply to a group of fields in related records or repeating fields.

Table 5.1   Aggregate Functions

Syntax	Data Type Returned
Average (field {; field...})	Number
Count (field {; field...})	Number
Max (field {; field...})	Text, Number, Date, Time, Timestamp
Min (field {; field...})	Text, Number, Date, Time, Timestamp
StDev (field {; field...})	Number
StDevP (field {; field...})	Number
Sum (field {; field...})	Number
Variance (field {; field...})	Number
VarianceP (field {; field...})	Number

Date Functions

FileMaker offers a range of date manipulation functions, including those for the Japanese calendar.

Table 5.2   Date Functions

Syntax	Data Type Returned
Date (month; day; year)	Date
Day (date)	Number
DayName (date)	Text
DayNameJ (date)	Text (Japanese)
DayOfWeek (date)	Number
DayOfYear (date)	Number

Table 5.2   Date Functions (continued)

Syntax	Data Type Returned
Month (date)	Number
MonthName (date)	Text
MonthNameJ (date)	Text (Japanese)
WeekOfYear (date)	Number
WeekOfYearFiscal (date; startingDay)	Number
Year (date)	Number
YearName (date; format)	Text (Japanese)

Design Functions

Design functions generally extract information about one's database and are helpful in debugging or for advanced scripting.

Table 5.3   Design Functions

Syntax	Data Type Returned
DatabaseNames	Text
FieldBounds (fileName; layoutName; fieldName)	Text
FieldComment (fileName; fieldName)	Text
FieldIDs (fileName; layoutName)	Text
FieldNames (fileName; layout/tableName)	Text
FieldRepetitions (fileName; layoutName; fieldName)	Text
FieldStyle (fileName; layoutName; fieldName)	Text
FieldType (fileName; fieldName)	Text
GetNextSerialValue (fileName; fieldName)	Text
LayoutIDs (fileName)	Text
LayoutNames (fileName)	Text
RelationInfo (fileName; tableOccurrence)	Text
ScriptIDs (fileName)	Text
ScriptNames (fileName)	Text
TableIDs (fileName)	Text
TableNames (fileName)	Text
ValueListIDs (fileName)	Text
ValueListItems (fileName; valueListName)	Text
ValueListNames (fileName)	Text
WindowNames {(filename)}	Text

External Functions

External functions originate from installed plug-ins and vary widely based on the plug-ins used.

Table 5.4   External Functions

Syntax	Data Type Returned
External (nameOfFunction; parameter)	Depends on the external function

Financial Functions

Financial functions assist with various specialized mortgage and interest calculations.

Table 5.5   Financial Functions

Syntax	Data Type Returned
FV (payment; interestRate; periods)	Number
NPV (payment; interestRate)	Number
PMT (principal; interestRate; term)	Number
PV (payment; interestRate; periods)	Number

Get Functions

Get functions generally pull information from a given user's current state, be it from within FileMaker, from one's computer, or from a given network.

Table 5.6   Get Functions

Syntax	Data Type Returned
Get (AccountName)	Text
Get (ActiveFieldContents)	Text, Number, Date, Time, Timestamp, Container
Get (ActiveFieldName)	Text
Get (ActiveFieldTableName)	Text
Get (ActiveModifierKeys)	Number
Get (ActiveRepetitionNumber)	Number
Get (ActiveSelectionSize)	Number
Get (ActiveSelectionStart)	Number
Get (AllowAbortState)	Number
Get (AllowToolbarState)	Number
Get (ApplicationLanguage)	Text

Table 5.6   Get Functions (continued)

Syntax	Data Type Returned
Get (ApplicationVersion)	Text
Get (CalculationRepetitionNumber)	Number
Get (CurrentDate)	Date
Get (CurrentHostTimestamp)	Timestamp
Get (CurrentTime)	Time
Get (CurrentTimestamp)	Timestamp
Get (CustomMenuSetName)	Text
Get (DesktopPath)	Text
Get (DocumentsPath)	Text
Get (ErrorCaptureState)	Number
Get (ExtendedPrivileges)	Text
Get (FileMakerPath)	Text
Get (FileName)	Text
Get (FilePath)	Text
Get (FileSize)	Number
Get (FoundCount)	Number
Get (HighContrastColor)	Text
Get (HighContrastState)	Number
Get (HostIPAddress)	Text
Get (HostName)	Text
Get (LastError)	Number
Get (LastMessageChoice)	Number
Get (LastODBCError)	Text
Get (LayoutAccess)	Number
Get (LayoutCount)	Number
Get (LayoutName)	Text
Get (LayoutNumber)	Number
Get (LayoutTableName)	Text
Get (LayoutViewState)	Number
Get (MultiUserState)	Number
Get (NetworkProtocol)	Text
Get (PageNumber)	Number
Get (PortalRowNumber)	Number
Get (PreferencesPath)	Text
Get (PrinterName)	Text
Get (PrivilegeSetName)	Text
Get (RecordAccess)	Number

Table 5.6   Get Functions (continued)

Syntax	Data Type Returned
Get (RecordID)	Number
Get (RecordModificationCount)	Number
Get (RecordNumber)	Number
Get (RecordOpenCount)	Number
Get (RecordOpenState)	Number
Get (RequestCount)	Number
Get (RequestOmitState)	Number
Get (ScreenDepth)	Number
Get (ScreenHeight)	Number
Get (ScreenWidth)	Number
Get (ScriptName)	Text
Get (ScriptParameter)	Text
Get (ScriptResult)	Text, Number, Date, Time, Timestamp, Container
Get (SortState)	Number
Get (StatusAreaState)	Number
Get (SystemDrive)	Text
Get (SystemIPAddress)	Text
Get (SystemLanguage)	Text
Get (SystemNICAddress)	Text
Get (SystemPlatform)	Number
Get (SystemVersion)	Text
Get (TextRulerVisible)	Number
Get (TotalRecordCount)	Number
Get (UserCount)	Number
Get (UserName)	Text
Get (UseSystemFormatsState)	Number
Get (WindowContentHeight)	Number
Get (WindowContentWidth)	Number
Get (WindowDesktopHeight)	Number
Get (WindowDesktopWidth)	Number
Get (WindowHeight)	Number
Get (WindowLeft)	Number
Get (WindowMode)	Number
Get (WindowName)	Text
Get (WindowTop)	Number
Get (WindowVisible)	Number
Get (WindowWidth)	Number
Get (WindowZoomLevel)	Text

Logical Functions

Logical functions allow comparative tests to be evaluated and return differing results based on those comparisons. They also allow you to work with variables.

Table 5.7   Logical Functions

Syntax	Data Type Returned
Case (test1; result1 {; test2; result2; defaultResult...})	Text, Number, Date, Time, Timestamp, Container
Choose (test; result0 {; result1; result2...})	Text, Number, Date, Time, Timestamp, Container
Evaluate (expression {; [field1; field2; ...]})	Text, Number, Date, Time, Timestamp, Container
EvaluationError (expression)	Number
GetAsBoolean (data)	Number
GetField (fieldName)	Text, Number, Date, Time, Timestamp, Container
GetNthRecord (fieldName; recordNumber)	Text, Number, Date, Time, Timestamp, Container
If (test; result1; result2)	Text, Number, Date, Time, Timestamp, Container
IsEmpty (expression)	Number
IsValid (expression)	Number
IsValidExpression (expression)	Number
Let ({[} var1=expression1 {; var2=expression2 ...] }; calculation)	Text, Number, Date, Time, Timestamp, Container
Lookup (sourceField {; failExpression })	Text, Number, Date, Time, Timestamp, Container
LookupNext (sourceField; lower/higher Flag)	Text, Number, Date, Time, Timestamp, Container
Quote (text)	Text

Number Functions

Number functions allow various mathematical expressions within FileMaker.

Table 5.8   Number Functions

Syntax	Data Type Returned
Abs (number)	Number, Time
Ceiling (number)	Number
Combination (setSize; numberOfChoices)	Number
Div (number; divisor)	Number
Exp (number)	Number
Factorial (number {; numberOfFactors })	Number
Floor (number)	Number

Table 5.8   Number Functions (continued)

Syntax	Data Type Returned
Int (number)	Number
Lg (number)	Number
Ln (number)	Number
Log (number)	Number
Mod (number; divisor)	Number
Random	Number
Round (number; precision)	Number
SetPrecision (expression; precision)	Number
Sign (number)	Number
Sqrt (number)	Number
Truncate (number; precision)	Number

Repeating Functions

Repeating functions facilitate working with repeating fields within other calculations.

Table 5.9   Repeating Functions

Syntax	Data Type Returned
Extend (non-repeatingField)	Text, Number, Date, Time, Timestamp, Container
GetRepetition (repeatingField; repetitionNumber)	Text, Number, Date, Time, Timestamp, Container
Last (field)	Text, Number, Date, Time, Timestamp, Container

Summary Functions

Summary functions operate across multiple records based on a break field (sort criteria). The function in this category is the analogue of the sub-summary part within reporting.

Table 5.10   Summary Functions

Syntax	Data Type Returned
GetSummary (summaryField; breakField)	Number, Date, Time, Timestamp

Text Functions

Text functions provide all the various text parsing tools within FileMaker, some specialized and some general.

Table 5.11   Text Functions

Syntax	Data Type Returned
Exact (originalText; comparisonText)	Number
Filter (textToFilter; filterText)	Text
FilterValues (textToFilter; filterValues)	Text
GetAsCSS (text)	Text
GetAsDate (text)	Date
GetAsNumber (text)	Number
GetAsSVG (text)	Text
GetAsText (data)	Text
GetAsTime (text)	Time
GetAsTimestamp (text)	Timestamp
GetValue (listOfValues; valueNumber)	Text
Hiragana (text)	Text (Japanese)
KanaHankaku (text)	Text (Japanese)
KanaZenkaku (text)	Text (Japanese)
KanjiNumeral (text)	Text (Japanese)
Katakana (text)	Text (Japanese)
Left (text; numberOfCharacters)	Text
LeftValues (text; numberOfValues)	Text
LeftWords (text; numberOfWords)	Text
Length (text)	Number
Lower (text)	Text
Middle (text; startCharacter; numberOfCharacters)	Text
MiddleValues (text; startingValue; numberOfValues)	Text
MiddleWords (text; startingWord; numberOfWords)	Text
NumToJText (number; separator; characterType)	Text (Japanese)
PatternCount (text; searchString)	Number
Position (text; searchString; start; occurrence)	Number
Proper (text)	Text
Replace (text; start; numberOfCharacters; replacementText)	Text
Right (text; numberOfCharacters)	Text
RightValues (text; numberOfValues)	Text
RightWords (text; numberOfWords)	Text
RomanHankaku (text)	Text (Japanese)
RomanZenkaku (text)	Text (Japanese)
SerialIncrement (text; incrementBy)	Text

Table 5.11   Text Functions (continued)

Syntax	Data Type Returned
Substitute (text; searchString; replaceString)	Text
Trim (text)	Text
TrimAll (text; trimSpaces; trimType)	Text
Upper (text)	Text
ValueCount (text)	Number
WordCount (text)	Number

Text Formatting Functions

Text formatting functions allow a routine or calculation to manipulate the actual formatting of data within text fields in FileMaker.

Table 5.12   Text Formatting Functions

Syntax	Data Type Returned
RGB (red; green; blue)	Number
TextColor (text; RGB (red; green; blue))	Text
TextColorRemove (text {; RGB (red; green; blue)})	Text
TextFont (text; fontName {; fontScript})	Text
TextFontRemove (text {; fontName; fontScript})	Text
TextFormatRemove (text)	Text
TextSize (text; fontSize)	Text
TextSizeRemove (text {; sizeToRemove})	Text
TextStyleAdd (text; style(s))	Text
TextStyleRemove (text; style(s))	Text

Time Functions

Time functions provide a means of manipulating time data within FileMaker.

Table 5.13   Time Functions

Syntax	Data Type Returned
Hour (time)	Number
Minute (time)	Number
Seconds (time)	Number
Time (hours; minutes; seconds)	Time

Timestamp Functions

The Timestamp function allows developers to exchange or transform data between date, time, and timestamp data types.

Table 5.14   Timestamp Functions

Syntax	Data Type Returned
Timestamp (date; time)	Timestamp

Trigonometric Functions

Trigonometric functions extend math and number functions within FileMaker to trigonometry.

Table 5.15   Trigonometric Functions

Syntax	Data Type Returned
Atan (number)	Number
Cos (number)	Number
Degrees (number)	Number
Pi	Number
Radians (angleInDegrees)	Number
Sin (angleInRadians)	Number
Tan (angleInRadians)	Number

## CHAPTER 6

Calculation Functions

Abs()

Category: **Number**

Syntax: **Abs (number)**

Parameters:

number—Any expression that resolves to a numeric value.

Data type returned: **Number, Time**

Description:

Returns the absolute value of number; absolute value is always a positive number.

Examples:

Function	Results
Abs (-92)	Returns 92.
Abs (Get (CurrentPlatform))	Returns 1 for MacOS and 2 for Windows.
Abs (RetailPrice - WholeSalePrice)	Returns the difference between the two prices, regardless of which one is larger.
Abs (2:15:00 – 3:30:00)	Returns 1:15:00.

Atan()

Category: **Trigonometric**

Syntax: **Atan (number)**

Parameters:

number—Any expression that resolves to a numeric value.

Data type returned: **Number**

Description:

The arc tangent of a number is the angle (measured in radians) whose tangent is the specified number. The range of values returned by the Atan function is -(pi/2) to pi/2.

If Atan (x) = y, then Tan (y) = x.

Atan (x) = Atan (-x).

Examples:

Atan (0) = 0

Atan (1) = .785398163

which is pi/4 radians, or 45 degrees.

Average()

Category: **Aggregate**

Syntax: **Average (field {; field...})**

Parameters:

field—Any related field, repeating field, or set of non-repeating fields that represent a collection of numbers. Parameters in curly braces { } are optional and may be repeated as needed, separated by a semicolon.

Data type returned: **Number**

Description:

Returns a numeric value that is the arithmetic mean of all non-blank values in the set designated by the parameter list. The arithmetic mean of a set of numbers is the sum of the numbers divided by the size of the set. Blank values are not considered as part of the set.

When the parameter list consists of two or more repeating fields, Average() generates a repeating field in which the corresponding repetitions from the specified fields are averaged separately. So, if a field Repeater1 has two values, 16 and 20, and another field, Repeater2, has two values, 14 and 25, Average (Repeater1; Repeater2) would return a repeating field with values 15 and 22.5.

Examples:

Function	Results
Average (field1; field2; field3)	Returns 2 when field1 = 1, field2 = 2, and field3 = 3.
Average (repeatingField) repeatingField[2]; repeatingField[3];)	Returns 2 when repetition1 = 1, repetition2 = 2, and repetition3 = 3.

Examples: *(continued)*

Function	Results
Average (repeatingField[1];	Returns 2 when repetition1 = 1, repetition2 = 2, and repetition3 = 3.
Average (Customer::InvoiceTotal)	Returns $450 when a customer has three related invoice records with invoice totals of $300, $500, and $550.

Case()

Category: **Logical**

Syntax: **Case (test1; result1 {; test2; result2; defaultResult...})**

Parameters:

test(n)—An expression that yields a Boolean result.

result(n)—The value to return if corresponding test is true.

defaultResult—The value to return if all tests are false. Parameters in curly braces { } are optional and may be repeated as needed, separated by a semicolon.

Data type returned: **Text, Number, Date, Time, Timestamp, Container**

Description:

The Case function returns one of several possible results based on a series of tests.

Each test expression is evaluated in order, and when the first true expression (one that resolves to a Boolean 1) is found, the value specified in the result for that expression is returned. The function stops evaluating as soon as it finds a true test.

The default result at the end of the parameter list is optional. If none of the tests evaluate to True, the function returns the value specified for defaultResult. If no default result is specified, the Case function returns an "empty" result. If you believe that one of the tests in the Case should always be true, we recommend using an explicit default case, possibly with a value of "default" or "error" to assist in error trapping.

Consider using hard returns in long Case() statements to make them more readable, and indent lines with tabs, as shown previously. (Note that this example makes repeated calls to Get(SystemLanguage); in practice it might be better to use Let() to make a single call to Get(SystemLanguage) so that it needs to be evaluated only once.)

In the last example, while all three tests resolve to true, only the first line is executed and its result returned. Using the **Case()** function, with its "short-circuiting" feature, can help with performance tuning.

Examples:

Function	Results
Case (IsEmpty (Contact_Name); 1)	Returns 1 if the Contact_Name field is empty.
	Note that a default value is not required, making the usage of Case() shorter than If().

```
Case (
Get(SystemLanguage) = "English"; "Welcome";
Get(SystemLanguage) = "French"; "Bienvenue";
Get(SystemLanguage) = "Italian"; "Benvenuto";
Get(SystemLanguage) = "German"; "Willkommen";
Get(SystemLanguage) = "Swedish"; "Välkommen";
Get(SystemLanguage) = "Spanish "; "Bienvenido",;
Get(SystemLanguage) = "Dutch"; "Welkom";
Get(SystemLanguage) = "Japanese"; "Irashaimasu" ;
"Sorry... not sure of your language." // default value
)
```

Returns a welcoming message in the language determined by the Get (SystemLanguage) function.

```
Case (
SalesTotal < 10; .1;
SalesTotal < 50; .2;
SalesTotal < 100; .3;
.35
)
```

Returns .1 when the value in the SalesTotal field is 5, and returns .2 when the value in the SalesTotal field is 12.

Ceiling()

Category: **Number**

Syntax: **Ceiling (number)**

Parameters:

number—Any expression that resolves to a numeric value.

Data type returned: **Number**

Description:

Returns number rounded up to the next integer.

One common use for the Ceiling function is finding out how many pages will be required to print *x* items if *y* items fit on a page. The formula for this is Ceiling (x / y). For instance, if you have 16 items, and 5 can print per page, you would need Ceiling (16/5) = Ceiling (3.2) = 4 pages.

Examples:

Ceiling (1.05) = 2

Ceiling (-4.6) = -4

Ceiling (3) = 3

Choose()

Category: **Logical**

Syntax: **Choose (test; result0 {; result1; result2...})**

Parameters:

test—An expression that returns a number greater than or equal to zero.

result(n)—The value returned or the expression that is evaluated based on the result of the test. Parameters in curly braces { } are optional and may be repeated as needed, separated by a semicolon.

Data type returned: **Text, Number, Date, Time, Timestamp, Container**

Description:

Returns one of the result values according to the integer value of test. FileMaker evaluates test to obtain an index number, which is used to then select the corresponding ordinal result.

The Choose function is a 0-based list. Choose (1; "a"; "b"; "c") will return "b".

Any fractional value of test is ignored (as opposed to rounded) when obtaining the index number. Choose (1.9; "a"; "b"; "c") will return "b".

If the index value returned by test exceeds the number of results available, the Choose function will not return any result—The field will be blank as opposed to having a "?" in it. There is no way to define a default value to use when the index value exceeds the number of results available.

Examples:

Function	Results
Choose (DayOfWeek(Get (CurrentDate)); ""; "Sun"; "Mon"; "Tue"; "Wed"; "Thu"; "Fri"; "Sat")	Returns a three-letter day name abbreviation for today's date.
Choose ((Month (myDate)/ 3.1); "Q1"; "Q2"; "Q3"; "Q4")	Returns "Q1" for the instance where myDate contains "2/1/2005".

The following formula converts decimal values to fractional notation, rounded to the nearest eighth. Assume an input from a field (or parameter), myNumber.

```
Let ([
    n = myNumber;
    int = int ( n );
    decimal = mod ( n; 1 );
    numberOfEighths = Round ( decimal/.125; 0 );
    intDisplay = Case ( Abs ( int ) > 0; int & Case ( Abs ( decimal ) > 0; " - "; "" ); "" );
    fraction = Choose( numberOfEighths;
            Floor ( n );
            intDisplay & "1/8";
            intDisplay & "1/4";
            intDisplay & "3/8";
            intDisplay & "1/2";
            intDisplay & "5/8";
            intDisplay & "3/4";
            intDisplay & "7/8";
            Ceiling ( n )
    ) // end choose
    ]; // end variables
    fraction
)
```

If myNumber contained 3.45, this function would return 3 - 1/2.

Combination()

Category: **Number**

Syntax: **Combination (setSize; numberOfChoices)**

Parameters:

setSize—Non-negative numeric value (or an expression that results in one).

numberOfChoices—Non-negative numeric value (or an expression that results in one).

Data type returned: **Number**

Description:

Returns the number of ways to uniquely choose numberOfChoices items from a set of size setSize.

The formula used to determine the Combination value is n! / (n-x)! * x!, where n = set size, x = number of choices.

The numbers returned by the Combination function are the coefficients of the binomial expansion series. Useful in statistics, combinatorics, and polynomial expansions, the values returned by this function are referred to as *combination coefficients*. They form Pascal's triangle.

$(x + y)^4 = 1x^4 + 4x^3y + 6x^2y^2 + 4xy^3 + 1y^4$
Combination (4; 0) = 1
Combination (4; 1) = 4
Combination (4; 2) = 6
Combination (4; 3) = 4
Combination (4; 4) = 1

Examples:

Function	Results
Combination (4; 2)	Returns 6 because there are six ways of selecting two items from a set of four items. Given set {A, B, C, D}, these subsets would be {AB, AC, AD, BC, BD, CD}.
Combination (x; 0)	Returns 1 for any x representing the empty set.
Combination (x; x)	Returns 1 for any x.
(13 * 12 * Combination (4; 2) * Combination (4; 3)) / Combination (52; 5)	Returns 0.00144057..., which is the probability of being dealt a full house in five-card poker (less than a 1% chance).

Cos()

Category: **Trigonometric**

Syntax: **Cos (number)**

Parameters:

number—Any expression that resolves to a numeric value that represents an angle measured in radians.

Data type returned: **Number**

Description:

Returns the cosine of the angle represented by the value of the parameter measured in radians. Cos is a periodic function with a range from -1 to 1.

In any right triangle, the cosine of the two non-right angles can be obtained by dividing the length of the side adjacent to the angle by the length of the hypotenuse.

You can convert an angle measured in degrees into radians by using the Radians() function, or by multiplying the value by Pi/180. One radian is slightly more than 57 degrees.

Examples:

Cos (0) = 0

Cos (Pi / 4) = .707106781 (which is 1 / Sqrt (2))

Cos (Radians (60)) = .5

Count()

Category: **Aggregate**

Syntax: **Count (field {; field...})**

Parameters:

field—Any related field, repeating field, or set of non-repeating fields; or an expression that returns a field, repeating field, or set of non-repeating fields. Parameters in curly braces { } are optional and may be repeated as needed, separated by a semicolon.

Data type returned: **Number**

Description:

Returns a count of the fields (or repetitions, in the case of repeating fields) in the parameter list that contain non-blank values.

When the parameter list consists of two or more repeating fields, Count() returns a repeating field in which the corresponding repetitions from the specified fields are counted separately. So if a field Repeater1 has three values, 16, 20, and 24, and another field, Repeater2, has two values, 14 and 25, Count (Repeater1; Repeater2) would return a repeating field with values 2, 2, and 1.

Examples:

Function	Results
Count (field1; field2; field3)	Returns 2 when field1 and field2 contain valid values, and field3 is empty.
Count (repeatingField)	Returns 2 when repetitions 1 and 2 contain valid values, and repetition 3 is empty.
Count (InvoiceItem::InvoiceID)	Returns 2 when the current record is related to two InvoiceItem records. When using the Count() function to count the number of related records, be sure to count a field that is guaranteed not to be blank, such as the table's primary key.

NEW FileMaker 8 modifies the Count() function to take portal and field context into account. For example, in a scenario where a Customer table occurrence is related one-to-many with an Invoice table occurrence that is then related one-to-many to a LineItem table occurrence, evaluating a Count() function from Customer to LineItem will yield *all* LineItem records for the current Customer record if the user's context is on the Customer TO; but if the user's context is on the Invoice TO (if a user clicks in an Invoice portal row, say, or a script navigates into the portal using a Go To Field script step), Count(LineItem::field) will return a count of just those line items related to the currently selected invoice. Given that calculation fields explicitly specify their evaluation context, this issue is most likely to arise in scripting.

DatabaseNames

Category: **Design**

Syntax: **DatabaseNames**

Parameters:

None

Data type returned: **Text**

Description: Returns a carriage return–delimited list of currently open databases (filenames), whether open as a client of another machine or open locally.

Note that on Windows, the .fp7 extension is not returned. This means that the function is consistent across both platforms.

Use caution when checking for hard-coded strings in calculations. If someone renames a file, any calculation containing the old value will no longer behave as before. Get (FileName) can be used in conjunction with a startup script to see whether a filename has been changed, and developers may want to consider establishing a centrally controlled custom function or variable for such checks.

Examples:

In a circumstance where three files are open, Customers, Invoices, and Invoice Line Items, DatabaseNames() will return Customers¶Invoices¶Invoice_Line_Items.

    PatternCount (DatabaseNames; "Customers")

Returns 1 if the Customers database is open.

Date()

Category: **Date**

Syntax: **Date (month; day; year)**

Parameters:

month—The month of the year (a number from 1 to 12).

day—The day of the month (a number from 1 to 31).

year—The year (four digits between 0001 and 4000). The year parameter should be passed as a four-digit number; if not, FileMaker will not infer or prepend a century. (1/10/05 = January 10, 0005.)

Note that regardless of your system settings, this function requires that its parameters be listed strictly in order: month, day, year. Localizations settings will not apply.

Data type returned: **Date**

Description:

Returns a valid date of data type date represented by the three parameters.

Values for month and day outside of normal ranges will be interpreted correctly. For instance, a month value of 13 returns a date in January of the following year. A day value of 0 returns the last day of the preceding month.

Parameters can be calculation expressions or fields; as long as the final result is valid, the date function will work correctly. Dates are stored internally as numbers (a unit of "1" represents one day); whole number math can be done on dates.

Be sure when returning dates as the result of calculation fields that you specify a calculation result of Date. If you were to define a field as Date (1; 1; 2000) and were to set the calculation result as Number, then you would see 730120 as the calculation value. Internally, FileMaker stores dates as the number of days since January 1, 0001, and that internal representation is returned if you incorrectly specify the return data type.

Examples:

Function	Results
Date (1; 1; 2000)	Returns January 1, 2000 (formatting is determined on the layout and by system preferences).

Math can be performed on dates:

Date(1; 1; 2000) - 1	Returns December 31, 1999.

The parameters in a Date function can be calculated:

Date (Month (Get (CurrentDate)); 1; Year (Get (CurrentDate)))	Returns the date of the first of the current month; if today is August 12, 1965, then August 1, 1965 is returned.

The parameters in a Date function can be fields:

Date (pickMonth; 1; Get (CurrentDate))	Returns the date of the first of a month specified by the value in the field pickMonth.

Category: **Date**

Syntax: **Day (date)**

Parameters:

Date—Any valid date (1/1/0001–12/31/4000), expression that returns a date, or field that contains a date.

Data type returned: **Number**

Description:

Returns the day of month (1–31) for any valid date.

Examples:

    Day ("1/15/2000") = 15

Other functions can be referenced in Day():

    Day (Get (CurrentDate))

returns the day of month for today.

Parameters in Day() can be calculated:

    Day (Get (CurrentDate) - 90)

Returns the day number for the date 90 days before today, which may not be the same as today's day number.

DayName()

Category: **Date**

Syntax: **DayName (date)**

Parameters:

Date—Any valid date (1/1/0001–12/31/4000), expression that returns a date, or field that contains a date. The parameter can also be the numeric representation of a date (1–1460970).

Data type returned: **Text**

Description:

Returns a text string containing the name of a weekday for any valid date (1/1/0001–12/31/4000).

Note that the year is optional. DayName ("12/1") will return the day name for December 1st in the current year.

Examples:

Function	Results
DayName ("11/24/2003")	Returns Monday.
DayName (dateField)	Returns the day of week for the date stored in the field dateField.
DayName (Get (CurrentDate) - 30)	Returns the day name for the date 30 days prior to today.

DayNameJ()

Category: **Date**

Syntax: **DayNameJ (date)**

Parameters:

Date—Any calendar date.

Data type returned: **text (Japanese)**

Description:

Returns a text string in Japanese that is the full name of the weekday for date.

To avoid errors when using dates, always use four-digit years. FileMaker will not infer or prepend a century on two-digit dates. (1/10/05 = January 10, 0005.)

Examples:

Function	Results
DayNameJ (Date (11; 1; 2005))	Returns Kaiyobi in whatever font/display preference a user's system supports.

DayOfWeek()

Category: **Date**

Syntax: **DayOfWeek (date)**

Parameters:

Date—Any valid date (1/1/0001–12/31/4000), expression that returns a date, or field that contains a date. The parameter can also be the numeric representation of a date (1–1460970).

Data type returned: **Number**

Description:

Returns a number from 1 to 7, representing the day of week (Sunday = 1, Saturday = 7) for any valid date (1/1/0001–12/31/4000).

DayOfWeek() can be used to perform conditional tests on days of week without concern for localization issues. The number returned is always the same regardless of what language version of FileMaker Pro the user is using. The number value returned by DayOfWeek() can also be used in mathematical calculations.

Note that the year is optional. DayOfWeek ("12/1") will return the appropriate integer for December 1st in the current year.

Examples:

Function	Results
DayOfWeek ("11/24/2003")	Returns 2 (Monday).
DayOfWeek (dateField)	Returns the day of week for the date stored in the field dateField.
DayOfWeek (Date (12; 25; Year (Get (CurrentDate))))	Returns the day number on which Christmas falls this year.

DayOfYear()

Category: **Date**

Syntax: **DayOfYear (date)**

Parameters:

Date—Any valid date (1/1/0001–12/31/4000), expression that returns a date, or field that contains a date. The parameter can also be the numeric representation of a date (1–1460970).

Data type returned: **Number**

Description:

Returns a number representing the day of year (1–366) for any valid date (1/1/0001–12/31/4000).

You can use the DayOfYear function to check whether a particular year is a leap year. Given a field Year, the formula DayOfYear (Date (12; 31; Year)) would return 366 if Year was a leap year, and 365 if it wasn't.

Note that the year is optional. DayOfYear ("12/1") will return the appropriate integer for December 1st in the current year.

Examples:

Function	Results
DayOfYear ("12/31/2000")	Returns 366 (leap year).
DayOfYear ("12/31/2001")	Returns 365 (non–leap year).
DayOfYear ("1/24/2004")	Returns 24.
DayOfYear (dateField)	Returns the day number for the date stored in dateField.
DayOfYear (Get (CurrentDate) + 30)	Returns the day of year for a date 30 days from now.

Degrees()

Category: **Trigonometric**

Syntax: **Degrees (number)**

Parameters:

number—A number representing an angle measured in radians.

Data type returned: **Number**

Description:

Converts an angle measured in radians to its equivalent in degrees. There are 2×Pi radians in 360°, so 1 radian is just over 57°.

Another way to convert radians to degrees is to multiply by 180/Pi.

Examples:

Function	Results
Degrees (0)	Returns 0.
Degrees (Pi / 4)	Returns 45.
Degrees (2 * Pi)	Returns 360.
Degrees (4 * Pi)	Returns 720.
Degrees (-Pi / 2)	Returns -90.

Div()

Category: **Number**

Syntax: **Div (number; divisor)**

Parameters:

number—Any expression that resolves to a numeric value.

divisor—Any expression that resolves to a numeric value.

Data type returned: **Number**

Description:

Returns the quotient resulting from the division of the numerator number by the denominator divisor.

The Div() function is equivalent to Floor (numerator / denominator).

To obtain the remainder when a numerator is divided by denominator, use the Mod function.

Examples:

Function	Results
Div (30; 4)	Returns 7 because 30/4 is 7, remainder 2.
Div (51; 8)	Returns 6 because 50/8 is 6, remainder 3.

Evaluate()

Category: **Logical**

Syntax: **Evaluate (expression {; [field1; field2; ...]})**

Parameters:

expression—Any valid calculation formula, field containing a valid formula, or expression returning a valid formula.

field(n)—A list of optional fields that can then serve to trigger a re-evaluation; the expression re-evaluates when any of the included fields are updated.

Parameters in curly braces { } are optional. The optional field list must be enclosed by square brackets when there are multiple parameters.

Data type returned: **Text, Number, Date, Time, Timestamp, Container**

Description:

The Evaluate() function returns the results obtained by evaluating expression.

The optional second parameter is a list of fields on which the calculation becomes dependent. When any of those fields are modified, the Evaluate() function re-evaluates the expression specified by the first parameter.

➔ *For more in-depth examples of the* Evaluate() *function,* **see** Special Edition Using FileMaker 8, *Chapter 14, "Advanced Calculation Techniques."*

The Evaluate() function expects that the first parameter passed to it is a string that contains a formula of some sort. If you are passing a literal string, as in the fourth of the following examples, using the Quote() function ensures that any quotation marks in the formula itself are properly encoded. If the first parameter is a field name or an expression, that field or expression is expected to return a formula, which the Evaluate() function then evaluates. In a nutshell, if the first parameter is *not* surrounded by quotation marks, the *result* of whatever field or expression is provided is evaluated.

Note that the execution of the expression does occur—in other words, do not think of Evaluate() as a "testing function" making use of its own memory space. If your expression modifies a global or local variable (using the Let() function), any applicable changes will be applied. If you need a calculation "scratch pad," consider using the Evaluate Now function of the FileMaker Advanced Data Viewer—though there again, any "side-effect" modifications of variables will occur "for real," a good example of why modifying variables from within calculations can be a questionable practice.

Examples:

Function	Results
Evaluate(MyFormula)	Returns 8 if MyFormula contains the string 5+3.
Evaluate(MyFormula)	Returns 4 if MyFormula contains the string Length (FirstName) and FirstName contains Fred.
Evaluate("MyFormula")	Returns a text string, "5+3" if MyFormula contains the string 5+3.
Evaluate(Quote ("The comment field was last updated on " & Get (CurrentDate) & " by " & Get (AccountName)); CommentField)	Returns a string containing information about the date and user who last modified the CommentField.

EvaluationError()

Category: **Logical**

Syntax: **EvaluationError (expression)**

Parameters:

expression—Any FileMaker calculation formula.

Data type returned: **Number**

Description:

Returns whatever error code an expression may generate if executed. If the expression executes properly, a zero (no error) will be returned.

Note that the expression is executed if it is syntactically correct. If your expression manipulates local or global variables, they will be affected by this EvaluationError() check. Note also that there are two kinds of errors returned: syntax errors, where the expression cannot be executed (and will not be executed by EvalutionError()), and runtime errors, where the expression is valid but, for example, a field or record may be missing.

Important: The EvaluationError() function must enclose the Evaluate() function to return any syntax errors.

Examples:

Function	Results
EvaluationError (Evaluate (Length (<missingfield>)))	Returns error 102 (field missing).
EvaluationError (Evaluate (Case (1 = 1))	Returns error 1201 (too few parameters).
EvaluationError (Case (1 = 1))	Returns error 0 since there were no runtime errors. If you want to ensure you always get error codes including this syntax error, be sure to use the nested Evaluate() function. Note that this error is impossible to get unless you're working with calculation formulas in fields: If you were to enter this example into a calculation dialog, FileMaker would not allow it to be saved and would prompt the developer to correct the syntax.

Exact()

Category: **Text**

Syntax: **Exact (originalText; comparisonText)**

Parameters:

originalText—Any text expression, text field, or container field.

comparisonText—Any text expression, text field, or container field.

Data type returned: **Number**

Description:

Compares the contents of any two text or container expressions. This function is case sensitive. If the expressions match, the result is 1 (True); otherwise, the result is 0 (False). For container fields, not only must the data be the same, but it must also be stored in the same manner (either embedded or stored by file reference). Note that for container fields it is the text representations of the file references being compared.

Remember that Exact() considers the case of the two strings, whereas the = operator does not. If you need to compare two values in a conditional test, consider using If (Exact (A; B); ... instead of If (A = B; ....

Examples:

Function	Results
Exact ("Smith"; "smith")	Returns 0 (False).
Exact (Proper (Salutation); Salutation)	Returns 1 if the contents of the Salutation field begin with initial caps.
Exact (Zip_Lookup::City_Name; City_Name)	Returns 1 if the value of City_Name is exactly the same as the one stored in a related ZIP Code table.

Exp()

Category: **Number**

Syntax: **Exp (number)**

Parameters:

number—Any expression that resolves to a numeric value.

Data type returned: **Number**

Description:

Returns the value of the constant *e* raised to the power of *number*. The Exp() function is the inverse of the Ln() function.

To return the value of the constant *e* itself, use Exp (1), which returns 2.7182818284590452. You can use the SetPrecision() function to return *e* with up to 400 digits of precision.

Examples:

Function	Results
Round (Exp (5); 3)	Returns 148.413.
Exp (Ln (5))	Returns 5.

Extend()

Category: **Repeating**

Syntax: **Extend (non-repeatingField)**

Parameters:

non-repeatingField—Any non-repeating field (a field defined to contain only one value).

Data type returned: **Text, Number, Date, Time, Timestamp, Container**

Description:

Allows a value in non-repeatingField to be applied to every repetition within a repeating field (most commonly a calculation field). Without using the Extend() function, only the first repetition of a repeating calculation field will properly reference the value in non-repeatingField.

Examples:

Given a number field RepCommission, defined to hold three repetitions, a non-repeating number field (SalePrice), and repeating calculation field (SalesCommission), defined as follows:

Round (RepCommision * Extend (SalePrice); 2)

RepCommission	SalePrice	SalesCommission
.10	18.00	1.80
.12		2.16
.15		2.40

Without the Extend() function, only the first repetition of SalesCommission would have returned the correct value.

External()

Category: **External**

Syntax: **External (nameOfFunction; parameter)**

Parameters:

nameOfFunction—The name of the external function being called.

parameter—The parameter that is being passed to the external function.

Data type returned: **Depends on the external function**

Description:

The External() function is used to call functions defined within a plug-in. A plug-in must be installed (located in the Extensions folder) and enabled (under the Plug-Ins tab of Preferences) for you to have access to its functions.

→ *For more detail on plug-ins, **see** Special Edition Using FileMaker 8, Chapter 24, "Deploying and Extending FileMaker."*

The function name and parameter syntax for an external function is defined by the plug-in developer. When calling external plug-ins, be sure to use the exact syntax specified in the documentation for the plug-in. The external function parameter can generally be passed as a field, as long as the contents of the field conform to the requirements set forth by the plug-in developer. Because only a single parameter may be passed to a function, parameters often consist of delimited lists of data, which are then parsed and interpreted inside the plug-in.

Examples:

External ("myPlugin"; "param1|param2|param3")

External ("myPlugin"; myParmField)

Factorial()

Category: **Number**

Syntax: **Factorial (number {; numberOfFactors })**

Parameters:

number—Any expression that resolves to a positive integer.

numberOfFactors—Any expression that resolves to a positive integer that represents how many factors to include in the multiplication.

Parameters in curly braces { } are optional.

Data type returned: **Number**

Description:

Returns the factorial of number, stopping either at 1 or stopping at the optional numberOfFactors. The factorial of a number n is defined as $n \times (n–1) \times (n–2) \times (n–3)\ldots\times 1$. Factorials are useful in statistics and combinatorics. In mathematics, factorials are usually represented by an exclamation mark. 4! = Factorial (4) = 4×3×2×1 = 24.

One application of factorials is to determine how many unique ways a set of objects can be ordered. For instance, a set of three objects {A, B, C} can be ordered 3! = 6 ways: {ABC, ACB, BAC, BCA, CAB, CBA}.

Examples:

Function	Results
Factorial (3)	Returns 6, which = 3×2×1.
Factorial (10; 3)	Returns 720, which = 10×9×8.

FieldBounds()

Category: **Design**

Syntax: **FieldBounds (fileName; layoutName; fieldName)**

Parameters:

fileName—Name of the file where the field resides.

layoutName—Name of the layout where the field resides.

fieldName—Name of the field open.

Data type returned: **Text**

Description:

Returns the physical position and rotation of a field that is described by the parameters. Note that the parameters are text and must either be references to fields or enclosed in quotation marks. Results are returned as a space-delimited text string in the form of "Left Top Right Bottom Rotation." The first four of these values represent the distance in pixels from either the left margin of the layout (in the case of Left and Right) or the top margin (in the case of Top and Right). The Rotation value will be 0, 90, 180, or 270, depending on the field's orientation on the layout.

The values returned are delimited by spaces; the MiddleWords() function can easily be used to parse them.

Be aware that changing the name of a file, layout, or field may cause literal references to them to be broken in functions that use FieldBounds.

The field name that is passed to FieldBounds() must be the name from Define Database (not the field label); if a field appears on layout more than once, the one that is furthest in the rear in the layering order will be used.

Related fields must be referenced by RelationshipName::FieldName or FileName::FieldName.

Examples:

Function	Results
FieldBounds (myFile; myLayout; myField)	Might return 444 84 697 98 0.

FieldComment()

Category: **Design**

Syntax: **FieldComment (fileName; fieldName)**

Parameters:

fileName—The name of the open file where the field is located.

fieldName—The name of the field for which to return comments.

Data type returned: **Text**

Description:

Returns the contents of any comment that has been entered in Define Database for the specified field. The syntax Table::fieldName is required to reference fields outside of the current table context. (The safest approach is to use this method in all cases.)

FieldComment() is useful for documenting a database. Care must be taken, however, because literal references to fields can be broken when file, table, or field names are changed. FieldNames() and TableNames() can be used to dynamically investigate all field names and load the results from FieldComment() into tables for browsing.

A field comment may contain a maximum of 30,000 characters, though it's doubtful such a large comment would constitute a sound development practice.

Examples:

Function	Results
FieldComment ("myDatabase"; "Contacts::FirstName")	Returns the comment, if any, for the FirstName field as it appears in the table definition.

FieldIDs()

Category: **Design**

Syntax: **FieldIDs (fileName; layoutName)**

Parameters:

fileName—The name of the open FileMaker database from which to return IDs.

layoutName—The name of the layout from which to return field IDs.

Data type returned: **Text**

Description:

Returns a list of all FileMaker internal field IDs in fileName and layoutName, separated by carriage returns. Fields outside the current table context are returned as TableID::RelatedFieldID. If layoutName is empty, then the field IDs of the first table created (the "default" table) are returned.

Calls to FieldIDs() can be broken when file and layout names are changed. Field IDs are assigned by FileMaker and cannot be changed. In our practice we do not recommend using Field IDs when other means may exist to accomplish your needs.

Examples:

Function	Results
FieldIDs ("Invoices"; "List View")	Returns IDs of all unique fields, including related fields, on the List View layout in Invoices. In this case the returned data might be 8::12. (Table with an ID of 8, field with ID of 12.)

FieldNames()

Category: **Design**

Syntax: **FieldNames (fileName; layout/tableName)**

Parameters:

fileName—The name of an open FileMaker database from which to return field names.

layout/tableName—The name of the layout or table to reference.

Data type returned: **Text**

Description:

Returns a carriage return–delimited list of field names.

When a table name is given (and is not also serving as a layout name), all fields for that table are returned. If a layout has the same name as a table, FileMaker will turn first to the layout in question and return only those fields that have been placed on that layout.

FieldNames() can be used to dynamically generate database structure information about any open FileMaker database.

When information about fields in a table is returned, the results are ordered according to the creation order of the fields. When the names of the fields on a particular layout are returned, the results are ordered according to the stacking order of the fields, from back to front. If an object appears on a layout more than once, it appears multiple times in the result list. Related fields appear as RelationshipName::FieldName.

Examples:

Function	Results
FieldNames (Get (FileName); "Customers")	Returns a list of fields found in the table named Customers in the current database (assuming there isn't a layout named "Customers").

FieldRepetitions()

Category: **Design**

Syntax: **FieldRepetitions (fileName; layoutName; fieldName)**

Parameters:

fileName—The name of the open file where the field to be referenced is located.

layoutName—The name of the layout where the field to be referenced is located.

fieldName—The name of the field for which to return repetition information.

Data type returned: **Text**

Description:

Returns a space-delimited text string that indicates the number of repetitions and orientation of the field in question. Note that you must pass a layout name. (A table name does not work.) The data is returned in the format of "NumRepetitions Orienation."

The MiddleWords() function can be used to extract either component of the result.

If literal names of objects are used, calls to the function may be broken when file or object names are changed. Functions such as Get(FileName), LayoutNames(), and FieldNames() can be used to dynamically return information about a database. Also remember that only the number of repetitions that appear on the layout are returned, not the number of repetitions defined in Define Database. Use FieldType() to return the number of repetitions specified in Define Database.

Examples:

Function	Results
FieldRepetitions (Get (FileName); "Invoice_Detail"; "Payment_History")	Might return a string like 10 vertical.

FieldStyle()

Category: **Design**

Syntax: **FieldStyle (fileName; layoutName; fieldName)**

Parameters:

fileName—The name of the open file where the field is located.

layoutName—The name of the layout where the field is used.

fieldName—The name of the field for which to return results.

Data type returned: **Text**

Description:

Returns a space-delimited string indicating the field style and any associated value list. The field styles are

  Standard
  Scrolling
  Popuplist
  Popupmenu
  Checkbox
  RadioButton
  Calendar

Calls to FieldStyle() that rely on literal object names may be broken if file, layout, or field names are changed.

Examples:

Function	Results
FieldStyle (Get (FileName); "Invoice_Detail"; "Notes")	Might return Scrolling for a notes field that has scrollbars turned on.
FieldStyle (Get (FileName); "Invoice_Detail"; "Paid")	Might return RadioButton Yes_No for a field formatted as a radio button that uses a value list called Yes_No.

FieldType()

Category: **Design**

Syntax: **FieldType (fileName; fieldName)**

Parameters:

fileName—The name of the open file where the field is located.

fieldName—The name of the field for which to return results.

Data type returned: **Text**

Description:

Returns a space-delimited string indicating the field type of the field specified by fieldName. There are four components to the string, each of which can contain several possible values. The possible values for each item are

Item 1: standard, storedcalc, summary, unstoredcalc, or global

Item 2: text, number, date, time, timestamp, or container

Item 3: indexed or unindexed

Item 4: Number of repetitions (1 for a non-repeating field)

fieldName must be specified as Table::Field when referencing fields in tables outside of the current table context.

Using the Table::Field method for referencing fields as a matter of course avoids broken references when the current table context changes.

Examples:

Function	Results
FieldType (Get (FileName); "Contacts::ContactID")	Might return values that look like this: standard number indexed 1.
FieldType (Get (FileName); "Contacts::gTempName")	Might return values that look like this: global text unindexed 1.

Filter()

Category: **Text**

Syntax: **Filter (textToFilter; filterText)**

Parameters:

textToFilter—Any expression that resolves to a text string.

filterText—The characters to preserve in the specified text.

Data type returned: **Text**

Description:

Strips from textToFilter all the characters not explicitly listed in filterText. All remaining characters are returned in the order in which they exist in textToFilter, including duplicates. If filterText doesn't have any characters, an empty string is returned, as opposed to a question mark. The Filter() function is case sensitive.

The Filter() function is frequently used to ensure that users have entered valid data into a field. The textToFilter parameter should contain any valid characters; the order of the characters within textToFilter isn't important.

Examples:

Function	Results
Filter ("ab123"; "abc")	Returns ab.
Filter (PhoneNumber; "0123456789")	Would strip any non-numeric characters from the PhoneNumber field.

FilterValues()

Category: **Text**

Syntax: **FilterValues (textToFilter; filterValues)**

Parameters:

textToFilter—A return-delimited text string or expression that generates a return-delimited text string.

filterValues—A return-delimited text string or expression that generates a return-delimited text string representing values that you want to preserve in the specified text.

Data type returned: **Text**

Description:

FilterValues() produces a return-delimited list of items in textToFilter that are included among the specified filterValues. The items must match exactly in order to be returned, with the exception of case; FilterValues() is not case sensitive.

Values are returned in the order they appear in textToFilter. If filterValues is an empty string, or if no items in textToFilter are contained in the filterValues list, then an empty string is returned.

FilterValues() can be used to determine whether a particular item is part of a return-delimited array. For instance, the WindowNames() function produces a return-delimited list of windows. If you wanted to know whether a window named Contact Detail existed, you could use the following formula:

ValueCount (FilterValues (WindowNames; "Contact Detail"))

If the value count is anything other than zero, that means the window name was found. The benefit of using FilterValues for this rather than PatternCount() is that Contact Detail - 2 would not be returned if Contact Detail were the filter.

Examples:

Function	Results
FilterValues(Offices; "San Francisco¶Chicago¶Philadelphia")	Returns Chicago¶Philadelphia when Offices contains: Chicago¶Philadelphia¶San Mateo.

Floor()

Category: **Number**

Syntax: **Floor (number)**

Parameters:

number—Any expression that resolves to a numeric value.

Data type returned: **Number**

Description:

Returns number rounded down to the next lower integer.

For positive numbers, Floor() and Int() return the same results; however, for negative numbers, Int() returns the next larger integer, whereas Floor() returns the next smaller integer.

Examples:

Function	Results
Floor (1.0005)	Returns 1.
Floor (-1.0005)	Returns –2.

FV()

Category: **Financial**

Syntax: **FV (payment; interestRate; periods)**

Parameters:

payment—The nominal amount of the payment.

interestRate—The per-period interest rate.

periods—The number of periods in the duration of the investment.

Data type returned: **Number**

Description:

Returns the future value of a periodic investment based on the payments and interest rate for the number of periods specified.

The FV() function doesn't account for the present value of your investment, and it assumes that payments are made at the end of each period.

Examples:

Function	Results
FV (50; .10; 2)	Returns 105, indicating the amount of money you would have after making two periodic deposits of $50 into an investment that paid 10% per period.

If the investment compounds monthly, divide the annual interestRate by 12 to express the periods as a number of months.

To figure out the future value of monthly investments of $250, earning 8% interest, for 10 years, you would use the formula

FV (250; .08/12; 10 * 12)   which returns 45736.51.

Get(AccountName)

Category: **Get**

Syntax: **Get (AccountName)**

Parameters: None

Data type returned: **Text**

Description:

Returns the name of the authenticated account being used by the current user of the database file. If a user is logged in under the default Admin account, Admin is returned. If a user is using the FileMaker Pro guest account, then [Guest] is returned.

For external server authentication, Get(AccountName) returns the name of the authenticated account being used by the current user of the database file, not the group to which the user belongs. (The group name appears in the Account list when you define accounts and privileges in FileMaker Pro.) If an individual belongs to more than one group (account), the first group name listed when you View By Authentication Order while defining accounts and privileges determines access for the user.

Get (AccountName) can be used to retrieve the account name of the current user for purposes of logging or auditing database access.

Examples:

Function	Results
Get (AccountName)	Returns klove when the current user is logged in with the klove account.

Get(ActiveFieldContents)

Category: **Get**

Syntax: **Get (ActiveFieldContents)**

Parameters: None

Data type returned: **Text, Number, Date, Time, Timestamp, Container**

Description:

Returns the contents of the field in which the cursor is currently placed. The contents of the field need not be highlighted.

Get (ActiveFieldContents) can return the contents of fields of any data type, but the field in which you place those contents may need to be of the same data type for it to display properly.

Note that in the case where the cursor is not placed in a field, a blank value is returned, as opposed to a question mark.

When using Get() functions within field definitions, in most cases you should set the storage option to be "unstored" so that the field always displays current data.

Examples:

Function	Results
Get (ActiveFieldContents)	Returns Rowena when the current field contains the name Rowena.

Get(ActiveFieldName)

Category: **Get**

Syntax: **Get (ActiveFieldName)**

Parameters: None

Data type returned: **Text**

Description:

Returns the name of the field in which the cursor is currently placed.

Even when the active field is a related or unrelated field from another table, Get (ActiveFieldName) simply returns the field's name. It does *not* use the double-colon syntax "relationshipName::FieldName."

Note that in the case where the cursor is not placed in a field, a blank value is returned, as opposed to a question mark.

When using Get() functions within field definitions, in most cases you should set the storage option to be "unstored" so that the field always displays current data.

Examples:

Function	Results
Get (ActiveFieldName)	Returns Name_First when the cursor is in the Name_First field.

Get(ActiveFieldTableName)

Category: Get

Syntax: **Get (ActiveFieldTableName)**

Parameters: None

Data type returned: **Text**

Description:

Returns the name of the table occurrence for the field in which the cursor is currently placed.

Note that the table occurrence name (from the Relationships Graph) is returned, rather than the source table name.

Note that in the case where the cursor is not placed in a field, a blank value is returned, as opposed to a question mark.

When using Get() functions within field definitions, in most cases you should set the storage option to be "unstored" so that the field always displays current data.

Examples:

Function	Results
Get (ActiveFieldTableName)	Might return Contacts2.

Get(ActiveModifierKeys)

Category: **Get**

Syntax: **Get (ActiveModifierKeys)**

Parameters: None

Data type returned: **Number**

Description:

Returns the sum of the constants that represent the modifier keys that the user is pressing on the keyboard. The constants for modifier keys are as follows:

1—Shift

2—Caps lock

4—Control

8—Alt (Windows) or Option (Mac OS)

16—Command key (Mac OS only)

When using Get() functions within field definitions, in most cases you should set the storage option to be "unstored" so that the field always displays current data.

Examples:

Get (ActiveModifierKeys)

Returns 4 if the Control key is being held down, and returns 7 (1+2+4) if the Shift, Caps Lock, and Control keys are being held down.

The following formula can be used to show text values for keys being held down; it can be used in a calculated field or a custom function:

```
Let ( keys = Get (ActiveModifierKeys);
        Case (Mod (keys;2); "Shift ") &
        Case (Int (Mod (keys;4)/2); "Caps Lock ") &
        Case (Int (Mod (keys;8)/4); "Control ") &
        Choose ( 2 * (Int (Mod (keys;16)/8)) +
            (Abs (Get(SystemPlatform)) - 1);
            "";""; "Option "; "Alt ")&
        Case (keys>=16; "Command")
)
```

If the user is holding down the Shift, Caps, and Control keys when this function is evaluated, the text values for those keys are returned in the form of Shift, Caps Lock, and Control.

Get(ActiveRepetitionNumber)

Category: **Get**

Syntax: **Get (ActiveRepetitionNumber)**

Parameters: None

Data type returned: **Number**

Description:

Returns the number of the active repetition (the repetition in which the cursor currently resides) for a repeating field. Repetition numbers start with 1.

If the cursor is not in a field, 0 is returned.

When using Get() functions within field definitions, in most cases you should set the storage option to be "unstored" so that the field always displays current data.

Examples:

Function	Results
Get (ActiveRepetitionNumber)	Would return 2 when a user was clicked into the second repetition of a field.

Get(ActiveSelectionSize)

Category: **Get**

Syntax: **Get (ActiveSelectionSize)**

Parameters: None

Data type returned: **Number**

Description:

Returns the number of characters that are highlighted in the current field. The function returns 0 if no characters are highlighted, and returns a blank value if no field is active. When multiple windows are open (which leads to the possibility of multiple highlighted selections), only the active window is considered.

Carriage returns, tabs, spaces, and other invisible characters are counted by Get (ActiveSelectionSize).

When using Get() functions within field definitions, in most cases you should set the storage option to be "unstored" so that the field always displays current data.

Examples:

Function	Results
Get (ActiveSelectionSize)	Would return 10 if a user had highlighted 10 characters in any field in the active window.

Get(ActiveSelectionStart)

Category: **Get**

Syntax: **Get (ActiveSelectionStart)**

Parameters: None

Data type returned: **Number**

Description:

Returns the position of the first character in the highlighted text of the current field. If no text is highlighted (that is, the user has simply clicked into a block of text), then the current position of the cursor is returned. It returns a blank value if no field is active. When multiple windows are open, only the active window is considered.

Remember that carriage returns, tabs, spaces, and other invisible characters are taken into account when evaluating Get (ActiveSelectionStart).

Used in conjunction with Get (ActiveSelectionSize), you can determine the string that a user has highlighted in any field, using the formula
    Middle (Get (ActiveFieldContents); Get (ActiveSelectionStart) ;
      Get (ActiveSelectionSize))

Examples:

Function	Results
Get (ActiveSelectionStart)	Returns 1 if the user has selected an entire field, or if the insertion point is at the beginning of a field.

Get(AllowAbortState)

Category: **Get**

Syntax: **Get (AllowAbortState)**

Parameters: None

Data type returned: **Number**

Description:

Returns 1 if Allow User Abort is On; returns 0 if Allow User Abort is Off.

If the setting for User Abort hasn't been explicitly set, a script runs as if Allow User Abort is On. Get (AllowAbortState) returns 1 in such cases.

Examples:

In the following script
    Allow User Abort [Off]
    Show Custom Dialog [Get (AllowAbortState)]

the custom dialog would display 0.

In the following script
    Allow User Abort [On]
    Show Custom Dialog [Get (AllowAbortState)]

the custom dialog would display 1.

Get(AllowToolbarState)

Category: **Get**

Syntax: **Get (AllowToolbarState)**

Parameters: None

Data type returned: **Number**

Description:

Developers may control whether or not users can make toolbars visible or not via the Allow Toolbars script step. This companion function returns a Boolean value representing whether toolbars are allowed to be visible. Returns 1 if toolbars are allowed, otherwise returns 0.

By default, toolbars are allowed.

Examples:

Function	Results
Get (AllowToolbarState)	Returns 1 if toolbars are allowed to be visible.

Get(ApplicationLanguage)

Category: **Get**

Syntax: **Get (ApplicationLanguage)**

Parameters: None

Data type returned: **Text**

Description:

Returns a text string representing the current application language. The possible results are as follows:

English

French

Italian

German

Swedish

Spanish

Dutch

Japanese

The string returned will always be in English, even in versions of the product based on other languages. That is, it returns German, not Deutsch, in the German language version of FileMaker.

Examples:

Function	Results
Get (ApplicationLanguage)	Would return English for users using an English-language version of FileMaker Pro.

Get(ApplicationVersion)

Category: **Get**

Syntax: **Get (ApplicationVersion)**

Parameters: None

Data type returned: **Text**

Description:

Returns a text string representing the application and version:

NEW Pro (version) for FileMaker Pro.

ProAdvanced (version) for FileMaker Advanced.

Runtime (version) for FileMaker Runtime.

Web (version) for FileMaker Web Client in cases where IWP is being hosted from FileMaker Pro or Pro Advanced.

Server (version) for FileMaker Web Server.

If you have allowed web access to a database, you may want to add conditional tests within some of your scripts so that they will behave differently for web and FileMaker Pro clients. To identify web users, use either of the following formulas:

PatternCount (Get (ApplicationVersion); "Web")

Position (Get (ApplicationVersion); "Web"; 1; 1)

If either of these return anything other than 0, the user is a web client.

Examples:

Get (ApplicationVersion)

Returns ProAdvanced 8.0v1 for FileMaker Pro Advanced 8.0v1.

If you add an unstored calculation field that performs Get(ApplicationVersion) to a database, and then extract the data as XML via Custom Web Publishing, you may get

```
<field name="AppVersion">
  <data>Web Publishing Engine 8.0v1</data>
</field>
```

Get(CalculationRepetitionNumber)

Category: **Get**

Syntax: **Get (CalculationRepetitionNumber)**

Parameters: None

Data type returned: **Number**

Description:

Returns the current repetition number of a calculation field. If the calculation is not set to allow more than one value, Get (CalculationRepetitionNumber) returns 1.

Get (CalculationRepetitionNumber) is nothing more than the repetition number.

You can use the repetition number in conditional tests involving repeating fields. For instance, the following formula

If (Get (CalculationRepetitionNumber) < 4; "foo"; "boo")

returns a repeating calculation field with values foo, foo, foo, boo, boo, and so on.

Examples:

Function	Results
Get (CalculationRepetitionNumber)	Returns 1 in the first repetition of a repeating field, 2 in the second repetition, and so on, up to the maximum number of repetitions the field has been defined to hold.

A calculation field defined to hold five repetitions and has the following formula

Get (CalculationRepetitionNumber) ^ 2

returns the repetition values 1, 4, 9, 16, 25.

Get(CurrentDate)

Category: **Get**

Syntax: **Get (CurrentDate)**

Parameters: None

Data type returned: **Date**

Description:

Returns the current date according to the operating system calendar.

The format of the result varies based on the date format that was in use when the database file was created. In the United States, dates are generally in the format

MM/DD/YYYY. You can change a computer's date format in the Regional Settings Control Panel (Windows 2000), the Date and Time Control Panel (Windows XP), or the Date & Time System Preference (Mac OS X).

If the result is displayed in a field, it is formatted according to the date format of the field in the current layout.

Examples:

Function	Results
DayName (Get (CurrentDate) - 30)	Returns the day name for the date 30 days prior to today.
Get (CurrentDate) - InvoiceDate	Returns the number of days outstanding for a given invoice.

Get(CurrentHostTimestamp)

Category: **Get**

Syntax: **Get (CurrentHostTimestamp)**

Parameters: None

Data type returned: **Timestamp**

Description:

Returns the current timestamp (date and time) according to the host's system clock, to the nearest second.

Get (CurrentHostTimeStamp) returns the date and time from the host machine, regardless of the date and time settings on the client machine. Get (CurrentHostTimestamp) is therefore useful for storing information about when records are created or edited because it disregards differences in time zones or improper settings of the client machines.

Function calls that run on the server may impact a network user's performance, especially when they are used in unstored calculations.

Examples:

Function	Results
Get (CurrentHostTimestamp)	Returns 1/1/2004 11:30:01 AM when the system clock on the host machine shows January 1, 2004, 11:30:01 AM.

Get(CurrentTime)

Category: **Get**

Syntax: **Get (CurrentTime)**

Parameters: None

Data type returned: **Time**

Description:

Returns the current time from the local system clock (on the client machine).

Note that the Time data type is stored internally as the number of seconds since midnight. Math can be performed on all Time() functions using multiples of seconds (60 = 1 minute, 3600 = 1 hour).

Remember that the time returned by Get (CurrentTime) is the local time on the system clock of the client machine. In cases where clients are accessing a database from different time zones, or someone has their clock set wrong, this data may be less useful than time extracted from the host machine's system clock with the Get (CurrentHostTimeStamp) function.

Examples:

Function	Results
Get (CurrentTime) + 3600	Returns the time one hour from now.
Get (CurrentTime)	Returns the current time from the local system clock.

Get(CurrentTimestamp)

Category: **Get**

Syntax: **Get (CurrentTimestamp)**

Parameters: None

Data type returned: **Timestamp**

Description:

Returns the current timestamp (date and time) according to the local system clock to the nearest second.

Note that a timestamp is stored internally as an integer that represents the number of seconds since 1/1/0001. Therefore, calculations that use seconds as the base unit can be performed on timestamp data types.

Get (CurrentTimeStamp) uses the date and time settings of the local machine (client) and may be less useful or accurate than Get (CurrentHostTimeStamp) in a database that is accessed by clients from different time zones.

Examples:

Function	Results
Get (CurrentTimeStamp)	Might return 1/25/2004 8:28:05 PM.
GetAsDate (CurrentTimeStamp)	Extracts the date from a timestamp.
GetAsTime (CurrentTimeStamp)	Extracts the time from a timestamp.

Get(CustomMenuSetName)

Category: **Get**

Syntax: **Get (CustomMenuSetName)**

Parameters: None

Data type returned: **Text**

Description:

Returns the name of the active custom menu set. If the active menu set is the Standard FileMaker Menus (which is the initial default for all files), a blank value is returned.

Examples:

Function	Results
Get (CustomMenuSetName)	Returns SalesMenuSet when a custom menu set called SalesMenuSet has been defined and is active.
	Returns an empty string when the [Standard FileMaker Menus] menu set is active.

Get(DesktopPath)

Category: **Get**

Syntax: **Get (DesktopPath)**

Parameters: None

Data type returned: **Text**

Description:

Returns the path to the desktop folder for the current user's computer. In Windows, the path format is /Drive:/Documents and Settings/UserName/Desktop/. In the Mac OS, the path format is /DriveName/Users/UserName/Desktop/.

Note that the user in this case is the operating system user account and should not be confused with the account with which a user logged in to a given database.

Examples:

Function	Results
Get (DesktopPath)	Might return /C:/Documents and Settings/Kai/Desktop/ for a user named Kai in Windows.
	Might return /MacintoshHD/Users/Erlend/Desktop/ for a user named Erlend in the Mac OS.

Get(DocumentsPath)

Category: **Get**

Syntax: **Get (DocumentsPath)**

Parameters: None

Data type returned: **Text**

Description:

Returns the path to the documents folder for the current user. In Windows, the path format is /Drive:/Documents and Settings/UserName/My Documents/. In the Mac OS, the path format is /DriveName/Users/UserName/Documents/.

Note that the user in this case is the operating system user account and should not be confused with the account with which a user logged in to a given database.

Examples:

Function	Results
Get (DocumentsPath)	Returns /C:/Documents and Settings/Kai/My Documents/ for a user named Kai in Windows.
	Returns /MacintoshHD/Users/Erlend/Documents/ for a user named Erlend in the Mac OS.

Get(ErrorCaptureState)

Category: **Get**

Syntax: **Get (ErrorCaptureState)**

Parameters: None

Data type returned: **Number**

Description:

Returns 1 if Set Error Capture has been set to On, and 0 if Set Error Capture was either not set or set to Off.

It is not possible to tell with the Get (ErrorCaptureState) function whether Error Capture was explicitly turned off or simply not set.

Examples:

In the following script
    Set Error Capture [Off]
    Show Custom Dialog [Get (ErrorCaptureState)]

the custom dialog displays 0.

In the following script
```
Set Error Capture [On]
Show Custom Dialog [ Get (ErrorCaptureState) ]
```

the custom dialog displays 1.

Get(ExtendedPrivileges)

Category: **Get**

Syntax: **Get (ExtendedPrivileges)**

Parameters: None

Data type returned: **Text**

Description:

Returns a delimited list of extended privileges, separated by carriage returns, currently assigned for use by the active account in a given database file. Extended privileges are additional access rights assigned to a privilege set; by default they control such things as access via the Web, via ODBC/JDBC, and via FileMaker Networking, but developers can add their own extended privileges as well.

If the user's privilege set doesn't have any extended privileges enabled, Get (ExtendedPrivileges) returns an empty list.

To test whether a user has a certain extended privilege, use one of the following formulas:

PatternCount (Get (ExtendedPrivileges); "salesNorthWestRegion")

If this function returns anything other than 0, then the user has the salesNorthWestRegion extended privilege.

The Position() function can also be used:

Position (Get (ExtendedPrivileges); "fmiwp"; 1; 1)

In this case, any value greater than 0 indicates the presence of the fmiwp privilege.

Examples:

If the currently logged-in account uses a privilege set that includes the extended privileges of Access via Instant Web Publishing (keyword fmiwp) and Access via FileMaker Network (keyword fmapp).

Function	Results
Get (ExtendedPrivileges)	Returns fmiwp¶fmapp.

Get(FileMakerPath)

Category: **Get**

Syntax: **Get (FileMakerPath)**

Parameters: None

Data type returned: **Text**

Description:

Returns the path to the folder of the currently running copy of FileMaker Pro. In Windows, the path format is /Drive:/Program Files/FileMaker/FileMaker Pro 8/. In the Mac OS, the path format is /DriveName/Applications/FileMaker Pro 8/. (The actual path may vary if FileMaker was installed in a non-standard location.)

Examples:

Function	Results
Get (FileMakerPath)	Returns /C:/Program Files/FileMaker/FileMaker Pro 8/ in Windows.
	Returns /MacintoshHD/Applications/FileMaker Pro 8/ in the Mac OS.

Get(FileName)

Category: **Get**

Syntax: **Get (FileName)**

Parameters: None

Data type returned: **Text**

Description:

Returns the filename of the current database file without the file extension.

Get(FileName) is useful in function calls that require a filename, even if the current file is being referenced. This way, if the filename changes, you don't need to change any of your calculation formulas.

If a field in file Alpha.fp7 contains the formula Get (FileName), and that field is displayed on a layout in another file, Beta.fp7, via an external table occurrence, the field value will still return Alpha. Its context is rightly applied.

Examples:

Function	Results
Get (FileName)	Returns the value Contacts when the current database file is named Contacts.fp7.
GetNextSerialValue (Get (FileName); "Contacts:: PrimaryContactID")	Returns the next PrimaryContactID from the Contacts table in the current file. This function call is far less fragile than hard-coding the filename into the preceding expression. If the filename changes at some point in the future, this expression will continue to work as expected.

Get(FilePath)

Category: **Get**

Syntax: **Get (FilePath)**

Parameters: None

Data type returned: **Text**

Description:

Returns the full path to the currently active database file, including the file extension.

Returns file:/driveletter:/databaseName for local files in Windows.

Returns file://volumename/myfoldername/databaseName for remote files in Windows.

Returns file:/path/databaseName for local and remote files in the Mac OS.

Returns fmnet:/networkaddress/databaseName for FileMaker Pro networked files.

Remember that Get (FilePath) includes the filename and extension. Text parsing functions can be used to extract just the file path from the results returned by Get (FilePath). This can be useful for building dynamic paths to objects that are in the same directory as the current file.

If a field in file Alpha.fp7 contains the formula Get (FilePath), and that field is displayed on a layout in another file, Beta.fp7, via an external table occurrence, the field value will still return the file path for file Alpha. Its context is rightly applied.

Examples:

Function	Results
Get (FilePath)	Returns the current file path.
Left (Get (FilePath); Position (Get (FilePath); Get (FileName); 1; 1) -1)	Returns just the path to the current file directory. The Position() function truncates the path before the filename.

Get(FileSize)

Category: **Get**

Syntax: **Get (FileSize)**

Parameters: None

Data type returned: **Number**

Description:

Returns the size of the current file in bytes.

Examples:

If the current file size is 1,404,928 bytes Get (FileSize) returns 1404928.

Function	Results
Round (Get (FileSize) / 1024; 0)	Returns 1372, the file size in KB.
Round (Get (FileSize) / 1048576; 2)	Returns 1.34, the file size in MB.

Get(FoundCount)

Category: **Get**

Syntax: **Get (FoundCount)**

Parameters: None

Data type returned: **Number**

Description:

Returns a number that represents the number of records in the current found set.

If multiple windows are open in the current database file, each window can have its own found set. If the Get (FoundCount) function is used in a script, it returns the found count of the active layout in the active window.

Get (FoundCount) is often used in scripts, following finds, to determine navigation paths. In the following script, if one record is found, the Detail layout is shown. If multiple records are found, the List layout is shown. Finally, if no records are found, the script notifies the user with a dialog box.

```
If[Get(FoundCount)=1]
  Go To Layout[Detail]
Else If[Get(FoundCount)>1]
  Go To Layout[List]
Else
  Show Custom Dialog ["Empty Set"; "No Records Found"]
End If
```

Examples:

If 240 records are in the found set, Get (FoundCount) returns 240.

Get(HighContrastColor)

Category: **Get**

Syntax: **Get (HighContrastColor)**

Parameters: None

Data type returned: **Text**

Description:

Windows only: Returns the name of the current high-contrast default color scheme. Returns an empty value (null) if Use High Contrast is unavailable, inactive, or if the function is called on the Mac OS.

Use High Contrast is an option under Control Panel, Accessibility Options, Display tab. The standard options increase default font sizes and heighten screen contrast to assist users with impaired vision.

Examples:

Function	Results
Get (HighContrastColor)	Returns High Contrast White (large) when the Use High Contrast option in Windows 2000 is active and Black on White is selected.
	Returns High Contrast Black (large) when the Use High Contrast option in Windows 2000 is active and White on Black is selected.
	Returns the name of the custom color scheme when the Use High Contrast option in Windows 2000 is active and a custom color scheme is selected.
	Returns null if the Use High Contrast option is not selected or if the computer is a Macintosh.

Get(HighContrastState)

Category: **Get**

Syntax: **Get (HighContrastState)**

Parameters: None

Data type returned: **Number**

Description:

Windows only: Returns a number representing the state of the Use High Contrast option in the Accessibility Options control panel.

Returns:

0 if Use High Contrast is unavailable, inactive, or if the function is used on the Mac OS.

1 if Use High Contrast is available and active.

Examples:

If you have users with impaired vision, you might create alternate versions of your layouts that are easier for them to use. If so, you can test in your navigation scripts whether Use High Contrast is active and go to an appropriate layout or zoom the window.

```
If [ Get (HighContrastState) = 1 ]
    Go to Layout ["ContactDetail (HC)"]
Else
    Go to Layout ["ContactDetail"]
End If
```

Get(HostIPAddress)

Category: **Get**

Syntax: **Get (HostIPAddress)**

Parameters: None

Data type returned: **Text**

Description:

Returns the IP address of the host computer for the current database. If the current database is open as a single-user non-hosted file, an empty string is returned.

Examples:

Returns 14.156.13.121 (as an example) when the current database is being hosted.

Get(HostName)

Category: **Get**

Syntax: **Get (HostName)**

Parameters: None

Data type returned: **Text**

Description:

Returns the registered name of the computer hosting the database file.

To change the registered name on a computer:

On Windows, the computer name is found on the Network Identification tab of the System Properties control panel. The Full Computer Name option displays the current registered name.

On Mac OS, the computer name is found within System Preferences, under the Sharing settings.

If a client connects to a file hosted by FileMaker Server, Get (HostName) returns the name of the server. The host name can be configured with the Server Administration tool. By default, FileMaker Server uses the system's name, but a custom name can be supplied instead.

We find it helpful in our practice to place a Get(HostName) display on a prominent layout within our solutions so that we can see during development whether or not we're working on a live version, a development version, or a scratch file on our local laptops.

Examples:

If the computer is named "Maturin"

    Get(HostName)

results in Maturin.

Get(LastError)

Category: **Get**

Syntax: **Get (LastError)**

Parameters: None

Data type returned: **Number**

Description:

Returns the number of the error generated by the most recent script step. If there was no error, then Get (LastError) returns 0. Use this function in combination with Set Error Capture [On] to trap and handle errors raised in scripts.

A common source of bugs in scripts is not remembering that the Get (LastError) function returns the error code from only the most recently executed script step. For example, in this script

    Perform Find
    If (Get(ErrorCaptureState) = 1)
       Show Custom Dialog (Get (LastError))
    End If

the Get (LastError) step returns the result of the execution of the If statement, not the error code generated by the Find step.

→ *For a complete listing of error codes, **see** Chapter 11, "FileMaker Error Codes."*

→ *For more discussion on debugging and troubleshooting, **see** Special Edition Using FileMaker 8, "Debugging and Troubleshooting."*

Note that if a script is running on the Mac OS and calls an AppleScript routine, any errors generated will also be passed through to and presented via this function.

Note too that if an error occurs in FileMaker while performing an SQL query, an SQL-STATE error will be returned by ODBC.

Examples:

Consider the following script:
```
Set Error Capture [On]
Print Setup[Restore]
SetVariable [$error; value: Get (LastError)]
```

If the user cancels out of the Print Setup dialog, Get (LastError) returns 1 (user canceled action). If the Print Setup step executes successfully, Get (LastError) returns 0.

Get(LastMessageChoice)

Category: **Get**

Syntax: **Get (LastMessageChoice)**

Parameters: None

Data type returned: **Number**

Description:

Returns a number corresponding to the button clicked as a result of the Show Custom Dialog script step.

Though it has a value of 1, the default button on a dialog is always on the far right side. For example, if there are three buttons, they will appear in 3-2-1 (Cancel, Maybe, OK) order.

Returns:

1 for the default button.

2 for the second button.

3 for the third button.

Examples:

For the following script step, where the default button is labeled OK, the second button is labeled Maybe, and the third button is labeled Cancel:

Show Custom Dialog ["test";"Proceed?"]

If the user chooses OK, Get (LastMessageChoice) returns 1.

If the user chooses Maybe, Get (LastMessageChoice) returns 2.

If the user chooses Cancel, Get (LastMessageChoice) returns 3.

You can then use an If() statement to handle each possibility appropriately.

Note that if a custom dialog has input fields, it is only when the user clicks the default right-most button will the data be inserted into the input field.

Get(LastODBCError)

Category: **Get**

Syntax: **Get (LastODBCError)**

Parameters: None

Data type returned: **Text**

Description:

Returns a string that shows the ODBC error state (SQLSTATE), as published by ODBC standards, based on ISO/IEF standards.

The ODBC error state is cleared at the time the next ODBC-related script step is performed. Anytime before that happens, you can check to see whether an ODBC error was generated.

By setting the Set Error Capture script step to On, you can suppress the error messages that a user sees during execution of a script that uses ODBC functions.

Examples:

When attempting to execute a SQL statement with an invalid field name, Get (LastODBCError) returns S0022.

If no error is encountered, Get (LastODBCError) returns 00000.

Get(LayoutAccess)

Category: **Get**

Syntax: **Get (LayoutAccess)**

Parameters: None

Data type returned: **Number**

Description:

Returns a number that represents the current user's record access privileges level for the current layout. Privileges are assigned in the Custom Layout Privileges dialog box

The Get (LayoutAccess) function can be used to alert users of restricted privileges at the layout level. Note that Get (LayoutAccess) returns information about only the current layout. Record access privileges for any other layout are not represented.

Note also that Get (LayoutAccess) does not return information about whether or not the layout itself is accessible, but rather what access the user has to edit record data via the current layout.

The Get (RecordAccess) function evaluates record access privileges independent of the Get (LayoutAccess) function. To fully evaluate record access, evaluate the return values of both the Get (LayoutAccess) and Get (RecordAccess) functions.

Examples:

Function	Results
Get(LayoutAccess)	Returns 0 if the custom layout privileges of an account's privilege set allow "no access" to records via this layout.
	Returns 1 if the custom layout privileges of an account's privilege set allow "view only" access to records via this layout.
	Returns 2 if the custom layout privileges of an account's privilege set allow "modifiable" access to records via this layout.

Get(LayoutCount)

Category: **Get**

Syntax: **Get (LayoutCount)**

Parameters: None

Data type returned: **Number**

Description:

Returns the total number of layouts in the current file.

Get(LayoutCount) returns the total number of layouts within a file, including hidden layouts and layouts the user doesn't have privileges to see.

Examples:

Function	Results
Get(LayoutCount)	Returns 3 when there are three layouts in a database file.

Get(LayoutName)

Category: **Get**

Syntax: **Get (LayoutName)**

Parameters: None

Data type returned: **Text**

Description:

Returns the name of the layout currently displayed in the active window.

To change the name of a layout, in Layout mode, go to the Layouts menu, select the Layout Setup menu item, and then click the General tab. Layouts do not need to be uniquely named.

Examples:

Function	Results
Get(LayoutName)	Returns Data Entry when the Data Entry layout is displayed.
	Returns Invoice List when the Invoice List layout is displayed.

Get(LayoutNumber)

Category: **Get**

Syntax: **Get (LayoutNumber)**

Parameters: None

Data type returned: **Number**

Description:

Returns the number of the layout currently displayed in the active window. The order of layouts can be set in Layout mode by going to the Layouts menu and selecting the Set Layout Order menu item.

Get (LayoutNumber) can be used to keep track of the last layout a user visited. The following script takes a user from one layout to another, allows the user to complete other tasks, and then returns the user to the original layout:

```
Set Field [temp; Get(LayoutNumber)]
Go to Layout ["Other Layout"]
[perform script, process, etc]
Go to Layout [temp]
```

Because the layout you navigate to might be associated with a different table than the calling layout, the temp field used to store the layout number should be set to have global storage.

Examples:

Function	Results
Get (LayoutNumber)	Returns 6 when the sixth layout on the Set Layout Order list is active.

Get(LayoutTableName)

Category: **Get**

Syntax: **Get (LayoutTableName)**

Parameters: None

Data type returned: **Text**

Description:

Returns the name of the table occurrence (not the source table) from which the current layout shows records.

Because there is no way of retrieving the name of the source table with which a layout is associated, consider prefixing the names of table occurrences with an abbreviation that represents the source table. For instance, you might name a table occurrence INV_CustomerInvoices. You can then use text parsing functions to retrieve the source table name from the results returned by the Get (LayoutTableName) function.

Note that when no windows are active or visible, an empty string is returned.

Examples:

Function	Results
Get(LayoutTableName)	Returns INV_Invoices when the current layout is attached to the table occurrence named INV_Invoices.
	Returns EMP_Employees when the current layout is attached to the table occurrence named EMP_Employees.

Get(LayoutViewState)

Category: **Get**

Syntax: **Get (LayoutViewState)**

Parameters: None

Data type returned: **Number**

Description:

Returns a number that represents the view mode for the current layout in the active window.

Get (LayoutViewState) is useful in scripts to test the state of the current layout. Unless a layout has been restricted not to be viewable in another state, users can manually change the state of the current layout, provided they have access to menu commands. You can detect whether the layout is in the proper state, and if necessary, change it with the View As script step.

Examples:

Get (LayoutViewState) returns 0, 1, or 2, depending on the current layout's view state:

    0 = View as Form

    1 = View as List

    2 = View as Table

Get(MultiUserState)

Category: **Get**

Syntax: **Get (MultiUserState)**

Parameters: None

Data type returned: **Number**

Description:

Returns a number that represents the FileMaker sharing/networking status for the current file.

Return 0 when network sharing is off, or when network sharing is on but no privilege sets have the [fmapp] Extended Privilege keyword enabled.

Returns 1 when network sharing is on, the database file is accessed from the host computer, and some or all users have the [fmapp] keyword enabled.

Returns 2 when network sharing is on, the database file is accessed from a client computer, and some or all users have the [fmapp] keyword enabled.

Examples:

Function	Results
Get (MultiUserState)	Returns 2 when network sharing is on.

Get(NetworkProtocol)

Category: **Get**

Syntax: **Get (NetworkProtocol)**

Parameters: None

Data type returned: **Text**

Description: Returns the name of the network protocol that FileMaker Pro is using on the current machine.

Unlike in previous versions of FileMaker, the only network protocol supported by FileMaker Pro 8 is TCP/IP. Get (NetworkProtocol) always returns TCP/IP, even if FileMaker Network sharing is off.

Examples:

Function	Results
Get (NetworkProtocol)	Returns TCP/IP.

Get(PageNumber)

Category: **Get**

Syntax: **Get (PageNumber)**

Parameters: None

Data type returned: **Number**

Description:

When printing or previewing a document, this function returns the current page number. If nothing is being printed or previewed, Get (PageNumber) returns 0.

If you are printing a report of unknown length and you want to determine the number of pages, you can have a script go to the last page in Preview mode and capture the value returned by Get (PageNumber) in a global field. This would then allow you to have something like "Page 2 of 5" appear in the footer of your report.

Examples:

Imagine you have an unstored calculation with the formula:

  "Page " & Get (PageNumber)

When printing a multi-page report, this field could be placed in the footer of the layout and it would return the proper page number when the report was previewed or printed.

Get(PortalRowNumber)

Category: **Get**

Syntax: **Get (PortalRowNumber)**

Parameters: None

Data type returned: **Number**

Description:

Returns the number of the currently selected portal row—A case where either the row itself is selected (highlighted in black) or the cursor is actively sitting within a field in the portal.

When no portal row is selected, Get (PortalRowNumber) returns 0.

Get(PortalRowNumber) should be used to determine with which row a user is working.
→   *See also "GetNthRecord()" later in this chapter.*

Examples:

When the user clicks on the third row of a portal,

   Get (PortalRowNumber)

returns 3.

When the user clicks out of the portal onto the layout itself,

   Get (PortalRowNumber)

returns 0.

Get(PreferencesPath)

NEW   *Category:* **Get**

   Syntax: **Get (PreferencesPath)**

   Parameters: None

   Data type returned: **Text**

Description:

Returns the operating system path to a user's preferences and default options folder. In Windows, the path format is /Drive:/Documents and Settings/UserName/Local Settings/Application Data/. In the Mac OS, the path format is /DriveName/Users/UserName/Library/Preferences/.

Note that the user in this case is the operating system user account and should not be confused with the account with which a user logged in to a given database.

Examples:

Returns /C:/Documents and Settings/Nate/Local Settings/Application Data/ for a user named Nate in Windows.

Returns /MacintoshHD/Users/Eleanor/Library/Preferences/ for a user named Eleanor in the Mac OS.

Get(PrinterName)

Category: **Get**

Syntax: **Get (PrinterName)**

Parameters: None

Data type returned: **Text**

Description:

Returns information about the currently selected printer.

In Windows, Get (PrinterName) returns a text string containing the printer name, driver name, and printer port, separated by commas.

In Mac OS, Get (PrinterName) returns a text string with the name or IP address of the printer, and the name of the print queue, as it appears in the Print Center.

If in either operating system the printer information is unavailable for whatever reason, <Unknown> is returned.

If there are certain print jobs that require that a specific printer be selected, you can test for Get (PrinterName) within a script and ask the user to select a different printer if necessary.

Examples:

In Windows,

    Get (PrinterName)

might return \\server1\Lexmark Optra M412 PS3, winspool,Ne02:.

In Mac OSX,

    Get (PrinterName)

may return the IP address 255.5.5.255.

Or it may return the name of the current printer (if the printer is not networked). For example, hp Laserjet 4200.

Get(PrivilegeSetName)

Category: **Get**

Syntax: **Get (PrivilegeSetName)**

Parameters: None

Data type returned: **Text**

Description:

Returns the name of the privilege set assigned to the active account.

Every account must be assigned one, and only one, privilege set.

Examples:

Function	Results
Get (PrivilegeSetName)	Returns [Full Access] if you haven't modified the security settings of a new database.
Get (PrivilegeSetName)	Returns Sales if the current user is logged in with an account assigned to the Sales privilege set.

Get(RecordAccess)

Category: **Get**

Syntax: **Get (RecordAccess)**

Parameters: None

Data type returned: **Number**

Description:

Returns a number that represents the current account's access privileges for the current record. Record privileges are assigned via privilege set.

Returns 0 if the user does not have View or Edit privileges for the current record.

Returns 1 if the user has view-only access to the current record. This could mean the View is set to Yes for the current table, or that View is set to Limited and that the calculation defined for Limited access returns a value of True.

Returns 2 if the user has edit access for the current record. This could mean that Edit is set to Yes for the current table, or that Edit is set to Limited and that the calculation defined for Limited access returns a value of True.

The Get (RecordAccess) function can be used to alert users of restricted privileges at the record level. Note that Get (RecordAccess) returns information only about table record privileges. Record access may be restricted through the layout access as well.

To fully evaluate current record access, evaluate both the return values of Get (LayoutAccess) and the Get (RecordAccess) function.

Examples:

Function	Results
Get (RecordAccess)	Returns 1 if a user can view, but potentially not edit, a given record.

Get(RecordID)

Category: **Get**

Syntax: **Get (RecordID)**

Parameters: None

Data type returned: **Number**

Description: Returns the unique, internal ID number of the current record. This number is generated automatically by FileMaker Pro and does not change.

The record ID is assigned sequentially within each table, beginning at 1. Record IDs are not reused; if a record is deleted, its ID is not reassigned.

When files are converted from previous versions, record IDs from the original file are preserved.

The record ID is required for editing and deleting records via Custom Web Publishing, as this is how the record to be changed or deleted must be identified.

Examples:

Function	Results
Get (RecordID)	Returns 275 when the FileMaker record ID is 275.

Get(RecordModificationCount)

Category: **Get**

Syntax: **Get (RecordModificationCount)**

Parameters: None

Data type returned: **Number**

Description:

Returns the total number of times the current record has been modified. A record change must be committed before the modification count updates.

Committing multiple field changes at once is considered a single record modification. Each time a change is committed, the modification count increases.

Get (RecordModificationCount) can be used by custom web applications to ensure that one user's changes do not overwrite another's. At the time the record is loaded into the web browser, the record modification count can be stored. When the record is saved, the current record modification count can be checked against the stored one to see whether another user has updated the record in the meantime.

Duplicated records retain the same record modification count as the record from which they were created; the count is not reset to zero. There's no way to alter or reset the modification count.

Examples:

Function	Results
Get (RecordModificationCount)	Returns 0 if a record has never been modified.
	Returns 17 if a record has been modified 17 times since it was originally created.

Get(RecordNumber)

Category: **Get**

Syntax: **Get (RecordNumber)**

Parameters: None

Data type returned: **Number**

Description:

Returns a number that represents the position of a record in the current found set. This value changes depending on the found set and the sort order.

Get (RecordNumber) tells you a record's position within the found set. This is useful if you want to create a calculation to display "X of Y records" on a given layout.

To determine FileMaker's unique internal record ID, use Get (RecordID).

Examples:

Function	Results
Get (RecordNumber)	Returns 1 for the first record in the found set.
	Returns 83 for the 83rd record in a found set of 322 records.

Get(RecordOpenCount)

Category: **Get**

Syntax: **Get (RecordOpenCount)**

Parameters: None

Data type returned: **Number**

Description:

Returns the total number of open, uncommitted records in the current found set. An open record is one in which changes have been made but not yet saved by the user or currently executing script.

This function is particularly useful when batch processes are necessary. For example, when exporting records, first check that Get(RecordOpenCount) is zero to ensure having the latest data.

Examples:

Returns 4 if there are four open records in the current found set that haven't been saved.

Get(RecordOpenState)

NEW *Category:* **Get**

Syntax: **Get (RecordOpenState)**

Parameters: None

Data type returned: **Number**

Description:

Returns a number representing the open/committed status of the current record.

Returns 0 for a closed or committed record.

Returns 1 for a new record that hasn't been committed.

Returns 2 for a modified record that hasn't been committed.

This is particularly useful for cases where you may have a script looping through a set of records making a change of some sort. If a user is editing a record, your script could skip over the record in question and, depending on the script and its error capture state, may make no note of it.

Examples:

Returns 1 if the current record is a new record that hasn't been saved.

Get(RequestCount)

Category: **Get**

Syntax: **Get (RequestCount)**

Parameters: None

Data type returned: **Number**

Description:

Returns the total number of find requests defined in the current window.

Get (RequestCount) can be used in scripted find routines to see whether the user has added any find requests to the default request. It is also useful as a boundary condition if you ever need to loop through all the find requests and either capture or set search parameters.

Examples:

If the current find request asks for invoices with values greater than $200.00,

    Get (RequestCount)

returns 1.

If the current find request asks for invoices with values greater than $200 or invoices with dates after 1/1/2004,

    Get (RequestCount)

returns 2.

Get(RequestOmitState)

Category: **Get**

Syntax: **Get (RequestOmitState)**

Parameters: None

Data type returned: **Number**

Description:

Returns 1 if the Omit checkbox is selected in Find mode, otherwise returns 0.

Examples:

Returns 1 when the Omit checkbox is selected in the current find request.

Get(ScreenDepth)

Category: **Get**

Syntax: **Get (ScreenDepth)**

Parameters: None

Data type returned: **Number**

Description:

Returns the number of bits needed to represent the color or shade of gray of a pixel on the user's monitor. A value of 8 represents 256 (equal to 2^8) colors or shades of gray.

Use Get (ScreenDepth) to alert users if their monitor color settings are set too low to view images correctly. For example,

```
If[Get(ScreenDepth)<32]
  Show Custom Dialog ["Color";"Your monitor should be set to "Millions
  of colors" to display images correctly"]
End If
```

Examples:

Function	Results
Get (ScreenDepth)	Returns 32 on a display showing millions (2^32) of colors.
	Returns 16 on a display showing thousands (2^16) of colors.
	Returns 4 on a VGA display.
	Returns 1 on a black-and-white display.

Get(ScreenHeight)

Category: **Get**

Syntax: **Get (ScreenHeight)**

Parameters: None

Data type returned: **Number**

Description:

Returns the number of pixels that are displayed vertically on the current screen. This corresponds to a user's operating system settings for display resolution.

Note when the active window spans more than one screen, this function calculates the value for the screen that contains the largest percentage of the window.

Use Get (ScreenHeight) and Get (ScreenWidth) to check minimum resolution settings on a user's computer.

```
If [Get (ScreenHeight)<1200 OR Get (ScreenWidth)<1600]
    Show Custom Dialog ["Resolution";"This application requires a minimum
    of 1600 x 1200 screen resolution."]
    Perform Script ["Close Solution Files"]
End If
```

Examples:

Function	Results
Get (ScreenHeight)	Returns 854 on a monitor set to display at 1280×854.

Get(ScreenWidth)

Category: **Get**

Syntax: **Get (ScreenWidth)**

Parameters: None

Data type returned: **Number**

Description:

Returns the number of pixels that are displayed horizontally on the active screen. This corresponds to a user's operating system settings for display resolution.

Note when the active window spans more than one screen, this function calculates the value for the screen that contains the largest percentage of the window.

See Get (ScreenHeight).

Examples:

Function	Results
Get (ScreenWidth) resolution.	Returns 1280 when the user's monitor is set to display at 1280×854

Get(ScriptName)

Category: **Get**

Syntax: **Get (ScriptName)**

Parameters: None

Data type returned: **Text**

Description:

Returns the name of the current script even if paused. When no script is running, Get (ScriptName) returns an empty string.

One use of Get (ScriptName) is to capture errors. In this example, the Log Error script takes the script name as a parameter.

```
If [Get(LastError) <> 0]
  Perform Script ["Log Error"; Parameter: Get (ScriptName)]
End If
```

Passing the current script's name as a script parameter can be useful anytime a subscript can be called by multiple scripts.

Examples:

Function	Results
Get(ScriptName)	Returns Calculate Invoice if the current script is Calculate Invoice.

Get(ScriptParameter)

Category: **Get**

Syntax: **Get (ScriptParameter)**

Parameters: None

Data type returned: **Text**

Description:

Retrieves the parameter that was passed to a currently running script.

The value of a script parameter can be retrieved anywhere within a script, regardless of subscript calls. Script parameters cannot be altered during execution of a script.

Subscripts do not inherit the script parameter of the calling script. Rather, they can be passed parameters of their own that exist only for the duration of the subscript. If you want a subscript to inherit a script parameter, pass Get (ScriptParameter) as the subscript's parameter.

Only one value can be passed as a script parameter, but that value can contain a delimited list, thus allowing multiple values to be passed.

> → *For more information on how to pass and parse multivalued script parameters,* **see** Special Edition Using FileMaker 8, *Chapter 15 "Advanced Scripting Techniques."*

Script parameters can be specified when scripts are performed via buttons and via subscripts, but not when scripts are called manually from the Scripts menu or via a startup or shutdown script.

Examples:

In this example, the Navigate script is called, with the parameter "West":

Perform Script ["Navigate"; "West"]

Within the Navigate script, the script parameter value ("West") is assigned to a variable ("$direction") through the use of the following script step:

Set Variable ["$direction"; Get (ScriptParameter)]

$direction now equals West.

Get(ScriptResult)

Category: **Get**

Syntax: **Get (ScriptResult)**

Parameters: None

Data type returned: **Text, Number, Date, Time, Timestamp, Container**

Description:

This function allows subscripts to pass results to their calling ("parent") script. Get(ScriptResult) returns whatever value was set by the Exit Script script step.

Note that once all scripts complete execution, no value is stored and Get(ScriptResult) will return a null (or blank) value.

Examples:

Consider a subscript that checks for duplicate records within a found set and passes a count of duplicates as a script result. Any number of scripts within a given solution can then call that subscript and perform a check like so:

    Case (Get(ScriptResult) > 1; "duplicates exist"; "no duplicates")

Get(SortState)

Category: **Get**

Syntax: **Get (SortState)**

Parameters: None

Data type returned: **Number**

Description:

Returns a number that represents the sort state of the active window.

Get (SortState) can be used in a customized interface where the Status Area is normally hidden from the user. Also, Get (SortState) can be used to correctly display sort icons in a customized interface.

A sorted found set becomes semi-sorted if new records are created. Omitting or deleting records does not cause the sort status to change, however. Subsummary reports may not show expected results when the found set is semi-sorted.

Examples:

Function	Results
Get (SortState)	Returns 0 if the found set in the active window is not sorted.
	Returns 1 if the found set in the active window is sorted.
	Returns 2 if the found set in the active window is partially sorted (semi-sorted).

Get(StatusAreaState)

Category: **Get**

Syntax: **Get (StatusAreaState)**

Parameters: None

Data type returned: **Number**

Description:

Returns a number that represents the state of the Status Area of the active window.

If you want a single test that will tell you whether the Status Area is hidden (regardless of whether it's locked or not), use Mod (Get (StatusAreaState); 3). When this returns 0, the Status Area is hidden; when it's anything else, the Status Area is visible.

Examples:

Function	Results
Get(StatusAreaState)	Returns 0 if the Status Area is hidden.
	Returns 1 if the Status Area is visible.
	Returns 2 if the Status Area is visible and locked.
	Returns 3 if the Status Area is hidden and locked.

Get(SystemDrive)

NEW

Category: **Get**

Syntax: **Get (SystemDrive)**

Parameters: None

Data type returned: **Text**

Description:

Returns the drive letter (Windows) or volume name (Mac OS) where the currently running operating system is located.

Examples:

Returns /C:/ in Windows when the operating system is on the C: drive.

Returns /MyDrive/ in the Mac OS when the operating system is on a volume named MyDrive.

Get(SystemIPAddress)

Category: **Get**

Syntax: **Get (SystemIPAddress)**

Parameters: None

Data type returned: **Text**

Description:

Produces a return-delimited list of the IP addresses of all the machines connected to a NIC (Network Interface Controller) card.

Examples:

Returns 202.27.78.34, for example, when only one machine is connected.

Get(SystemLanguage)

Category: **Get**

Syntax: **Get (SystemLanguage)**

Parameters: None

Data type returned: **Text**

Description:

Returns the language setting of the user's machine. The returned text is the English language name for a language, regardless of system settings.

Examples:

Function	Results
Get (SystemLanguage)	Returns English on a system set to use English, returns German for a system set to use Deutsch.

Get(SystemNICAddress)

Category: **Get**

Syntax: **Get (SystemNICAddress)**

Parameters: None

Data type returned: **Text**

Description:

Produces a return-delimited list containing the hardware addresses of all the NIC (Network Interface Controller) cards connected to the machine.

In Windows, you can find this address by typing **ipconfig /All** from a command prompt. On Mac OS X, you can find the NIC address by using the Apple System Profiler utility.

If the user's machine has multiple NIC cards, Get (SystemNICAddress) generates a return-delimited list of all their addresses. You might, for instance, have both a built-in Ethernet card and a wireless networking card installed in a laptop. Or, a server might have multiple built-in Ethernet ports. In both of these cases, Get (SystemNICAddress) returns the addresses of both devices.

Examples:

Function	Results
Get (SystemNICAddress)	Returns 00:30:65:cf:df:98.

Get(SystemPlatform)

Category: **Get**

Syntax: **Get (SystemPlatform)**

Parameters: None

Data type returned: **Number**

Description:

Returns a number that represents the current platform on a user's computer.

Because FileMaker tends to change or add to the values in the platform-checking function (as new versions of operating systems become supported), checks against this function should be performed in a single, central location for ease of future updates. The results of the function may be stored in a global variable during startup, and then referred to for subsequent platform checks throughout the rest of the database. We recommend using a custom function for this purpose.

The reason that this function returns negative numbers is for backward compatibility. Positive 1 and 2 were used for operating systems that are no longer supported by FileMaker Pro.

Examples:

Function	Results
Get (SystemPlatform)	Returns -1 if the current platform is Mac OS X.
	Returns -2 if the platform is Windows 2000 or Windows XP.

Get(SystemVersion)

Category: **Get**

Syntax: **Get (SystemVersion)**

Parameters: None

Data type returned: **Text**

Description:

Returns the current operating system version level.

The values returned by Get (SystemVersion) will change as new versions of operating systems become available. As with checks against Get (SystemPlatform), you should try to perform tests of the system version in a single, central location within your files so that it will be easy to update in the future. We recommend using a custom function for this purpose.

Examples:

Function	Results
Get (SystemVersion)	Returns **10.3.3** for Mac OS X version 10.3.3.
	Returns **5.0** for Windows 2000.
	Returns **5.1** for Windows XP.

Get(TextRulerVisible)

Category: **Get**

Syntax: **Get (TextRulerVisible)**

Parameters: None

Data type returned: **Number**

Description:

Returns a Boolean value by which to determine whether or not the text ruler is visible. Returns 1 if the text ruler is displayed, otherwise returns 0.

Examples:

Returns 1 when the text ruler is visible.

Get(TotalRecordCount)

Category: **Get**

Syntax: **Get (TotalRecordCount)**

Parameters: None

Data type returned: **Number**

Description:

Returns the total number of records in the current table (not table occurrence), regardless of the state of the found set.

The Get (TotalRecordCount) function is most often used in unstored calculations and scripts. Be sure to navigate to a layout that establishes the correct table context before referencing the function.

The total record count includes records that have been created but not yet committed. If such records are reverted, the total record count is decreased.

Examples:

Function	Results
Get (TotalRecordCount)	Returns **283** when there are 283 records in the current table, regardless of the size of the current found set.

Get(UserCount)

Category: **Get**

Syntax: **Get (UserCount)**

Parameters: None

Data type returned: **Number**

Description:

Returns the number of clients currently accessing the file, including the current user.

Only FileMaker Pro client connections are counted by the Get (UserCount) function. Web, ODBC, and JDBC connections are not counted.

Examples:

Function	Results
Get (UserCount)	Returns 1 if FileMaker Network sharing is turned off. If it is turned on, returns 1 plus the number of networked clients.

If a file is hosted by FileMaker Server 7, Get (UserCount) returns the number of client connections to the current file and does not count the server.

Get(UserName)

Category: **Get**

Syntax: **Get (UserName)**

Parameters: None

Data type returned: **Text**

Description:

Returns the username that has been established for the current user's copy of FileMaker Pro. This username is specified on the General tab of the Preferences dialog and can be set to return either the system name or a custom name.

The returned name is the same for anyone opening any database on the machine, regardless of what account name and password they've used. It's an application-level setting, not a document-level setting. The username can always be manually changed, regardless of whatever security you've set up. For these reasons we recommend against using it.

For greater security, use Get (AccountName) to track and manage user access; a user cannot change the account name used to log in to a database file.

Examples:

Function	Results
Get (UserName)	Returns Delilah Bean when the user-specified name is "Delilah Bean."

Get(UseSystemFormatsState)

NEW *Category:* **Get**

Syntax: **Get (UseSystemFormatsState)**

Parameters: None

Data type returned: **Number**

Description:

This function is used to determine if the option to Use System Formats (in the File Menu, File Options dialog, Text tab) is explicitly turned on. It returns a Boolean value representing the state of the Use System Formats option: 1 if Use System Formats is on, otherwise returns 0.

Note that developers can use the Set Use System Formats script step to control this setting as well.

Examples:

Returns 1 when Use System Formats is on.

Get(WindowContentHeight)

Category: **Get**

Syntax: **Get (WindowContentHeight)**

Parameters: None

Data type returned: **Number**

Description:

Returns the height, in pixels, of the content area of the current window. The content area is the area inside a window's frame, and doesn't include the title bar, scroll bars, or the Status Area.

The relationship of the content area dimensions to the overall window dimensions are different on each platform.

➔ *For a thorough discussion on the differences,* **see** *Special Edition Using FileMaker 8, Chapter 15, "Advanced Scripting Techniques."*

Examples:

Function	Results
Get (WindowContentHeight)	On the Mac OS, returns 563 when the current window height is 600. The title bar and bottom scroll bar make up the other 37 pixels.

Get(WindowContentWidth)

Category: **Get**

Syntax: **Get (WindowContentWidth)**

Parameters: None

Data type returned: **Number**

Description:

Returns the width, in pixels, of the content area of the current window. The content area is the area inside a window's frame, and doesn't include the title bar, scroll bars, or the Status Area.

The relationship of the content area dimensions to the overall window dimensions are different on each platform.

→ *For a thorough discussion on the differences, **see** Special Edition Using FileMaker 8, Chapter 15, "Advanced Scripting Techniques..*

Examples:

Function	Results
Get(WindowContentWidth)	On the Mac OS, returns 782 when the current window width is 800 and the Status Area is not showing.

Get(WindowDesktopHeight)

Category: **Get**

Syntax: **Get (WindowDesktopHeight)**

Parameters: None

Data type returned: **Number**

Description:

Returns the height, in pixels, of the desktop space.

In Windows, the desktop space is the FileMaker Pro application window. Get (WindowDesktopHeight) measures the total vertical space used by the application window. If the application is maximized, the application window height is the screen height, minus the height of the Start menu (if it's placed on the bottom of the screen).

On Mac OS X, the desktop space includes everything on the screen except the top menu bar and the Dock.

You cannot programmatically set the window desktop height or width, nor on Windows can you tell where the application window has been positioned on the user's monitor.

Examples:

Function	Results
Get (WindowDesktopHeight)	Returns 746 in the Mac OS when the current monitor's resolution is set to 1152×768. The menu bar accounts for the other 22 pixels of height, and in this case the Dock is not showing.

Get(WindowDesktopWidth)

Category: **Get**

Syntax: **Get (WindowDesktopWidth)**

Parameters: None

Data type returned: **Number**

Description:

Returns the width, in pixels, of the desktop space.

In Windows, the desktop space is the FileMaker Pro application window. Get (WindowDesktopWindow) measures the total horizontal space used by the application window. If the application is maximized, the application window width is the screen width, minus the width of the Start menu (if it's placed on the side of the screen).

On Mac OS X, the desktop space includes everything on the screen except the top menu bar and the Dock.

You cannot programmatically set the window desktop height or width, nor on Windows can you tell where the application window has been positioned on the user's monitor.

Examples:

Function	Results
Get (WindowDesktopWidth)	Returns 1152 in the Mac OS when the current monitor's resolution is set to 1152×768 and the Dock is not showing.

Get(WindowHeight)

Category: **Get**

Syntax: **Get (WindowHeight)**

Parameters: None

Data type returned: **Number**

Description:

Returns the total height, in pixels, of the current window. The current window is usually the active window, but it's also possible for a script to run in a window that isn't the active foreground window.

The window height and width return the outside dimensions of a window. So, if you make a new window and specify a height and width of 300, then the Get (WindowHeight) and Get (WindowWidth) would both return 300.

Be aware that the window height and width are different from the window content height and width, which return the inside dimensions of a window.

Examples:

Function	Results
Get (WindowHeight)	Returns 541 when the window that is being acted upon is 541 pixels tall.

Get(WindowLeft)

Category: **Get**

Syntax: **Get (WindowLeft)**

Parameters: None

Data type returned: **Number**

Description:

Returns the horizontal distance, in pixels, from the outer left edge of a window to the left edge of the application window on Windows or screen on Mac OS.

See Get (WindowDesktopHeight) for a discussion of how the application window is defined for each platform.

If any docked toolbars are placed along the left edge of the application window, the position of the origin shifts inward. The Get (WindowLeft) function is relative to the inside edge of the application window, inclusive of docked toolbars.

Get (WindowLeft) can return negative numbers. This may indicate the window is located on a second monitor positioned to the left of the first, or it may mean that a portion of the left side of the window is hidden.

Examples:

Function	Results
Get (WindowLeft)	Returns 0 when the left edge of the window being acted upon is flush with the left edge of the application window.

Get(WindowMode)

Category: **Get**

Syntax: **Get (WindowMode)**

Parameters: None

Data type returned: **Number**

Description:

Returns a number that indicates in what mode the active window is.

Returns 0 for Browse mode.

Returns 1 for Find mode.

Returns 2 for Preview mode.

Returns 3 if printing is in progress.

Notice that this function can never return a value indicating that a window is in Layout mode. If a script ever attempts to operate within the context of a window that is in Layout mode, the window is automatically switched to Browse mode and the script continues as expected.

Examples:

Function	Results
Get (WindowMode)	Assuming a window is in Browse mode, returns 0.

Get(WindowName)

Category: **Get**

Syntax: **Get (WindowName)**

Parameters: None

Data type returned: **Text**

Description:

Returns the name of the active window.

The name of a window is the text string that appears in the window's title bar. A window's name can be specified when it is created with the New Window script step. It can also be altered with the Set Window Title script step.

Window names do not need to be unique. If a user manually creates a new window, the name of the new window will be the same as the active window at the time the user selected New Window, but will have a - 2 (or higher number if necessary) appended to it.

Examples:

Function	Results
Get (WindowName)	Returns Contacts if the window being acted upon is named Contacts.

Get(WindowTop)

Category: **Get**

Syntax: **Get (WindowTop)**

Parameters: None

Data type returned: **Number**

Description:

Returns the vertical distance, in pixels, from the top edge of a window to the inside of the top of the application window.

See Get (WindowDesktopHeight) for a discussion of how the application window is defined for each platform.

If any docked toolbars are placed along the top of the application window, this shifts the location of the inside edge of the application window.

Get (WindowTop) can return negative numbers. This may indicate the window is located on a second monitor positioned above the first, or it may mean that a portion of the top of the window is hidden.

Examples:

Function	Results
Get (WindowTop)	Returns 0 when the top edge of a window is positioned flush to the top of the application window.

Get(WindowVisible)

Category: **Get**

Syntax: **Get (WindowVisible)**

Parameters: None

Data type returned: **Number**

Description:

Returns a number indicating whether the current window is visible or hidden.

Returns 1 if the window is visible.

Returns 0 if the window is hidden.

When you call a subscript in another file, it operates from the context of the front-most window in that file, but that window does not need to become the active window. The current window can therefore be different from the active, foreground window, and it can either be hidden or visible.

Examples:

Function	Results
Get (WindowVisible)	Returns 1, assuming the current window is visible.

Get(WindowWidth)

Category: **Get**

Syntax: **Get (WindowWidth)**

Parameters: None

Data type returned: **Number**

Description:

Returns the total width, in pixels, of the current window. A window retains all its properties, such as height and width, even if it is hidden.

The window height and width measures the outside dimensions of a window, whereas the window content height and window content width measure the inside dimensions of a window.

Window height and width can be assigned when creating and resizing windows.

Examples:

Function	Results
Get (WindowWidth)	Returns 650 when the window that is being acted upon is 650 pixels wide.

Get(WindowZoomLevel)

Category: **Get**

Syntax: **Get (WindowZoomLevel)**

Parameters: None

Data type returned: **Text**

Description:

Returns the zoom state (percentage) for the current window.

In Windows, an asterisk appears next to the zoom percentage when the Enlarge Window Contents to Improve Readability option is selected in the General tab of the Preferences dialog box.

Examples:

Returns 400 when the current window's zoom percentage is set to 400.

Returns 200* in Windows when the current window's zoom percentage is set to 200 and the Enlarge Window Contents to Improve Readability option is selected.

GetAsBoolean()

Category: **Data**

Syntax: **GetAsBoolean (data)**

Parameters:

data—Any text, number, date, time, timestamp, or container, or a string containing text, a number, date, time, timestamp, or container.

Data type returned: **Number**

Description:

Returns a 1 if the expression or data passed into the function is not zero nor empty, otherwise zero and null values return 0.

GetAsBoolean() is somewhat different than the also common test not IsEmpty (data). The important distinction is that a GetAsBoolean() test will treat zero as a false result.

Examples:

Function	Results
GetAsBoolean (myField) where myField = "hello":	Returns 1.
GetAsBoolean (myField) where myField = -1000:	Returns 1.
GetAsBoolean (myField) where myField = 0:	Returns 0.
GetAsBoolean (myField) where myField is empty:	Returns 0.

GetAsCSS()

Category: **Text**

Syntax: **GetAsCSS (text)**

Parameters:

text—Any expression that resolves to a text string.

Data type returned: **Text**

Description:

GetAsCSS() returns a representation of the specified text string, marked up with CSS (Cascading Style Sheet) tags. CSS can capture rich text formatting that has been applied to a text string.

Representing formatted text as CSS means that you can export stylized text and have it rendered properly by CSS-aware applications, such as web browsers.

GetAsCSS() is also useful within FileMaker itself because you can determine what special formatting, if any, has been applied to a field.

Examples:

The field myField contains Go Team and has manually been formatted as follows:

Font = Helvetica, Font Size = 36 points, Font Color = red, Font Style = bold.

GetAsCSS (myField) returns
```
<SPAN STYLE= "font-size: 36px;color: #AA0000;font-weight: bold; >
text-align: left;"Go Team</SPAN>
```

GetAsDate()

Category: **Text**

Syntax: **GetAsDate (text)**

Parameters:

text—Any text expression or text field that returns a date, formatted the same as the date format on the system where the file was created.

Data type returned: **Date**

Description:

GetAsDate() interprets a text string that contains a date as an actual date. Anytime you use a date constant within a calculation formula, you should use the GetAsDate() or Date() functions to ensure that the date is interpreted correctly.

Note: In order to avoid errors, we recommend always using four-digit years; however, GetAsDate ("1/1") will resolve to 1/1/2006 assuming the current year is 2006. GetAsDate ("1/1/05") will resolve to 1/1/0005.

Examples:

Function	Results
GetAsDate ("1/1/2004")	Returns 1/1/2004 stored internally as a date.
GetAsDate ("1/1/2004") + 8	Returns 1/9/2004. In this case, had the GetAsDate() function not been used, "1/1/2004" + 8 would have returned 112012.

GetAsNumber()

Category: **Text**

Syntax: **GetAsNumber (text)**

Parameters:

text—Any valid text expression that contains numbers.

Data type returned: **Number**

Description:

GetAsNumber() returns only the numbers from a text string, as a data type number. All non-numeric characters are dropped from the string.

Use GetAsNumber() to strip all non-numeric characters out of a text string. For instance, you might have a phone number field to which you want to apply some formatting. GetAsNumber (PhoneNumber) returns just the numeric characters from the field, stripping all punctuation and spaces, so that you can then apply whatever new formatting you wish.

GetAsNumber() can also be applied to date and time fields to coerce the data into its integer representation. For instance,

   GetAsNumber (Get (CurrentDate))

returns 731689 when the date is 4/18/2004.

Examples:

Function	Results
GetAsNumber ("abc123")	Returns 123.
GetAsNumber ("$100.10")	Returns 100.1.

GetAsSVG()

Category: **Text**

Syntax: **GetAsSVG (text)**

Parameters:

text—Any expression that resolves to a text string.

Data type returned: **Text**

Description:

GetAsSVG() returns a representation of the text string, marked up in SVG (Scalable Vector Graphics) format. SVG can capture rich text formatting that has been applied to a text string.

SVG format can be used to transfer formatted text from FileMaker to other applications. You can also test an SVG-formatted version of a text string to determine what, if any, formatting has been applied to the string.

Examples:

The field myField contains two phrases, Go Team and Hello World!, each with some text formatting applied to it.

   GetAsSVG (myField)

Might return:
```
<StyleList>
<Style#0>"font-size: 36px;color: #AA0000;font-weight: bold;text-align: left;",
Begin: 1, End: 8</Style>
<Style#1>"color: #000000;font-weight: normal;font-style:normal;text-align:
left;", Begin: 9, End: 20</Style>
</StyleList>
<Data>
<Span style="0">Go Team </Span>
<Span style="1">Hello World!</Span>
</Data>
```

GetAsText()

Category: **Text**

Syntax: **GetAsText (data)**

Parameters:

data—Any field or expression that returns a number, date, time, timestamp, or container.

Data type returned: **Text**

Description: GetAsText() returns the text equivalent of data in any other data type. You can then manipulate the data as you would any other text string.

When applied to a container field that stores a reference to an object, GetAsText() returns the path to the container data. If the container data is embedded in the database, GetAsText() returns a question mark.

One frequent use of GetAsText() is to get the path and filename information for container data stored as a reference. You can then parse the path information and build links to other objects in the same location.

In most cases, you do not need to explicitly coerce number, date, and time data into text before performing text operations on the data. Text functions operate on numbers, dates, and times as if they were text strings, even if you don't wrap the data with GetAsText().

Examples:

Function	Results
GetAsText (Get (CurrentDate))	Might return 3/8/2004.

GetAsTime()

Category: **Text**

Syntax: **GetAsTime (text)**

Parameters:

text—Any text expression or text field containing a time.

Data type returned: **Time**

Description:

GetAsTime() returns the data specified in the text string as data-type time. The value can then be manipulated like any other time data.

GetAsTime() can be used to convert an integer representing a number of seconds into an elapsed time, as demonstrated in the third of the following examples.

Examples:

Function	Results
GetAsTime ("01:30:30")	Returns 1:30:30 AM when you specify Time as the calculation result.
GetAsTime ("01:30:30")	Returns 1/1/0001 1:30:30 AM when you specify Timestamp as the calculation result.
GetAsTime (48000)	Returns 8:53:20.

Using GetAsTime() when working with literal time strings in calculation formulas

    GetAsTime ("15:30:00") - FinishTime

would yield the elapsed time between 3:30 p.m. and the FinishTime.

GetAsTimestamp()

Category: **Text**

Syntax: **GetAsTimestamp (text)**

Parameters:

text—Any text string or expression that returns a text string that contains a timestamp.

Data type returned: **Timestamp**

Description:

GetAsTimestamp() converts a timestamp contained in a text string into a data-type timestamp. It can then be used in formulas as any other timestamp would be.

GetAsTimestamp() also converts numbers into timestamps. See the Timestamp() function for more information on how timestamps can be represented as numbers.

Use GetAsTimestamp() anytime you include a literal string containing a timestamp. For instance, to find out the amount of time that has elapsed between a fixed time in the past and now, you would use the following formula:

    Timestamp (Get(CurrentDate); Get (CurrentTime) - GetAsTimestamp
    ("6/29/1969 4:23:56 PM"))

Examples:

Function	Results
GetAsTimestamp ("1/1/2004 1:10:10")	Returns 1/1/2004 1:10:10.
GetAsTimeStamp (61997169000)	Returns 8/12/1965 7:50:00 pm.

GetField()

Category: **Logical**

Syntax: **GetField (fieldName)**

Parameters:

fieldName—A text string, or field or expression that returns a text string, which contains the name of a field.

Data type returned: **Text, Number, Date, Time, Timestamp, Container**

Description:

Returns the contents of the fieldName field.

Essentially, GetField() provides a level of abstraction when retrieving the contents of a field. Instead of saying "Give me the value of the FirstName field," for instance, it's like saying "Give me the value of the field whose name is in the gWhatField field." By putting a different field name in the gWhatField field, you can retrieve the contents of a different field.

The Evaluate() function can always be used in place of the GetField(). In this example, for instance, Evaluate (gSelectColumn) and GetField (gSelectColumn) both return the same result. The opposite is not true, however. Evaluate() can perform complex evaluations and can have trigger conditions defined, whereas GetField() can retrieve only the contents of a field.

Examples:

Function	Results
GetField ("myField")	Returns the contents of myField.
GetField (myField)	Returns the contents of FirstName, when myField contains the string "FirstName".
GetField (MiddleValues (fieldList; counter ;1))	Returns the contents of the LastName field, when fieldList is a return-delimited list of field names containing "FirstName¶LastName¶City¶State¶Zip" and counter is 2.

GetNextSerialValue()

Category: **Design**

Syntax: **GetNextSerialValue (fileName; fieldName)**

Parameters:

fileName—A string or text expression that represents the name of an open file.

fieldName—A string or text expression that represents the name of the field for which to return results.

Data type returned: **Text**

Description:

Returns the next value for a field defined to auto-enter a serialized value.

It's good practice to use the TableOccurrence::FieldName syntax to reference the field in this formula so that it can be evaluated in any context. Without explicitly naming a table occurrence, this function assumes the field can be found in the current context, which may not be the case. Because the auto-entered serial number is defined at the table level, it doesn't matter which of a table's occurrences you reference, as they will all return the same result.

Examples:

Function	Results
GetNextSerialValue ("Invoices"; "InvoiceID")	Might return 5435.
GetNextSerialValue (Get (FileName); "Contacts::ContactID")	Might return 84.

GetNthRecord()

Category: **Logical**

NEW

Syntax: **GetNthRecord (fieldName; recordNumber)**

Parameters:

fieldName—Any related field or repeating field, or an expression that returns a field or a repeating field.

recordNumber—An integer representing the record number from which you want data.

Data type returned: **Text, Number, Date, Time, Timestamp, Container**

Description:

Returns the contents of fieldName from the provided recordNumber.

Note that the rules governing storage and indexing for related calculation values apply to GetNthRecord() just as they do for other functions: The result of an expression containing GetNthRecord() will not update when a related value is referenced unless it is set to be an unstored calculation or unless the relationship is reset/refreshed somehow.

Examples:

Function	Results
GetNthRecord(First Name; 2)	Returns the contents of the First Name field for record 2 in the current table.
GetNthRecord(First Name; Get(RecordNumber)+ 1)	Returns the contents of the First Name field for the next record in the current table. Using this technique, you might set a tool tip to show the next and previous names in a found set.
GetNthRecord(Contacts::First Name; 2)	Returns the contents of the First Name field for record 2 in the Contacts table.
GetNthRecord(Contacts::Phone[2]; 2)	Returns the contents of the second repetition of the Phone field for record 2 in the Contacts table.

GetRepetition()

Category: **Repeating**

Syntax: **GetRepetition (repeatingField; repetitionNumber)**

Parameters:

repeatingField—Any repeating field, or an expression that returns a reference to a repeating field.

repetitionNumber—A positive integer representing the repetition number to retrieve.

Data type returned: **Text, Number, Date, Time, Timestamp, Container**

Description:

Returns the contents of the specified repetition of a repeating field.

A shorthand notation can be used in place of the GetRepetition() function. The repetition number can be placed in square brackets after the name of the repeating field. For instance, GetRepetition (myField; 6) is the same as myField[6].

Examples:

Function	Results
GetRepetition (RepPercentage; 2)	Returns the contents of the second repetition of the RepPercentage field.

If you had a repeating text field called QuoteOfTheDay that contained 20 repetitions, you could extract a random quote using the following formula:

```
Let (repNumber = Ceiling (Random * 20) ;
  GetRepetition (QuoteOfTheDay; repNumber)
)
```

GetSummary()

Category: **Summary**

Syntax: **GetSummary (summaryField; breakField)**

Parameters:

summaryField—A field of type summary, or an expression that returns a reference to one.

breakField—A field, or an expression that returns a reference to one.

Data type returned: **Number, Date, Time, Timestamp**

Description:

The GetSummary() function returns the value of summaryField when summarized by breakField. The found set must be sorted by breakField for GetSummary() to return the proper value.

GetSummary() returns the same values that you would see if you were to place the specified summary field in a subsummary report. GetSummary() is necessary when you need to use summarized values in calculation formulas or for display purposes while in Browse mode.

Note, you could also achive similar results using a self-join relationship and aggregate functions.

To calculate a grand summary value, use the same summary field for both the summary field and the break field parameters.

➜ *For more detail on reporting and subsummary parts,* ***see*** Special Edition Using FileMaker 8, Chapter 10, "Getting Started with Reporting."

Examples:

Given the following record set, sorted by Country, and a summary field called Sum_Sales defined as the Total of Sales:

Country	Region	Sales
U.S.	North	55,000
U.S.	South	45,000
China	North	35,000
China	South	40,000

A field SalesByCountry defined as

GetSummary (Sum_Sales; Country)

returns 100,000 for the two U.S. records and returns 75,000 for the two China records.

GetValue()

NEW

Category: **Text**

Syntax: **GetValue (listOfValues; valueNumber)**

Parameters:

listOfValues—A list of carriage return–delimited values.

valueNumber—The value to return from the list.

Data type returned: **Text**

Description:

Returns from a list of carriage return–delimited values a single value. Value lists in FileMaker are comprised of any line of data followed by a pilcrow or paragraph return character (¶). You can treat value lists as simple arrays and extract lines as needed using GetValue().

Examples:

Function	Results
GetValue("Red¶Green¶Light Green";2)	Returns Green.

Hiragana()

Category: **Text**

Syntax: **Hiragana (text)**

Parameters:

text—Any text expression or text field.

Data type returned: **Text (Japanese)**

Description:

Converts written Japanese Katakana (Hankaku and Zenkaku) text to Hiragana.

Japanese has four written alphabets where it is possible to represent a syllable in a number of different ways. The Hiragana() function, along with the KanaHankaku(), KanaZenkaku(), and Katakana() functions, all enable conversion from one set of alphabetic glyphs to another.

Examples:

Hiragana (アイウエオ) returns あいうえお

Hour()

Category: **Time**

Syntax: **Hour (time)**

Parameters:

time—Any valid time value or expression that returns a valid time value.

Data type returned: **Number**

Description:

The Hour() function returns an integer representing the number of hours specified by the time parameter.

When its parameter represents a specific time of day, the Hour() function returns a value from 0 to 23. To map this into the more familiar 1 to 12 range, you can use the following formula:

   Mod (Hour (time) -1; 12) + 1

The Hour() function can return an integer value outside of the 0 to 23 range when its parameter represents a duration rather than a specific time of day. For instance, Hour ("65:12:53") returns 65.

Examples:

Function	Results
Hour ("10:45:20")	Returns 10.
Hour ("12:15 am")	Returns 0.
Hour ("11:15 pm")	Returns 23.
Hour (Get (CurrentTime))	Will return a value from 0 to 23.

If()

Category: **Logical**

Syntax: **If (test; result1; result2)**

Parameters:

test—A logical expression that returns True (1) or False (0); result1—The expression to evaluate if test is true; result2—The expression to evaluate if test is false.

Data type returned: **Text, Number, Date, Time, Timestamp, Container**

Description:

The If() function returns one of two possible results depending on whether the test supplied as the first parameter is true or false. Result1 is returned if the test is true; Result2 is returned if the test is false.

The test parameter should be an expression that returns a numeric or Boolean result. For numeric results, zero and null are both considered false; all other values are considered true.

If the test contains multiple conditions separated by "and" or "or," FileMaker stops evaluating the conditions as soon as it can determine the overall truthfulness of the test. For instance, if the test parameter is IsEmpty(FieldA) and IsEmpty(FieldB), if Field A is not empty, there's no way that the entire expression could be true. FileMaker will not evaluate the other condition involving FieldB, and will return the false result.

You can nest If() statements within one another, but it is usually more efficient to use a Case() statement rather than an If() in such cases.

Examples:
```
If( DayOfWeek (Get (CurrentDate))) = 1 ;
   "It's Sunday, no work!"; // true result
   "Get back to work!" // false result
)
```


```
If ( myFlagField; graphicTrue; graphicFalse)
```
Looks for a true value (non-zero, non-blank) in myFlagField, and displays the correct graphic container.
```
If (not IsEmpty (Taxable) and TaxRate > 0;
   Price + (Price * TaxRate);
   Price
)
```

Int()

Category: **Number**

Syntax: **Int (number)**

Parameters:

number—Any expression that resolves to a numeric value.

Data type returned: **Number**

Description:

Returns the whole number (integer) part of the number parameter without rounding. Digits to the right of the decimal point are dropped.

Note that for positive numbers, Floor() and Int() return the same results; however, for negative numbers, Int() returns the next larger integer, whereas Floor() returns the next smaller integer.

There are many practical uses for the Int() function. For instance, given any date, to find the date of the Sunday preceding it, use the formula GetAsDate (Int (myDate/7) * 7). Similarly, to test whether an integer is odd or even, you can test whether Int (num/2) = num/2.

Examples:

Function	Results
Int (1.0005)	Returns 1.
Int (-1.0005)	Returns -1.

IsEmpty()

Category: **Logical**

Syntax: **IsEmpty (expression)**

Parameters:

expression—Typically a field name, but can be any valid FileMaker Pro calculation formula.

Data type returned: **Number**

Description:

Returns 1 (True) if the referenced field is empty or if the expression returns an empty string. Returns 0 (False) if the field or expression is not empty.

Remember that zero is a valid entry for a number field. If a number field contains a 0, it is not considered to be empty. If you need to test for zero or null, use GetAsBoolean().

Examples:

Function	Results
IsEmpty (myField)	Returns 1 if myField is empty.
IsEmpty (Name_First & Name_Last)	Returns 1 if the result of concatenating the two fields together is an empty string.

IsValid()

Category: **Logical**

Syntax: **IsValid (expression)**

Parameters:

expression—Typically a field name, but can be any valid FileMaker Pro calculation formula.

Data type returned: **Number**

Description:

Returns either a 1 (True) or a 0 (False), depending on whether the field or expression returns valid data.

IsValid returns a **0** if there is a data type mismatch (for example, text in a date field) or if FileMaker cannot locate the table or field that is referenced.

Otherwise it returns 1, indicating that the data is valid.

Examples:

Function	Results
IsValid (myField)	Returns 1 (True) when myField is present and contains data appropriate to its defined data type.
IsValid (Contacts::Name)	Returns 0 (False) if the current record has no related records in the Contacts table, or if the fields in the records in question all contain invalid data.

IsValidExpression()

Category: **Logical**

Syntax: **IsValidExpression (expression)**

Parameters:

expression—A text string containing a calculation expression, or a field or expression that returns a text string that contains a calculation expression.

Data type returned: **Number**

Description:

Returns 1 (True) if the expression syntax is correct. Returns 0 (False) if the expression has a syntax error.

The IsValidExpression() function is often used in conjunction with the Evaluate() function to ensure that Evaluate() is passed a valid expression. For instance, if users are allowed to enter a formula into a field called myFormula, and you want to have another field express the results of that formula, you could use the following:

```
If (IsValidExpression (myFormula); Evaluate (myFormula); "Invalid formula: "
& TextColor (myFormula; RBG (255; 0; 0)))
```

An expression is considered invalid if it contains syntax errors or if any of the referenced fields cannot be found. Errors that might occur only during execution of the expression, such as record access restrictions, are not detected by the IsValidExpression() formula.

Examples:

Function	Results
IsValidExpression ("Length (SideA)")	Returns 1 (True) as long as there is, in fact, a field named SideA.
IsValidExpression ("Middle (myField; 1)")	Returns 0 (False) because the Middle function requires three parameters to be considered valid syntax.
IsValidExpression (myFormula)	Returns 1 (True) if the contents of myFormula would be considered a valid calculation expression.

KanaHankaku()

Category: **Text**

Syntax: **KanaHankaku (text)**

Parameters:

text—Any text expression or text field.

Data type returned: **Text (Japanese)**

Description:

Converts Zenkaku Katakana to Hankaku Katakana.

Japanese has four written alphabets where it is possible to represent a syllable in a number of different ways. The KanaHankaku() function, along with the KanaZenkaku(), Hiragana(), and Katakana() functions, all enable conversion from one set of alphabetic glyphs to another.

Examples:

KanaHankaku (データベース) returns ﾃﾞｰﾀﾍﾞｰｽ

KanaZenkaku()

Category: **Text**

Syntax: **KanaZenkaku (text)**

Parameters:

text—Any text expression or text field.

Data type returned: **Text (Japanese)**

Description:

Converts Hankaku Katakana to Zenkaku Katakana.

Japanese has four written alphabets where it is possible to represent a syllable in a number of different ways. The KanaZenkaku() function, along with the KanaHankaku(), Hiragana(), and Katakana() functions, all enable conversion from one set of alphabetic glyphs to another.

Examples:

KanaZenkaku ("ﾃﾞｰﾀﾍﾞｰｽﾞ") returns データベース

KanjiNumeral()

Category: **Text**

Syntax: **KanjiNumeral (text)**

Parameters:

text—Any text expression or text field.

Data type returned: **Text (Japanese)**

Description:

Converts Arabic numerals to Kanji numerals.

In Japanese, numbers are represented by either the Arabic "123… etc." character glyphs or by their Kanji equivalents. KanjiNumeral enables converting from Arabic to Kanji.

Note to convert in the opposite direction from Kanji to Arabic, one can use the GetAsNumber() function.

Examples:

KanjiNumeral (富士見台２の３の２５) returns 富士見台二の三の二五

Katakana()

Category: **Text**

Syntax: **Katakana (text)**

Parameters:

text—Any text expression or text field.

Data type returned: **Text (Japanese)**

Description:

Converts from Hiragana to Zenkaku Katakana.

Japanese has four written alphabets where it is possible to represent a syllable in a number of different ways. The Katakana() function, along with the Hiragana(), KanaHankaku(), and KanaZenkaku() functions, all enable conversion from one set of alphabetic glyphs to another.

Examples:

Katakana (あいうえお) returns アイウエオ

Last()

Category: **Repeating**

Syntax: **Last (field)**

Parameters:

field—Any repeating field or related field.

Data type returned: **Text, Number, Date, Time, Timestamp, Container**

Description:

If the specified field is a repeating field, Last() returns the value from the last valid, non-blank repetition. If the specified field is a related field, it returns the last non-blank value from the set of related records. The order of the set of related records is determined by the sort order of the relationship. If no sort order has been specified, then the creation order is used.

Examples:

When RepPercentage is a repeating field with the values .04, .05, and .06, Last (RepPercentage) returns .06.

  Last (PhoneNumber::Number)

returns the most recent phone number entry, assuming no sort is specified for the relationship.

LayoutIDs()

Category: **Design**

Syntax: **LayoutIDs (fileName)**

Parameters:

fileName—A string or text expression that represents the name of an open file. It can include a file extension, but doesn't need one.

Data type returned: **Text**

Description:

Returns a carriage return–delimited list of all the internal layout IDs for the specified file. The list is ordered according to the current layout order, not the creation order.

LayoutIDs are assigned in sequential order beginning at 1. The original file's LayoutIDs are retained when older databases are converted to FileMaker Pro 8.

Examples:

Function	Results
LayoutIDs (Get(FileName))	Might return a list of values that looks like this: 3 9 10 24 13 28

LayoutNames()

Category: **Design**

Syntax: **LayoutNames (fileName)**

Parameters:

fileName—A string or text expression that represents the name of an open file. It can include a file extension, but doesn't need one.

Data type returned: **Text**

Description:

Returns a carriage return–delimited list of layout names for the specified file.

As with the LayoutIDs() function, the order of the layout names is determined by the current order of the layouts, not their creation order.

If you wanted to find out a particular layout's ID (say, the Contact_Detail layout), you can use the LayoutNames() and LayoutIDs() functions together, as follows:

```
Let ([
LNs = LayoutNames (Get(FileName));
LIs = LayoutIDs (Get(FileName));
pos = Position (LNs; "Contact_Detail"; 1; 1);
num = PatternCount (Left(LNs, pos); "¶") + 1 ] ;
GetAsNumber (MiddleValues (LIs; num; 1))
)
```

Examples:

Function	Results
LayoutNames (Get (FileName))	Might return a list of values that looks like this: Contact_List Contact_Detail Invoice_List Invoice_Detail

Left()

Category: **Text**

Syntax: **Left (text; numberOfCharacters)**

Parameters:

text—Any expression that resolves to a text string.

numberOfCharacters—Any expression that resolves to a positive integer.

Data type returned: **Text**

Description:

Returns a string containing the first *n* characters from the specified text string, where *n* is the number specified in the numberOfCharacters parameter. If the string is shorter than numberOfCharacters, the entire string is returned. If numberOfCharacters is less than 1, an empty string is returned.

The Left() function is commonly used in text parsing routines to extract portions of a text string. It is often used in conjunction with other text functions. For example, to extract the City portion of a field (called "CSZ") containing "City, State Zip" data, you could use the following formula:

```
Let (commaPosition = Position (CSZ; ","; 1; 1); Left (CSZ;
commaPosition - 1))
```

Examples:

Function	Results
Left ("Hello"; 2)	Returns He.
Left (FirstName; 1)	Returns the first character of the FirstName field.

LeftValues()

Category: **Text**

Syntax: **LeftValues (text; numberOfValues)**

Parameters:

text—A return-delimited text string or expression that returns a return-delimited text string.

numberOfValues—Any positive number or expression that returns a positive number.

Data type returned: **Text**

Description:

Returns the specified number of items from the beginning of the text parameter.

The LeftValues() function returns the first *n* items from a return-delimited array, where *n* is the number specified in the text parameter. The items will themselves be a return-delimited array, and there will always be a trailing return at the end of the last item.

You can remove the trailing return in a number of ways. If you are extracting a single item from the beginning of a list, you can use the Substitute() function to remove any return characters—for instance, Substitute (LeftValues (text; 1); "¶"; ""). You would not use this method when returning multiple items because the internal delimiters would be lost as well. Instead, the following function returns everything except the last character of the extracted list:

> Let (x = LeftValues (text; n); Left (x; Length (x) - 1))

Another option is the following:

> LeftWords (LeftValues (text; n); 999999)

This function takes advantage of the fact that the LeftWords() function ignores any leading or trailing delimiters. Be aware that this function also ignores leading or trailing delimiters (including punctuation symbols) from the actual items in the array, so in some cases this function does not return the desired result. The safest function to use in all cases is the Let() function (described ahead).

Examples:

Function	Results
LeftValues("A¶B¶C¶D¶E";3)	Returns the following list: A B C
LeftValues (WindowNames;1)	Returns the name of the active window.

LeftWords()

Category: **Text**

Syntax: **LeftWords (text; numberOfWords)**

Parameters:

text—Any expression that resolves to a text field.

numberOfWords—Any positive number or expression that returns a positive number.

Data type returned: **Text**

Description:

Returns the first *n* number of words in a text expression, where *n* is the number specified in the numberOfWords parameter.

Be aware of what symbols are considered to be word breaks by FileMaker Pro. Spaces, return characters, and most punctuation symbols are considered to be word breaks. Multiple word breaks next to each other (for example, two spaces, a comma, and a space) are considered as a single word break.

Certain punctuation symbols are word breaks when separating alpha characters, but not when separating numeric characters. These include the colon (:), slash (/), period (.), comma (,), and dash (-). For instance, LeftWords ("54.6"; 1) returns 54.6, but LeftWords ("x.y"; 1) returns x. The reason for this behavior is that those symbols are valid date, time, and number separators.

Leading and trailing punctuation around a word may be ignored by the LeftWords() function. For example, LeftWords ("John Q. Public, Jr."; 2) returns John Q, but LeftWords ("John Q. Public, Jr."; 3) returns John Q. Public.

Examples:

Function	Results
LeftWords("the quick brown fox jumps"; 3)	Returns the quick brown.
LeftWords(FullName; 1)	Returns Davie when FullName contains "Davie Jacques".

Length()

Category: **Text**

Syntax: **Length (text)**

Parameters:

text—Any expression that resolves to a text string.

Data type returned: **Number**

Description:

Returns the number of characters in the specified text string. Numbers, letters, punctuation, spaces, and carriage returns are all considered as characters.

Length() also serves a second function in that it returns the byte size of the object data found in a container field.

The Length() function is often used as part of data validation rules. For instance, if you want to make sure that users enter phone numbers with either 7 or 10 digits, you could set up a validation by calculation rule as follows:

```
Length ( GetAsNumber ( Phone )) = 7 or Length ( GetAsNumber ( Phone )) = 10
```

Examples:

Function	Results
Length ("Hello there!")	Returns 12.
Length (LastName)	Returns 8 when LastName contains "Humphrey".
Length (Get (CurrentDate))	Returns 9 when the date is 3/27/2004.
	Note that in versions of FileMaker prior to 7, this last example would have returned 6, because the serialized numeric value for the current date would have been used (as opposed to the "3/27/2004)" formula). To achieve that same result, use the following formula: Length (GetAsNumber (Get (CurrentDate)))
Length (myContainer)	Returns 156862 when the myContainer field holds an image that is approximately 157KB in size. (Operating systems report file size slightly differently. It is not unlikely that this function will return a slightly different number than that of your operating system.)

Let()

Category: **Logical**

Syntax: **Let ({[} var1=expression1 {; var2=expression2 ...] }; calculation)**

Parameters:

var(n)—Any valid variable name. The rules for naming variables are the same as for defining fields.

expression(n)—Any calculation formula, the results of which are assigned to the var(n) variable.

calculation—Any calculation formula.

Parameters in curly braces { } are optional and may be repeated as needed, separated by a semicolon.

Data type returned: **Text, Number, Date, Time, Timestamp, Container**

Description:

The Let() function enables you to declare local variables within a calculation formula. The variables exist only within the boundaries of the Let() function itself.

The first parameter of the Let() function is a list of variable names and expressions. If multiple variables are declared, the list needs to be enclosed in square brackets. The items in the list are separated by semicolons. The variables are set in the order in which they appear. This means that you can use previously defined variables as part of the expression to define another variable.

The final parameter, calculation, is some expression that you want to evaluate. That formula can reference any of the variables declared in the first half of the function.

Duplicate variable names are allowed and variables can be named the same as existing fields. If this happens, the value assigned to the variable, not the field, will be used in future references to the variable within the Let() function.

Let() can be used to simplify complex, nested calculation formulas. We cannot advocate its use strongly enough.

In the case where a subexpression is used many times within a formula, the Let() function may also provide a performance benefit because the subexpression is evaluated only once when it is assigned to the variable.

You can also use the Let() function to set script variables like so:

```
Let ([
    $var = 100;
    $$var = 500
    ];
    expression
)
```

Keeping track of functions that overlap scope—in this case overlapping the scope of a calculation expression with that of script or global variables—can often lead to code that is extrememly difficult to work with and maintain. While the preceding is entirely possible, we generally do not recommend it as a practice.

Note also that it is possible to use the Let() function to set a local script variable while no script is running. This in effect allows you to manipulate variables in a "null script" space that then do not exist while scripts run. A fairly obscure point, but interesting nonetheless.

Examples:

The following formula extracts the domain name from an email address:

```
Let( [
    start = Position (eMail ;"@" ;1 ;1);
    numberOfCharacters = Length (eMail) - start];
    Right ( eMail; numberOfCharacters)
)
```

The following example produces a summary of a student's grades:

```
Let ([
  TotalGradePoints = Sum (Grades::GradePoints);
  CreditPoints = Sum (Classes::CreditPoints);
  GPA = Round (TotalGradePoints/CreditPoints; 2)] ;
  "Total Grade Points: "& TotalGradePoints & "¶" &
  "Available Credit Points: " & CreditPoints & "¶" &
  "Your GPA is: " & GPA
)
```

The final example formula returns the volume of a pyramid:

```
Let(
  SideOfBase = 2 * Sqrt(2 * SlantHeight^2 - Height^2;
  SideOfBase^2 * Height/3
)
```

Lg()

Category: **Number**

Syntax: **Lg (number)**

Parameters:

number—Any expression that resolves to a positive numeric value or a field containing a numeric expression.

Data type returned: **Number**

Description:

Returns the base-2 logarithm of number. Negative values for number return an error.

The base-2 logarithm (often called the *binary logarithm*) of a number is the power of 2 that you would need to generate the number. Thus, if $2^x = y$, then $Lg(y) = x$. The value returned by the Lg() function is increased by 1 every time that x is doubled.

Examples:

Lg (1) = 0

Lg (2) = 1

Lg (32) = 5

Ln()

Category: **Number**

Syntax: **Ln (number)**

Parameters:

number—Any positive number or expression that returns a positive number.

Data type returned: **Number**

Description:

Returns the natural logarithm of the specified number. The natural logarithm uses the transcendental number *e* as its base. The value of *e* is approximately 2.71828.

Exp() and Ln() are inverse functions of one another.

The Log() and Lg() functions produce base-10 and base-2 logarithms, respectively. The Ln() function produces base-*e* logarithms, but it can also be used to solve a logarithm of any base. Log (base-x) of y is equivalent to Ln (y) / Ln (x).

Examples:

Function	Results
Ln (2.7182818)	Returns .9999999895305023.
Ln (Exp(1))	Returns 1.
Ln (100)	Returns 4.6051701859880914.
Ln (Exp(5))	Returns 5.

Log()

Category: **Number**

Syntax: **Log (number)**

Parameters:

number—Any positive number or expression that returns a positive number.

Data type returned: **Number**

Description:

Returns the base-10 logarithm of number.

Logarithms are used to determined the power to which a number must be raised to equal some other number. If x^n = y, then n = Log_x(y). The Log() function assumes a base (the variable *x* in the preceding formula) of 10. The Lg() function uses a base of 2, whereas the Ln() function uses a base of *e*.

The Log() and Lg() functions produce base-10 and base-2 logarithms, respectively. The Ln() function produces base-*e* logarithms, but it can also be used to solve a logarithm of any base. Log (base-x) of y is equivalent to Ln (y) / Ln (x).

Examples:

Function	Results
Log (1)	Returns 0 because 10^0 = 1.
Log (100)	Returns 2 because 10^2 = 100.
Log (1000)	Returns 3 because 10^3 = 1000.

Lookup()

Category: **Logical**

Syntax: **Lookup (sourceField {; failExpression })**

Parameters:

sourceField—Any related field.

failExpression—An expression to evaluate and return if the lookup fails. This is an optional parameter.

Data type returned: **Text, Number, Date, Time, Timestamp, Container**

Description:

Returns the contents of sourceField, or if no related record is found, the result of the failExpression. The table containing the sourceField must be related to the table where the Lookup() is defined.

A calculation field that contains a Lookup() function can be stored or unstored. If it is unstored, then anytime the sourceField changes, the calculation field updates. If the calculation is stored, which is typically why you want to use a Lookup in the first place, then changes to the sourceField do not cascade automatically through to the calculation field. Lookup() is retriggered when any of the relationship's match fields (in the current table, not the source table) are modified, or when a relookup is triggered on any of those fields.

Lookup() is invaluable for addressing performance issues caused by interacting with related (and hence unindexed) values.

Examples:

Imagine you have a stored calculation field in an Invoice table called CustomerNameLookup, defined as follows:

```
Lookup (Customer::CustomerName;"<Missing Customer>")
```

Assume that the Invoice and Customer tables are related on the CustomerID. Whenever the CustomerID field is modified in the Invoice table, this triggers the lookup, and the name of the customer is copied into CustomerNameLookup. If an invalid CustomerID is entered, <Missing Customer> is returned. Because CustomerNameLookup is stored, indexed searches can be performed on it.

Be aware, however, that if the CustomerName field is updated in the Customer table, the change does not cascade automatically through to the Invoice table.

LookupNext()

Category: **Logical**

Syntax: **LookupNext (sourceField; lower/higher Flag)**

Parameters:

sourceField—Any related field.

lower/higher Flag—Keyword that indicates whether to take the next lower or higher value if no direct match is found.

Data type returned: **Text, Number, Date, Time, Timestamp, Container**

Description:

Returns the contents of sourceField, or if no related record is found, the next lower or higher match value. The table containing the sourceField must be related to the table where the LookupNext() function is defined.

The LookupNext() function is very similar to the Lookup() function; they differ only in how they handle the case of no matching record. The Lookup() function returns a fail expression in such cases, whereas the LookupNext() returns the value associated with the next lower or higher match.

The Lower and Higher flags are keywords and should not be placed in quotation marks.

See the Lookup() function to learn about how a lookup is triggered and how the storage options determine how often the LookupNext() function is to be refreshed.

Looking up a value from the next higher or lower matching record is desirable when mapping a continuous variable onto a categorical variable. Think, for instance, of how student grades typically map to letter grades. A grade of 90 to 100 is considered an A, 80 to 89 is a B, 70 to 79 is a C, and so on. The percentage value is a continuous variable, whereas the letter grades are categorical.

Using the Lookup() function, if you wanted to use the student's percentage score to retrieve the letter grade, you would need to have records for every possible combination of percentage and letter grade.

The LookupNext() function makes it possible to have records representing only the border conditions. For student grades, you would need to have five records in your lookup table: 90 is an A, 80 is a B, 70 is a C, 60 is a D, and 0 is an F. You could then relate a student's percentage score to this table, and define the following formula as the StudentLetterGrade:

```
LookupNext (GradeLookup::LetterGrade; Lower)
```

Given a percentage score of 88, which has no exact match, the next lower match would return a letter grade of B.

Examples:

Function	Results
Lookup (ShipRates::ShippingCost; Higher)	Returns the contents of the ShippingCost field from the ShipRates table. If no exact match is found, the next highest match is returned.

Lower()

Category: **Text**

Syntax: **Lower (text)**

Parameters:

text—Any expression that resolves to a text string.

Data type returned: **Text**

Description:

Returns an all-lowercase version of the specified text string.

The Lower() function is one of three functions FileMaker has for changing the case of a text string. The other two are Upper() and Proper().

The following formula can be used to test whether a given text string is already written with all lowercase characters:

    Exact (text; Lower(text))

Examples:

Function	Results
Lower ("This is a test")	Returns this is a test.
Lower (Name)	Returns mary smith when the Name field contains "MARY Smith".

Max()

Category: **Aggregate**

Syntax: **Max (field {; field...})**

Parameters:

field—Any related field, repeating field, or set of non-repeating fields that represent a set of numbers. Parameters in curly braces { } are optional and may be repeated as needed, separated by a semicolon.

Data type returned: **Text, Number, Date, Time, Timestamp**

Description:

Returns the largest valid, non-blank value from the set of values specified by the field parameter.

When the parameter list consists of two or more repeating fields, Max() returns a repeating field in which the corresponding repetitions from the specified fields are evaluated separately. So, if a field Repeater1 has three values, 16, 20, and 24, and another field, Repeater2, has two values, 14 and 25, Max (Repeater1; Repeater2) would return a repeating field with values 16, 25, and 24.

Because dates, times, and timestamps are represented internally as numbers, the Max() function can be used to compare data of these data types. For instance, to return the later of two dates, you could use the following type of formula:

GetAsDate (Max (Date (4; 1; 2005); Get (CurrentDate)))

This would return either 4/1/2005 or the current date, whichever is greater.

Examples:

Function	Results
Max (44; 129; 25)	Returns 129.
Max (repeatingField)	Returns 54 (when repetition 1 = 18, repetition 2 = 10, and repetition 3 = 54).
Max (Invoice:InvoiceAmount)	Returns the largest invoice amount found in the set of related Invoice records.

Middle()

Category: **Text**

Syntax: **Middle (text; startCharacter; numberOfCharacters)**

Parameters:

text—Any expression that resolves to a text string.

startCharacter—Any expression that resolves to a numeric value.

numberOfCharacters—Any expression that resolves to a numeric value.

Data type returned: **Text**

Description:

Returns a substring from the middle of the specified text parameter. The substring begins at startCharacter and extracts the numberOfCharacters characters following it. If the end of the string is encountered before the specified number of characters has been extracted, the function returns everything from the start position though the end of the string.

The Middle() function is often used in conjunction with other text functions as part of text parsing routines. For instance, if you had a field containing city, state, and ZIP data where the entries were consistently entered as "city, state zip", you could extract the state portion of the string with the following formula:

    Let ([commaPosition = Position(CSZ; ","; 1; 1); Middle
    (CSZ; commaPosition + 2; 2))

Examples:

Function	Results
Middle ("hello world"; 3; 5)	Returns llo w.
Middle (FirstName; 2; 99999)	Returns everything except the first character of the first name.

MiddleValues()

Category: **Text**

Syntax: **MiddleValues (text; startingValue; numberOfValues)**

Parameters:

text—Any return-delimited string or expression that generates a return-delimited string.

startingValue—Any positive integer or expression that returns a positive integer.

numberOfValues—Any positive number or expression that returns a positive integer.

Data type returned: **Text**

Description:

Returns the specified number of items from the middle of the text parameter, starting at the value specified in the startingValue parameter.

The MiddleValues() function returns a slice from the middle of a return-delimited array. The output itself will be a return-delimited array, and there will always be a trailing return at the end of the last item.

See the LeftValues() function for a discussion of methods to remove the trailing return from the output of the MiddleValues() function.

The MiddleValues() function is used frequently in scripts to loop over the items in an array. Each time through the loop, you can extract the next value from the array by incrementing a counter. For instance:

    Set Variable [$counter; 1]
    Loop
      Set Variable [$value; MiddleValues ($myArray; $counter; 1)
    { ... some set of operations involving the extracted item }
      Exit Loop If [$counter = ValueCount ($myArray)]
    End Loop

Examples:

Function	Results
MiddleValues ("A¶B¶C¶D¶E"; 2; 3)	Returns the following: B C D
MiddleValues (test; 3; 1)	Returns the following: C When test contains: A B C D

MiddleWords()

Category: **Text**

Syntax: **MiddleWords (text; startingWord; numberOfWords)**

Parameters:

text—Any expression that resolves to a text string.

startingWord—Any positive number or expression that returns a positive number.

numberOfWords—Any positive number or expression that returns a positive number.

Data type returned: **Text**

Description:

The MiddleWords() function extracts a substring from the middle of a text string. The substring begins with the *n*th word of the text string (where *n* represents the startingWord parameter) and extends for the number of words specified by the third parameter.

MiddleWords(text; 1; 1) and LeftWords(text; 1) are equivalent functions.

Be aware of what symbols are considered to be word breaks by FileMaker Pro. Spaces, return characters, and most punctuation symbols are considered to be word breaks. Multiple word breaks next to each other (for example, two spaces, a comma, and a space) are considered as a single word break.

Certain punctuation symbols are word breaks when separating alpha characters but not when separating numeric characters. These include the colon (:), slash (/), period (.), comma (,), and dash (-). The reason for this behavior is that those symbols are valid date, time, and number separators.

Leading and trailing punctuation around a word may be ignored by the MiddleWords() function. For example, MiddleWords ("John Q. Public, Jr."; 2; 1) returns Q, but MiddleWords ("John Q. Public, Jr."; 2; 1) returns Q. Public.

Examples:

Function	Results
MiddleWords ("the quick brown fox jumps"; 3; 2)	Returns brown fox.
MiddleWords (FullName"; 2; 1)	Returns Allan when FullName contains "Edgar Allan Poe."

Min()

Category: **Aggregate**

Syntax: **Min (field {; field...})**

Parameters:

field—Any related field, repeating field, or set of non-repeating fields that represent a set of numbers. Parameters in curly braces { } are optional.

Data type returned: **Text, Number, Date, Time, Timestamp**

Description:

Returns the lowest valid, non-blank value from the set of values specified by the field parameter.

When the parameter list consists of two or more repeating fields, Min() returns a repeating field in which the corresponding repetitions from the specified fields are evaluated separately. So, if a field Repeater1 has three values, 16, 20, and 24, and another field, Repeater2, has two values, 14 and 25, Min (Repeater1; Repeater2) would return a repeating field with values 14, 20, and 24.

Because dates, times, and timestamps are represented internally as numbers, the Min() function can be used to compare data of these data types. For instance, to return the earlier of two dates, you could use the following type of formula:

GetAsDate (Min (Date (4; 1; 2005); Get (CurrentDate)))

This example would return either 4/1/2005 or the current date, whichever is less.

Examples:

Function	Results
Min (44; 25; 129)	Returns 25.
Min (repeatingField)	Returns 10 (when repetition 1 = 18, repetition 2 = 10, and repetition 3 = 54).
Min(Invoice:InvoiceAmount)	Returns the lowest invoice amount found in the set of related Invoice records.

Minute()

Category: **Time**

Syntax: **Minute (time)**

Parameters:

time—Any valid time value or expression that returns a valid time value.

Data type returned: **Number**

Description:

The Minute() function returns an integer representing the number of minutes from the given time value.

The Minute() function always returns an integer in the range from 0 to 59. If you want the output of this function to be expressed always as a two-character string (for example, 07 instead of 7 when the time is 4:07 p.m.), use the following formula:

  Right ("00" & Minute (time); 2)

Examples:

Function	Results
Minute ("10:45:20")	Returns 45.
Minute ("12:07 am")	Returns 7.
Minute (Get (CurrentTime))	Returns a value from 0 to 59.

Mod()

Category: **Number**

Syntax: **Mod (number; divisor)**

Parameters:

number—Any expression that resolves to a numeric value.

divisor—Any expression that resolves to a numeric value.

Data type returned: **Number**

Description:

Returns the remainder after number is divided by divisor.

Mod() is related to the Div() function; Div() returns the whole number portion of x divided by y, whereas Mod() returns the remainder.

There are many practical uses for the Mod() function. For instance, when x is an integer, Mod (x; 2) returns 0 if x is even, and 1 if x is odd. Mod (x; 1) returns just the decimal portion of a number.

Examples:

Function	Results
Mod (7; 5)	Returns 2.
Mod (-7; 5)	Returns 3.
Mod (13; 3)	Returns 1.
Mod (1.43; 1)	Returns .43.

Month()

Category: **Date**

Syntax: **Month (date)**

Parameters:

date—Any valid date (1/1/0001–12/31/4000). The parameter should be a string containing a date (for example, "3/17/2004"), an expression with a date result (for example, Date (6, 29, 1969)), or an integer that represents a serialized date value (for example, 718977).

Data type returned: **Number**

Description:

Returns the month number (1–12) for any valid date (1/1/0001–12/31/4000).

The numeric value returned by Month() can be used in mathematical calculations as well as within the Date() function to construct a new date.

One common use of the Month() function is to build a formula that returns the quarter of a given date:

```
Case(
  Month(myDate) < 4, "First Quarter",
  Month(myDate) < 7, "Second Quarter",
  Month(myDate) < 9, "Third Quarter",
  "Fourth Quarter"
)
```

Examples:

Function	Results
Month ("5/1/2000")	Returns 5.
Month (718977)	Returns 6.
Month (Get (CurrentDate))	Returns 3 (if the current date is in March).

MonthName()

Category: **Date**

Syntax: **MonthName (date)**

Parameters:

date—Any valid date (1/1/0001–12/31/4000). The parameter should be a string containing a date (for example, "3/17/2004"), an expression with a date result (for example, Date (6, 29, 1969)), or an integer that represents a serialized date value (for example, 718977).

Data type returned: **Text**

Description:

Returns the month name of the specified date.

The MonthName() is frequently used for display purposes in subsummary reports. Although you display the name of the month, be sure that you summarize based on the month number (obtained with the Month() function). If you don't, your report will be summarized alphabetically by month rather than chronologically by month.

Examples:

Function	Results
MonthName ("1/1/2000")	Returns January.
MonthName ("5/20/2003")	Returns May.
MonthName (Get (CurrentDate))	Might return March.

MonthNameJ()

Category: **Date**

Syntax: **MonthNameJ (date)**

Parameters:

date—Any calendar date.

Data type returned: **Text (Japanese)**

Description:

Returns the name of the month in Japanese.

To avoid errors when using dates, always use four-digit years.

Examples:

Function	Results
MonthNameJ("6/6/2003")	Returns Rokugatsu in whatever alphabet the field is formatted to display.

NPV()

Category: **Financial**

Syntax: **NPV (payment; interestRate)**

Parameters:

payment—A repeating field that contains one or more values representing loan and payment amounts.

interestRate—An interest rate, expressed as a decimal number.

Data type returned: **Number**

Description:

Returns the Net Present Value of a series of unequal payments made at regular intervals, assuming a fixed interestRate per interval. The repeating field specified in the first parameter should contain all loan and payment amounts.

Examples:

Imagine someone borrows $300 from you and repays you $100, $50, $100, and $125 at regular intervals.

Assuming an interest rate of 5%, the NPV() function can tell you the actual profit, in today's dollars, that will be realized from this transaction. To calculate this, you would place the following values in a repeating number field: -300, 100, 50, 100, and 125. Then, use the formula

    Round (NPV (Payments; .05)),

which returns $28.39. Your actual profit on the transaction would be $75 (simply the sum of the payments minus the original loan). That $75, however, is collected over time, so the present value is discounted by the assumed interest rate. The higher the interest rate, the less the NPV of the $75.

NumToJText()

Category: **Text**

Syntax: **NumToJText (number; separator; characterType)**

Parameters:

number—Any numeric expression or field containing a number.

separator—A number from 0–3 representing a separator.

characterType—A number from 0–3 representing a type.

Data type returned: **Text (Japanese)**

Description:

Converts Roman numbers in the number parameter to Japanese text. If the value for separator and characterType are blank or other than 0 to 3, then 0 is used.

Separator:

0—No separator

1—Every 3 digits (thousands)

2—Ten thousands (万) and millions (億) unit

3—Tens (十), hundreds (百), thousands (千), ten thousands (万), and millions (億) unit

Type:

0—Half width (Hankaku) number

1—Full width (Zenkaku) number

2—Kanji character number (一二三)

3—Traditional-old-style Kanji character number (壱弐参)

Examples:

Function	Results
NumToJText(123456789;2;0)	Returns 1億2345万6789.
NumToJText(123456789;3;2)	Returns 一億二千三百四十五万六千七百八十九.

PatternCount()

Category: **Text**

Syntax: **PatternCount (text; searchString)**

Parameters:

text—Any expression that resolves to a text string.

searchString—Any expression that resolves to a text string, representing the substring for which you want to search within the text string.

Data type returned: **Number**

Description:

Returns the number of times that searchString appears in the text string. PatternCount() returns 0 if the searchString is not found.

Only non-overlapping occurrences of searchString are counted by PatternCount(). PatternCount() is not case sensitive.

Even though PatternCount() is designed to answer the question "how many?", it is often used simply to determine whether one string is contained within another. If it returns any value other than zero, the search string is found.

Examples:

Function	Results
PatternCount ("This is a test"; "is")	Returns 2.
PatternCount (WindowNames; "¶") + 1	Returns the number of carriage returns in the list returned by the WindowNames() function. This could be used to determine the number of windows that are available. The ValueCount() function could also be used for this purpose.
PatternCount ("ababababa"; "Aba")	Returns 2.

Pi

Category: **Trigonometric**

Syntax: **Pi**

Parameters: None

Description:

Returns the value of the trigonometric constant Pi, which is approximately 3.1415926535897932. Pi is defined as the ratio of the circumference to the diameter of any circle.

Pi is most often used in conjunction with other trigonometric functions, such as Sin(), Cos(), and Tan(), which each require an angle measured in radians as a parameter. There are 2×Pi radians in 360 degrees.

Examples:

Function	Results
Pi / 2	Returns 1.5707963267948966.
SetPrecision (Pi; 25)	Returns 3.141592653589793238462643 4.

PMT()

Category: **Financial**

Syntax: **PMT (principal; interestRate; term)**

Parameters:

principal—A number (or numeric expression) representing the initial amount borrowed.

interestRate—A decimal number (or numeric expression), representing the monthly interest rate used to amortize the principal amount. Given an annual interest rate, you can divide by 12 to get the monthly interest rate.

term—A number (or numeric expression) representing the period of loan, expressed in months.

Data type returned: **Number**

Description:

Returns the monthly payment that would be required to pay off the principal based on the interestRate and term specified.

The PMT calculation makes it easy to see the effect of interest rates on the monthly payment of an installment loan. For instance, buying a $20,000 car at 6.9% for 48 months would require a $478.00 monthly payment, but at 3.9%, the payment would be $450.68.

Examples:

Someone borrows $1,000 from you, and you want to set up a payment schedule whereby the loan is paid off in 2 years at an interest rate of 6%. To determine the monthly payment,

    PMT (1000; .06/12; 24)

returns $44.32.

Position()

Category: **Text**

Syntax: **Position (text ; searchString ; start ; occurrence)**

Parameters:

text—Any expression that resolves to a text string in which you want to search.

searchString—Any expression that resolves to a text string for which to search.

start—An integer representing the character number at which to begin searching.

occurrence—An integer representing which occurrence of searchString to locate. A negative number causes the search to proceed backward from the start character.

Data type returned: **Number**

Description:

Returns the character number where the searchString is found within the specified text string. If the searchString is not found, the Position() function returns a 0.

In most cases, the Position() function is used to find the first occurrence of some substring within a string. Both the start and occurrence parameters will simply be 1 in such instances.

To find the *last* occurrence of a substring within a string, set the start parameter to be the length of the string and the occurrence parameter to be -1, indicating that the function should search backward from the end of the string for the first occurrence of the substring.

The Position() function is not case sensitive.

Examples:

Function	Results
Position ("This is a est"; "is"; 1; 1)	Returns 3.
Position ("This is a test"; "is"; 1; 2)	Returns 6.
Position ("Let (myString = "This is a test"; Position (myString; " "; Length (myString); -1))	Returns 10, which is the position of the last space in myString.

Proper()

Category: **Text**

Syntax: **Proper (text)**

Parameters:

text—Any expression that resolves to a text string.

Data type returned: **Text**

Description:

Returns the specified text string with the initial letter of each word capitalized and all other letters as lowercase.

The Proper() function is one of three case-changing functions in FileMaker. The other two are Lower() and Upper().

The Proper() function is often used as part of an auto-entered calculation formula to reformat a user's entry with the desired case. For instance, in a City field, where you would expect the first letter of each word to be capitalized, you could set up an auto-entry option to enter Proper(City) and uncheck the option to not replace existing value. Then, if a user were to type SAN FRANCISCO, upon exiting the field the entry would be reset to San Francisco.

Examples:

Function	Results
Proper ("this is a TEST")	Returns This Is A Test.
Proper (Address)	Returns 123 Main Street when Address contains "123 main street".

PV()

Category: **Financial**

Syntax: **PV (payment; interestRate; periods)**

Parameters:

payment—A number (or numeric expression) representing a payment amount made per period.

interestRate—A decimal number (or numeric expression) representing the interest rate per period.

periods—The number of periods of the loan.

Data type returned: **Number**

Description:

The Present Value formula tells you what money expected in the future is worth today. The PV() function returns the present value of a series of equal payments made at regular intervals, and assumes a fixed interestRate per interval.

Examples:

Imagine you have won $1,000,000 in a lottery. You have been offered either $50,000 per year for the next 20 years, or a one-time lump sum payment now of $700,000. Which option should you choose?

Assuming an inflation rate of 3% per year, the present value of the future payments is determined by

PV (50000; .03; 20)

which returns 743873.74.

If you assume a 4% inflation rate, the present value of the future payments decreases to 679516.31. So, depending on your assumptions about inflation rates, you may or not be better off taking the lump sum payment.

As another example, consider the question of whether it would be better for someone to give you $10 today, or $1 per year for the next 10 years. You can use the PV() function to tell you the present value of receiving $1 for 10 years. Assuming an inflation rate of 3%, the formula PV (1, .03, 10) shows that the present value of the future income is only $8.53.

Quote()

Category: **Logical**

Syntax: **Quote (text)**

Parameters:

text—Any expression that resolves to a text string.

Data type returned: **Text**

Description:

The Quote() function returns the specified text string enclosed in quotation marks. To escape any special characters within the text string, such as quotation marks and double backslashes, place a backslash before them in the text string.

The Quote() function is used primarily in conjunction with the Evaluate() function, which can evaluate a dynamically generated formula. If the formula you are assembling contains a literal text string enclosed by quotation marks, or if it includes field contents that may potentially have quotation marks in it, then use the Quote() function to ensure that all internal quotation marks are escaped properly.

Examples:

If the FullName field contains the name Billy "Joe" Smith, then Quote (FullName) would return "Billy \"Joe\" Smith". The absence and presence of quotation marks here is deliberate; the quotation marks are part of the returned string.

Radians()

Category: **Trigonometric**

Syntax: **Radians (angleInDegrees)**

Parameters:

angleInDegrees—A number representing an angle measured in degrees.

Data type returned: **Number**

Description:

The Radians() function converts an angle measured in degrees into an angle measured in radians.

The trigonometric functions Sin(), Cos(), and Tan() all take an angle measured in radians as their parameter. To find, say, the cosine of a 180° angle, you could use the formula Cos (Radians (180)). There are 2×Pi radians in 360°.

Examples:

Function	Results
Radians (60)	Returns 1.0471975511965977 (= Pi/3).
Radians (180)	Returns 3.1415926535897932 (= Pi).

Random

Category: **Number**

Syntax: **Random**

Parameters: None

Data type returned: **Number**

Description:

Returns a random decimal between zero and one (but will not return 1 nor 0.) When used in a field definition, a new value is generated when the formula is updated. It is also updated anytime the formula re-evaluates, such as when other field values referenced in the formula change. In an unstored calculation, the Random() function re-evaluates each time the field is displayed.

If you want to generate a random integer in a certain range, multiply the result returned by the random function by the range you want to produce; then use the Int(), Floor(), Ceiling(), Round(), or Truncate() functions to remove the decimals.

For instance, to return a random number from 1 to 6 (as in the roll of a die), use the formula:

    Ceiling (Random * 6)

If you need to specify a lower bound for the random number, just add the bound to the results of the random number. For instance, to return a random number between 10 and 100, inclusive, use the following formula:

    Int (Random * 91) + 10

Examples:

Function	Results
Round (Random; 5)	Might return .07156.

RelationInfo()

Category: **Design**

Syntax: **RelationInfo (fileName; tableOccurrence)**

Parameters:

fileName—A string or text expression representing the name of an open file.

tableOccurrence—A string or text expression representing the name of a particular table occurrence in fileName.

Data type returned: **Text**

Description:

Returns a list of information about all the table occurrences that are related to the specified tableOccurrence.

The results are formatted as

FileName
Related Table Reference::Related Field
Local Related Field
Options for "right" side of relationship ("Delete", "Create" and/or "Sorted")

Repeat above four lines for each relationship.

The RelationInfo() function returns four lines for each table occurrence that's related to the one you specify. If there are no options selected on the "right" side of the relationship, the fourth line is blank.

Examples:

RelationInfo (Get(FileName);"Contacts 2") might return values that look like this:

MyDatabase
Invoice_Line::ContactID_fk
ContactID_pk
Delete Sorted
MyDatabase
Phone_Nums::ContactID_fk
ContactID_pk
Delete

Replace()

Category: **Text**

Syntax: **Replace (text; start; numberOfCharacters; replacementText)**

Parameters:

text—Any expression that resolves to a text string.

start—Any positive number or expression that returns a positive number.

numberOfCharacters—Any positive number or expression that returns a positive number.

replacementText—Any expression that resolves to a text string.

Data type returned: **Text**

Description:

The Replace() function extracts a segment of a text string and replaces it with some other string. The segment to extract begins with the start character number and extends for numberOfCharacters. The replacement string is specified by the replacementText parameter.

The extracted segment and the replacement text do not need to be the same length.

The Replace() and Substitute() functions are often confused with one another. Substitute() replaces all occurrences of a particular substring with another string, whereas Replace() replaces a specified range of characters with another string.

Replace() is often used for manipulation of delimited text arrays. There is no function that will directly replace the contents of a particular item in an array with another. The Replace() function can do this by finding the appropriate delimiters and inserting the replacement item. For instance, if you have a pipe-delimited list of numbers (for example, 34|888|150|43) and you wish to increase the third item in the list by 18, you could use the following formula:

```
Let ([
    item = 3;
    increase = 18;
    start = Position (myArray; "|"; 1; (item-1)) + 1;
    end = Position (myArray; "|"; 1; item);
    itemValue = Middle (myArray; start; end-start);
    newValue = itemValue + increase ];
    Replace (myArray; start; end-start; newValue)
)
```

Given the example string as myArray, this would produce the string 34|888|168|43. Typically, the item and increase values would be supplied by other fields and not hard-coded into the formula.

Another great use of the Replace() function is to use it as an "Insert" function: Pass a zero as the number of characters and you will simply insert some amount of text without having to use a combination of Left(), Middle(), and Right() functions.

Examples:

Function	Results
Replace ("abcdef"; 4; 2; "TEST")	Returns abcTESTf.
Replace ("Fred Smith"; 1; 4; "Joe")	Returns Joe Smith.
Replace ("leftright"; 5; 0; "middle")	Returns leftmiddleright.

RGB()

Category: **Text Formatting**

Syntax: **RGB (red; green; blue)**

Parameters:

red—Any number or numeric expression containing a value ranging from 0 to 255.

green—Any number or numeric expression containing a value ranging from 0 to 255.

blue—Any number or numeric expression containing a value ranging from 0 to 255.

Data type returned: **Number**

Description:

Returns a number that represents a color.

To calculate this integer, the red, green, and blue values are combined using the following formula:

$$(\text{red} * 256^2) + (\text{green} * 256) + \text{blue}$$

Use the RGB() function in conjunction with the TextColor() function to format text.

If a number above 255 is supplied as the parameter, the formula in the example still computes a result. If the result of the formula returns a value above the expected 0 to 16777215 range, the Mod (result; 16777216) is used to map the result into the expected range. So RGB (255; 255; 256), which returns a value one higher than white, returns the color black, just as 0 does.

Examples:

Table 6.1 lists the RGB values of some common colors.

Table 6.1   RGB Values

Function	Integer Result	Color
RGB (255; 0; 0)	16711680	Red
RGB (0; 255; 0)	65280	Green
RGB (0; 0; 255)	255	Blue
RGB (255; 255; 255)	16777215	White
RGB (0; 0; 0)	0	Black
RGB (24; 162; 75)	1614411	Dark Green
RGB (7; 13; 78)	462158	Dark Purple
RGB (23; 100; 148)	1533076	Bright Blue

Right()

Category: **Text**

Syntax: **Right (text; numberOfCharacters)**

Parameters:

text—Any expression that resolves to a text string.

numberOfCharacters—Any expression that resolves to a numeric value.

Data type returned: **Text**

Description:

Returns a string containing the last *n* characters from the specified text string. If the string is shorter than numberOfCharacters, the entire string is returned. If numberOfCharacters is less than 1, an empty string is returned.

The Right() function is commonly used in text parsing routines to extract portions of a text string.

Examples:

Function	Results
Right ("Hello"; 2)	Returns lo.
Right (FirstName; 1)	Returns the last character of the FirstName field.

RightValues()

Category: **Text**

Syntax: **RightValues (text; numberOfValues)**

Parameters:

text—Any return-delimited text string or expression that generates a return-delimited string.

numberOfValues—Any positive number or expression that returns a positive number.

Data type returned: **Text**

Description:

Returns the specified number of items from the end of the text parameter.

The RightValues() function returns the last *n* items from a return-delimited array. The items themselves will be a return-delimited array, and there will always be a trailing return at the end of the last item.

See the LeftValues() function for a discussion of methods to remove the trailing return from the output of the RightValues() function.

Examples:

Function	Results
RightValues("A¶B¶C¶D¶E";3)	Returns the following: C D E
RightValues(test;1)	Returns C when test contains A B C

RightWords()

Category: **Text**

Syntax: **RightWords (text; numberOfWords)**

Parameters:

text—Any expression that resolves to a text string.

numberOfWords—Any positive number or expression that returns a positive number.

Data type returned: **Text**

Description:

Returns the last *n* number of words in a text expression, where *n* is the number specified in the numberOfWords parameter.

Be aware of what symbols are considered to be word breaks by FileMaker Pro. Spaces, return characters, and most punctuation symbols are considered to be word breaks. Multiple word breaks next to each other (for example, two spaces, a comma, and a space) are considered as a single word break.

Certain punctuation symbols are word breaks when separating alpha characters, but not when separating numeric characters. These include the colon (:), slash (/), period (.), comma (,), and dash (-). For instance, RightWords ("54.6"; 1) returns 54.6, but RightWords ("x.y"; 1) returns y. The reason for this behavior is that those symbols are valid date, time, and number separators.

Leading and trailing punctuation around a word will be ignored by the RightWords() function. For example, RightWords ("John Q. Public, Jr."; 2) returns Public, Jr, and RightWords ("John Q. Public, Jr."; 3) returns Q. Public, Jr.

Examples:

Function	Results
RightWords ("the quick brown fox jumps"; 3)	Returns brown fox jumps.
RightWords (FullName; 1)	Returns Smith when the FullName field contains Joe Smith.

RomanHankaku()

Category: **Text**

Syntax: **RomanHankaku (text)**

Parameters:

text—Any text expression or text field.

Data type returned: **Text (Japanese)**

Description:

Converts from Zenkaku alphanumeric and symbols to Hankaku alphanumeric and symbols. Zenkaku alphanumeric and symbols represent Roman alphanumeric and symbols using Japanese Unicode characters.

Examples:

Function	Results
RomanHankaku("M a c i n t o s h")	Returns Macintosh.

RomanZenkaku()

Category: **Text**

Syntax: **RomanZenkaku (text)**

Parameters:

text—Any text expression or text field.

Data type returned: **Text (Japanese)**

Description:

Converts from Hankaku alphanumeric and symbols to Zenkaku alphanumeric and symbols. Zenkaku alphanumeric and symbols represent Roman alphanumeric and symbols using Japanese Unicode characters.

Examples:

Function	Results
RomanZenkaku("Macintosh")	Returns M a c i n t o s h.

Round()

Category: **Number**

Syntax: **Round (number; precision)**

Parameters:

number—Any expression that resolves to a numeric value.

precision—Any number or numeric expression representing the number of decimal points to which to round the number.

Data type returned: **Number**

Description:

Returns the specified number rounded off to the number of decimal points specified by the precision parameter. The Round() function rounds numbers from 5 to 9 upward, and from 0 to 4 downward.

A precision of 0 rounds to the nearest integer. A negative number for the precision causes the number to be rounded to the nearest ten, hundred, thousand, and so on.

Examples:

Function	Results
Round (62.566; 2)	Returns 62.57.
Round (62.563; 2)	Returns 62.56.
Round (92.4; 0)	Returns 92.
Round (32343.98; -3)	Returns 32000.
Round (505.999; -1)	Returns 510.

ScriptIDs()

Category: **Design**

Syntax: **ScriptIDs (fileName)**

Parameters:

fileName—A string or text expression that represents the name of an open file.

Data type returned: **Text**

Description:

Returns a carriage return–delimited list of script IDs from the specified file.

ScriptIDs are assigned sequentially by FileMaker, starting at 1 for each new file. The results returned by the ScriptIDs function are ordered according to the current order within ScriptMaker, not the creation order of the scripts.

When you convert a solution developed in an earlier version of FileMaker, the ScriptIDs of the original file are retained after conversion.

Any scripts that are set to "no access" for the current user's privilege set are not included in the list.

Examples:

Function	Results
ScriptIDs ("myFile")	Returns a list of script IDs for the current file that might look like this: 21 22 24 25

ScriptNames()

Category: **Design**

Syntax: **ScriptNames (fileName)**

Parameters:

fileName—A string or text expression that represents the name of an open file.

Data type returned: **Text**

Description:

Returns a carriage return–delimited list of script names from the specified file.

As with the ScriptIDs() function, the order of the list returned by ScriptNames() is the current order of the scripts within ScriptMaker.

Any scripts that are set to "no access" for the current user's privilege set are not included in the list.

Examples:

Function	Results
ScriptNames (Get (FileName))	Returns a list of script names for the current file that might look like this: Contact_Nav Invoice_Nav - Contact_New Invoice_New - Contact_Delete Invoice_Delete

Seconds()

Category: **Time**

Syntax: **Seconds (time)**

Parameters:

time—Any valid time value or expression that returns a valid time value.

Data type returned: **Number**

Description:

The Seconds() function returns an integer representing the number of seconds specified by the time parameter.

This function always returns a value from 0 to 59.

If you want to express the output of this function as a two-character string rather than as an integer (for example, 03 rather than 3), use the following formula:

Right ("00" & Seconds (Time); 2)

If the time parameter has a seconds value greater than 59, the Seconds() function returns the Mod-60 result of that value. For instance, Seconds ("12:42:87") returns 27. Note that the "overflow" of the seconds value is applied to the minutes value: Minute ("12:42:87") returns 43.

Examples:

Function	Results
Seconds ("10:45:20")	Returns 20.
Seconds ("12:15 am")	Returns 0.

SerialIncrement()

Category: **Text**

Syntax: **SerialIncrement (text; incrementBy)**

Parameters:

text—Any text or text expression that contains an alphanumeric string.

incrementBy—A number or numeric expression with which to increment the text value.

Data type returned: **Text**

Description:

Returns the combined text and number from the text value, where the numeric portion of the text has been incremented by the value specified in the incrementBy parameter.

The incrementBy value is truncated to an integer when incrementing. Positive and negative numbers are accepted.

Examples:

Function	Results
SerialIncrement ("test1"; 2)	Returns test3.
SerialIncrement ("project_plan_v12.3"; -1)	Returns project_plan_v12.2.
SerialIncrement ("2hithere3"; 3)	Returns 2hithere6.

SetPrecision()

Category: **Number**

Syntax: **SetPrecision (expression; precision)**

Parameters:

expression—Any number or expression that returns a number.

precision—An integer from 1 to 400.

Data type returned: **Number**

Description:

FileMaker normally computes decimals with 16 digits of precision. The SetPrecision() function allows you to specify with up to 400 digits of precision.

The expression specified in the first parameter is rounded at the digit specified by the second parameter.

The trigonometric functions do not support extended precision.

You can specify a number below 17 as the precision, but FileMaker still returns 16 digits of precision regardless. Use the Round() function instead to specify a precision up to 16.

Examples:

Function	Results
SetPrecision(Pi;28)	Returns 3.1415926535897932384626433833.
SetPrecision(Pi;29)	Returns 3.14159265358979323846264338328.

Sign()

Category: **Number**

Syntax: **Sign (number)**

Parameters:

number—Any expression that resolves to a numeric value.

Data type returned: **Text**

Description:

Returns a value that represents the sign of number:

    -1 when number is negative
    0 when number is zero
    1 when number is positive

For any x other than 0, multiplying x by Sign(x) yields the Abs(x).

Examples:

Function	Results
Sign (0)	Returns 0.
Sign (100)	Returns 1.
Sign(-100)	Returns -1 for the formula If (Sign (BalanceDue) = -1; "Please pay now!"; "Thanks for your payment!").

Sin()

Category: **Trigonometric**

Syntax: **Sin (angleInRadians)**

Parameters:

angleInRadians—Any numeric expression or field containing a numeric expression, in radians.

Data type returned: **Number**

Description:

Returns the sine of angleInRadians expressed in radians.

In any right triangle, the sine of the two non-right angles can be obtained by dividing the length of the side opposite the angle by the length of the hypotenuse.

Examples:

Function	Results
Sin (Radians(60))	Returns .86602.
Sin (.610865)	Returns .57357624....

Sqrt()

Category: **Number**

Syntax: **Sqrt (number)**

Parameters:

number—Any expression that resolves to a positive number.

Data type returned: **Number**

Description:

Returns the square root of number.

Examples:

Function	Results
Sqrt (64)	Returns 8.
Sqrt (2)	Returns 1.414213562373095.

StDev()

Category: **Aggregate**

Syntax: **StDev (field {; field...})**

Parameters:

field—Any related field, repeating field, or set of non-repeating fields that represent a collection of numbers. Parameters in curly braces { } are optional.

Data type returned: **Number**

Description:

Returns the standard deviation of the non-blank values represented in the parameter list. Standard deviation is a statistical measurement of how spread out a collection of values is. In a normal distribution, about 68% of the values are within one standard deviation of the mean, and about 95% are within two standard deviations of the mean.

The difference between the StDevP() and StDev() functions is that StDev divides the sum of the squares by n-1 instead of by n.

StDev() can also be calculated as the square root of the Variance() of a set of numbers.

Examples:

There are several ways you can manually calculate the standard deviation of a set of numbers. One is to take the square root of the sum of the squares of each value's distance from the mean, divided by n-1, where n is the number of values in the set.

For instance, given the set of numbers 8, 10, and 12, the mean of this set is 10. The distances of each value from the mean are therefore -2, 0, and 2. The squares of these are 4, 0, and 4. The sum of the squares is 8. The standard deviation of the population is Sqrt (8/(3-1)), which is 2.

    StDev (8; 10; 12)

returns 2.

Given a portal that contains a field called Scores with the following values (64, 72, 75, 59, 67),

    StDev (People::Scores)

returns 6.35.

StDevP()

Category: **Aggregate**

Syntax: **StDevP (field {; field...})**

Parameters:

field—Any related field, repeating field, or set of non-repeating fields that represent a collection of numbers. Parameters in curly braces { } are optional.

Data type returned: **Number**

Description:

Returns the standard deviation of a population represented by the non-blank values represented in the parameter list. Standard deviation is a statistical measurement of how spread out a collection of values is. In a normal distribution, about 68% of the values are within one standard deviation of the mean, and about 95% are within two standard deviations of the mean.

The difference between the StDevP() and StDev() functions is that StDev() divides the sum of the squares by n-1 instead of by n.

StDevP() can also be calculated as the square root of the VarianceP() of a set of numbers.

Examples:

There are several ways you can manually calculate the standard deviation of a population. One is to take the square root of the sum of the squares of each value's distance from the mean, divided by the number of values.

For instance, given the set of numbers 8, 10, and 12, the mean of this set is 10. The distances of each value from the mean are therefore -2, 0, and 2. The squares of these are 4, 0, and 4. The sum of the squares is 8. The standard deviation of the population is Sqrt (8/3), which is 1.633.

   StDevP (8; 10; 12)

returns 1.633.

Given a portal that displays the heights of a set of people (64, 72, 75, 59, 67),

   StDevP (People::Heights)

returns 5.68.

Substitute()

Category: **Text**

Syntax: **Substitute (text; searchString; replaceString)**

Parameters:

text—Any text string or expression that returns a text string.

searchString—Any text string or expression that returns a text string.

replaceString—Any text string or expression that returns a text string.

Data type returned: **Text**

Description:

Returns a text string in which all instances of searchString in the text parameter are replaced with the replaceString.

Multiple substitutions may occur in the same Substitute() function:

Substitute ("This is a test"; ["i"; "q"]; ["s"; "$"])

returns Thq$ q$ a te$t.

The Substitute() function is case sensitive.

Examples:

Function	Results
Substitute ("Happy Anniversary!"; "Anniversary"; "Birthday")	Returns Happy Birthday!.
Substitute ("This is a test"; "i"; "q")	Returns Thqs qs a test.

Sum()

Category: **Aggregate**

Syntax: **Sum (field {; field...})**

Parameters:

field—Any related field, repeating field, or set of non-repeating fields that represent a collection of numbers. Parameters in curly braces { } are optional.

Data type returned: **Number**

Description:

Returns the sum of all valid values represented by the fields in the parameter list.

The Sum() function is most often used to add up a column of numbers in a related table.

Examples:

Function	Results
Sum (field1; field2; field3)	Returns 6 (when field1 = 1, field2 = 2, and field3 = 3).
Sum (repeatingField)	Returns 6 (when repetition 1 = 1, repetition 2 = 2, and repetition 3 = 3).

Function	Results
Sum (repeatingField1; repeatingField2)	Returns a repeating calculation field where the first value equals the sum of the values in repeatingField1, and the second repitition contains the sum of the values in repeatingField2.
Sum (Customer::InvoiceTotal)	Returns 420 (when the sum of InvoiceTotal in the related set of data is 420).

TableIDs()

Category: **Design**

Syntax: **TableIDs (fileName)**

Parameters:

fileName—A string or text expression that represents the name of an open file.

Data type returned: **Text**

Description:

Returns a carriage return–delimited list of table occurrence IDs from the specified file.

Note that TableIDs() returns the IDs of table occurrences from the Relationships Graph, not the actual data tables. A database table may appear in the Relationships Graph more than once.

A unique TableID is assigned by FileMaker whenever a table occurrence is added to the Relationships Graph. The order of the IDs in the list is based on the alphabetic ordering of the table occurrence names themselves.

Examples:

Function	Results
TableIDs (Get (FileName))	Returns a list of table occurrence IDs for the current file that might look like this: 100021 100049 100002

TableNames()

Category: **Design**

Syntax: **TableNames (fileName)**

Parameters:

fileName—A string or text expression that represents the name of an open file.

Data type returned: **Text**

Description:

Returns a carriage return–delimited list of table occurrence names from the specified file.

Note that TableNames() returns the names of table occurrences from the Relationships Graph, not the actual data tables. A database table may appear in the Relationships Graph more than once.

The list returned by the TableNames() function is ordered alphabetically.

Examples:

Function	Results
TableNames (Get (FileName))	Would return a list of table occurrence names for the current file that might look like this: Contacts Contact2 Invoice Lines Invoices

Tan()

Category: **Trigonometric**

Syntax: **Tan (angleInRadians)**

Parameters:

number—Any number representing the size of an angle measured in radians.

Data type returned: **Number**

Description:

Returns the tangent of the specified angle.

The tangent of an angle can also be obtained by dividing the sine of the angle by its cosine. In any right triangle, the tangent of the two non-right angles can be obtained by dividing the length of the side opposite the angle by the length of the adjacent side.

Examples:

Function	Results
Tan (0)	Returns 0.
Tan (Pi / 6)	Returns .5773502691896257.
Tan (Radians (45))	Returns 1.

TextColor()

Category: **Text Formatting**

Syntax: **TextColor (text; RGB (red; green; blue))**

Parameters:

text—Any text string or expression that returns a text string.

RGB (red;green;blue)—A function that accepts three parameters from 0 to 255 and returns a number representing a color. See the RGB() definition.

Data type returned: **Text**

Description:

Returns the text string in the color specified by the RGB parameter. Use the TextColor() function within text expressions to emphasize words:

```
"We will have " & TextColor (NumberItems;RGB (255;0;0)) & " errors per cycle.
Unacceptable!"
```

TextColor() can also be used for conditional text formatting. The following calculation highlights losses in red:

```
Let (Profit = GetAsText (Earnings – Expenditures);
  Case (
    Profit > 0; TextColor (Profit; RGB(0;0;0));
    Profit < 0; TextColor (Profit; RGB(255;0;0));
    "")
)
```

If a field is formatted in the Number Format dialog, some options override the TextColor() function. For example, conditional color for negative numbers overrides TextColor, unless the user has clicked into the field being formatted.

Examples:

Function	Results
TextColor ("this text will be blue"; RGB (0;0;255))	Returns this text will be blue, formatted in blue.
TextColor ("this text will be red"; 16711680)	Returns this text will be red, formatted in red.

TextColorRemove()

Category: **Text Formatting**

Syntax: **TextColorRemove (text {; RGB (red; green; blue)})**

Parameters:

text—Any text expression or text field.

RGB(red; green; blue)—Any integer number from 0 to 16777215 obtained by combining the red, green, and blue values (each ranging from 0 to 255) to represent a color.

Parameters in curly braces { } are optional.

Data type returned: **Text**

Description:

Removes all font colors in text, or removes instances of a specific font color as an optional parameter, leaving others unchanged.

Note that text formatting options will not be applied if the data type that is returned is something other than text.

Examples:

Function	Results
TextColorRemove ("This should be boring monochromatic stuff")	Returns This should be boring monochromatic stuff without a color specified; it will then adopt whatever default text color is set for the layout object in which it is displayed.
TextColorRemove ("No More Red Eye"; RGB(255;0;0))	Returns No More Red Eye without the specific red indicated by RGB (255;0;0), should there be any applied within the text.

TextFont()

Category: Text Formatting

Syntax: **TextFont (text; fontName {; fontScript})**

Parameters:

text—Any text string or expression that returns a text string.

fontName—Any font name available on the system. Must be enclosed in quotation marks.

fontScript—The name of a character set (for example, Cyrillic, Greek, Roman). This is an optional parameter; quotation marks should not be used around the script name. Parameters in curly braces { } are optional.

Data type returned: **Text**

Description:

Changes the text font to the specified fontName and optional fontScript. Font names are case sensitive.

If no matches for the specified font and script exist, FileMaker first looks for the font script and associated font in the Fonts tab of the Preferences dialog box. If the script is not specified in the Fonts tab, the TextFont() function uses the default font for the system. This font script might not be the same as the specified script.

A list of font scripts is available in the online help system.

When TextFont() is used as part of the definition of a calculation field, the calculation should be set to return a text result. Text formatting options are lost if the data type returned is anything other than text.

Examples:

Function	Results
TextFont ("testing 123"; "Courier")	Returns the string testing 123 in Courier font.

TextFontRemove()

Category: **Text Formatting**

Syntax: **TextFontRemove (text {; fontName; fontScript})**

Parameters:

text—Any text expression or text field.

fontName—Any font name expressed in text.

fontScript—The name of a character set that contains characters required for writing in the specified language.

Parameters in curly braces { } are optional.

Note that the fontScript parameter is not enclosed in quotation marks (" ") and requires the specific keywords listed later.

Data type returned: **Text**

Description:

Removes all fonts applied to text, or removes only fonts and font scripts as specified by the two optional parameters, fontName and fontScript. Once fonts have been removed, the data is displayed and treated as text entered into any FileMaker field by adopting whatever font attributes have been applied to the layout objects in question.

Note that font names are case sensitive and need to be entered correctly in order for the function to work properly.

Note also that font formatting functions only work on data returned as text.

The following font scripts are available:
Roman
Greek
Cyrillic
CentralEurope
ShiftJIS
TraditionalChinese
SimplifiedChinese
OEM
Symbol
Other

Examples:

Function	Results
TextFontRemove ("Nuke all fonts")	Returns Nuke all fonts displayed in a layout object's default font.
TextFontRemove ("Two fonts enter, one font leaves"; "Comic Sans MS")	Returns Two fonts enter, one font leaves with the Comic Sans MS font removed (assuming the original text string made use of it).
TextFontRemove ("How's your Russian?"; "Arial"; Cyrillic)	Returns How's your Russian? with the Arial font removed from any Cyrillic character sets.

TextFormatRemove()

NEW *Category:* **Text Formatting**

Syntax: **TextFormatRemove (text)**

Parameters:

text—Any text expression or text field.

Data type returned: **Text**

Description:

Removes all formatting from text including all fonts, styles, font sizes, and font colors.

Examples:

Function	Results
TextFormatRemove ("Enough is enough")	Returns the text Enough is enough without any text formatting applied. It will then derive display attributes from the layout object in which it appears.

TextSize()

Category: **Text Formatting**

Syntax: **TextSize (text; fontSize)**

Parameters:

text—Any text string or expression that returns a text string.

fontSize—Any font size expressed in pixels as an integer.

Data type returned: **Text**

Description:

Returns the text string at the specified font size.

When TextSize() is used as part of the definition of a calculation field, the calculation should be set to return a text result. Text formatting options are lost if the data type returned is anything other than text.

Examples:

Function	Results
TextSize ("Hello, world!"; 8)	Returns Hello, world! in 8pt font.
TextSize ("Large print book"; 18)	Returns Large print book.

TextSizeRemove()

NEW *Category:* **Text Formatting**

Syntax: **TextSizeRemove (text {; sizeToRemove})**

Parameters:

text—Any text expression or text field.

sizeToRemove—Any font size expressed as an integer.

Parameters in curly braces { } are optional.

Data type returned: **Text**

Description:

Removes all font size applications in text, or removes just the font size specified by sizeToRemove. The text in question will then adopt whatever font size has been specified for the layout object in which it displays.

Note that text formatting functions only work for data returned as text.

Examples:

Function	Results
TextSizeRemove ("It should be 8pt anyway")	Returns It should be 8pt anyway without font sizes specified. It then will display in the field's default font size.
TextSizeRemove ("It's too small!!"; 6)	Returns It's too small!! with the 6 point font size removed.

TextStyleAdd()

Category: **Text Formatting**

Syntax: **TextStyleAdd (text; style(s))**

Parameters:

text—Any text string or expression that returns a text string.

style—Any named style or list of styles separated by a plus (+) sign, or an integer that represents a combination of styles. Named styles should not be placed in quotation marks and cannot be passed as field contents.

Data type returned: **Text**

Description:

Returns a text string that has the specified style(s) applied to it.

The style names are reserved keywords in FileMaker Pro and should not be placed within quotes. You also cannot place a keyword in a field and use the field as the style parameter within TextStyleAdd(). Styles can be specified as local variables within Let functions.

All the style names have numeric equivalents that you can use instead of the names. To combine multiple styles, simply add the numeric equivalents together. The numeric equivalent can be specified by a field, so use this method if you need to dynamically specify a text style.

The list of styles and their numeric equivalents is shown in Table 6.2:

Table 6.2   Style Names and Numeric Equivalent

Style Name	Numeric Equivalent
Plain	0
Strikethrough	1
Smallcaps	2
Superscript	4
Subscript	8
Uppercase	16

Table 6.2   Style Names and Numeric Equivalent (continued)

Style Name	Numeric Equivalent
Lowercase	32
Titlecase	48
Wordunderline	64
Doubleunderline	128
Bold	256
Italic	512
Underline	1024
Condense	8192
Extend	16384
Allstyles	32767

Examples:

Function	Results
TextStyleAdd ("word underline."; WordUnderline)	Returns word underline.
TextStyleAdd ("bold italic!"; bold+italic)	Returns ***bold italic!***.
TextStyleAdd ("Plain text"; Plain)	Removes all styles from the text. If the "Plain" style is combined with any other styles, "Plain" is ignored.

TextStyleRemove()

Category: **Text Formatting**

Syntax: **TextStyleRemove (text; style(s))**

Parameters:

text—Any text string or expression that returns a text string.

style—Any named style or list of styles separated by a plus (+) sign, or an integer that represents a combination of styles. Named styles should not be placed in quotation marks and cannot be passed as field contents.

Data type returned: **Text**

Description:

Removes the specified styles from formatted text.

Removing AllStyles with TextStyleRemove() accomplishes the same thing as adding Plain with TextStyleAdd().

See TextStyleAdd() for a complete list of styles and a discussion of their numeric equivalents.

Examples:

Function	Results
TextStyleRemove ("word underline"; WordUnderline)	Removes the word underline formatting from the phrase "word underline".
TextStyleRemove ("bold italic!"; bold+italic)	Removes the bold and italic formatting from the phrase "bold italic!".
TextStyleRemove (sampleText; AllStyles)	Removes all formatting styles from the contents of the variable sampleText.

Time()

Category: **Time**

Syntax: **Time (hours; minutes; seconds)**

Parameters:

hours—A number representing the hours portion of the desired time value.

minutes—A number representing the minutes portion of the desired time value.

seconds—A number representing the seconds portion of the desired time value.

Data type returned: **Time**

Description:

Returns a time value built from the specified hours, minutes, and seconds parameters. The resulting value accurately calculates the effect of fractional parameters. Similarly, although the typical range for the minutes and seconds parameters is from 0 to 59, any values above or below are compensated for in the resulting time value.

The Time() function is often used in conjunction with the Hour(), Minute(), and Seconds() functions. For instance, the following formula takes the current time and returns the time of the next lowest hour:

Time (Hour (Get (CurrentTime));0;0))

Examples:

Function	Results
Time (8; 34; 15)	Returns 8:34:15.
Time (15.25; 0; 0)	Returns 15:15:00.
Time (22; 70; 70)	Returns 23:11:10.
Time (12; -30; 0)	Returns 11:30:00.

Timestamp()

Category: **Timestamp**

Syntax: **Timestamp (date; time)**

Parameters:

date—Any calendar date or expression that returns a date. The date parameter can also be an integer from 1 to 1460970, representing the number of days since January 1, 0001.

time—Any time value or expression that returns a time value. The time parameter can also be an integer representing the number of seconds since midnight.

Data type returned: **Timestamp**

Description:

Returns a timestamp from the two parameters in the format "12/12/2005 10:45:00 AM".

You can use text parsing functions or mathematical operations to extract the pieces of a timestamp. You can also use the GetAsDate() and GetAsTime() functions to retrieve just the date or time.

Internally, FileMaker Pro stores timestamp data as the number of seconds since 1/1/0001 12:00 a.m. You can use the GetAsNumber() function to see the numeric representation. For instance, GetAsNumber (Timestamp ("4/18/2004"; 12:00pm)) returns 63217886400.

You can manually calculate the integer value of a timestamp by using the following formula:

    (GetAsNumber (myDate)-1) * 86400 + GetAsNumber (myTime)

Examples:

Function	Results
Timestamp ("10/11/2005"; "10:20 AM")	Returns 10/11/2005 10:20 AM.
Timestamp ("10/11/2005"; "20:20:20")	Returns 10/11/2005 8:20:20 PM.
Timestamp (Date (10;11;2005); Time (10;20;00))	Returns 10/11/2005 10:20 AM.
Timestamp (laborDay; 0)	Returns 9/5/2005 12:00:00 AM when laborDay is equal to 9/5/2005.
Timestamp (1; 0)	Returns 1/1/0001 12:00 AM.

Trim()

Category: **Text**

Syntax: **Trim (text)**

Parameters:

text—Any expression that resolves to a text string.

Data type returned: **Text**

Description:

Returns the specified text string with any leading or trailing spaces removed.

The Trim() function removes only leading and trailing spaces and not any other characters (such as carriage returns).

Trim() can be used to reformat data where users have inadvertently typed spaces at the end of an entry. This happens frequently with fields containing first names. To automatically have the entry reformatted when the user exits the field, have the field auto-enter Trim (FirstName) and uncheck the option not to replace any existing value in the field. Thus, if a user enters "Fred " into the FirstName field, it is replaced with "Fred" when the user exits the field.

Trim() is also used frequently to clean up fixed-width data that has been imported from some other data source. In such cases, fields have been padded with leading or trailing spaces to be a certain length. Remove them after importing by doing calculated replaces in the appropriate fields.

Examples:

Function	Results
Trim (" This is a test ")	Returns This is a test.

TrimAll()

Category: **Text**

Syntax: **TrimAll (text; trimSpaces; trimType)**

Parameters:

text—Any text expression or text field.

trimSpaces—0 (False), 1 (True).

trimType—0 through 3 depending on the trim style.

Data type returned: **Text**

Description:

Returns text with all leading and trailing spaces removed, and takes into account different Unicode representations of spaces.

Set trimSpaces to 1 if you want to include the removal of full-width spaces between non-Roman and Roman characters. Set trimSpaces to 0 if you do not.

Characters are considered Roman if their Unicode values are less than U+2F00. Characters with values values greater than or equal to U+2F00 are considered non-Roman.

Characters within the Roman range belong to the following character blocks: Latin, Latin-1 Supplement, Latin Extended-A & B, IPA Extensions, Spacing Modifier Letters, Combining Diacritical Marks, Greek, Cyrillic, Armenian, Hebrew, Arabic, Devanagari, Bengali, Gurmukhi, Gujarati, Oriya, Tamil, Telugu, Kannada, Malayalam, Thai, Lao, Tibetan, Georgian, Hangul Jamo, and additional Latin and Greek extended blocks.

Symbols within the Roman range include punctuation characters, superscripts, subscripts, currency symbols, combining marks for symbols, letter-like symbols, number forms, arrows, math operators, control pictures, geometric shapes, dingbats, and so on.

Characters within the non-Roman range are those belonging to the CJK symbols/punctuations area, Hiragana, Katakana, Bopomofo, Hangul compatibility Jamo, Kanbun, CJK unified ideographs, and so on.

The trimType parameter controls how the function returns text in the following ways:

0   Removes spaces between non-Roman and Roman characters and always leaves one space between Roman words.

1   Always includes a half-width space between non-Roman and Roman characters and always leaves one space between Roman words.

2   Removes spaces between non-Roman characters (reducing multiple spaces between non-Roman and Roman words to 1 space) and leaves one space between Roman words.

3   Removes all spaces everywhere.

In all cases, spaces between non-Roman characters are removed.

Examples:

Function	Results
TrimAll(Full_Name,1,0)	Returns James Aloysius Kinsella when the value of Full_Name is "James Aloysius Kinsella ". It is useful for stripping extra spaces out of lengthy text fields.
TrimAll(" 名前,1,0)	Returns 山田太郎 when the value of 名前,1,0 is 山田　太郎 .

Truncate()

Category: **Number**

Syntax: **Truncate (number; precision)**

Parameters:

number—Any expression that resolves to a numeric value.

precision—Any expression that resolves to a numeric value.

Data type returned: **Number**

Description:

Returns the specified number truncated to the specified number of decimal places (precision). Unlike the Round() function, the Truncate() function simply discards further digits without performing any sort of rounding.

Truncating a number by using a precision parameter of 0 has the same effect as taking the Int() of that number. Truncate (x; 0) = Int (x).

Negative values can be used for the precision parameter in the Truncate() function. For instance, Truncate (1234.1234; -1) returns 1230. Truncate (1234.1234; -2) returns 1200.

Examples:

Function	Results
Truncate (Pi; 6)	Returns 3.141592.
Truncate (Amount; 2)	Returns 54.65 when Amount contains 54.651259.
Truncate (1234.1234; 0)	Returns 1234.
Truncate (-1234.1234; 0)	Returns –1234.

Upper()

Category: **Text**

Syntax: **Upper (text)**

Parameters:

text—A string or text expression.

Data type returned: **text**

Description:

Returns a completely uppercase version of the specified text string.

The Upper() function is one of three functions FileMaker Pro has for changing the case of a text string. The other two are Lower() and Proper().

The Upper() function is often used to reformat user-entered data to ensure consistent data entry. Sometimes when exporting data that is to be used by external applications, you need to format the data entirely as uppercase characters to be consistent with data in the other system.

The following formula checks whether a given text string is already written in all upper-case characters:

Exact (text; Upper(text))

Examples:

Function	Results
Upper ("This is a test")	Returns THIS IS A TEST.
Upper (AccessCode)	Returns 1ABC-2XYZ when AccessCode contains "1abc-2XYz".

ValueCount()

Category: **Text**

Syntax: **ValueCount (text)**

Parameters:

text—Any return-delimited string or expression that generates a return-delimited list.

Data type returned: **Number**

Description:

Returns a count of the number of values in the text provided.

The presence or absence of a trailing return after the last item in the return-delimited list does not affect the result returned by ValueCount. For instance, ValueCount ("Blue¶Green") and ValueCount ("Blue¶Green¶") both return 2.

If there are multiple returns at any point in the list, the ValueCount() function recognizes the empty items as valid items. For instance, ValueCount ("¶¶Blue¶¶Green¶¶") returns 6. Note that this behavior is different from how the WordCount() function treats multiple delimiters. There, multiple delimiters in a row are considered to be a single delimiter.

Examples:

Function	Results
ValueCount ("A¶B¶C¶D¶E")	Returns 5.
ValueCount (officeList)	Returns 3 when officeList is equal to Chicago Philadelphia San Francisco

ValueListIDs()

Category: **Design**

Syntax: **ValueListIDs (fileName)**

Parameters:

fileName—A string or text expression that represents the name of an open file.

Data type returned: **Text**

Description:

Returns a carriage return–delimited list of value list IDs from the specified file.

FileMaker assigns a serial number to each value list created in a file. The order of the list returned by the ValueListIDs() function is the same as that in which the value lists are ordered in the Define Value Lists dialog when the order is set to Custom Order. Changing the Custom Order changes the way the results are ordered, but selecting one of the other choices (Creation Order, Source, Value List Name) does not affect the order.

Examples:

Function	Results
ValueListIDs (Get (FileName))	Returns a list of value list IDs for the current file that might look like this:
	21
	92
	90
	108
	15

ValueListItems()

Category: **Design**

Syntax: **ValueListItems (fileName; valueListName)**

Parameters:

fileName—A string or text expression that represents the name of an open file.

valueList—The name of a value list in fileName.

Data type returned: **Text**

Description:

Returns a carriage return–delimited list of the items in the specified value list.

The ValueListItems() function is often used to consolidate information about a set of related records. For instance, in an invoice file, you might have a value list called Products_Ordered that's defined to return the ProductName field from a related set of records in the InvoiceItem table. ValueListItems (Get (FileName); "Products_Ordered") would return a list of all the products ordered on the current invoice.

As with many design functions, we recommend against hard-coding specific text strings into calculations, but in this case it cannot be avoided. One practice we follow in our work is to name value lists that are referenced elsewhere by name with a suffix "DNR" for "do not rename." Another approach is to create a custom function that returns value list names and thus provides a single place to control edits.

Examples:

Function	Results
ValueListItems (Get (FileName); "Phone_Label")	Returns a list of values from the value list Phone_Label in the current file that might look like this: Home Work Cell Fax

ValueListNames()

Category: **Design**

Syntax: **ValueListNames (fileName)**

Parameters:

fileName—A string or text expression that represents the name of an open file.

Data type returned: **Text**

Description:

Returns a carriage return–delimited list of value list names from the specified file.

The order of the list returned by the ValueListNames() function is the same as that in which the value lists are ordered in the Define Value Lists dialog when the order is set to Custom Order. Changing the Custom Order changes the way the results are ordered, but selecting one of the other choices (Creation Order, Source, Value List Name) does not.

Examples:

Function	Results
ValueListNames (Get (FileName))	Returns a list of value list names from the current file that might look like this: Phone_Label Location Type Category

Variance()

Category: **Aggregate**

Syntax: **Variance (field {; field...})**

Parameters:

field—Any related field, repeating field, or set of non-repeating fields that represent a collection of numbers.

Data type returned: **Number**

Description:

Returns the variance of the non-blank values represented in the parameter list. Variance is a statistical measure of how spread out a set of values is.

The StDev() of a set of numbers is the square root of the Variance() of the set.

The difference between the Variance() and VarianceP() functions is that the Variance divides the sum of the squares by n-1 instead of by n.

Examples:

The Variance of a set of numbers can be calculated by summing the squares of the distance of each value from the mean, then dividing by n-1, where n is the number of values.

For instance, given the set of numbers 8, 10, and 12, the mean of the set is 10. The distance of each value from the mean is -2, 0, and 2. The squares of these distances are 4, 0, and 4, and the sum of the squares is 8. The Variance is 8 divided by (3–1), which is 4.

    Variance (8; 10; 12)

Returns 4.

    Variance (7; 11; 15)

Returns 16.

VarianceP()

Category: **Aggregate**

Syntax: **VarianceP (field {; field...})**

Parameters:

field—Any related field, repeating field, or set of non-repeating fields that represent a collection of numbers.

Data type returned: **Number**

Description:

Returns the variance of a population represented by the non-blank values in the parameter list. Variance of population is a statistical measure of how spread out a set of values is.

The StDevP() of a set of numbers is the square root of the VarianceP() of the set.

Examples:

The variance of a population represented by a set of numbers can be calculated by summing the squares of the distance of each value from the mean, then dividing by *n*, where *n* is the number of values.

For instance, given the set of numbers 8, 10, and 12, the mean of the set is 10. The distance of each value from the mean is -2, 0, and 2. The squares of these distances are 4, 0, and 4, and the sum of the squares is 8. The VarianceP is 8 divided by (3), which is 2.67.

VarianceP (8; 10; 12)

Returns 2.67.

VarianceP (7; 11; 15)

Returns 10.66.

WeekOfYear()

Category: **Date**

Syntax: **WeekOfYear (date)**

Parameters:

date—Any valid date (1/1/0001–12/31/4000). The parameter should be a string containing a date (for example, "3/17/2004"), an expression with a date result (for example, Date (6, 29, 1969)), or an integer that represents a serialized date value (for example, 718977).

Data type returned: **Number**

Description:

Returns the week number of the specified date. Weeks are defined as starting on Sunday and ending on Saturday. A partial week at the beginning of the year is considered as week 1, so the WeekOfYear() function can return values from 1 to 54.

WeekOfYear() can be used to return the approximate number of weeks between two dates in the same year. For instance, WeekOfYear("6/1/2001") - WeekOfYear("5/1/2001") returns 4.

January 1st of any given year is always part of week 1, no matter on what day of the week it falls.

Examples:

Function	Results
WeekOfYear ("3/12/2004")	Returns 11.
WeekOfYear ("12/31/2001")	Returns 53.

WeekOfYearFiscal()

Category: **Date**

Syntax: **WeekOfYearFiscal (date; startingDay)**

Parameters:

date—Any valid date (1/1/0001–12/31/4000). The parameter should be a string containing a date (for example, "3/17/2004"), an expression with a date result (for example, Date (6, 29, 1969)), or an integer that represents a serialized date value (for example, 718977).

startingDay—A numeric value between 1 (Sunday) and 7 (Saturday).

Data type returned: **Number**

Description:

The WeekOfYearFiscal() function returns an integer from 1 to 53 that represents the week number of the year of the specified date. Weeks are defined as starting on the day of week specified by the startingDay parameter.

The first week of a year is defined as the first week that contains four or more days of that year. For instance, January 1, 2004 was a Thursday. Using a startingDay of 5, the first fiscal week of the year would be considered as 1/1/2004 through 1/7/2004. The second fiscal week would begin on Thursday, 1/8/2004. However, if you used a startingDay of 1 (Sunday), then the first day of the fiscal year would be 1/4/2004. In the previous week (12/28/03–1/3/2004), only three days are in 2004, so that would be considered as the 53rd fiscal week of 2003.

WeekOfYearFiscal() and WeekOfYear() often yield different results. WeekOfYear() is always based on a week defined as Sunday through Saturday, whereas WeekOfYearFiscal() can begin on whatever day you specify. Even when it begins on Sunday, however, you might have discrepancies because of the rule that the first week must have four or more days in the current year. Whereas WeekOfYearFiscal("1/1/2004") returns 53, WeekOfYear("1/1/2004") returns 1.

Examples:

Function	Results
WeekOfYearFiscal ("3/21/2004", 4)	Returns 12.
WeekOfYearFiscal ("1/1/2004", 1)	Returns 53.
WeekOfYearFiscal ("1/1/2004", 2)	Returns 1.

WindowNames

Category: **Design**

Syntax: **WindowNames {(filename)}**

Parameters: Optional filename as text.

Data type returned: **Text**

Description:

Returns a carriage return–delimited list of open window names.

Note that WindowNames returns window names from all open FileMaker files or just the file specified by the optional parameter. Window names do not need to be unique. The order of the list is determined by the stacking order of the windows, with the topmost window (the active window) listed first. Hidden windows are listed, but not any window that appears in the window list surrounded by parentheses. This indicates a file that is open but that doesn't have any windows, hidden or visible. Visible windows are listed first, then minimized windows, then hidden windows.

Examples:

Function	Results
WindowNames	Might return a list of values that looks like this:
	Customers
	Invoices
	myDatabase
	Invoices - 2

WordCount()

Category: **Text**

Syntax: **WordCount (text)**

Parameters:

text—Any expression that resolves to a text string.

Data type returned: **Number**

Description:

Returns a count of the number of words in text.

Spaces, return characters, and most punctuation symbols are considered to be word breaks by FileMaker Pro. Multiple word breaks next to each other (for example, two spaces, a comma, and a space) are considered as a single word break.

Certain punctuation symbols are word breaks when separating alpha characters, but not when separating numeric characters. These include the colon (:), slash (/), period (.), comma (,), and dash (-). For instance, WordCount ("54.6") returns 1, but WordCount ("x.y") returns 2. The reason for this behavior is that those symbols are valid date, time, and number separators.

Examples:

Function	Results
WordCount ("The quick brown fox jumps over the lazy dog.")	Returns 9.
WordCount (FullName)	Returns 4 when FullName contains "John Q. Public, Jr."

Year()

Category: **Date**

Syntax: **Year (date)**

Parameters:

date—Any valid date (1/1/0001–12/31/4000). The parameter should be a string containing a date (for example, "3/17/2004"), an expression with a date result (for example, Date (6, 29, 1969)), or an integer that represents a serialized date value (for example, 718977).

Data type returned: **Number**

Description:

Returns the year portion of the date parameter.

The Year() function is often used in conjunction with the Date() function to assemble new date values. For instance, if you have a field called DateOfBirth that contains someone's birthdate, you can calculate the date of that person's birthday in the current year as follows:

    Date (Month (DateOfBirth), Day (DateOfBirth), Year (Get (CurrentDate)))

Examples:

Function	Results
Year ("1/1/2004")	Returns 2004.
Year (Get(CurrentDate))	Returns the current year.
Year (myBirthdate)	Returns the year portion of the field myBirthdate.

YearName()

Category: **Date**

Syntax: **YearName (date; format)**

Parameters:

date—Any calendar date.

format—A number (0, 1, or 2) that controls the display format.

Data type returned: **Text (Japanese)**

Description:

Returns the Japanese year name for the date specified.

The formats control how the name of Emperor is displayed: 0 = Long, 1 = Abbreviated, 2 = 2-byte Roman. "Seireki" is returned when date falls before Emperial names have been applied.

0 - Meiji (明治) 8, Taisho (大正) 8, Showa (昭和) 8, Heisei (平成) 8 (before 1868.9.8, Seireki (西暦xxxx)

1 - Mei (明) 8, Tai (大) 8, Sho (昭) 8, Hei (平) 8 (before 1868.9.8, Sei (西暦xxxx)

2 - M8, T8, S8, H8 (before 1868.9.8, A.D.xxxx)

Examples:

Function	Results
YearName(DateField;0)	Returns 平成 14 when DateField contains 7/17/2002.

PART 3

Custom Functions

## CHAPTER 7

Custom Functions Primer

Custom functions are without a doubt one of the most powerful features in FileMaker; we cannot advocate their use strongly enough.

Simply described, custom functions become available in the calculation dialog as additional functions for use within expressions. They are snippets of code that, just as FileMaker's pre-established functions do, accept parameters and produce output. One example might be

```
fnCommission ( unitPrice; quantity; discount )
```

This function would then presumably return a dollar amount based on some formula that multiplied unitPrice and quantity, subtracted a discount from the total, and then applied a percentage or some internal factoring to arrive as a sales commission.

Note that as a developer using the function, we need not even know what that formula might be. All we require is, when fed the three parameters in question, that the function return a meaningful and consistent result.

For example, if ever an organization's commission rates needed to change, the developer could edit a single custom function and all the calculations based on that function would immediately (depending on their storage settings) reflect and make use of the change.

Custom functions allow developers to abstract portions of their code, independent from database schema or scripts, where it's possible to reuse a particular piece of logic throughout one's database (or, by recreating the function in other files, across dozens of databases).

Custom functions can also serve as permanent "system variables" that are not subject to session issues as global fields and global variables are. The values within a custom function do not expire at the end of a user's session, they are consistent across all users of a database, and a developer can change them centrally as needed.

→ For more detail and explanation on custom functions, **see** Chapter 14, "Advanced Calculation Techniques," in our companion book, Special Edition Using FileMaker 8.

The Custom Function Interface

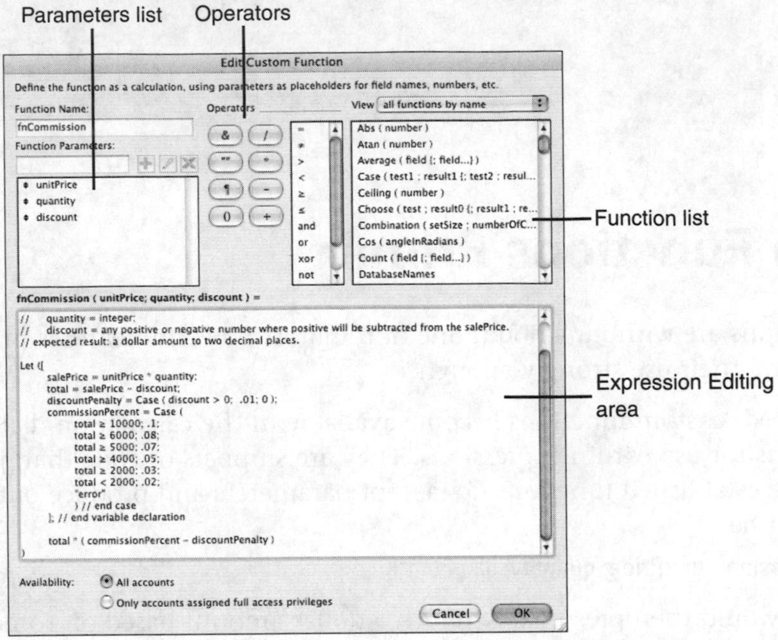

Parameters list   Operators

Function list

Expression Editing area

Figure 7.1
The Custom Function dialog allows developers to define parameters that then serve as input for an expression that is then written to reference those parameters.

Custom Functions: Things to Remember

Custom functions work much like calculations, but it's important to understand the following aspects of custom functions:

- Custom functions follow the same rules for syntax that calculation functions follow.

  → *For a review of calculation syntax,* **see** *Chapter 4 "Working with Calculations Primer."*

- Instead of referencing schema information (data fields), custom functions make use of parameters. Values for these parameters are passed into the custom function from elsewhere in one's database via the calculations dialog.
- Custom functions return a single result.
- Custom functions cannot directly incorporate use of container data.
- Writing custom functions requires FileMaker Pro Advanced; however, once written, anyone with access to a calculation dialog can make use of a custom function.
- Custom functions can make use of all the functions built into FileMaker, including other custom functions and external functions.

- It is possible to make use of schema data fields by using the Evaluate() function. The following example illustrates a scenario where a sales commission is referenced:

```
fnSalesCommission ( unitPrice; quantity; discount )
// function to calculate the sales commission for various transaction totals.
// expected input:
//      unitPrice = dollar amount to two decimal places;
//      quantity = integer;
//      discount = any number (positive = discount)
// expected result: a dollar amount.

Let ([
      salePrice = unitPrice * quantity;
      total = salePrice - discount;
      discountPenalty = Case ( discount > 0;  .01; 0 );
      commissionPercent = Evaluate ( "ProductRate::Commission" ) - discountPenalty
      ]; // end variable declaration
      total * ( commissionPercent - discountPenalty )
)
```

- Just as custom functions can reference other functions, they can reference themselves as well. This allows you to write recursive functions in FileMaker.

  If no exit condition exists or an error in logic occurs, the maximum number of recursions a function can make is 50,000 deep. If you create multiple branches of recursion, the most branches a custom function can perform is 10,000.

  The following is an example of a simple recursive function that reorders a carriage return–delimited list from bottom to top:

```
fnListBackwards ( valueList )
// function to reverse-order a ¶-delimited list
// expected input:
//      valuelist = text values delimited by ¶
// expected result: a valuelist of text values delimited by ¶ in reverse order

Let ([
      numOfValues = PatternCount ( valuelist; "¶");
      firstValue = LeftValues ( valuelist; 1 )
      remainingList = RightValues ( valuelist; numOfValues - 1 );
      resultList = Case ( numOfValues = 1; ""; fnListBackwards ( remainingList ) );
      ]; // end variables
      resultList & firstValue
)
```

- Custom functions can interact with global and local variables. In the case of local variables ($myVar), FileMaker will store values specific to a currently running script. In the case of a global variable ($$myVar), the value in the variable will be updated and maintained throughout the file.

If you wish to create or set variables within a custom function, use the Let() function:

```
Let ([
     myInternalVariable = $$globalVariable + 1;
     $$newVariable = 1 + 1;
     result = $$newVariable + myInternalVariable
     ]; // end variables
     result
)
```

Custom functions are extremely powerful tools for building abstract units of logic that can then be reused throughout a solution. Indeed, once a custom function has been created (and tested!) it's easy enough to recreate them in other files and use them throughout all your solutions. We strongly recommend you create a library of tools to refine and reuse over time. To that end, visit the next chapter for a selection of some of our favorites.

## CHAPTER 8

Useful Custom Functions

This chapter presents a sampling of custom functions that we've found useful, or that we feel serve as good examples of functions we use in our day-to-day practice. They're broken into groups according to their purpose, much as Filemaker's calculation functions are.

Please note that these functions are meant as examples—we've not tested them exhaustively, nor is this collection meant to be comprehensive. We hope you'll find some of them helpful directly, or that reading and analyzing others might provide a springboard for your own ideas.

→ *We use a couple of icons to denote specific types of custom functions:*

 This icon shows that the function participates in a "sub-function" relationship: the function in question either calls or is called by other custom functions.

 This icon shows that the function is recursive: in other words, under certain circumstances, it calls itself.

Number Calculations

fnHypotenuse (leg1Length; leg2Length)

Although FileMaker includes many common mathematical operations and formulas, no list can be exhaustive. This function applies the Pythagorean Theorem ($a^2 + b^2 = c^2$) to generate the length of a hypotenuse (the leg of a right triangle opposite the right angle).

Example:

fnHypotenuse (3; 4) returns **5**.

Code:

```
// returns the length of a hypotenuse based on the Pythagorean
Theorem ( a^2 + b%2 = c%2 )
// input: two numbers
// output: number
Let ([
   a2 = leg1Length * leg1Length;
   b2 = leg2Length * leg2Length;
```

```
    c2 = a2 + b2
    ];
    Sqrt ( c2 )
)
```

fnNthRoot (number; root)

FileMaker provides a built-in function for calculating the square root of a number, but not the nth root.

Example:

fnNthRoot (8; 3) returns **2**.

fnNthRoot (256; 4) returns **4**.

Code:
```
// returns the nth root of number
// input: two numbers
// output: number
Exp ( Ln ( number ) / root )
```

fnPolyAreaFromRadius(numberOfSides; radius)

This function computes the area of a regular polygon, given the number of sides and the radius of the polygon. (A regular polygon is a polygon in which all sides are of equal length.) The radius is the distance from the center of the polygon to any vertex. In other words, the radius of the polygon is the radius of a circle that exactly circumscribes the polygon.

Examples:

A pentagon with a radius of three meters would be evaluated like so: **fnPolyAreaBySide (5 ; 3)** which returns **21.399** (rounded) square meters.

An equilateral triangle with a radius of 4 inches: **fnPolyAreaByRadius (3 ; 4)** returns **20.723** square inches (rounded).

Code:
```
// computes the area of a regular polygon
// input:
//    numberOfSides = the number of the polygon's sides
//    radius = distance from the center of the polygon to a vertex
// output: area of the polygon in aquare units
// requires fnPolyAreaFromSideLength

Let ([
    n = numberOfSides;
```

```
    r = radius;
    sideLength = 2 * r * Sin ( Pi / n );
    result = fnPolyAreaFromSideLength ( n ; sideLength )
    ];
    result
)
```

fnPolyAreaFromSideLength(numberOfSides; sideLength)

This function computes the area of a regular polygon, given the number of sides and the length of each side.

Examples:

A hexagon with sides of length 3: **fnPolyAreaBySide (6 ; 3)** returns **23.382** (rounded) units squared.

An equilateral triangle with sides of length 4: **fnPolyAreaBySide (3 ; 4)** returns **6.928** (rounded) units squared.

Code:

```
// computes the area of a regular polygon
// input:
//    numberOfSides = the number of the polygon's sides
//    sideLength = the length of one side
// output: area of the polygon in units squared

Let ([
    n = numberOfSides;
    l = sideLength;
    result = ( n * l^2) / ( 4 * Tan( Pi / n ) )
    ];
    result
)
```

fnRandomInRange (lowNumber; highNumber)

The Random function in FileMaker returns a value from 0 to 1, but developers almost always need a random number within a range of numbers. For example, if you need a number between 10 and 50, the formula would be

```
Int ( Random * 41 ) + 10
```

This makes code somewhat difficult to read and requires that you think through the formula each time you need it. The **fnRandomInRange()** function hides this logic in an easy-to-use function.

Example:

fnRandomInRange (3; 7) might return **4**.

Code:
```
// returns a random number from low to high range
// input: two numbers
// output: a random number within the range between the two
Int ( Random * ( highNumber - lowNumber + 1 )) + lowNumber
```

---

fnSphericalDistance (lat1; long1; lat2; long2; units)

This function computes the distance between two points on the surface of the Earth, given in terms of decimal latitude and longitude. The coordinates must be decimal—in other words, 45.5, not 45 degrees 30 minutes—and must be given in degrees.

The function can return results in miles or kilometers. Any "units" value beginning with "m" will yield miles; otherwise, the function will return kilometers.

The computation is based on the "haversine formula" and assumes a reasonable degree of mathematical precision in the software, which FileMaker possesses.

See http://en.wikipedia.org/wiki/Haversine_formula for further details.

Example:

The distance between San Francisco and Chicago in miles is **fnSphericalDistance (37.799; 122.461; 41.886; 87.623; "miles")**, which returns **1856.62**.

Code:
```
// computes distance between two points on Earth's surface
// input:
//   lat1, long2, lat2, long2 = lat and long of two points, in DECIMAL DEGREES
//   units = "miles" or "km"
// output: distance between the two points in miles or kilometers

Let([
  D = Case( Trim(Lower(Left(units;1))) = "m"; 3958.75; 6367.45 );
    // diameter of Earth in miles or km
  lat1R =   Radians(lat1);
  lat2R =   Radians(lat2);
  long1R =   Radians(long1);
  long2R =   Radians(long2);
  dlat =   lat2R - lat1R;
  dlong =   long2R - long1R;
  a = (Sin(dlat/2))^2 + Cos(lat1R) * Cos(lat2R) * (Sin(dlong/2))^2;
  c = 2 * Atan(Sqrt(a)/Sqrt(1-a));
```

```
    result = D * c
    ];
    result
)
```

Date Calculations

fnAgeInYears (dateOfBirth)

This function calculates an age in years.

The **GetAsDate()** function is used to ensure that whatever is passed in—a date, an integer, or raw text—gets converted to a date and thus accounts for data type issues.

Example:

fnAgeInYears ("6/6/1967") returns **38**.

Code:
```
// calculates age in years
// input: date
// output: integer
Div (Get ( CurrentDate ) - GetAsDate ( dateofbirth ) ; 365.25)
```

fnDateMonthEnd (calendarDate)

This particular function determines the last day of the month for a given date. Note that in FileMaker, subtracting one from the first day of a month results in the last day of the prior month.

Example:

fnDateMonthEnd ("1/1/2005") will return **1/31/2005**.

Code:
```
// calculates the last day of the month for a given date
// input: date
// output: date
date ( month ( calendarDate ) + 1 ; 1; year ( calendarDate )) - 1
```

fnDateQuarter (calendarDate)

This function returns numerals; if you wanted it to return text along the lines of "1st Quarter", "2nd Quarter", and so on, you'd need a formula that might make use of the **Choose()** function.

You could also use this function to calculate fiscal quarters by adding a number at the end of the custom function's formula for whatever month begins the fiscal year for a given company.

Example:

fnDateQuarter (12/1/2006) returns **4**.

Code:

```
// function returns in which calendar quarter a date falls
// input: date
// output: text

Ceiling ( Month ( calendarDate ) / 3 )

/*


Here's an alternative that returns text:
Choose ( Ceiling ( Month ( calendarDate ) / 3 ) - 1;
   "1st Quarter"; "2nd Quarter"; "3rd Quarter"; "4th Quarter" )
*/
```

fnDateRepetitions (calendarDate; period; numberOfRepetitions)

While we'd never recommend trying to replicate the full functionality of a calendaring program like Outlook in FileMaker, we do often need to create date ranges in list form. This function will generate a delimited list of dates; you can then extract individual dates using the **GetValue()** function.

Note that the function requires specific keyword inputs and returns an error message if it does not recognize the value passed for its period parameter.

Example:

fnDateReptitions ("1/1/2005"; "quarterly"; 6) returns

1/1/2005

4/1/2005

7/1/2005

10/1/2005

1/1/2006

4/1/2006

Code:

```
// assembles a valuelist of repeating dates based on a period keyword
// input:
//    calendarDate = date
//    period = "daily"; "weekly"; "monthly"; "quarterly"; "yearly"
//    numberOfRepetitions = integer
// output: return-delimited list of dates as a text string

Let ([
    startDate =  GetAsDate ( calendarDate );
    m = month (startdate);
    d = day (startdate);
    y = year (startdate);
    nextDate = Case (
       period = "daily" ; startDate + 1 ;
       period = "weekly" ; startDate + 7 ;
       period = "monthly" ; Date ( m + 1 ; d ; y);
       period = "quarterly" ; Date ( m + 3 ; d ; y);
       period = "yearly" ; Date ( m  ; d ; y + 1)
       )

];

Case ( numberofrepetitions > 0 ;
    startdate & "¶" &
    fndaterepetitions (nextdate ; period ; numberofrepetitions - 1);
    "error - period not recognized"
    )
)
```

fnNextDayOfWeek (calendarDate; numDayOfWeek)

This function returns a future next date based on a day of week provided. For example, from a starting date of 11/2/2005, the next Friday is 11/4/2005. We often need this sort of function for reporting based on a "standard" week (week starting Friday, week starting Saturday, and the like).

The second parameter is an integer that corresponds to a day of the week. 1 = Sunday, 2 = Monday, and so on through to 7 = Saturday.

Examples:

fnNextDayOfWeek ("6/28/2006"; 7) returns the Saturday following 6/28/2006 = 7/1/2006.

fnNextDayOfWeek ("4/1/2006"; 2) returns the Monday following April Fools' Day = 4/3/2006.

Code:

```
// returns the date of the next day of week requested
// input:
//   calendarDate = date
//   dayOfWeek = integer, 1 for Sunday ... 7 for Saturday

Let ([
  varDate = GetAsDate ( calendarDate )
  ];
  varDate + Mod ( numDayOfWeek - DayOfWeek ( varDate ); 7 )
)
```

Text and Data Conversions

fnConvertLengthUnits (number; unitFrom; unitTo)

Converting data between various unit types is a common need in database systems. This function serves as an example of converting length units between the various Metric and Imperial forms.

Note that it uses recursion to save dozens of lines of code. In its first pass, it converts its input into meters, and then in its second pass, converts meters to whichever unit the calling calculation has requested. This technique saves the function from having to create a massive matrix of 15 $*$ 15 different options.

Examples:

fnConvertLengthUnits (9; "in"; "m") returns **.2286**.

fnConvertLengthUnits (2.33; "ft"; "in") returns **27.9599999714808**.

fnConvertLengthUnits (5; "km"; "cm") returns **500000**.

Code:

```
// converts common length units
// input:
//   number
//   unitFrom = specific text keyword
//   ( microinch | in | ft | yd | mile | league | league nautical |
//   μm | mm | cm | dm | m | dam | hm | km )
//   unitTo = same as above.
// output: number

Case (
  unitFrom = "microinch"";
    fnConvertLengthUnits ( number * .0000000254; "m"; unitTo );
  unitFrom = "in"";
```

```
   fnConvertLengthUnits ( number * .0254; "m"; unitTo );
unitFrom = "ft"";
   fnConvertLengthUnits ( number * .3048; "m"; unitTo );
unitFrom = "yd"";
   fnConvertLengthUnits ( number * .9144; "m"; unitTo );
unitFrom = "mile"";
   fnConvertLengthUnits ( number * 1609.3; "m"; unitTo );
unitFrom = "league"";
   fnConvertLengthUnits ( number * 4828.0417; "m"; unitTo );
unitFrom = "league nautical"";
   fnConvertLengthUnits ( number * 5556; "m"; unitTo );

unitFrom = "µm"; fnConvertLengthUnits ( number * .000001; "m"; unitTo );
unitFrom = "mm"; fnConvertLengthUnits ( number * .001; "m"; unitTo );
unitFrom = "cm"; fnConvertLengthUnits ( number * .01; "m"; unitTo );
unitFrom = "dm"; fnConvertLengthUnits ( number * .1; "m"; unitTo );
unitFrom = "dam"; fnConvertLengthUnits ( number * 10; "m"; unitTo );
unitFrom = "hm"; fnConvertLengthUnits ( number * 100; "m"; unitTo );
unitFrom = "km"; fnConvertLengthUnits ( number * 1000; "m"; unitTo );

unitFrom = "m" and unitTo = "µm"; number * 1000000;
unitFrom = "m" and unitTo = "mm"; number * 1000;
unitFrom = "m" and unitTo = "cm"; number * 100;
unitFrom = "m" and unitTo = "dm"; number * 10;
unitFrom = "m" and unitTo = "m"; number * 1;
unitFrom = "m" and unitTo = "dam"; number * .1;
unitFrom = "m" and unitTo = "hm"; number * .01;
unitFrom = "m" and unitTo = "km"; number * .001;

unitFrom = "m" and unitTo = "microinch"; number * 39370078.7401575;
unitFrom = "m" and unitTo = "in"; number * 39.3700787;
unitFrom = "m" and unitTo = "ft"; number * 3.2808399;
unitFrom = "m" and unitTo = "yd"; number * 1.0936133;
unitFrom = "m" and unitTo = "mile"; number * 0.0006214;
unitFrom = "m" and unitTo = "league"; number * 0.0002071;
unitFrom = "m" and unitTo = "league nautical"; number * 0.00018;

)
```

fnConvertTemperature (number; inputUnit)

Function converts between Celsius to Fahrenheit.

Notice the fail condition for the **Case()** function. Given the specific values the **inputUnit** parameter requires, it's always best to test for errors.

Examples:

fnConvertTemperature (65; "F") returns **18**.

fnConvertTemperature (40; "C") returns **104**.

Code:

```
// Converts celsius to fahrenheit and vice-versa
// input:
//   temperature = number
//   inputUnit = "C" | "F"
// output: temperature in text with unit notation

Case (
   inputUnit = "F" ; Round ( ( temperature - 32 ) * 5/9 ; 0 );
   inputUnit = "C" ; Round ( ( temperature * 9/5 ) + 32 ; 0 );
   "error - inputUnit not recognized"
)
```

fnConverttoUSAbrvState (text)

There's nothing particularly magical about this function; it converts long state names for the United States into their abbreviated form. It is useful only because once written it never has to be written again.

Note that to save space and avoid belaboring the obvious, we didn't include its partner, **fnUSAStateConverttoLong()**. That function can be found in the electronic files included with this book.

One could argue that this kind of lookup table is a good candidate for solving with a database structure. But it requires more work to reuse a database structure, and this list is closed-ended, meaning it is going to change very slowly, if at all. If there were hundreds of data pairs and they changed frequently, a custom function might not be the ideal choice.

Examples:

fnConverttoUSAbrvState ("California") returns **CA**.

fnConverttoUSAbrvState ("Ican'tspell") returns **Ican'tspell**.

Code:

```
// Converts long US State names to 2-char abbreviations

Case (
   text = "Alabama"; "AL";
   text = "Alaska"; "AK";
   text = "Arizona"; "AZ";
   text = "Arkansas"; "AR";
```

```
    text = "California"; "CA";
    text = "Colorado"; "CO";
...
...
    text = "Wyoming"; "WY";
    text  // default do nothing
)
```

Note: List trimmed to save space. Please refer to the electronic files included with this book for the complete code.

---

fnExplodeText (text)

Exploded text allows developers to create multiline keys within FileMaker and then to use those keys in relationships often established for filtering portal contents.

Examples:

"Zaphod" becomes:

Z

Za

Zap

Zaph

Zapho

Zaphod

→ *To learn more about using multiline keys and how to construct filtered portals, see Chapter 16, "Advanced Portal Techniques," in our companion book,* Special Edition Using FileMaker 8.

Note that exploded text will significantly increase the size of an index for a given field. If you are concerned about performance or file size, consider adding a limiter to this function: an integer that controls how many characters deep the function should extract text.

Code:

```
// returns a delimited list of all the possible left substrings
within a text string
// input: text
// output: delimited text
// note: if a field containing this data is indexed, it can result
in very large storage blocks.
// note: 49999 iterations is the maximum permitted by FileMaker
```

```
Let ([
  textLength = Length ( text )
  ];
  Case ( textLength > 1;
    fnExplodeText ( Left ( text; textLength - 1 ) ) & "¶" & text;
    text
  )
)

/* Alternate function for character limited results:
// requires a second parameter: characterLimit
Let ([
  newText = Left ( text; characterLimit );
  textLength = Length ( newText )
  ];
  Case ( textLength > 1;
    fnExplodeText ( Left ( text; textLength - 1 ); characterLimit )
      & "¶" & newText;
    newText
  )
)
*/
```

fnFormatDollars (number)

The following function uses the **fnInsertRepeatingCharacters()** function to format a number into U.S. currency.

Note the isolation of logic: This function manages how to handle negative numbers and decimals, along with to what degree to round. The **fnInsertRepeatingCharacters()** function only takes care of comma placement. This preserves flexibility and reusability in both functions.

Examples:

fnFormatDollars (111) returns **$111**.

fnFormatDollars (33222111) returns **$33,222,111**.

fnFormatDollars (-4333.222) returns **-$4,333.22**.

Code:

```
// converts number data into data with commas and $ symbol
// input: number
// output: text
// dependencies: fnInsertRepeatingString
```

```
Let ([

    positiveInteger = Abs ( Int ( number ));
    decimal = Abs ( number ) - positiveInteger
    ];

    Case ( number < 0; "-$"; "$" ) &
     fnInsertRepeatingString ( positiveInteger; ","; 3; "right") &
    Case ( decimal ≠ 0; Round ( decimal; 2 ); ".00" )
)
```

fnFormatPhone (text)

Based on how much it consumes the attention of developers, one might assume phone number formatting to be a favorite pastime. This function represents an attempt to put the functionality to bed, once and for all.

This function is most often used in conjunction with the Auto-Enter by Calculation field option. If you turn off the "Do Not Replace Existing Value" checkbox associated with that option, the field in question will automatically reformat itself whenever someone enters new data or edits its contents.

You can extend this function in a variety of ways: You could add recognition of an override character (say, for example, a "+" character) that would leave data entered exactly "as is" if users prefix the input with that override. Another modification could be to change the mask or style attributes of the function to refer to one or more preferences fields on a user record, if your system has a such a thing—allowing users to control phone formats dynamically.

This is where custom functions show their strengths: by abstracting the logic of this functionality into a central location, developers can efficiently modify and expand upon it.

Examples:

fnFormatPhone ("1234567890111"; "usa_standard") returns **(123) 456-7890 x111**.

fnFormatPhone ("1234567890"; "usa_dot") returns **123.456.7890**.

fnFormatPhone ("1122aabb"; "usa_dot") returns **error - too few numerals: 1122aabb** in red colored text.

Code:

```
// reformats phone numbers based on a mask style
// dependencies:
//   fnTextColor() & fnMaskReplace()
// input:
//   text = text string assumed to contain at least 10 numeral digits
//   style = specific keywords to allow for different
```

styles (international) within the same database
// output:
//　text string
// note: error returned in red if < 10 digits
// note: strings assume no more than 20 characters

```
Let ([
    minimumDigits = 10;
    digitsOnly = Filter ( text; "0123456789" );
    digitCount = Length ( digitsOnly );
    errorCheck = Case ( digitCount < minimumDigits;
        fnTextColor ( "error - too few numerals: " & text; "red" );
        0 );
    formatText = Case (
      style = "usa_standard""";
        fnMaskReplace ( "(***) ***-**** x***********"; text; "*" );
      style = "usa_dot""";
        fnMaskReplace ( "***.***.**** x***********"; text; "*" );
      style = "japan_alternate""";
        fnMaskReplace ( "* ** ***-**** x***********"; text; "*" );
      style = "japan_standard""";
        fnMaskReplace ( "** ****-**** x***********"; text; "*" );
        fnMaskReplace ( "*** ***-**** x***********"; text; "*" )
      ); // end case { formatText }
    finalBlackText = fnTextColor ( formatText; "black" )
    ]; // end variables
    Case ( errorCheck ? 0; errorCheck; finalBlackText )
  ) // end let
```

fnInsertRepeatingCharacters (text; insertString; numberOfCharacters; startDirection)

Converting data into currency, or formatting a number with commas, requires some function that can make character insertions at regular intervals. Rather than write a function that only manages a specific currency or situation, this function is more generic. It allows you to specify what character set you wish to insert into some other body of text, the interval at which you need it inserted, and finally from which direction to begin counting. This function will then be used by others when setting up specific cases of, for example, a number formatted with commas or dealing with currency.

Note that FileMaker can display numbers with commas and with currency symbols, but these displays do not manipulate the actual data in question. This function operates at a data level, not a display level. It actually changes your data.

Note also that this function does not make any logical assumptions about what sort of data you've passed it: It will simply iterate through **N** number of characters.

Examples:

fnInsertRepeatingText ("Azeroth"; "*"; 2; "left") returns **Az*er*ot*h**.

fnInsertRepeatingText ("Ironforge"; "*"; 3; "left") returns **Iro*nfo*rge**.

fnInsertRepeatingText ("Darnassus"; "*"; 4; "right") returns **D*arna*ssus**.

fnInsertRepeatingText ("1222333"; ","; 3; "right") returns **1,222,333**.

fnInsertRepeatingText ("1222333.444"; ","; 3; "right") returns **12,223,33.,444**.

Code:

```
// converts a number into currency text complete with commas.

// input: a number
//   text = source string
//   insertString = text to insert at intervals
//   numberOfCharacters = interval
//   startDirection = "right" or "left"
// output: text string

Let ([
   lengthText = Length ( text );
   remainder = Mod ( lengthText; numberOfCharacters )
   ];

   Case (
     startDirection = "left" or remainder = 0;

         Case ( lengthText > numberOfCharacters;
           Left ( text; numberOfCharacters ) & insertString & fnInsertRepeatingString ( Right ( text;
lengthText - numberOfCharacters ); insertString; numberOfCharacters; startDirection );
           Right ( text; lengthText )
         );

     startDirection = "right";

         Case ( lengthText > numberOfCharacters;
           Left ( text; remainder ) & insertString & fnInsertRepeatingString ( Right ( text; lengthText -
remainder ); insertString; numberOfCharacters; "left" );
           Right ( text; lengthText )
         );

     "error - startDirection not recognized"
   )
)
```

fnIsWhitespace (text)

This function looks for "filler" characters in a block of text and returns a 1 or 0 if that block of text is only comprised of filler characters. In this example we've used a tab, return carriage, and space for filler characters, but you could add whatever other characters to the **Filter()** function as you wish.

Examples:

fnIsWhitespace ("hello   ") returns **0**.

fnIsWhitespace ("   ") returns **1**.

Code:

```
// determines if a block of text contains nothing other than spaces,
 tabs and pilcrow characters
// input: text
// output: 1 or 0
// dependencies: uses fnTab

Let ([
   filtered = Filter ( text; " ¶" & fnTab )
   ];
   If ( filtered = text; 1; 0 )
)
```

fnMaskReplace (maskText; replacementText; wildcardCharacter)

This function is often called by other functions like **fnFormatPhone()** and **fnFormatSSN()**. It allows developers to create a character mask of some sort and insert characters into that mask.

Note that this function is recursive and passes two altered bits of data back into itself in each pass:

pass one—("***hello***"; "123456"; "*")

pass two—("1**hello***"; "23456"; "*")

pass one—("12*hello***"; "3456"; "*")

pass one—("123hello***"; "456"; "*")

...and so on.

Examples:

Where a field, myPhone, contains 1234567890, **fnMaskReplace ("(xxx) xxx-xxxx"; myPhone; "x")** would return **(123) 456-7890**.

Another example might derive from a product name: AB12301Widget (pack of 10). In that case, **fnMaskReplace ("**-**-*** *******************************"; productSKU; "*"**) might return **AB-12-301 Widget (pack of 10)**.

Code:

```
// replaces wildcard characters within a text string with the characters
in a replacement string
// input:
//    maskText = text string with some number of wildcard characters
//    replacementText = text string meant to replace wildcard
characters one for one
//    wildcardCharacter = the specific char used as a wildcard
// output:
//    text string
// note: if there are too many wildcard characters, they will be stripped out
// note: if there are too many replacement characters, the excess will be ignored
// note: recursive stack can manage up to 49,999 characters.

Let ([
    charReplaceCount = Length ( replacementText );
    charWildcardCount = Length ( Filter ( maskText; wildcardCharacter ));
    firstWildcardPosition = Position ( maskText; wildcardCharacter; 1; 1 );
    firstReplaceChar = Left ( replacementText; 1 );
    remainingReplaceChars =
      Right ( replacementText; Length ( replacementText ) - 1 );
    oneCharReplaced =
      Replace ( maskText; firstWildcardPosition; 1; firstReplaceChar );
    returnText = Case ( charReplaceCount > 1 and charWildcardCount > 1 ;
      fnMaskReplace ( oneCharReplaced; remainingReplaceChars;
        wildcardCharacter );
      oneCharReplaced
      ); // end case
    cleanText = Substitute ( returnText; wildcardCharacter; "" )
    ]; // end variables
    cleanText
)


/* Example:
fnMaskReplace ( "***hello***"; "123456"; "*")
returns: "123hello456"

fnMaskReplace ( "***hello********"; "123"; "*")
returns: "123hello"

fnMaskReplace ( "***hello*"; "1234567"; "*")
returns: "123hello4"
*/
```

fnPadCharacters (text; padLength; padCharacter; side)

We often face situations where a given text string, or more often a number, needs to be a fixed number of characters in length. This function will allow a developer to pad a string of data with some sort of pad character.

It makes use of the **fnRepeatText** function. This simplifies the function significantly and is a good example of using a subfunction effectively.

Notice also that the side parameter requires specific values.

Example:

fnPadCharacters ("999"; 8; "0"; "start") returns **00000999**.

Code:

```
// function adds characters to either the right or left of a text string.
// dependencies: fnRepeatText()
// input:
//    text
//    padLength = total characters the string should reach
//    padCharacter = character to use in padding
//    side = "left"|"right"
// output: text
// note: in the case that text > padLength, function will truncate

Let ([
    textLength = Length ( text );
    padString = fnRepeatText ( padCharacter; padLength - textLength )
    ];
    Case (
        textLength > padLength; Left ( text; padLength );
        side = "left"; padString & text;
        side = "right"; text & padString;
        "error: side not recognized."
    )
)
```

fnRecordMetaDisplay (Create_Name; Create_Timestamp; Modify_Name; Modify_Timestamp)

We recommend that for every table in a database, developers create what we've referred to as housekeeping fields: meta information stored about when a record was last created and/or modified and by whom. These four fields, fed by auto-enter field options, track this information for all records.

Once this information is available for a given table, we find it useful to place it somewhere innocuous on a layout. Often users benefit from knowing when something has been edited, and so on. To that end, this function creates a display that is easy for users to read.

Example:

fnRecordMetaDisplay ("slove"; "11/10/2005 6:45:22 AM"; "slane"; "11/10/2005 4:15:02 PM") will return **Created November 10, 2005 (6:45am) by slove; modified November 10, 2005 (4:15pm) by slane**.

Code:

```
// creates the record housekeeping field display
// input: creator name, created timestamp, modifier name, modified timestamp
// output: display text

// create portion
"Created " &

MonthName ( Create_Timestamp ) & " " &
Day ( Create_Timestamp ) & ", " &
Year ( Create_Timestamp ) & " (" &

// format time
Case (
   Hour ( Create_Timestamp ) > 12 ;
      ( Hour ( Create_Timestamp ) - 12 ) & ":" &
      ( Right ( "0" & Minute ( Create_Timestamp ) ; 2 ) ) & "pm" ;
       Hour ( Create_Timestamp ) & ":" &
      (Right ( "0" & Minute ( Create_Timestamp ) ; 2 )) & "am"
   ) // end case
& ") by " & Create_Name &
//modify portion
Case (
   not IsEmpty ( Modify_Timestamp );
      "; modified " & MonthName ( Modify_Timestamp ) & " " &
      Day ( Modify_Timestamp ) & ", " & Year ( Modify_Timestamp )
      & " (" &
      // format time
      Case (
         Hour ( Modify_Timestamp ) > 12 ;
            ( Hour ( Modify_Timestamp ) - 12 ) & ":" &
         ( Right ( "0" & Minute ( Modify_Timestamp ) ; 2 ) ) & "pm" ;
            Hour ( Modify_Timestamp ) & ":" & ( Right ( "0" &
         Minute ( Modify_Timestamp ) ; 2 ) ) & "am"
         ) // end case
      & ") by " & Modify_Name ; ""
   ) // end case
& "."
```

fnRepeatText (text; numberOfRepetitions)

This is a great function to tinker with if you're new to recursive functions. Notice that it simply stacks its own results on top of each other, decrementing the **numberOfRepetitions** parameter until it reaches a **numberOfRepetitions** of 1.

Examples:

fnRepeatText ("|"; 5) returns **|||||**.

fnRepeatText ("hello"; 3) returns **hellohellohello**.

Code:
```
// duplicates a text string n times
// input:
//   text
//   integer
// output: text

text & Case ( numberOfRepetitions > 1;
   fnRepeatText ( text; numberOfRepetitions - 1 ); "" )
```

fnTrimCharacters (text; trimCharacter; side)

FileMaker's **Trim()** function strips leading and trailing spaces from a block of text, but there are times when we need it to recognize other characters as well. This function allows a developer to define what padded character he or she needs stripped away, and whether or not to strip from the start, end, or both sides of a text string.

Note that this function is not case sensitive. To make it so, use the **Exact()** function when comparing **leftChar** or **rightChar** to **trimCharacter**.

Examples:

fnTrimCharacters ("xxxMarzenxxxxxx"; "x"; "both") returns **Marzen**.

fnTrimCharacters ("00001234"; "0"; "start") returns **1234**.

Code:
```
// removes leading and trailing character multiples
// input:
//   text
//   trimCharacter = character to be trimmed away
//   side: "left"|"right"|"both"
// output: text
// note: this function is NOT case sensitive
```

```
Let ([
    leftChar = Left ( text; 1 );
    rightChar = Right ( text; 1 );
    remainderLength = Length ( text ) - 1
    ];
    Case (
        ( side = "left" or side = "both" ) and leftChar = trimCharacter;
            fnTrimCharacters ( Right ( text; remainderLength );
                trimCharacter; side );
        ( side = "right" or side = "both" ) and rightChar = trimCharacter;
            fnTrimCharacters( Left ( text; remainderLength );
                trimCharacter; side );
        text
    )
)
```

fnTrimReturns (text)

This function is a common tool for doing data cleanup, especially when involving email. Text that has been hard-wrapped can sometimes end up formatted poorly. This function removes single line breaks but preseves double line breaks.

Note that this function does not insert or remove spaces. If a line ends with a carriage return but then does not include a space before the next word, the two words on either side of the line break will be concatenated.

Example:

Consider a field, **originalText**, with the following:

Hello. This is my

raw text. Notice that

it wraps poorly.

It also has two

paragraphs that

should be on two

lines.

fnTrimReturns (originalText) will return

Hello. This is my raw text. Notice that it wraps poorly.

It also has two paragraphs that should be on two lines.

Code:

```
// removes single line breaks but preserves double line breaks
// input: text
// output: text with ¶ line breaks removed

Substitute ( text ; ["¶¶"; "*#*#*#*#"];["¶";""];["*#*#*#*#";"¶¶"] )
```

Email Tools

fnEmailIsValid (text)

This function checks for a few common problems with email addresses and returns a 1 or 0 depending on whether or not a submitted block of text passes its tests.

Note that the function makes use of the **fnEmailTLDs** (Top Level Domains) function.

The function isn't meant to be exhaustive: It is still entirely possible to enter an invalid email address; we encourage you to add further conditions to the case function that handles testing.

Also note that the function as written returns a 1 or 0. Using the **fnErrorHandler** (discussed later in this chapter), you could derive more information from the function when an error condition existed. We wrote this as a **Case()** test rather than one long concatenated series of tests joined by **and** operators to explicitly test for each error and allow for the possibility of adding more error handling logic.

Examples:

fnEmailIsValid (**"kathiel@soliantconsulting.com"**) returns **1**.

fnEmailIsValid (**"kathielsoliantconsulting.com"**) returns **0**.

fnEmailIsValid (**"kathiel@soliant@consultingcom"**) returns **0**.

Code:

```
// tests for valid email address formatting and domain
// dependencies: fnEmailTLDs
// input: text (presumably an email address)
// output: 1 or 0

Let ([
   lengthText = Length ( text );
   positionAt = Position ( text; "@"; 1; 1 );
   positionLastDot = Position ( text; "."; lengthText; -1);
```

```
validCharacters =
   ".0123456789abcdefghijklmnopqrstuvwxyzABCDEFGHIJKLMNOPQRSTUVWXYZ";
userBlock = Left ( text; positionAt - 1 );
domainBlock = Right ( text; lengthText - PositionAt );
topLevelDomain = Right ( text; lengthText - positionLastDot );

errorCondition = Case (
   lengthText < 1; 0;              // text parameter is empty
   positionAt = 0; 0;             // no @ symbol
   positionLastDot = 0; 0;        // no dot
   Filter ( userBlock; validCharacters )  serBlock; 0;   // invalid chars in user block
   Filter ( domainBlock; validCharacters )  domainBlock; 0;
      // invalid chars in domain block
   PatternCount ( fnEmailTLDs; topLevelDomain & "¶" ) < 1; 0;
      // top level domain not recognized
   1                   // if no error condition is met, return 1.
   )
];
errorCondition
)
```

fnEmailTLDs ()

This function serves as a system constant (we discuss that term later in the chapter) and holds simply a value list of top-level domains. It is easy to keep the list up-to-date in this form and prevents developers from having to enter this rather unwieldy block of information in more than this one place (or within a larger, more complex function).

Notice that the **fnEmailIsValid** function requires that a return carriage follow each domain.

Code:

```
// function contains a text block of return-delimited list of top level domains.
"ac
ad
ae
aero

// other values removed to save space. Please refer to the electronic
files included with this book for a complete listing.

zm
zw
"
```

List Handlers

In FileMaker a list is defined as a return-delimited group of values. Most often developers will encounter them in value lists, but they are also often used as simple one-dimensional arrays of data. FileMaker has a set of functions for manipulating list data (**GetValues()**, **LeftValues()**, **RightValues()**, **MiddleValues()**) and the following represent some useful additions.

fnBubbleSort (list)

This function sorts a list of values using the "bubble sort" algorithm. It isn't an efficient sort (we've included an implementation of the "merge sort" algorithm, **fnMergeSort()**, which is generally much quicker), but it's a good example of some useful programming techniques.

This function is actually just a wrapper around a "helper" or "auxiliary" function that does the real work. The internal function is a recursive function that keeps track of some extra information, which it passes to itself as a parameter. In some cases FileMaker will need to pass information to itself in recursive functions that otherwise might confuse developers and need not be exposed to them. For that reason this master function was created so that the actual sort function, **fnBubbleSort_iterations()**, can be called with the proper parameters.

Example:

Consider a field, list, with the following values:

fish

goat

bird

dog

fnBubbleSort (list) will result in

bird

dog

fish

goat

Code:

```
// calls fnBubbleSort_iterations
// necessary to avoid exposing the seed parameter

fnBubbleSort_iterations ( list; ValueCount ( list ) )
```

fnBubbleSort_iterations (list; values)

This function is called by the master **fnBubbleSort()** function. It is this function that performs the sort and results in a final sorted list. The purpose of the master function is to avoid having to pass the iterations parameter directly.

Consider a value list that contains

fish

goat

bird

dog

fnBubbleSort_iterations (list; 4) will result in

bird

dog

fish

goat

Code:
```
// sorts list items
// input:
//    list = group of values to be shifted one iteration
//    values = starting number of values ( seed )
// output: modified list

Case ( values > 1; fnBubbleSort_values ( fnBubbleSort_shift ( list; 1 ); values - 1); list )
```

fnBubbleSort_shift (list; shift)

This function performs the inner comparison for a classic bubble sort. It should be called by **fnBubbleSort_iterations()**.

Consider a list that contains:

fish

goat

bird

dog

fnBubbleSort_shift (list; 1) will result in

fish

bird

dog

goat

Code:

```
// performs an inner shift for fnBubbleSort
// input:
//   list = group of values to be shifted one iteration
//   shift = list item (integer) to be shifted
// output: modified list

Let ([
   numOfValues = ValueCount ( list )
   ];
   Case ( shift < numOfValues;
      fnBubbleSort_shift ( Case ( MiddleValues ( list; shift; 1 ) >
         MiddleValues ( list; shift + 1; 1 );
            LeftValues ( list; shift - 1) &
            MiddleValues ( list; shift + 1 ; 1 ) &
            MiddleValues ( list; shift; 1 ) &
            RightValues ( list; numOfValues - ( shift + 1 ));
         list
         );
      shift + 1 );
   list )
)
```

fnMergeSort(list)

This function sorts a return-delimited list of values using the "merge sort" technique. The function is recursive. It operates by first splitting the list in two, and then sorting each sublist and merging the results back together into a single sorted list. It relies on the helper function **fnMergeLists()**, which is responsible for merging two sorted lists into one.

Code:

```
// sort a return-delimited list using the "mergesort" algorithm
// input: a return-delimited list of values
// output: the same list, sorted
// requires the fnMergeLists function
// http://en.wikipedia.org/wiki/Mergesort
```

```
Case(
    ValueCount(list)  = 1; // if only one value left in the list ...
    LeftValues ( list ; 1 );   // then just return that value
    Let (                    // else ...

    [

        length = ValueCount(list) ;
        // split the list in two ...
        leftLength = Floor(length/2);
        rightLength = length - leftLength;
        leftList = LeftValues(list; leftLength);
        rightList = RightValues(list; rightLength);
        sortedLeft = fnMergeSort(leftList);        // sort each sub-list ...
        sortedRight = fnMergeSort(rightList);
        mergedList = fnMergeLists( sortedLeft; sortedright )
        // and merge the two sorted lists

    ];

    mergedList )
)
```

fnMergeSortedValues (list1; list2)

This function merges two sorted, return-delimited lists of values into a single sorted, return-delimited list. It's probably useful in its own right but is provided here as a necessary "helper" function for the **fnMergeSort** function.

Code:

```
// merges two sorted lists into a single sorted list
// input: two sorted, return-delimited lists
// output: a single sorted return-delimited list

Case (
    ValueCount ( list1 ) = 0 and ValueCount ( list2 ) = 0 ; "";
    ValueCount ( list1 ) = 0; list2;
    ValueCount ( list2 ) = 0; list1;

    Let ([
        first = LeftValues ( list1; 1 );
        second = LeftValues ( list2; 1 );
        lesser = Case ( first = second; first; second );
        firstRemaining = Case ( first = lesser; RightValues ( list1; ValueCount ( list1 ) - 1 ); list1 );
        secondRemaining = Case ( second = lesser; RightValues ( list2; ValueCount ( list2 ) - 1 ); list2 );
        result = lesser & fnMergeSortedValues ( firstRemaining; secondRemaining )
```

```
        ];
        result
    ) // end let
)
```

fnValuesBackwards (list)

[fn] List arrays can store simple data in cases where a database table would be overkill or inappropriate, they can be manipulated by a range of functions in FileMaker, and they're fairly easy to decipher. This function takes a list and flips the order of its values.

If the concept of recursion is a little opaque to you, this is a nice, "clean" recursion that would serve well for study purposes.

Example:

fnValuesBackwards ("red¶green¶blue¶yellow¶") returns

yellow

blue

green

red

Code:
```
    // function to reverse-order a ¶-delimited list
    // expected input:
    //    list = text values delimited by ¶
    // expected result:  a list of text values delimited by ¶ in reverse order

    Let ([
        numOfValues = ValueCount ( list );
        newList = RightValues ( list; numOfValues - 1 );
        resultList = Case ( numOfValues = 1; ""; fnValuesBackwards ( newList ) );
        firstValue = LeftValues ( list; 1 )
        ]; // end variables

        resultList & firstValue
    )
```

fnValuesCrossProduct (list1; list2)

[fn][fn] This function creates a cross product between two functions. It will output concatenated combinations of each value. For example, take one list **(hello¶goodbye¶)** and **(1¶2¶3¶)**. The result of the function will be **(hello1¶hello2¶hello3¶goodbye1¶ goodbye2¶goodbye3¶)**.

This function is a master function that calls a subfunction. The subfunction is a recursive function that requires an initialized counter, and rather than have developers guess on what that initial value needs to be (or better yet, refer to documentation), we created this parent function that takes care of that for them.

Consider this the "public" version of the function. The other is a "private" subfunction and is meant to stay in the background to be called only by this controlling function.

Code:

```
// this function exists only to call fnValuesCrossProduct_sub.
// input: two lists
// output: output from fnValuesCrossProduct_sub

fnValuesCrossProduct_sub ( list1; list2; 1 )
```

fnValuesCrossProduct_sub (list1; list2; counter)

The cross product of two sets is a set containing all the two-element sets that can be created by taking one element of each set. For example, if **Set1** contained **{A, B}** and **Set2** contained **{P, Q, R, S}**, then their cross product would consist of **{AP, AQ, AR, AS, BP, BQ, BR, BS}**. The number of elements in the cross product is the product of the number of elements in each of the two sets.

The **fnValuesCrossProduct_sub()** function "loops," incrementing a counter as it goes, until the counter is no longer less than the number of elements expected in the result set. With **Set1** and **Set2** from the previously mentioned scenario, the function would iterate 8 times. If it were on iteration 5, the function will work with the second item from the first list (because Ceiling (5/4) = 2) is "B," and the first item from the second list (because Mod (4; 4) + 1 = 1) is "P." "BP" becomes the fifth element of the result set.

Notice also that this function, besides recursively calling itself, also calls the **fnTrimCharacters()** function available also in this section.

Examples:

fnValuesCrossProduct_sub ("A¶B¶C"; "1¶2¶3¶4"; 1) returns
A1¶A2¶A3¶A4¶B1¶B2¶B3¶B4¶C1¶C2¶C3¶C4¶.

fnValuesCrossProduct_sub ("One¶Two¶Red¶Blue"; " fish") returns

One fish

Two fish

Red fish

Blue fish

Code:

```
// function combines two lists into concatenated cross-product lines
// dependencies: fnTrimCharacters
// input:
//    list1 = return delimited list of values
//    list2 = return delimited list of values
//    counter = should initially be set to 1; function then
calls itself and increments
// output: return delimited list of values

Let ([
    array1count = ValueCount ( list1 );
    array2count = ValueCount ( list2 );
    limit = array1count * array2count;

    pos1 = Ceiling (counter / array2count) ;
    pos2 = Mod (counter - 1; array2count ) + 1;

    item1 = fnTrimCharacters ( MiddleValues ( list1; pos1; 1 ); "¶" ; "end" );
    item2 = fnTrimCharacters ( MiddleValues ( list2; pos2; 1 ); "¶" ; "end" )
    ];

    Case ( counter = limit ;
    item1 & item2 & "¶" & fnValuesCrossProduct_sub (list1; list2; counter + 1 ) )
)
```

fnValuesRemove (list; valuesToRemove)

fn This function extends what developers can do with lists. It allows a developer to remove one or more values from a given list.

Example:

Consider a field, **myList**, holding the following list:

Black

Green

Yellow

Pink

Purple

Black

White

fnValuesRemove (myList; "Pink¶Black¶Yellow") will return

Green

Purple

White

Code:

```
// removes from the first return-delimited list parameter a
second return-delimited set of values
// input:
//   list: return-delimited list of text
//   valuesToRemove: return-delimited set of text values to
be removed from list
// output:
//   list of return-delimited text items
// note: This function is NOT case sensitive.

Let ([

   listcount = ValueCount ( list );
   compare = PatternCount ( valuesToRemove ; GetValue ( list; listcount ));
      // compares the last list value against values
   newList = LeftValues ( list; listcount - 1 );

   includeValue =
      Case ( compare = 0;
         GetValue ( list; listcount ) & "¶";
         ""
      );   // end case {includeValue}

   resultList =
      Case ( vCount > 1;
         fnValuesRemove ( newList; valuesToRemove )
            & includeValue;
         includeValue
      )   // end case {resultList}

   ];   // end variable declarations

   resultList

) // end let
```

Developer Tools

The following functions are those that tend not to do anything for users directly but represent some of our most used behind-the-scenes tools.

fnErrorHandler (errorCode)

When adding error checking to functions—and we strongly recommend that you do—you will need to consider a few issues. First, is it necessary in every function to test for valid or non-Empty parameters? FileMaker's standard functions don't, so in some cases we will opt to follow that approach and assume that the developer in question will test his or her code and be able to detect any error conditions in such cases.

However, for functions that veer off the beaten path—for example, by requiring specific keywords or employing complex logic—we will often add some reasonable level of error checking.

One then needs to decide how to manage the error results themselves. You might, if you wish, return an error message as the result of your function. In all the examples we've provided in this book, that is the path we've chosen. It is the most straightforward to write into the code of your functions and it reduces the complexity of the material we're presenting; however, some software developers may argue that error results belong in a different memory space than function results. We tend to agree.

In solutions that use more than a handful of custom functions (which, naturally, comprise almost all the solutions we produce), we add this **fnErrorHandler()** function in order to keep the error clutter in other functions to a minimum and to centralize the implementation of what a given system should do once it discovers an error.

Notice that this function contains no error checking logic (other than its own)—in other words, it will not test other functions. Instead it is meant to manage an error once another function encounters one.

Note also that this function sets a global variable to the error code passed into it, including zero (no error). This allows developers to check for errors after they've run routines that reference functions that in turn make use of this error handler.

For an example of how one might use this error handler from another function, please refer to **fnErrorHandlerExample()**.

Code:
```
// function does two separate things: returns a text explanation
of what error corresponds to which error code and secondly sets a
global variable with that code.
// input: integer that corresponds to an error code within FileMaker
or a custom error code established by another custom function.
// output: text description and also sets $$lastErrorCode
```

```
Let([
  $$lastErrorCode = errorCode
  ];

  Case (
    errorCode = 0; "no error";

    // custom error codes
    errorCode = 90100; "fnMyCustomFunction encountered an error";
    errorCode = 90101;
        "input does not match the expected parameter keyword for fnErrorHandlerExample";
    // create as many error codes as you need here.
    // The two above are simply examples.

    // filemaker error codes
    errorCode = -1; "Unknown error";
    errorCode = 1; "User canceled action";
    errorCode = 2; "Memory error";
    errorCode = 401; "No records match Find request";
    // others omitted to save space...
    // refer to the electronic files for a complete listing

    // not recognized default value for case()
    "error not recognized by fnErrorHandler"
  )
)
```

fnErrorHandlerExample (text)

This function serves as an example of using a central error handler instead of passing error messages directly from your functions. Instead of intermingling error messages with all your functions (and being faced with maintaining consistency across possibly dozens of functions), this approach places the logic for presenting errors in a single place.

Notice in the case of an error, this function returns an error message derived from **fnErrorHandler** and also sets a **$$errorHandler** global variable to 90101.

Note also that you need not return the results of **fnErrorHandler()** if you wish. This function does so, but the purpose of setting **$$errorHandler** is so that a developer can opt to not commingle error messages with function results if he or she wishes.

Please refer to **fnErrorHandler()** for more detail on error handling with custom functions.

Code:
```
// example of how to work with the fnErrorHandler() function.
// this function will always return an error, unless exactly
 the value "hello" is passed into it.

Case (
  Exact ( "hello"; text ) = 1;
    "All's well that ends well.";
    fnErrorHandler ( 90101 )
)

/* Here's another approach that does not return any error message
as a result of this function:

Let ([
  test = Exact ( "hello"; text );

  result = Case ( test = 1;
    "All's well that ends well.";
    ""
  );

  error = Case ( test = 0;
    fnErrorHandler ( 90101 );
    ""
  )

  result
)
*/
```

fnModifierKeys ()

This function returns a return-delimited list of text descriptors for the modifier keys held down whenever it is evaluated. This is useful for those of us who can't remember which numbers correspond to which key combinations. Developers can use this function in scripts or elsewhere by testing for the presence of "shift" in **fnModifierKeys** instead of having always to use **Get(ActiveModifierKeys) = 1**.

Examples:

In the case where a user has the Shift key pressed, **fnModifierKeys** returns **Shift**.

In the case where a user has both the Shift and Ctrl keys pressed, **fnModifierKeys** returns

Shift

Control

Code:
```
// identifies active modifier keys by text
// input: none
// output:
//    text value list <cr> corresponding to active mod keys

Let ([
    keys = Get (ActiveModifierKeys)
    ];
    Case ( Mod ( keys; 2 ) = 1; "Shift¶"; "" ) &
    Case ( Int ( Mod ( keys; 4 ) / 2 ) = 1; "Caps Lock¶"; "" ) &
    Case ( Int ( Mod ( keys; 8 ) / 4 ) = 1; "Control¶"; "" ) &
    Choose ( 2 * ( Int ( Mod ( keys; 16 ) / 8 )) +
        ( Abs (Get (SystemPlatform) ) - 1 ); "";""; "Option¶"; "Alt¶" ) &
    Case ( keys >= 16; "Command¶"; "" )
)
```

System Constants

A system constant is a value that developers place in a custom function that then becomes permanent. It doesn't "evaporate" at the end of a session (as global field values and global variables do), nor does its value vary from user to user. Developers can count on them being persistent and can easily edit them as needed.

fnSolutionVersion ()

We find it valuable to track version numbers of our systems and at times need to use logical (script) routines that reference or make use of those version numbers. Rather than adding a field to the data schema of a solution, use a custom function.

We recommend also creating a similar **fnSolutionNamespace()** function.

Examples:

In all cases, **fnSolutionVersion** returns **1.003**. Developers will want to update the hardcoded value as appropriate.

Code:
```
// returns version of database solution and name
// input: none
// output: version number or text

1.003

/* version history
...etc...
```

fnTab ()

FileMaker uses a pilcrow character ("¶") to represent carriage returns but there's no analog for tab characters. This custom function is simple but vital if you need to do formatting with tab characters. The alternative is seeing blank space within your formulas and being left to wonder what is in the space: Space characters? Tabs? Odd characters that can't display?

Note that Ctrl-tab inserts a tab character on Windows and Opt-tab on the Mac OS. The two are cross-platform compatible.

Code:

```
// tab character

"   "
```

fnTextColor (text; color)

With this function you can save yourself a bit of hassle by allowing the use of familiar terms for colors, rather than being forced to look up RGB numbers, but the real value here is in making use of the central nature of custom functions: If ever you need to change a color in your system you have one single place to do so. Tweak one of the RGB numbers in the function and your database will reflect that change throughout (however, some calculation results may be indexed). This custom function also ensures consistency. By virtue of having only one instance of a color, you never get confused on which red you're using in a given system.

Examples:

fnTextColor ("hello world"; "blue") returns **"hello world"** as blue text.

fnTextColor ("hello world"; "purple") returns **"color not recognized"**.

Code:

```
// returns colored text
// input:
//    text = text string
//    color = keywords defined below
// output:
//    text (w/color)

Let ([
  rgbValue = Case (
    color = "red"; RGB ( 255; 0; 0 );
    color = "green"; RGB ( 0; 255; 0 );
    color = "blue"; RGB ( 0; 0; 255 );
    color = "soliant"; RGB ( 231; 188; 19 );
```

```
        color = "ltgray"; RGB ( 170; 170; 170 );
        color = "dkgray"; RGB ( 120; 120; 120 );
        "color not recognized"
        )
    ]; // end variables

    Case ( rgbValue = "color not recognized";
      rgbValue;
      TextColor ( text; rgbValue )
      )
  )
```

Toolkit for Complex Data Structures

This last group of custom functions requires some explanation, and perhaps some evangelism as well. These functions are complex; our intent was to demonstrate, with a set of real examples from our own work, how it's possible to use custom functions and the power under the hood of this often under-appreciated feature.

Data API Within FileMaker

This **fnXML***** set of functions all exist to help manipulate a block of XML data, stored in a text field or variable. Together they represent a kind of small API (Application Programming Interface), and support some specific programming methodologies. In that way, this suite of functions is less general purpose than the earlier ones in this chapter.

The strength of these functions lie in their capability for manipulating complex data structures. You can add, delete, update, and extract data from a tree of nested data.

An API is a term borrowed (perhaps with a degree of liberty) from other programming environments like C# and Java. It refers to a set of instructions that are largely independent and allow programmers to accomplish some set of functions without having to know how the API itself was constructed. Both Apple and Microsoft provide a large range of APIs with their operating systems, there's an Apache API for extending its capabilities as a web server, and there's even a FileMaker API for writing plug-ins. The idea here is that an API provides a framework and hooks into some set of functionality that you as a developer intend to leverage and reuse, without necessarily needing to understand all the details of how it works internally.

Data Tree

A data tree is a powerful programming concept also borrowed from other environments. Abstractly, it is essentially a data structure that can hold multiple values. These values can be referenced by their positions within the tree (or perhaps array, if you accept a loose interpretation of the term) and related in similar ways to a set of FileMaker tables. In crude terms, this data structure can be thought of as a database within a database.

Data trees and arrays are useful for a variety of things, including storing a simple list of values, efficiently moving multiple values as a single block from place to place in a system, and for dealing with variable length data structures where it would be impractical or impossible to define fields or variables enough to hold them.

Perhaps an example would help; this is a simple one-dimensional array, and represents a simple one-level hierarchy of tiered data:

[red | green | blue | yellow]

In this scenario, most FileMaker developers would choose—rightly—to work with either a repeating variable or a return-delimited list and the **GetValues()** function. (We've included list handlers in this book as well.)

But there are times when a one-dimensional array isn't enough for your needs. Consider a scenario where you need to store colors and, say, shirt sizes and quantities. Your pipe-delimited array will need some new delimiter characters:

[red; large; 20 | green; large; 10 | blue; medium; 15 ... and so on]

As you can see, even a two-dimensional array can start to feel complex.

This is where XML can come in. How does one describe an N-dimensional data structure in a way that can be interpreted by both humans and across multiple platforms?

Note that the issue is twofold: XML holds information about its data, as well as providing a structure in which to store it.

Using XML As a Data Structure

Entire books have been written on XML and a complete discussion of it extends beyond the scope of this book; however, suffice it to say we chose XML for three reasons. First, it's self-documenting: Instead of identifying something by its position within an array, XML uses tags to clearly label data. **<quantity>10</quantity>** is a far more clear description than the preceding example using pipe and semicolon delimiters. Second, XML is an industry standard and has emerged as a leading means to transfer and express data between platforms and applications. Third, XML allows for "deep" data structures. Note that the following example represents a four-dimensional tree:

```
<inventory>
  <shirt>
    <shirtName>SiliconValleyT</shirtName>
    <shirtID>122</shirtID>
    <color>red</color>
    <sizes>
      <size>
        <sizeName>Extra Large</sizeName>
        <quantity>100</quantity>
      </size>
```

```
        <size>
           <sizeName>Large</sizeName>
           <quantity>200</quantity>
        </size>
      </sizes>
   </shirt>
</inventory>
<orders>
   <order>
      <orderNumber>1010</orderNumber>
      <shirtID>122</shirtID>
   </order>
   <order>
      <orderNumber>1011</orderNumber>
      <shirtID>142</shirtID>
   </order>
</orders>
```

Imagine trying to represent that data structure in a flat, delimited text list, and the mind boggles. Note too that even if you're unfamiliar with XML or with the data that this block is meant to express, you can infer a great deal by simply reading it.

Path-Based Selections

Having now decided on an API to manage a data tree, and having selected XML as a data format, this now brings us to FileMaker. We've worked with various sorts of arrays and trees for many years, but working with return-delimited lists or temporarily shoving things into makeshift data tables has never completely fit the need.

FileMaker 7 introduced script parameters and FileMaker 8 introduced script variables. Neither of them support anything other than one value (which can admittedly be a repeating value); if you want to pass more than one piece of data by either of these two features of FileMaker, you'll need to use a block of text and delimit it somehow. Then the second part of the process will be writing a parsing routine that extracts your multiple values from this data block.

This problem is a good candidate for one or more custom functions. Rather than writing a series of parsing routines throughout a database, we suggest building a set of array handlers that can abstract and centralize the entire set of functionality you need.

The approach we've developed here is admittedly complex. We wanted to get more than just a simple container of one or two dimensional data: We wanted to be able to name the values in our data and to hierarchically organize them to N layers deep. We have created a path syntax (inspired by XPath, for those of you familiar with it— http://en.wikipedia.org/wiki/Xpath) that can pull a variety of structured data from an XML source.

The six main functions do the following:

fnXMLselect—Extracts a block of data from an XML source.

fnXMLupdate—Replaces a block of data within an XML source with a new value.

fnXMLinsert—Inserts a new block of XML into an XML source.

fnXMLdelete—Deletes a block of XML from within an XML source.

fnXMLclean—Strips an XML block of extraneous characters and formatting.

fnXMLformat—Adds tab characters and return carriages to a block of XML for easy display/reading.

fnXMLselect() is the most powerful of the four functions and is used by three of the others. It takes two parameters, **xmlSource** and **path**, and returns a block of XML extracted from the value passed into **xmlSource**.

The path syntax is specific and is the key to understanding how to use all four functions. An example (referring to the preceding shirt inventory example) might be:

inventory/shirt/color

This path would return the value for the first color element of the first shirt of the first inventory it finds. Think of this path exactly like a tree or a file directory structure. In the preceding case, this path would return

red

The path inventory/shirt/sizes would return from the XML on pages 240-241:

```
<size>
    <sizeName>Extra Large</sizeName>
    <quantity>100</quantity>
</size>
<size>
    <sizeName>Large</sizeName>
    <quantity>200</quantity>
</size>
```

The path syntax here is specific and drives the logic of what data you manipulate within the block of XML. Valid syntax includes

```
node/subnode
```

(a tree of any depth comprised of simple path nodes)

```
node/subnode/
```

(function will strip trailing slashes)

```
node[2]/subnode
```

(specify an integer to take the Nth occurrence of a node; 1-based)

```
node[attribute="foo"]/subnode
```

You can specify finding an occurrence of a node where a child attribute node contains specified data.

Note: This syntax does *not* support XML attributes.

Supported: **<tag><name>foo</name></tag>**

Not supported: **<tag name ="foo">value</tag>**

This syntax also does *not* support the empty/close shortcut style: **<tag/>**.

This syntax supports the use of carriage returns, tabs, and spaces within XML values. It will not strip them out, and shouldn't produce bugs when encountered; however, using **fnXMLinsert()** and **fnXMLdelete()** in combination with XML formatted with such characters may end up looking fairly ugly. It should retain functionality, however.

Imagine a scenario where you want to create an audit trail. (Using auto-enter by calculation functions, you can trigger a second field to update itself when a given field is updated by the user.)

Rather than having to create double the amount of fields in your database, you'll want to store the audit information likely in one field. Likewise, you need to be able to store multiple values for a single field: who edited a field, what the old value was, what the new value is, and so on.

These functions would be perfectly suited for just such a scenario: use **fnXMLinsert** to store information into the audit trail field, and then use **fnXMLselect** to extract it for a rollback if necessary. The data structure might look something like this:

```
<audittrail>
  <record>
    <id>12</id>
    <field>
      <name>CustomerID</name>
      <value>1001</value>
    </field>
    <field>
      <name>Address</name>
      <oldValue>123 Main Street</oldValue>
      <newValue>100 Center Drive</newValue>
      <editedBy>Molly Tully</editedBy>
      <editedTime>11/12/2005 11:10:14</editedTime>
    </field>
  </record>
</audittrail>
```

You can then extract the old value with a query like so:

```
fnXMLselect
  ( auditTrail; audittrail/record[id=12]/field[name=Address]/oldValue )
```

This function will return: 123 Main Street.

The Functions

The following, finally, are the functions that comprise the suite of tools within this API.

fnXMLclean (xmlSource)

 This function calls the **fnXMLclean_sub()** function and is used to supply default initial values to that function.

Example:

Assume a field exists, xmlSource, that includes XML data formatted with return characters and tabs or spaces:

```
<state>
  <name>California</name>
  <city>
    <name>San Mateo</name>
    <district>downtown</district>
  </city>
</state>
```

fnXMLclean (xmlSource) returns
```
<state><name>California</name><city><name>San
Mateo</name><district>downtown</district></city></state>
```

Note that all text formatting (font, size, style, and color) will be removed as well.

Code:
```
// strips extraneous characters between end tags and start tags
// input: text with proper <tag>value</tag> XML embedded
// output: cleaned XML
// dependencies: this is the calling function to fnXMLclean_sub that
needs a second parameter initialized

TextFormatRemove ( fnXMLclean_sub ( xmlSource; 1 ))
```

fnXMLclean_sub (xmlSource; afterStartTag)

This function takes a block of XML with some amount of extraneous characters sitting between end tags and start tags in the form of spaces, tabs, and carriage returns, and returns a block of XML stripped of all such detritus.

Note that it uses a subfunction to determine white space characters. If ever one's logic needed to be extended, this would easily allow for such.

Example:

Assume a field exists, **xmlSource**, that includes XML data formatted with return characters and tabs or spaces:

```
<state>
  <name>California</name>
  <city>
    <name>San Mateo</name>
    <district>downtown</district>
  </city>
</state>
```

fnXMLclean (xmlSource) returns

```
<state><name>California</name><city><name>San
Mateo</name><district>downtown</district></city></state>
```

Code:

```
// iterates through a block of XML and removes extraneous characters
// between close and open tags.
// input: text block of XML
//   afterStartTag = initial value should be 1. 1 if the prior tag
was a start tag (or at the start of the processing of the data), 0 if
the prior tag was an end tag.
// output: text - clean XML
// dependencies: uses fnIsWhitespace

Let ([
      nexttag = Position(xmlSource;"<";1;1);
      ending = Position(xmlSource;">";1+nexttag;1);
      isStartTag = If(Middle(xmlSource;nexttag+1;1)="/"; 0; 1)
   ];
  If(nexttag = 0 or ending=0;  // Error case, or when source is empty
    If( fnIsWhitespace ( xmlSource ); "" ; xmlSource);
    Let ([
      rest = fnXMLclean_sub
    (Right(xmlSource;Length(xmlSource)-ending);isStartTag);
      start = Left(xmlSource;nexttag-1);
      tag = Middle(xmlSource;nexttag; ending-nexttag+1)
    ];
      Case (isStartTag=0 and afterStartTag = 1; start;
            fnIsWhitespace(start); "";
            start) // end Case
    & tag & rest
   ) // end Let
  ) // end If
) // end Let
```

fnXMLdelete (xmlSource; path)

This function, along with its sibling functions **fnXMLselect**, **fnXMLupdate()**, **fnXMLinsert()**, exists to help manipulate an XML data structure.

This particular function will remove a block of data as controlled by the path parameter.

Examples:

fnXMLdelete (xmlSource; "first_name")

The result would be that within **xmlSource**, the **<first_name>** block would be removed, including the enclosing tags.

Consider the following source XML:

```
source XML =
  <root>
    <branch>
      <num>100</num>
      <text>foo</text>
    </branch>
  </root>
```

for **fnXMLdelete (xmlSource; "root/branch")** the result would be

```
<root>
</root>
```

Code:

```
// Function removes a block of XML as controlled by a path.
// dependencies
//   makes use of two global vars => $$xmlSourceValueStart and
$$xmlSourceValueEnd. Needs to initialize them to ZERO.
//   uses fnXMLselect to find the proper position within xmlSource
// input:
//   xmlSource = a block of xml. Syntax is strict. Only use <tag></tag> pairs.
//   path = text string defining the hierarchical tree that should be used to
point to a specific branch or node within the block of XML.
//     see fnXMLselect comments for syntax options and examples.
// output:
//   xmlSource with data removed

Let ([
  $$xmlSourceValueStart = 0;
  $$xmlSourceValueEnd = 0;
```

```
        vValueLength = 0;
        vSourceLength = Length ( xmlSource );

        vBlock = fnXMLselect ( xmlSource ; path );

        vValuePosition =Position(xmlSource;"<"; $$xmlSourceValueStart;-1)-1;
        vBlockLength = $$xmlSourceValueEnd +
          ($$xmlSourceValueStart-vValuePosition)*2+1;
                end_position = vValuePosition + vBlockLength + 1;
                position_of_following_CR = Position(xmlSource;"¶";end_position;1);
                size_of_trailing_string = position_of_following_CR- end_position;
                trailing_string =
          Middle(xmlSource;end_position;size_of_trailing_string+1);
                vBlockLength =
If(Trim(trailing_string)="¶";vBlockLength+size_of_trailing_string+1;vBlockLength)

        ]; // end variable declaration

        Left ( xmlSource; vValuePosition ) &
          Middle ( xmlSource; vValuePosition + vBlockLength + 1;
              vSourceLength + vValueLength)
        ) // end let
```

fnXMLformat (xmlSource)

This function calls the **fnXMLformat_sub()** function and is used to populate default initial values.

Example:

Assume a field exists, **xmlSource**, that holds
```
<state><name>California</name><city><name>San
Mateo</name><district>downtown</district></city></state>
```

fnXMLformat_sub (xmlSource) returns
```
<state>
  <name>California</name>
  <city>
    <name>San Mateo</name>
    <district>downtown</district>
  </city>
</state>
```

Code:
```
Replace ( fnXMLformat_sub ( xmlSource; 1 ; "" );1;1;"")
```

fnXMLformat_sub (xmlSource; afterStartTag; indent)

This function is used to format a block of XML into an easy-to-read form. It inserts tab and carriage return characters, and colors the XML tags.

Notice that it uses subfunctions for the color choice, tab character, and for determining if there is already some whitespace (spaces, tabs, and return characters) in the block of XML.

Further, this function uses two parameters for keeping track of its recursions. This is a subfunction that should never be called by anything other than its enclosing **fnXMLformat()** function.

Example:

Assume a field exists, **xmlSource**, that holds

```
<state><name>California</name><city><name>San
Mateo</name><district>downtown</district></city></state>
```

fnXMLformat_sub (xmlSource; 1; "") returns

```
<state>
  <name>California</name>
  <city>
    <name>San Mateo</name>
    <district>downtown</district>
  </city>
</state>
```

Code:

```
// formats xmlSource with tab and return characters
// input:
//   xmlSource = text block of raw, unformatted xml
//   afterStartTag = initial value should be 1. 1 if the prior
tag was a start tag (or at the start of the processing of the data),
 0 if the prior tag was an end tag.
//   indent = initial value should be set to ""; used for recursion
to store iterative data
// output: formatted xmlSource
// dependencies: uses fnTab, fnIsWhitespace, fnTextColor

Let ([
      nexttag = Position(xmlSource;"<";1;1);
      ending = Position(xmlSource;">";1+nexttag;1);
      isStartTag = If(Middle(xmlSource;nexttag+1;1)="/"; 0; 1);
      indentStep = fnTab
   ];
```

```
If(nexttag = 0 or ending=0;  // Error case, or when source is empty
  If(fnIsWhitespace(xmlSource); "" ; xmlSource);
  Let ([
    newIndent = If(isStartTag; indent & indentStep; Left(indent;Length(indent)-Length(indentStep)));
    rest = fnXMLformat_sub
     (Right(xmlSource;Length(xmlSource)-ending);isStartTag;newIndent);
    start = Left(xmlSource;nexttag-1);
    tag = Middle(xmlSource;nexttag+1; ending-nexttag-1)
  ] ;
    Case (isStartTag=0 and afterStartTag = 1; start;
          fnIsWhitespace(start); ¶ & If (isStartTag; indent; newIndent);
          start)  // end Case
   & "<" & fnTextColor(tag;"blue") & ">" & rest
  ) // end Let
 ) // end If
) // end Let
```

fnXMLinsert (xmlSource; path; value)

This particular function will create a block of data as controlled by the path and value parameters.

Examples:

fnXMLinsert (xmlSource; "first_name"; "Alexander")

The result would be that within xmlSource, a new **<first_name>** block would be created and given a value of **"Alexander"**.

Consider the following source XML:

```
source XML =
    <root>
      <branch>
        <num>100</num>
        <text>foo</text>
      </branch>
    </root>
```

for **fnXMLinsert (xmlSource; "root/branch;
"<data>999</data><date>11/20/2005</date>)** the result would be

```
    <root>
      <branch>
        <num>500</num><text>foo</text><data>999</data><date>11/20/2005</date>
      </branch>
    </root>
```

Code:

```
// Function creates a block of XML with value as controlled by a path.
// dependencies
//   makes use of two global vars =>
//   $$xmlSourceValueStart and $$xmlSourceValueEnd. Needs to initialize them to ZERO.
//   uses fnXMLselect to find the proper position within xmlSource
// input:
//   xmlSource = a block of xml. Syntax is somewhat strict.
//   Only use <tag></tag> pairs.
//   path = text string defining the hierarchical tree
//   that should be used to point to a specific branch
//   or node within the block of XML.
//     see fnXMLselect comments for syntax options and examples.
//   value = a block of text or xml
// output:
//   xmlSource with new data

Let ([
   $$xmlSourceValueStart = 0;
   $$xmlSourceValueEnd = 0;

   vValueLength = Length ( value );
   vSourceLength = Length ( xmlSource );

   vBlock = fnXMLselect ( xmlSource ; path );

   vValuePosition = $$xmlSourceValueStart;
   vBlockLength = $$xmlSourceValueEnd

   ]; // end variable declaration

   Left ( xmlSource; vValuePosition ) &
      value & Middle ( xmlSource; vValuePosition + vBlockLength + 1;
      vSourceLength + vValueLength) & "¶position:"& vvalueposition

) // end let
```

fnXMLselect (xmlSource; path)

fnXMLselect() serves as both a subfunction for three of the other XML-parsing functions and as the means by which developers can extract data from an XML block.

Its primary mission is to take a path parameter (discussed in detail in the preceding pages) and return a block of XML extracted from a larger XML data source.

It also makes use of two global variables to keep track of where within the source XML a given block starts and ends.

Examples:

fnXMLselect (xmlSource; "last_name")

which might return Smith.

Another call might look like this:

fnXMLselect (xmlSource; "new_record_request/invoice/fkey_customer")

and might return C_10012 as a customer ID.

Another approach can make use of filtering, using a square bracket construction similar to an XPath predicate:

fnXMLselect (xmlSource; "new_record_request/invoice[date="11/11/2005"]/fkey_ customer")

This might return a different customer ID.

Consider the following source XML:

```
source XML =
    <root>
        <branch>
            <num>100</num>
            <text>foo</text>
        </branch>
        <branch>
            <num>200</num>
            <text>xyz</text>
        </branch>
    </root>
```

for **path root/branch**:

```
result =
    <num>100</num>
        <text>foo</text>
```

for **path root/branch/num**:

```
result =
    100
```

for **path root/branch[2]**:

result =
   <num>200</num>
      <text>xyz</text>

for **path root/branch[num="200"]**:

result =
   <num>200</num>
      <text>xyz</text>

for **path root/branch[num="200"]/text**:

result =
   xyz

Code:
```
// Function returns a block of XML as controlled by a path.
// It recursively iterates through a block of XML until it reaches
the end of the path parameter and returns a "child" block of XML.
// dependencies: makes use of two global vars =>
//   $$xmlSourceValueStart and $$xmlSourceValueEnd.
//   Expects them to start at ZERO
// input:
//   xmlSource = a block of xml. Syntax is somewhat strict. Only
use <tag></tag> pairs.
//   path = text string defining the hierarchical tree that should
be used to point to a specific branch or node within the block of XML.
//      see below for syntax options and examples.
// output:
//   text = a block of text as extracted from xmlSource

Let ([
     // Path Values
   vPathLength = Length ( path );
   vPath = Case ( Right ( path; 1) = """"/";
     Left ( path; vPathLength - 1); path );
        // strips trailing slash if necessary
   vPathNodeCount = PatternCount ( vPath; "/") + 1;
      // counts the nodes in the path provided
   vPathSlashPosition = Position ( vPath; "/"; 1; 1);
   vPathNew = Middle ( vPath; vPathSlashPosition + 1;
     vPathLength - vPathSlashPosition );
        // crops the first root of the path out...
```

```
      // this will be passed recursively back into the function
vPathFirstNode = Case ( vPathNodeCount > 1 ;
   Left ( vPath; vPathSlashPosition - 1 ); vPath );
      // the inverse of vPathNew, takes the first node and drops the rest


   // Isolate Expression Info
vPathLBracketPosition = Position ( vPathFirstNode; "["; 1; 1 );
vPathRBracketPosition = Position ( vPathFirstNode; "]"; 1; 1 );
vPathExpression = Middle ( vPath; vPathLBracketPosition + 1;
   vPathRBracketPosition - vPathLBracketPosition - 1 );


   // Isolate First Tag within Path
vPathRTagPosition = Case ( vPathLBracketPosition > 1;
   vPathLBracketPosition - 1; Length ( vPathFirstNode ) );
vPathTag = Left ( vPath; vPathRTagPosition );


   // Expression Checks
   // test to see if bracketValue is an INTEGER
   // or if it is a NAME-VALUE pair, by checking for an "=" char.
   // in the case that it's a name-value pair, extract the
   // search tag in question.
vExpressionValue = Case ( PatternCount ( vPathExpression; "=" ) > 0;
   Let ([
      vExpressionTagEnd = Position ( vPathExpression; "="; 1; 1) - 1;
      vExpressionTag = Trim ( Left ( vPathExpression; vExpressionTagEnd ) );
      vExpressionLPosition = Position ( vPathExpression; "="; 1; 1) + 2;
      vExpressionValueLength = Length ( vPathExpression ) - vExpressionLPosition;
      vExpressionValue = Trim ( Middle ( vPathExpression; vExpressionLPosition;
         vExpressionValueLength ));
      vExpressionResult = "<" & vExpressionTag & ">" & vExpressionValue &
         "</" & vExpressionTag & ">"
      ]; // end variable declaration
      vExpressionResult
   ); // end let
   // else if there is no "=" within vPathExpression
   // return "IsInteger" as a control check for blockOccurence
   "IsInteger"
); // end case { vExpressionValue }


   // vParentCount will determine which parent node contains
   // the search string in question. should end up with an integer
   // to be used as an occurrence variable.
vExpressionTagPosition = Position ( xmlSource; vExpressionValue; 1; 1);
vCropSource = Left ( xmlSource; vExpressionTagPosition );
vParentCount = PatternCount ( vCropSource; "<" & vPathTag & ">" );
```

```
// Set Occurrence
// The following is used in the position functions below
// for extracting blocks. This controls which of a given block
// is taken, the first, second, third, etc.
// If vPathExpression is an integer, use that for blockOccurrence.
// If there's something in searchTagString, use the vParentCount as
// blockOccurrence. Otherwise use 1.
vBlockOccurrence = Case (
  vExpressionValue ? "IsInteger"; vParentCount;
  vPathExpression > 1; vPathExpression;
  1    // default to 1
);   // end case { vBlockOccurrence }


  // Extract XML between vPath tags
vBlockStartChar = Position ( xmlSource; "<" & vPathTag & ">"; 1;
  vBlockOccurrence) + Length ( "<" & vPathTag & ">" );
vBlockEndChar = Position ( xmlSource; "</" & vPathTag & ">"; vBlockStartChar ; 1);
vBlockLength = vBlockEndChar - vBlockStartChar ;
vBlockRaw = Middle ( xmlSource ; vBlockStartChar ; vBlockLength );


  // Trim excess ¶ and space chars by excluding all but the block itself
vBlockPositionStart = Position ( vBlockRaw; "<"; 1; 1);
vBlockCountClose = PatternCount ( vBlockRaw; ">" );
vBlockPositionEnd = Case ( vPathNodeCount = 1;
  Length ( vBlockRaw ); Position ( vBlockRaw; ">"; 1; vBlockCountClose) );
vBlockTrimmed = Middle ( vBlockRaw; vBlockPositionStart;
  vBlockPositionEnd - vBlockPositionStart + 1 );


  // update global pointer to track beginning position
  // of block and value within xmlSource
  // ( allows for update, delete, insert )

$$xmlSourceValueStart = $$xmlSourceValueStart + vBlockStartChar - 1;
$$xmlSourceValueEnd = vBlockLength;


  // Error Checking
vErrorHasCloseTag = vBlockEndChar;
vErrorHasTag = PatternCount ( xmlSource; "<" & vPathTag & ">");
vErrorHasNameValueMatch = Case ( vExpressionValue = "IsInteger"";
  "Ignore"; Case ( PatternCount ( xmlSource; vExpressionValue ) > 0;
    "Ignore"; "No Match") );
vErrorOutOfBounds = Case ( vExpressionValue ? "IsInteger"";
  "Ignore"; Case ( PatternCount ( xmlSource; "<" & vPathTag & """>")
  < vBlockOccurrence; "Out Of Bounds"; "Ignore") );


  //Result
```

```
    //--> if you need to debug, just comment out the case below
    // and place one of your variables next to result.
  vResult =

    Case (
            IsEmpty ( xmlSource ) and IsEmpty ( path );
          "Error: Missing Parameters ( xmlSource; path )";
        IsEmpty ( xmlSource ); "Error: Missing Parameter ( xmlSource )";
        IsEmpty ( path ); "Error: Missing Parameter ( path )";
        vErrorHasTag = 0; "Error: Invalid Tag (" & vPathTag & ")";
        vErrorHasCloseTag = 0; "Error: No Close Tag (" & vPathTag & ")";
        vErrorHasNameValueMatch ? "Ignore"; "Error: Invalid Name/Value "("
          & vExpressionValue & ")";
        vErrorOutOfBounds = "Out Of Bounds"";
          "Error: Invalid Index (" & vPathTag & "[" & vBlockOccurrence & "])";
          // now return valid xml block in the case that
          // no error is returned; recursive if additional nodes exist
        vPathNodeCount > 1; fnXMLselect ( vBlockRaw; vPathNew );
        vBlockTrimmed    // default to value
    )  // end case {result}

  ];  // end variable declaration

  vResult

) // end let
```

fnXMLupdate (xmlSource; path; value)

This particular function will replace a block of data within the source XML with the contents of the "value" parameter.

Examples:

fnXMLupdate (xmlSource; "last_name"; "Smith")

The result would be that within xmlSource, the first **<last_name>** block encountered would be given a value of "Smith".

Consider the following source XML:

```
source XML =
    <root>
      <branch>
        <num>100</num>
        <text>foo</text>
      </branch>
```

```
    <branch>
      <num>200</num>
      <text>xyz</text>
    </branch>
  </root>
```

for **fnXMLupdate (xmlSource; "root/branch/num"; 500)** the result would be

```
<root>
  <branch>
    <num>500</num>
    <text>foo</text>
  </branch>
  <branch>
    <num>200</num>
    <text>xyz</text>
  </branch>
</root>
```

Code:

```
// Function replaces a block of XML with value as controlled by a path.
// dependencies
//    makes use of two global vars =>
//    $$xmlSourceValueStart and $$xmlSourceValueEnd.
//    Needs to initialize them to ZERO.
//    uses fnXMLselect to find the proper position within xmlSource
// input:
//    xmlSource = a block of xml. Syntax is somewhat strict.
//    Only use <tag></tag> pairs.
//    path = text string defining the hierarchical tree
//    that should be used to point to a specific branch or
//    node within the block of XML.
//       see  fnXMLselect comments for syntax options and examples.
//    value = a block of text or xml
// output:
//    xmlSource with new data

Let ([
  $$xmlSourceValueStart = 0;
  $$xmlSourceValueEnd = 0;

  vValueLength = Length ( value );
  vSourceLength = Length ( xmlSource );

  vBlock = fnXMLselect ( xmlSource ; path );
```

```
      vValuePosition = $$xmlSourceValueStart;
      vBlockLength = $$xmlSourceValueEnd

   ];  // end variable declaration

   Left ( xmlSource; vValuePosition ) & value &
      Middle ( xmlSource; vValuePosition + vBlockLength + 1;
      vSourceLength + vValueLength) & "¶position:" & vvalueposition
) // end let
```

PART 4

Script Steps

## CHAPTER 9

Scripting Primer

About FileMaker Scripting

Scripts are the lifeblood of an interactive FileMaker solution. In this section we try to distill FileMaker scripting down to its essentials.

The ScriptMaker Interface

All script editing is done within the FileMaker ScriptMaker, shown in Figures 9.1 and 9.2. ScriptMaker lives in the Scripts menu and is accessible from the keyboard via ⌘-Shift-S or Ctrl-Shift-S.

The interface depicted is the one available in FileMaker Pro Advanced (FMPA). FMPA has some scripting features not available in the regular FileMaker Pro client, such as the capability to copy and paste scripts and script steps, and to disable script steps. These differences are called out in the diagrams.

There are a large number of time-saving shortcuts available in ScriptMaker. We list these in the section of this book devoted to shortcuts.

> → *For more information on shortcuts available within ScriptMaker, please **see** "Scripting" in Chapter 12, "FileMaker Keyboard Shortcuts."*

Where Scripts Live

Scripts are attached to an individual file (no matter how many tables the file has). Though one script may call a script in another file, a given script may only act directly on data and records that are contained or referenced in the same file as the script.

Scripts may also be moved between files in several ways. From within ScriptMaker, it's possible to import scripts from another file. Simply click the Import button in ScriptMaker, navigate to the file containing the scripts you want to import, and then click a checkbox for each script you want to bring over, and import. FileMaker will move the scripts and do its best to resolve any references they contain (references to files, scripts, or value lists, for example), though you should still check over the scripts and fix any references that might not have translated correctly.

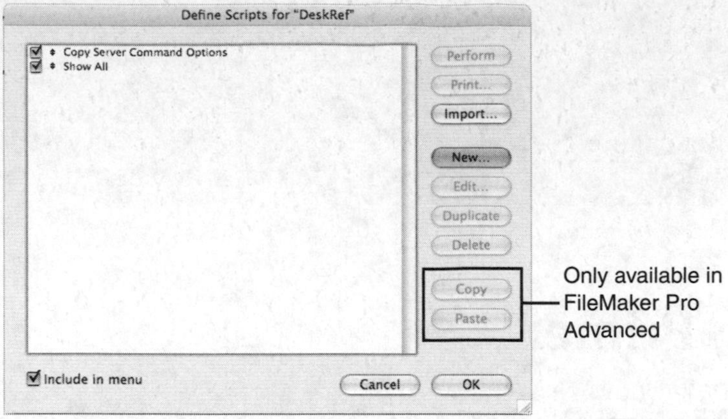

Figure 9.1
The main ScriptMaker dialog shows a list of scripts for a given file. Use this dialog to manage your list of scripts.

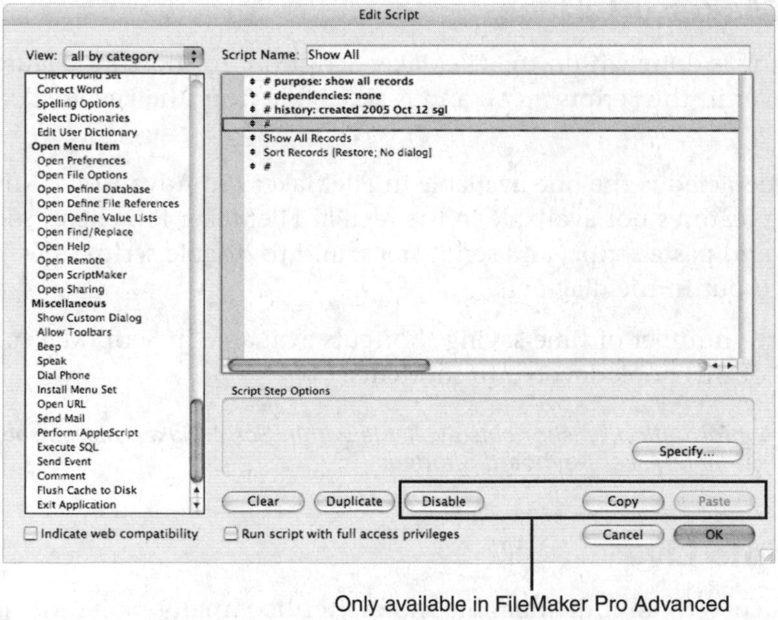

Figure 9.2
The ScriptMaker script editing dialog allows you to edit a single script.

Using FileMaker Advanced, it's also possible to copy and paste scripts, either singly or in blocks, both between files and within the same file (where the effect is the same as duplicating the scripts). Copying scripts between files is identical to the older import mechanism, but might feel more natural or convenient to some.

Script Privileges

Access to scripts is controlled via FileMaker's Accounts and Privileges setting. A given privilege set may be allowed to edit and execute scripts, to execute only, or may not be permitted to use scripts at all. These settings can be customized on a per-privilege-set, per-script basis.

When a script is executed, it will run with the privileges of the current user. For example, if a script tries to delete a record, and the user running that script does not have sufficient privileges to delete that record, the script step will fail.

This hurdle can be overcome by checking the Run Script with Full Access Privileges checkbox within ScriptMaker, for a specific script. When this option is selected, the script will run as though the current user has the [Full Access] privilege set. Note that if you use a function such as Get(PrivilegeSetName) while such a script is running, the function will return [Full Access]. It will *not* return the name of the privilege set normally associated with the current user's account.

Organizing Scripts

Unlike other parts of the FileMaker development environment, ScriptMaker has relatively few tools for organizing scripts. In particular, it's not possible to sort scripts in any way. Rather than relying on a built-in feature of ScriptMaker, you'll need to devise a scheme for keeping your scripts organized manually. Here are a few common methods for organizing scripts:

- Keep all scripts in alphabetical order.
- Break scripts into "functional groups" (navigation, record creation, and so forth) and separate these groups using "header" scripts (dummy scripts with a descriptive name but containing no script steps) that serve only to label a group of scripts within ScriptMaker.
- Use dummy scripts with a single hyphen (-) for the name. If displayed in the Scripts menu, such scripts will create a separator line within the menu.

Debugging Scripts

FileMaker Pro Advanced contains some powerful script debugging tools: the Script Debugger and the Data Viewer. The Script Debugger enables you to step through running scripts line by line, with fine-grained control over execution, while the Data Viewer enables you to watch the values of selected fields and expressions, and will often be used along with the Script Debugger to watch the values of data and expressions as a given script executes. Figure 9.3 shows the Script Debugger interface.

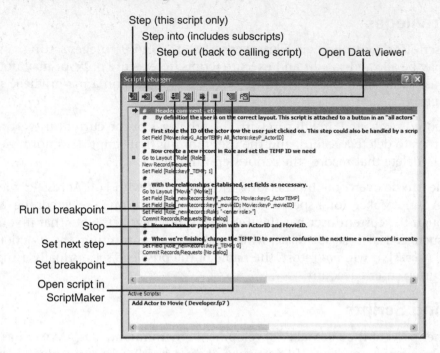

Step (this script only)
Step into (includes subscripts)
Step out (back to calling script)   Open Data Viewer

Run to breakpoint
Stop
Set next step
Set breakpoint
Open script in
ScriptMaker

Figure 9.3
The Script Debugger enables you to step through a script with fine-grained control over execution.

A full explanation of these tools is beyond the scope of this reference, though we do list the essential Script Debugger shortcuts in the chapter of this book that pertains to short-cuts.

➔ *For further exploration of script debugging,* **see** *Chapter 17, "Debugging and Troubleshooting," in our companion book,* Special Edition Using FileMaker 8.

FileMaker Pro Advanced includes one other useful addition for script troubleshooting: the Disable Script Step feature. If you select one or more script steps and click the Disable but-ton in ScriptMaker, those steps will be disabled and will not execute. This allows you to quickly "comment out" sections of a script as part of a troubleshooting effort.

Scripting for the Web

Scripts can be invoked from a web-published FileMaker database, both via Instant Web Publishing (IWP) and via Custom Web Publishing (CWP). But not all script steps can be run from the Web. ScriptMaker's "Show Web Compatibility" checkbox provides a visual indication of which steps will and will not work on the Web. (In general, any script step that requires user interaction, such as a confirmation dialog, or a script step that opens some element of the FileMaker interface such as the Define Database dialog, will not be web-compatible.)

If a script executed from the Web contains one or more non-web-compatible script steps, the non-compatible script steps will either be skipped, or else the script will stop in its entirety. Which of these occurs depends on whether Allow User Abort is set to On or Off in the script. If Allow User Abort is set to Off, unsupported script steps will be skipped. If Allow User Abort is set to On, an unsupported script step will cause the script to stop completely.

## CHAPTER 10

Script Step Reference

About the Script Step Reference

The script step reference is a detailed guide to all the FileMaker Pro script steps. It is similar in layout to FileMaker's online help system, but adds more detailed examples and commentary where possible. The listing for each script step also indicates its platform compatibility, any menu equivalent, and whether the script step is web compatible. A number of web-compatible steps are marked with an asterisk. This indicates that although the step as a whole is web compatible, one or more specific options of the step are not.

NEW **A note on menu equivalents:** With the introduction of custom menu sets in FileMaker Pro 8 Advanced, it's possible to customize the look and behavior of FileMaker's menus almost completely. Accordingly, the menu equivalents listed here all assume that the standard FileMaker menu set is active.

→ *For further discussion of custom menus, **see** Special Edition Using FileMaker 8, Chapter 13, "Advanced Interface Techniques."*

Add Account

Compatibility: 🍎 🪟 🌐

Menu Equivalent: None

Syntax: **Add Account [Account Name: <account name>; Password: <password>; Privilege Set: "<privilege set>"; Expire password]**

Options:

Account Name is the account name. Literal text can be entered or Specify can be clicked to create a new account name from a calculation.

Password is the new password. Literal text can be entered or Specify can be clicked to create a new password from a calculation.

Privilege Set allows you to assign a pre-existing privilege set for the user or to create a new one. (Full Access cannot be assigned via this script step. Accounts with Full Access must be created manually.)

User Must Change Password on Next Login: When selected, this option forces users to change their password the next time they log in to the database.

Examples:

Add Account [Account Name: "User_Account"; Password: "User_Password"; Privilege Set: "[Data Entry Only]"; Expire password]

Description:

This script step adds an account name, password, and privilege set to a database's security configuration. Account and password text may be defined in a calculation or typed into the script step itself. The account name must be unique, and full access to the file is required to execute this step.

Comments:

It might be desirable to allow access to this functionality via a script if certain users or user groups have limited access to the FileMaker menus because of security configurations. See the Change Password script step for a fuller discussion.

Note that there are circumstances where you should not set an account to force the user to change his password at next login. If the user will not have a direct means to do this, the option should not be set. The best example is an account that will be used to access a FileMaker database via Instant Web Publishing: IWP provides no means for a user to change her password, so this setting will lock the user out of the database. Similarly, if the account is externally authenticated, it may be risky to tie the account to a privilege set requiring that the password be changed at some point, or have a minimum length.

→ *For further discussion of security,* **see** Special Edition Using FileMaker 8, *Chapter 12, "Implementing Security."*

Adjust Window

Compatibility:

Menu Equivalent: None

Syntax: **Adjust Window [Resize to fit/Maximize/Minimize/Restore/Hide]**

Options:

Resize to Fit shrinks a window to the minimum possible size while including all layout elements.

Maximize expands the current window to the size of the user's screen or the application window in Windows. In Windows, the database window controls and scroll bar will disappear and be incorporated into the application window.

Minimize minimizes the current window to an icon or a minimized window bar at the bottom of the application window in Windows.

Restore returns the current window to the size it was before the last resize.

Hide hides the current database window.

Examples:
Go to Layout ["Detail"]
Adjust Window [Maximize]

Description:

This script step hides or otherwise controls the size of the current database window. It is important to note that the size and position of a window cannot be relied upon unless one has explicitly set them, or users are explicitly prohibited from modifying them.

Note that in Windows, FileMaker opens all database windows within an application window. The Adjust Window script step will affect only database windows. There are no controls by which a developer can manipulate the application-level window.

Note also that in Windows if a user minimizes or resizes an existing window or opens a new window, any maximized window will be restored to its previous state. In solutions where you expect to use multiple windows, we recommend against using the maximize command.

Allow Toolbars

Compatibility: 🍎 🪟

Menu Equivalent: None

Syntax: **Allow Toolbars [<On/Off>]**

Options:

On allows FileMaker's native toolbars to be utilized.

Off hides and makes inaccessible FileMaker's toolbars as well as the toolbar submenu options in the view menu.

Examples:
Allow Toolbars [Off]

Description:

This script step hides and shows the FileMaker Pro toolbars and menu options. This is often used to control the amount of screen space available in a given database screen. This script step takes effect only while the file that calls this script is active. This option has no effect in Kiosk mode because toolbars are always hidden in Kiosk mode.

Allow User Abort

Compatibility: 🍎 🖥 ⊕

Menu Equivalent: None

Syntax: **Allow User Abort [<on or off>]**

Options:

On allows users to halt the execution of a script by pressing the Esc key (or ⌘-period on Mac OS machines).

Off disables the halting of scripts by users.

Examples:
Allow User Abort[Off]

Description:

Allow User Abort is used to control the user's ability to cancel scripts by using the Esc key (or the ⌘-period key combination on Mac OS systems). This script step is typically used in scripts whose operation should not be arbitrarily canceled by the user, such as login logic, data import/export, or any script that must process a set of records without any interruption. Most of FileMaker's menu options are also unavailable while a script is running in the Allow User Abort [Off] state.

Comments:

If a script involves any processes that could work with large record sets, such as sorting, looping, or running a Replace script step, the user sees a progress dialog for the duration of that operation. If Allow User Abort is on, as it is by default, users can cancel the script and disrupt those operations, leaving them partially complete. If a script contains any process that must not be interrupted before completion, it should use Allow User Abort[Off] to ensure that these processes are able to finish without user interruption.

Arrange All Windows

Compatibility: 🍎 🖥

Menu Equivalent: Windows (various choices)

Syntax: **Arrange All Windows [Tile Horizontally/Tile Vertically/Cascade Window/ Bring All to Front]**

Options:

Tile Horizontally positions open windows from left to right across the screen. They are resized to avoid any overlaps.

Tile Vertically positions open windows from top to bottom down the screen. They are resized to avoid any overlaps.

Cascade Window positions windows overlapping diagonally from upper left to lower right. The idea of this arrangement is, presumably, to allow the reading of the title bar of each window. The windows are resized to fit the available screen space.

Bring All to Front (Mac OS only) brings all open windows to the front without resizing or otherwise moving or rearranging them. In the event that any open FileMaker windows have been hidden by (that is, are behind) any other application's windows, this step ensures that all FileMaker windows are above other application windows.

Examples:
New Window [Name: "Trees"; Height: 200; Width: 600; Top: 16; Left: 16]
Arrange All Windows [Tile Vertically]

Description:

This script step resizes and/or repositions open windows, but does not affect which window has focus. The active record also remains the same.

Beep

Compatibility:

Menu Equivalent: None

Syntax: **Beep**

Options:

None

Examples:
Set Error Capture [On]
Perform Find [Restore]
If [Get (FoundCount) = 0]
    Beep
    Show Custom Dialog ["No records were found that match your find criteria."]
End

Description:

This script step plays a beep noise. The beep is played at the default volume of the machine on which it is played.

Comments:

You may want to use the beep as an extra alert noise. (We've even heard of an intrepid FileMaker developer, on the road without an alarm clock, who programmed himself an alarm clock in FileMaker with the Beep step.)

Change Password

Compatibility: ⬤ ▦ ⊕*

Menu Equivalent: File, Change Password

Syntax: **Change Password [Old Password: <old password>; New Password: <new password>; No dialog]**

Options:

Old Password is the current account's current password. It can be the result of a specified calculation or typed in.

New Password is the desired new password for the current account. It can be the result of a specified calculation or typed in.

Perform Without Dialog suppresses the Change Password dialog for this action. Rather than prompting the user for old and new passwords, the script step will use whatever values have been specified and stored with the script step.

Examples:

The following script uses a custom Change Password dialog, rather than the standard dialog used by FileMaker.

Change Password [Old Password: 'OldpasswOrd'; New Password: New_Password; No Dialog]
// Change Password can be used in conjunction with "Show Custom Dialog" to cascade password changes throughout several files:
Allow User Abort [Off]
Set Error Capture [On]
#
Show Custom Dialog [Title: "Password Change"; Buttons: "OK", "Cancel";
Input #1: zgPassword_Old. t, "Old Password:";
Input #2: zgPassword_New. t, "New Password:"]
#
If [Get(LastMessageChoice)=1]
  Change Password [Old Password: zgPassword_Old. t;
New Password: zgPassword_New. t]
  # send password change to other files
  Perform Script ["Change Password"; from file "Contacts" Parameter:
 zgPassword_Old. t&"¶"&zgPassword_New. t]
  Perform Script ["Change Password"; from file "Invoices" Parameter:
 zgPassword_Old. t&"¶"&zgPassword_New. t]
End If
# be sure to clear the globals for security reasons
Set Field [zgPassword_Old. t; ""]
Set Field [zgPassword_New. t; ""]

Description:

This script step changes the password for the current account. By default, a Change Password dialog is displayed unless the Perform Without Dialog option is selected. If Error Capture has been enabled (in the Set Error Capture script step) and Perform Without Dialog is not selected, then the user is given five attempts at changing his password. If Error Capture has not been enabled and Perform Without Dialog is not selected, then the user is given only one attempt at changing the password. Run Script with Full Access Privileges enables a user to change the password for the current account even if she lacks the explicit permission to do so.

Comments:

A number of FileMaker script steps perform functions similar or identical to choices that are available in the FileMaker menus. For reasons of security or solution design, a developer might choose to limit user access to the FileMaker menus. Menu access can be configured differently for each privilege set in a file. If access to menus is limited, it may be necessary or desirable to reproduce some functionality available through menus by creating a scripted interface instead. A user without access to menus might instead then see a Change Password button or clickable link, which invokes the Change Password script step.

When programming for the Web, be sure to select Perform Without Dialog. Leaving the box unchecked is not web compatible and does not work on the Web.

→ *For more information on creating and editing privilege sets,* **see** Special Edition Using FileMaker 8, *Chapter 12, "Implementing Security."*

Check Found Set

Compatibility:

Menu Equivalent: Edit, Spelling, Check All

Syntax: **Check Found Set**

Options:

None

Examples:
Perform Find [Restore]
Check Found Set

Description:

This script step uses FileMaker Pro's spelling checker to check the spelling of the contents of text fields in all the records currently being browsed. The step checks spelling in all fields of type Text, and all calculation fields with a calculation result type of Text. It is an interactive script step that displays the familiar spelling dialog for every questionable spelling that the system finds.

Comments:

This option is normally available via the FileMaker menus. If one or more users have limited access to menu items, it may be necessary to write scripts that give them access to functionality normally available through menus, such as spell check functions. See the Change Password script step for further discussion of this point.

Check Record

Compatibility:  ⌂

Menu Equivalent: Edit, Spelling, Check Record

Syntax: **Check Record**

Options:

None

> *Examples:*
> Go to Record/Request/Page [First]
> Loop
>   Check Record
>   Go to Record/Request/Page [Next; Exit after last]
> End Loop

Description:

This script step uses FileMaker Pro's spelling checker to check the spelling of the contents of text fields in every record in the current record. The step checks spelling in all fields of type Text, and all calculation fields with a calculation result type of Text. It is an interactive script step that displays the familiar spelling dialog for every questionable spelling that the system finds. See also the Check Found Set script step for further discussion.

Comments:

This option is normally available via the FileMaker menus. If one or more users have limited access to menu items, it may be necessary to write scripts that give them access to functionality normally available through menus, such as spell check functions. See the Change Password script step for further discussion of this point.

Check Selection

Compatibility:  ⌂

Menu Equivalent: Edit, Spelling, Check Selection

Syntax: **Check Selection [Select; table::field]**

Options:

Select Entire Contents checks the spelling of the entire contents of the designated field. If this option is not chosen, then only the text that has been selected (highlighted) is checked.

Go to Target Field allows for the selection of the field to spell check.

Examples:
Check Selection [Select; Product::Description]

Description:

This script step uses FileMaker Pro's spelling checker to check the spelling of the contents of a single field. The step can check spelling in all fields of type Text, and all calculation fields with a calculation result type of Text. It is an interactive script step that displays the familiar spelling dialog for every questionable spelling that the system finds.

Comments:

This option is normally available via the FileMaker menus. If one or more users have limited access to menu items, it may be necessary to write scripts that give them access to functionality normally available through menus, such as spell check functions. See the Change Password script step for further discussion of this point.

Clear

Compatibility: ✎ ⍓ ⊕

Menu Equivalent: Edit, Clear

Syntax: **Clear [Select; <table::field>]**

Options:

Select Entire Contents allows for the deletion of the entire contents of a field, regardless of what portion of its contents have been selected (highlighted) by the user.

Go to Target Field specifies which field is to have its contents or selected contents deleted.

Examples:
#The following example clears the values in a repeating field with
three repetitions.
Clear [Select, table::field[3]]
Clear [Select, table::field[2]]
Clear [Select, table::field]

Description:

This script step removes either the entire contents of a field (if the Select Entire Contents option has been designated) or the selected portion of a field (if the Select Entire Contents option has not been designated). It is important to note that Clear is distinct from the Cut operation in that it does not place the deleted content on the clipboard. In a web-published database, it is necessary to use a Commit Record/Request script step to update the record that had one (or more) of its fields cleared.

Comments:

Clear is one of a number of script steps that depend on the presence of specific fields on the current layout. For these steps to take effect, the targeted field must be present on the current layout and the current mode must be Browse mode. Note, however, that these script steps take effect even if the field has been marked as not enterable in Browse mode. Other script steps with the same limitations include Cut, Copy, Paste, and Set Selection.

Close File

Compatibility:

Menu Equivalent: File, Close

Syntax: **Close File [Current File/"<filename>"]**

Options:

Specify allows you to select a FileMaker Pro file to close from among the list of existing predefined file references.

Add File Reference allows the selection of a file to close while at the same time adding it to the list of defined file references.

Define File References allows for existing file references to be modified or deleted.

> *Examples:*
> Close ["Line_Items"]

Description:

This script step closes the specified file. The target file may be specified via a file reference. If no file reference is designated, then the file in which the script is running is closed. (This also has the effect of halting the execution of the script that contains the Close File step.)

Comments:

If you used File, File Options to specify a script that should run when a file is closed, that script is triggered when the Close File script step is run.

Close Window

Compatibility:

Menu Equivalent: None

Syntax: **Close Window [Current Window or Name: <name of window>]**

Options:

Specify allows you to choose a window to close, either by typing its name explicitly, or by drawing the name from a calculation.

 Current file only causes FileMaker to search only within windows based on table occurrences from within the current file.

Examples:
Close Window [Name: "Sales records"]

Description:

This script step closes either the currently active window or a window designated by name. The name may be a string literal typed into the script itself or generated as the result of a calculation.

Comments:

Closing the last open window in a database closes the database and halts execution of the currently running script. This also triggers any script that has been set to run when the file closes.

NEW **Current file only** is a window management option that's new to FileMaker 8. In FileMaker 7, window management script steps could sometimes be "fooled" by the presence of windows from other files with the same name as the desired script step target, causing the script step to act on a window different from the desired one. In FileMaker 8, the developer can restrict the scope of window management script steps to consider only windows based on the current file.

Comment

Compatibility: 🍎 🪟 🌐

Menu Equivalent: None

Syntax: **#<comment text>**

Options:

Specify allows for the entry of comment text in a dialog box.

Examples:
Clear Globals for Login
#
Script authored by : Tom
Last modified on 1/12/2004
#
Clear [Select, table::gCurrentUserID]
Clear [Select, table::gCurrentUserName]
Clear [Select, table::gCurrentUserEmail]

Description:

This script step allows for the addition of comments to scripts. You can see these comments only when a script is viewed in ScriptMaker, or when a script is printed and the comments are bold text preceded by a #. Comments print as italics.

Comments:

Properly commented code helps greatly in legibility and debugging. Script comments are somewhat different from calculation comments, in that calculation comments are inserted in the body of a calculation's text, and can be preceded with // or wrapped in /* .. . */ comment delimiters.

→ *For further discussion of script commenting, **see** Special Edition Using FileMaker 8, Chapter 9 "Getting Started with Scripting," and Chapter 17, "Debugging and Troubleshooting."*

Commit Records/Requests

Compatibility: 🍎 🖥 ⊕*

Menu Equivalent: None

Syntax: **Commit Records/Requests [No dialog]**

Options:

Skip Data Entry Validation will override any data entry validation options set for fields and commit the record regardless of any errors. This option skips validation only for fields set with the Only During Data Entry validation option in the Options for Field dialog box; fields set to Always Validate still validate, even if the Skip Data Entry Validation option is selected in this script step.

Examples:
```
Show Custom Dialog ["Commit record?";
"Click 'Commit' to save your changes."]
If [Get(LastMessageChoice) = 1]
   Commit Records/Requests
Else
   Revert Record/Request [No dialog]
End
```

Description:

This script step commits a record. In other words, it exits the current record or find request and updates the field data for the record. It has the effect of causing the user to exit the record, in the sense that no field will be active on the current layout once the record is committed. Exiting a record in this fashion will also have the effect of saving any changes made to it. Exiting/committing a record can be accomplished in many non-scripted ways as well, including changing to another record or merely clicking on a layout outside of any field so that no field is selected. See the Revert Record/Request script step for more discussion.

Comments:

While a user is editing a record, any changes she makes to the record can't be seen by other users of the database. Only when she commits the record are her changes saved to the database and broadcast to other users. This script step has wide applicability. Any time you change data in a record via a script, it's a good idea to commit the record explicitly. This is especially true if the changes will result in significant screen updates. For example, if data changes in a record would lead to different data being displayed in a portal on the current layout, it's very important to make sure the data changes are explicitly committed. As a best practice we recommend using this step in any script where record data is altered. It's also necessary (not just desirable) to add this script step to scripts that are called from the Web, if those scripts change record data.

It's also critical to use this step liberally when the Set Field step is used in a script. Lack of an appropriate commit can leave a record in a locked state. For example, if the last step in a script is a Set Field step, you should finish the script with a Commit Records/Requests step. Otherwise, the affected record will remain "open" and will be locked until committed. Similarly, we recommend you perform Commit Records/Requests after any Set Field steps that may precede a Perform Script step to ensure the changes take effect before the next script runs. Problems with record locking in these circumstances are common in complex, scripted systems converted from FileMaker Pro 6.

→ *For further discussion of concurrency and committing records,* **see** Special Edition Using FileMaker 8, *Chapter 11, "Developing for Multi-User Deployment."*

When programming for the Web, be sure to select Perform Without Dialog. Leaving the box unchecked is not web compatible and does not work on the Web.

Constrain Found Set

Compatibility: 🍎 🖥 ⊕

Menu Equivalent: Requests, Constrain Found Set

Syntax: **Constrain Found Set [Restore]**

Options:

Specify Find Requests creates and stores a find request with the script step. See the Perform Find script step for more information.

Examples:
```
# Find all employees older than 60 years of age.
Enter Find Mode [ ]
Set Field [Age; ">60" ]
Perform Find []
# Now find which of these want early retirement
Enter Find Mode [ ]
Set Field [Early_Retire; "Yes" ]
Constrain Found Set[]
```

Description:

This script step specifies a find request that will be used to narrow the current found set. This is equivalent to applying the last find request with the new find request appended via a logical AND operator.

Comments:

Constrain[] is useful when searching unindexed fields as part of a complex find. If a search includes criteria for both stored and unstored fields, a performance gain may be achieved by first performing a find on the indexed fields, and then using Constrain[] to limit the search for the unindexed criteria to the smaller found set.

Convert File

Compatibility: 🍎 🖥

Menu Equivalent: None

Syntax: **Convert File ["<filename>"]**

Options:

Specify Data Source allows for the designation of a data source to be converted into a FileMaker Pro 7 file.

The possible data sources are File, XML, and ODBC.

Examples:
Convert File ["datafile.fp5"]

Description:

This script step converts a file from a variety of supported formats into a FileMaker 7 file. This command works on only one file at a time. Supported data formats are BASIC format, Comma-Separated Text format, dBase III and IV DBF format, DIF format, FileMaker Pro format, HTML Table format, Lotus 1-2-3 WK1/WKS formats, Merge format, Microsoft Excel format, SYLK format, Tab-Separated Text format, and XML format. Designation of various data sources follows the same procedures as an import. See the Import Records script step for further discussion.

Comments:

This step is analogous to the effects of using File, Open to open a non-FileMaker 7/8 file. A variety of formats can be opened/converted, each with its own set of options.

→ *For further discussion,* **see** *Special Edition Using FileMaker 8, Chapter 18, "Converting Systems from Previous Versions of FileMaker Pro," and Chapter 19 "Importing Data into FileMaker."*

Copy

Compatibility: 🍎 ▥ ⊕

Menu Equivalent: Edit, Copy

Syntax: **Copy [Select; <table::field>]**

Options:

Select Entire Contents copies the entire contents of a field to the Clipboard rather than just the selected portion of the designated field's contents.

Go to Target Field or **Specify** allow you to select the field from which you wish to copy the contents to the clipboard. If no field is specified and nothing is selected, FileMaker Pro copies the values from all fields of the current record.

> *Examples:*
> Go To Layout["Customer Entry" (Customer)]
> Copy [Select; CustomerTable::Shipping_Address]
> Paste [Select; CustomerTable::Billing_Address]

Description:

This script step places the contents of the specified field onto the clipboard. If no field is specified, all fields from the current record are copied, causing the step to function identically to the Copy Record step.

Comments:

Copy is generally a poor way to move data within scripts. It requires that the current layout contain the field to be copied. (This is fragile because the script malfunctions if the field is removed.) Additionally, the contents of the clipboard are overwritten, without the consent of the user. Copy does have some interesting uses, however. When in Preview Mode, Copy takes an image of the screen, and this image can then be pasted into a container field. Copy is one of a number of script steps that depend on the presence of specific fields on the current layout. Other script steps with the same limitations include Cut, Copy, Paste, and Set Selection.

Copy All Records/Requests

Compatibility: 🍎 ▥ ⊕

Menu Equivalent: None

Syntax: **Copy All Records/Requests**

Options:

None

Examples:
```
# Copy Records in Found Set
Go To Layout ["Detail"]
Copy All Records/Requests
# Place all records in log field
Go To Layout ["Log"]
New Record/Request
Paste [Select; Log Table::Log]
```

Description:

This script step copies the values of all fields in all the records in the current found set to the clipboard in a tab-delimited export format. Styles and formatting are not copied. The field values are exported in the order in which they appear on the current layout. Only those fields that appear in the current layout are included. With a record, individual fields are separated by tabs, and records are delimited by carriage returns. Repeating field values are separated by a group separator character between each repetition. Carriage returns within a field are copied to the clipboard as the "vertical tab" character (ASCII value 11), just as they are when being exported.

Comments:

Copy All Records/Requests is one of a number of script steps that depend on the presence of specific fields on the current layout. Other script steps with the same limitations include Cut, Copy, Paste, and Set Selection.

NEW In previous versions of FileMaker it was often necessary to use this script step to copy a set of record keys and paste them into a field that would act as a "multi-key," capable of relating to many records in another file at once. This technique was often used to navigate multistep relationship chains. The new relational capabilities of FileMaker 7 make it unlikely that this step will need to be used in this way, and the new Go to Related Records from found set capability of FileMaker 8 probably further limit the earlier need for such a technique. It does remain a very handy feature for copying record data in order to paste it into a program like Microsoft Word or Excel, where it can readily be formatted as a table.

Copy Record/Request

Compatibility: 🍎 🖥 ⊕

Menu Equivalent: None

Syntax: **Copy Record/Request**

Options:

None

> *Examples:*
> # Copy Current Record
> Go To Layout ["Detail"]
> Copy Record/Request
> # Place record in log field
> Go To Layout ["Log"]
> New Record/Request
> Paste [Select; Log Table::Log]

Description:

This script step copies the values of all fields in the current record to the clipboard in a tab-delimited export format. Styles and formatting are not copied. The field values are exported in the order in which they appear on the current layout. Only those fields that appear in the current layout are included. With a record, individual fields are separated by tabs, and records are delimited by carriage returns. Repeating field values are separated by a group separator character between each repetition. Carriage returns within a field are copied to the clipboard as the "vertical tab" character (ASCII value 11), just as they are when being exported.

Comments:

Copy Record/Request is one of a number of script steps that depend on the presence of specific fields on the current layout. Other script steps with the same limitations include Cut, Copy, Paste, and Set Selection.

Correct Word

Compatibility: 🍎 🪟

Menu Equivalent: Edit, Spelling, Correct Word

Syntax: **Correct Word**

Options:

None

> *Examples:*
> Check Selection [Select; Product::Description]
> Correct Word

Description:

This script step opens the spelling dialog box to allow for the correction of the spelling of a word that has been identified as having been misspelled by the FileMaker Pro spell check operation. The option to Check Spelling As You Type must be selected. A word can be corrected only if FileMaker has identified it as being misspelled.

Comments:

This option is normally available via the FileMaker menus. If one or more users have limited access to menu items, it may be necessary to write scripts that give them access to functionality normally available through menus, such as spell check functions. See the Change Password script step for further discussion of this point.

Cut

Compatibility: 🍎 🖥 ⊕

Menu Equivalent: Edit, Cut

Syntax: **Cut [Select; <table::field>]**

Options:

Select Entire Contents copies the entire contents of a field to the Clipboard, rather than just the selected portion of the designated field's contents. The field is cleared of its contents.

Go to Target Field or **Specify** allow you to select the field from which you wish to cut the contents to the clipboard. If no field is specified and nothing is selected, FileMaker Pro cuts the values from all fields of the current record.

> *Examples:*
> Enter Browse Mode [ ]
> Cut [Select, Table1::Recent Notes]
> Paste [Table1::Previous Notes]

Description:

This script step places the contents of the selected field (or of all fields on the current layout if no field is selected or designated within the script itself) onto the clipboard and then clears the contents of that field.

Comments:

Cut is generally a script step that bears avoiding. It requires that the current layout contain the field to be cut. (This is fragile because the script malfunctions if the field is removed.) Additionally, the contents of the clipboard are overwritten without the consent of the user. Think carefully about whether the intended effect could be accomplished in a layout-independent, less intrusive fashion. Other script steps with the same limitations include Copy, Paste, and Set Selection.

Delete Account

Compatibility: 🍎 🖥 ⊕

Menu Equivalent: None

Syntax: **Delete Account [Account Name: <account name>]**

Options:

Specify allows for the selection or input of the account to be deleted.

Examples:
Delete Account [Account Name: "Regional Sales"]

Description:

This script step deletes the specified account in the current database. Full access is required to complete this operation and an account with full access may not be deleted with this script step. It is possible to specify Run Script with Full Access Privileges to ensure that any user can execute this script. However, care must be taken to ensure that such usage does not create a security hole. After Run Script with Full Access Privileges has been checked, any user who can see the script can run it, including those who have external access from other FileMaker files and web access.

Comments:

It might be desirable to allow access to this functionality via a script if certain users or user groups have limited access to the FileMaker menus because of security configurations. See the Change Password script step for a fuller discussion.

Delete All Records

Compatibility: ⌥ ⊞ ⊕*

Menu Equivalent: Records, Delete All Records

Syntax: **Delete All Records [No dialog]**

Options:

Perform Without Dialog allows for the deletion of all records in the current found set without user intervention.

Examples:
Show All Records
Delete All Records
// use a custom dialog to warn user before deleting all records
Allow User Abort [Off]
Set Error Capture [On]
Show Custom Dialog [Title: "Delete All Records";
Message: "Are you really sure you want to delete all records?"; Buttons:
 "Cancel", "Delete"]
If [Get(LastMessageChoice)=2]
the user still wants to delete
  Show Custom Dialog [Title: "Delete All Records";
  Message: "Do you have a current backup?"; Buttons: "No", "Yes"]
If [Get(LastMessageChoice)=2]

```
# after they confirmed twice, go ahead with delete
Show All Records
Delete All Records[ No dialog ]
End If
End If
```

Description:

This script step deletes all records in the current found set. It can be set to operate without user approval if you select the Perform Without Dialog option. Special care should be exercised in the use of this script step because it is not possible to undo the operation after it has been completed.

Comments:

Note that any records that are "in use" by other users are not deleted by this step. Records are considered to be in use if other users are actively editing them and have not committed/saved their changes, or if they have been left open as a result of script actions. You may want to check explicitly whether this has occurred, either by using the Get (RecordOpenCount) function, or by using Get(LastError) to check for a script error. You should also decide how you want to handle cases where the step doesn't execute completely for reasons such as these. Note that this script step is context-dependent. The current layout determines which table is active, which determines from which table the records are deleted.

When programming for the Web, be sure to select Perform Without Dialog. Leaving the box unchecked is not web compatible and does not work on the Web.

Delete Portal Row

Compatibility: 🍎 🗑 ⊕

Menu Equivalent: None

Syntax: **Delete Portal Row [No dialog]**

Options:

Perform Without Dialog allows for the deletion of the current related record without user approval.

```
Examples:
Go to Portal Row [Last]
Delete Portal Row [No dialog]
```

Description:

This script step deletes the currently selected portal row. In other words, it deletes a record that's related to the current record, and is displayed in a portal on the current layout. It can be set to operate without user approval if you select the Perform Without Dialog option. Special care should be exercised in the use of this script step because it is not possible to undo the operation after it has been completed.

Comments:

Performance of this step can be inhibited if the record represented by the specified portal row is in use by another user. See the Delete All Records script step for further discussion. Note that this script step deletes a portal row even if the Allow Deletion of Portal Records check box in the Portal Setup dialog box is unchecked.

When programming for the Web, be sure to select Perform Without Dialog. Leaving the box unchecked is not web compatible and does not work on the Web.

Delete Record/Request

Compatibility: ⌘ 🖳 ⊕

Menu Equivalent: Records, Delete Record/Request

Syntax: **Delete Record/Request [No dialog]**

Options:

Perform Without Dialog allows for the deletion of the current record or find request without user approval.

Examples:
Go to Record/Request [Last]
Delete Record/Request [No dialog]

Description:

This script step deletes the current record (when in Browse mode) or current find request (when in Find mode). It can be set to operate without user approval if you select the Perform Without Dialog option. Special care should be exercised in the use of this script step because it is not possible to undo the operation after it has been completed.

Comments:

If the current layout has a portal and a portal row is selected, the user is prompted to specify whether the master record or the related record should be deleted. If the step is performed without a dialog, the action automatically applies to the master record. If a portal row is selected and the portal is not set to Allow Deletion of Portal Records, the option to delete a related record never appears. Note that this is in contrast to the Delete Portal Row step, which deletes an active portal row regardless of whether Allow Deletion of Portal Records is enabled or not. Performance of this step can be inhibited if the record is in use by another user. See the Delete All Records script step for further discussion. Note that this script step is context-dependent. The current layout determines which table is active, which determines from which table the record is deleted.

When programming for the Web, be sure to select Perform Without Dialog. Leaving the box unchecked is not web compatible and does not work on the Web.

Dial Phone

Compatibility: 📇

Menu Equivalent: None

Syntax: **Dial Phone [No dialog; <phone number>]**

Options:

Perform Without Dialog prevents the Dial Phone dialog from displaying when this script step executes.

Specify displays the Dial Phone options.

- **Phone Number** allows the entry of a telephone number.
- **Specify** allows the creation of a calculation to generate the telephone number to be dialed.
- **Use Dialing Preferences** applies the pre-established telephone dialing preferences to the number to be dialed, based on the designated location information.

Examples:
Dial Phone [No Dialog, Contacts::Phone_Home]

Description:

This script step allows FileMaker Pro to dial a telephone number from within a script. The number to be dialed may be entered within the script itself, contained within a field, or generated by a specified calculation. Current telephone dialing preferences can be applied optionally based on location information. Letters within telephone numbers are translated into the appropriate numbers (q and z being, of course, omitted). Note: This script step does not work on Mac OS.

Comments:

You might use this script step if you want to be able to dial the phone numbers of people or organizations whose contact information is stored in FileMaker. You might also use it to perform more low-level serial-line tasks, in conjunction with a plug-in that can communicate directly with a computer's serial port.

Duplicate Record/Request

Compatibility: 🍎 📇 🌐

Menu Equivalent: Records, Duplicate Record/Request

Syntax: **Duplicate Record/Request**

Options:

None

> *Examples:*
> Go to Portal Row [Last]
> Duplicate Record/Request

Description:

This script step duplicates the current record while in Browse mode and the current find request in Find mode. Values in fields with auto-entry options are not duplicated; new values are generated for these fields, according to the details of the specific auto-entry options. If this script step is used when a portal row is selected, and the portal relationship allows for the creation of related records, then the related record is duplicated, rather than the master record.

Comments:

If there are certain fields you want to make certain are never duplicated, you can set them to auto-enter an empty string (""). On duplication, the auto-entry option will take effect and clear the field in the new record.

Edit User Dictionary

Compatibility: 🍎 🖳

Menu Equivalent: Edit, Spelling, Edit User Dictionary

Syntax: **Edit User Dictionary**

Options:

None

> *Examples:*
> Show Custom Dialog ["Edit the user dictionary?"]
> If [Get (LastMessageChoice) = 1]
>   Edit User Dictionary
> End If

Description:

This script step opens the User Dictionary dialog box. This is often used to display the User Dictionary dialog box when user privileges do not allow for the dialog to be chosen directly from the FileMaker menus.

Else

Compatibility: 🍎 🖳 🌐

Menu Equivalent: None

Syntax: **Else**

Options:

None

Examples:
If [gUsername = "Tom"]
    Show Custom Dialog ["Hello Tom"]
Else If [gUsername = "Raul"]
    Show Custom Dialog ["Hola Raul"]
Else If [gUsername = "Guido"]
    Show Custom Dialog ["Ciao Guido"]
Else
    Show Custom Dialog ["I don't know who you are!"]
End If

Description:

This script step can be placed after an If or Else If statement and immediately before an End If statement. The designated code block for the Else statement is executed only if all the previous If and Else If statements have evaluated as false. It is thus often used as a way to deal with values that do not fit within expected parameters or as a default action.

Else If

Compatibility: 🍎 🖥 🌐

Menu Equivalent: None

Syntax: **Else If [<Boolean calculation>]**

Options:

Specify allows for any available fields, functions, and operators to be used to enter the Boolean calculation into the Specify Calculation dialog box. Only a zero (0), false, or null (empty) result is construed as a Boolean false.

Examples:
If [gUsername = "Tom"]
    Show Custom Dialog ["Hello Tom"]
Else if [gUsername = "Raul"]
    Show Custom Dialog ["Hola Raul"]
Else If [gUsername = "Guido"]
    Show Custom Dialog ["Ciao Guido"]
Else
    Show Custom Dialog ["I don't know who you are!"]
End If

Description:

This script step must follow the If script step or the Else If script step. It performs an action or actions based on the value of the Boolean calculation. The statements in the Else If block are executed only if none of the previous If or Else If statements are true.

Comments:

There can be an arbitrary number of Else If statements between an If statement and an End If statement. Their Boolean calculations are evaluated in the sequence in which they appear. If one should happen to evaluate to True, then its code block is executed and all subsequent Else If and Else clauses that appear before the End If are ignored.

Enable Account

Compatibility: 🍎 🖥 ⊕

Menu Equivalent: None

Syntax: **Enable Account [Account Name: <account name>; Activate/Deactivate]**

Options:

Specify displays the Enable Account Options dialog box.

- **Account Name** allows either the manual entry of or designation of a calculation to generate an account name.
- **Activate Account** enables the specified account.
- **Deactivate Account** disables the specified account.

> *Examples:*
> Enable Account [Account Name:"UserAccount"; Activate/Deactivate]

Description:

This script step enables or disables a specific pre-existing account. For this script step to be performed, the user must be assigned the Full Access privilege set or the Run Script with Full Access Privileges option must be selected. Accounts with Full Access may not be deactivated with this script step.

Comments:

It might be desirable to allow access to this functionality via a script if certain users or user groups have limited access to the FileMaker menus because of security configurations. See the Change Password script step for a fuller discussion.

End If

Compatibility: 🍎 🖥 ⊕

Menu Equivalent: None

Syntax: **End If**

Options:

None

Examples:
If [gUsername = "Tom"]
  Show Custom Dialog ["Hello Tom"]
Else If [gUsername = "Raul"]
  Show Custom Dialog ["Hola Raul"]
Else If [gUsername = "Guido"]
  Show Custom Dialog ["Ciao Guido"]
Else
  Show Custom Dialog ["I don't know who you are!"]
End If

Description:

This script step designates the end of an If/Else If/Else structure. See Else and Else If for more information.

End Loop

Compatibility:  🛒 ⚘

Menu Equivalent: None

Syntax: **End Loop**

Options:

None

Examples:
Set Variable [$counter; "0"]
Loop
  New Record/Request
  Set Variable [$counter; $counter + 1]
  Exit Loop If [$counter > 10]
End Loop

Description:

This script step marks the end of a Loop structure. The steps between Loop and End Loop are executed until the loop is explicitly exited. This step passes control to the step immediately following the Loop command preceding it.

Comments:

Note that this step doesn't cause a loop to stop executing. Without termination logic, a loop will run forever. Use the Exit Loop If script step to establish the conditions under which the loop will stop running and control will pass to the script step immediately following.

Enter Browse Mode

Compatibility: 🍎 🖥 ⊕

Menu Equivalent: View, Browse Mode

Syntax: **Enter Browse Mode [Pause]**

Options:

Pause stops the script step's execution to allow for user data entry and record navigation. The user may resume the script by clicking the Continue button in the Status Area, or by executing a Resume Script script step through a button or directly through the FileMaker Scripts menu.

Examples:
Allow User Abort [Off]
Set Error Capture [On]
Go To Layout ["Monthly Report']
Enter Preview Mode [Pause]
Go to Layout [Original Layout]
Enter Browse Mode []

Description:

This script step places the current window into Browse mode.

Enter Find Mode

Compatibility: 🍎 🖥 ⊕

Menu Equivalent: View, Find Mode

Syntax: **Enter Find Mode [Restore; Pause]**

Options:

Pause stops the script step's execution to allow for user data entry and record navigation. The user may resume the script by clicking the Continue button in the Status Area, or executing a Resume Script script step through a button or directly through the FileMaker Scripts menu.

Specify Find Requests enables you to create and edit find requests for use with the script step.

Examples:
#an example of a find that is executed from requests stored with the script
Go to Layout ["Detail View"]
Enter Find Mode [Restore]
Perform Find []

```
#this example waits for the user to enter find criteria and execute the find
Go to Layout ["Detail View"]
Enter Find Mode [Pause]
Perform Find[]
```

Description:

This script step places the current layout into Find mode. In Find mode, find requests may be created, edited, deleted, and duplicated. In addition, find requests can be stored with the script step if you check the Restore check box and using the Specify dialog. String multiple find requests together to create complex find requests. A single find request may either omit records from or add them to the existing found set.

Comments:

Enter Find Mode is one of several script steps that is capable of saving complex options along with the script step. Other such script steps are Perform Find, Sort Records, Import Records, Export Records, and Print Setup. Use the Pause option if you want the user to be able to enter his own search criteria, or modify a search that's saved with the script. If the status area is visible, the user sees a Continue button, as well as a Cancel button if Allow User Abort is set to "on" in the script. Be sure to set Allow User Abort to "off" if you don't want to offer an option to cancel the script at that point. If the status area is hidden, these buttons won't be accessible, and the user needs to either show the status area or use keyboard equivalents for Continue (Enter or Return) or Cancel (Escape or ⌘-period).

→ *For further discussion of saved script step options, **see** Special Edition Using FileMaker 8, Chapter 9, "Getting Started with Scripting."*

Enter Preview Mode

Compatibility: 🍎 🖥

Menu Equivalent: View, Preview Mode

Syntax: **Enter Preview Mode [Pause]**

Options:

Pause stops the script step's execution to allow for user inspection of the preview for the designated layout. The user may resume the script by clicking the Continue button.

```
Examples:
Enter Preview Mode [Pause]
```

Description:

This script step places the current layout into Preview mode, where an approximation of what a layout will look like when it is printed out is displayed. Preview mode is helpful for viewing layouts that use special layout parts for reporting, title headers, leading grand summaries, subsummaries, trailing grand summaries, and title footers. Preview is the only FileMaker mode that displays all layout parts correctly. (Subsummary parts do not display correctly in Browse mode.)

Comments:

Use the Pause option if you want the user to be able to spend time in Preview mode working with the displayed data. If the status area is visible, the user sees a Continue button, as well as a Cancel button, if Allow User Abort is set to "on" in the script. Be sure to set Allow User Abort to "off" if you don't want to offer an option to cancel the script at that point. If the status area is hidden, these buttons aren't accessible, and the user needs to either show the status area or use keyboard equivalents for Continue (Enter or Return) or Cancel (Escape or ⌘-period).

→   *For further discussion of Preview mode, **see** Special Edition Using FileMaker 8, Chapter 4, "Working with Layouts," and Chapter 10 "Getting Started with Reporting."*

Execute SQL

Compatibility: 🍎 🖳

Menu Equivalent: None

Syntax: **Execute SQL [No Dialog; ODBC: <datasource name>; <native SQL or calculated SQL>]**

Options:

Perform Without Dialog prevents the Specify SQL dialog box, the Select ODBC Data Source dialog box, and the Password dialog box from displaying when the script step executes.

Specify displays the Specify SQL dialog box, where you can set the following options:

- **Specify** displays the Select ODBC Data Source dialog box. This allows for the selection of an ODBC connection and allows for the entry of the appropriate username and password.
- **Calculated SQL Text** allows for the creation of a calculation to generate the desired SQL query.
- **SQL Text** allows for the direct entry of a text SQL query.

Examples:
Execute SQL [No Dialog; ODBC: SQL_Server; "UPDATE Customers SET Status = '" & Customer::Status & "' where CustID = '" & Customer::CustomerID & "' ;"]

Description:

This script step executes a designated SQL query over a selected ODBC connection. This allows for manipulation of SQL data sources through standard queries. A script can contain multiple Execute SQL steps that act on different SQL data sources.

Comments:

The Execute SQL step opens a great many avenues in FileMaker development.

→ *For further discussion, **see** Special Edition Using FileMaker 8, Chapter 20, "Exporting Data from FileMaker."*

Exit Application

Compatibility: 🍎 🪟 ⊕

Menu Equivalent: FileMaker Pro, Quit FileMaker Pro (Mac OS); File, Exit (Windows)

Syntax: **Exit Application**

Options:

None

> *Examples:*
> Exit Application

Description:

This script step closes all open files and exits the FileMaker Pro Application.

Comments:

The Exit application triggers the closing scripts of any files that have a closing script attached.

Exit Loop If

Compatibility: 🍎 🪟 ⊕

Menu Equivalent: None

Syntax: **Exit Loop If [<Boolean calculation>]**

Options:

Specify allows for the definition of the Boolean calculation that decides whether the loop is exited or not.

> *Examples:*
> Set Field [Table1::gCounter; "0"]
> Loop
>   New Record/Request
>   Set Field [Table1::gCounter; Table1::gCounter + 1]
>   Exit Loop If [gCounter > 10]
> End

Description:

This script step terminates a loop if the Boolean calculation evaluates to True (non-zero and non-null). Upon termination, control is passed to the next script step after the End Loop script step that applies to the current script step. If the Boolean calculation evaluates to False (zero or null), then control is passed to the next script step, or to the step at the beginning of the loop if no further steps are specified within the loop.

Comments:

You'll probably want to have at least one Exit Loop If script step inside any loop you write. Without at least one such statement, it's difficult to exit the loop, except by performing a subscript that performs a Halt Script or using a Go To Record/Request/Page [Next; Exit after last] script step.

Exit Script

Compatibility: 🍎 🖥 ⊕

Menu Equivalent: None

NEW *Syntax:* **Exit Script [Result]**

Options:

You can use **Specify** to specify a value to be returned from the script as the *script result*. This result will be accessible via the Get(ScriptResult) function.

Examples:
Perform Find [Restore]
If [Get (CurrentFoundCount)=0]
    Show All Records
    Go to Layout ["Detail View"]
    Exit Script
Else
    Print []
End

Description:

Exit Script forces the current script to stop executing. No further script steps in the current script will execute. If the current script was called by another script, the remaining script steps in the calling script will continue to execute.

Comments:

It's important to distinguish this script step from the related script step Halt Script. Halt Script forces the termination of *all* currently running scripts, whereas Exit Script simply exits the current script.

NEW The capability to return a script result is an important new feature of FileMaker 8. A script result is accessed via the Get(ScriptResult) function. Note that the Exit Script step is the only way to return a result from a script.

→ *For more information on this important new capability, **see** Special Edition Using FileMaker 8, Chapter 15, "Advanced Scripting Techniques."*

Export Field Contents

Compatibility: 🍎 🖥

Menu Equivalent: Edit, Export Field Contents

Syntax: **Export Field Contents [<table::field>; "<filename>"]**

Options:

Specify Target Field allows for the specification of the field whose contents are to be exported.

Specify Output File allows the desired filename and file path for the exported data to be specified.

> *Examples:*
> Go to Layout [Pictures::Agent_Picture]
> Export Field Contents [Pictures::Picture_Full; Pictures::filename]

Description:

Export Field Contents creates a named file on disk with the contents of the specified field.

Comments:

Export Field Contents is a very powerful and flexible command when used in conjunction with container fields. FileMaker Pro allows the user to store a file of any type in a container field (including FileMaker Pro files). Export Field Contents writes the file out to disk in its native format, where the file can then be opened with the appropriate application. Any type of file, including images, of course, can be saved in a FileMaker database and written out to disk.

NEW Using the new script variables feature of FileMaker 8, it is possible to set the name and path of the output file dynamically, rather than hard-coding a file reference within the script.

→ *For further discussion of exporting, **see** Special Edition Using FileMaker 8, Chapter 20, "Exporting Data from FileMaker."*

→ *For more information on dynamic file paths, **see** Special Edition Using FileMaker 8, Chapter 15, "Advanced Scripting Techniques."*

Export Records

Compatibility:

Menu Equivalent: File, Export Records

Syntax: **Export records [No dialog; "<output filename>"]**

Options:

Perform Without Dialog prevents the display of dialog boxes that let the user set new export criteria when the script step executes.

Specify Output File allows the desired filename and file path for the exported data to be specified as well as its file type. If XML Export is selected, then the XML Export Options dialog is displayed and allows the selection of an appropriate XML grammar and stylesheet for the export.

NEW In FileMaker 8, you can export records directly to the Excel file format by choosing Excel from among the available file types. **Specify Export Order** displays the export order that was in effect when you added the script step. The last export order used in the file appears as the default and can be edited or deleted.

Examples:
Export Records [No dialog, "Contracts"]

Description:

This script step exports records from the current found set to a specified file in a specified format. The current sort order of the found set is used for the export order of the records. Note that Group By works only for fields that are included in the current sort order. (Sorted fields appear in the Group By box; check off any fields in which you want to group by.)

Comments:

NEW Using the new script variables feature of FileMaker 8, it is possible to set the name and path of the output file dynamically, rather than hard-coding a file reference within the script.

Because it's possible to create FileMaker field names that are not valid names for XML elements, use extreme caution when exporting in the FMPDSORESULT grammar; the resulting XML may be invalid. FMPDSORESULT is deprecated in this version of FileMaker Pro and should probably be avoided.

→ *For more information about XML grammars,* **see** *Special Edition Using FileMaker 8, Chapter 22,   "FileMaker and Web Services."*

→ *For more information about exporting,* **see** *Special Edition Using FileMaker 8, Chapter 20,"Exporting Data from FileMaker."*

Extend Found Set

Compatibility: 🍎 🖥 🌐

Menu Equivalent: Requests, Extend Found Set

Syntax: **Extend Found Set [Restore]**

Options:

Specify Find Requests allows for the creation and storage of find requests with the script step.

Examples:
```
#This script finds employees that are local or have a specific zip code
Set Error Capture [On]
Allow User Abort [Off]
Enter Find Mode [ ]
Set Field [Local; "Yes"]
Perform Find [ ]
Enter Find Mode [ ]
Set Field [Zip; "94965"]
Extend Found Set[]
```

Description:

This script step allows the current found set to be extended if you append additional search criteria to the previous search or, put differently, if you apply designated search criteria only to records *not* included in the current found set. (This is equivalent to a logical OR search combined with the results of the previously executed search.)

Comments:

Similar to the Constrain Found Set script step, this step enables you to combine the results of more than one search. Whereas Constrain Found Set enables you to limit the results of one found set by the results of a second search (an operation known as an *intersection*), the Extend Found Set command enables you to add the results of one search to the results of another search (an operation known as a *union*).

Flush Cache to Disk

Compatibility: 🍎 🖥

Menu Equivalent: None

Syntax: **Flush Cache to Disk**

Options:

None

Examples:
Replace Field Contents [Line_Items::ProductID; Line_Items::NewProductID]
Flush Cache to Disk

Description:

This script step causes FileMaker Pro's internal disk cache to be written to disk. This operation is normally performed periodically or after structural changes such as defining fields or modifying calculation definitions. Flush Cache to Disk enables the developer to explicitly write out the contents of memory.

Comments:

Note that this script step flushes the contents of the cache for a local client copy of FileMaker Pro. It has no effect on the cache of any instance of FileMaker Server.

→ *For more information about configuring FileMaker Server, **see** Special Edition Using FileMaker 8, Chapter 25, "FileMaker Server and Server Advanced."*

Freeze Window

Compatibility:

Menu Equivalent: None

Syntax: **Freeze Window**

Options:

None

Examples:
Freeze Window
Replace Field Contents [Line_Items::ProductID; Line_Items::NewProductID]
Sort [Restore; No Dialog]
Refresh Window

Description:

This script step halts the updating of the active window as script steps are performed. The window resumes refreshing either at the end of the script where it was frozen or after a Refresh Window script step is executed within a script.

Comments:

Freeze Window is useful in creating more professional-looking applications because it prevents the screen from flashing or redrawing while other script steps execute (for example, those that navigate to "utility" layouts, perform some work there, and then return to a main interface layout). It's also possible to realize some performance gains from freezing a window; scripts that would otherwise cause changes to the contents or appearance of the active window run more quickly if the active window doesn't need to be refreshed.

Go to Field

Compatibility: 🍎 🖳 ⊕

Menu Equivalent: None

Syntax: **Go to Field [Select/perform; <table::field>]**

Options:

Select/Perform directs FileMaker to select all contents of the designated field. If the field is a container field and an action is associated with that field (such as playing a movie or sound file), then that action is performed.

Go to Target Field allows for the specification of the field to go to, using the standard FileMaker Pro field selection dialog box.

Examples:
Enter Browse Mode []
Go to Layout ["Contracts"]
New Record/Request
Go to Field [Contracts::Signatory]

Description:

This script step selects a specified field in the current layout. If the Select/Perform option is selected, then if an action is associated with a field, that action is performed. (Actions would be associated with container field types, such as sound files or movies—in these cases, the associated action would be to play the sound or movie file.) In cases where there is no implied action, the entire contents of the field are selected.

Comments:

Go to Field allows the developer to insert the cursor into a specific field after a record has been created from a script.

Like other script steps such as Cut, Copy, and Paste, this step depends on the specified field being present on the current layout.

Go to Layout

Compatibility: 🍎 🖳 ⊕

Menu Equivalent: None

Syntax: **Go to Layout ["<layout name or layout number>"]**

Options:

Specify allows the target layout to be selected. The following choices are available:

- **Original Layout** refers to the layout that was active when the script was initiated.
- **Layout Name by Calculation** enables you to enter a calculation that generates the name of the desired layout.

- **Layout Number by Calculation** enables you to enter a calculation that will generate the number of the desired layout. Layout numbers correspond to the order in which layouts are listed.

An existing layout may also be specified directly by name.

Examples:
Go to Layout ["Contracts"]
Copy [Select; DataTable1::ID_Number]
Go To Layout [Original Layout]

Description:

This script step makes the specified layout active in the current file. This step can navigate only to layouts in the currently active file. In the case where multiple layouts have the same name, the first match is selected for a calculated layout name.

Comments:

This script step is vital for establishing the proper context for any subsequent script steps that operate on record data. Any script steps that directly deal with FileMaker data or records will do so in the context of the table occurrence of the currently active layout.

It's also possible to draw either the name or the number of a layout from a calculation.

→ *For an extended example of the use of this script step in a custom navigation mechanism,* **see** Special Edition Using FileMaker 8, *Chapter 13, "Advanced Interface Techniques."*

Go to Next Field

Compatibility: 🍎 🖥 🌐

Menu Equivalent: None

Syntax: **Go to Next Field**

Options:

None

Examples:
Go to Field [Table1::First Name]
Set Field [Table1::gCounter; "0"]
Loop
  Set Field [Table1::gCounter; Table1::gCounter + 1]
  Exit Loop If [gCounter > Table1::ActiveField]
  Go To Next Field
End Loop

Description:

This script step moves to the next field in the established tab order for the current layout. If no field is selected, the first field in the established tab order for the current layout is selected. If the user regains control, either by pausing in Browse mode or by exiting the script, the cursor remains in the selected field. If there is no tab order on the layout, the fields are traversed in the order in which they were added to the layout.

Comments:

Note that this script can override the effect of field behaviors that prevent entry into a field.

Go to Portal Row

Compatibility:

Menu Equivalent: None

Syntax: **Go to Portal Row [<first/last/previous/next/by calculation>]**

Options:

First selects the first row of the currently active portal.

Last selects the last row of the currently active portal.

Previous selects the previous row of the currently active portal. If the Exit After Last option is selected and the script is currently performing a loop, then an Exit Loop action is performed when the first row in the designated portal is reached.

Next selects the next row of the currently active portal. If the Exit After Last option is selected and the script is currently performing a loop, then an Exit Loop action is performed when the last row in the designated portal is reached.

By Calculation selects the row number determined by the designated calculation.

Examples:
Go to Portal Row [Select, First]

Description:

This script step allows navigation among related records in the active portal on the current layout. If no portal is active, then the first portal in the layout stacking order is assumed. This step attempts to maintain the selected portal field when it changes rows. If no field is selected, the first enterable field is selected in the new row.

Go to Previous Field

Compatibility:

Menu Equivalent: None

Syntax: **Go to Previous Field**

Options:

None

Examples:
Go to Previous Field

Description:

This script step moves focus to the previous field in the current layout's tab order. If no field is selected, then the last field in the current layout's tab order is selected. If the user regains control, either by pausing in Browse mode or by exiting the script, the cursor will remain in the selected field. If there is no tab order on the layout, the fields are traversed in the order in which they were added to the layout.

Comments:

Note that this script can override the effect of field behaviors that prevent entry into a field.

Go to Record/Request/Page

Compatibility: 🍎 🗔 ⊕

Menu Equivalent: None

Syntax: **Go to Record/Request/Page [<first/last/previous/next/bycalculation>]**

Options:

First moves to the first record in the current found set, displays the first find request, or moves to the first page of the currently displayed report if in Preview mode.

Last moves to the last record in the current found set, displays the last find request, or moves to the last page of the currently displayed report.

Previous moves to the previous record in the current found set, displays the previous find request, or moves to the previous page of the currently displayed report. If the Exit After Last option is selected and the script is currently performing a loop, then an Exit Loop action is performed when the first record is reached; otherwise no action is taken. If the record pointer is already on the first page, FileMaker generates an error code of 101, which is not reported to the user.

Next moves to the next record in the current found set, displays the next find request, or moves to the next page of the currently displayed report. If the Exit After Last option is selected and the script is currently performing a loop, then an Exit Loop action is performed when the last record is reached; otherwise no action is taken. If the record pointer is already on the last page, FileMaker generates an error code of 101, which is not reported to the user.

By Calculation selects the record, find request, or report page determined by the designated calculation.

Examples:
```
# A very inefficient way of counting records
Go To Record/Request/Page [First]
Set Variable [$count; "0"]
Loop
    Set Variable [$count; $count + 1]
    Go To Record/Request/Page [Next; Exit After Last]
End Loop
# $count now contains the number of records in the found set.
# This could have been more easily accomplished by:
# Set Variable [$count; Get(FoundCount)]
```

Description:

This script step moves to a record in the found set if the file running the script is in Browse mode, to a find request if it is in Find mode, and to a report page if it is in Preview mode. This step can also be configured to exit a loop when either the first or last record has been reached.

Go to Related Record

Compatibility: 🍎 🪟 🌐

Menu Equivalent: None

Syntax: **Go to Related Record [From table: "<table name>";
    Using layout "<layout name>"]**

Options:

Get Related Record From allows the selection of a table that's related to the current table. If an appropriate table is not in the list or if you need to add or change a relationship, Define Database displays the Define Database dialog box, where you can create or edit relationships.

Use External Table's Layouts opens the file containing the external table you specify and displays any related record(s), using the specified layout in that file.

Show Record Using Layout displays related record(s), using the specified layout in the current file.

Show Related Records Only creates a found set in the related table containing only related records. For example, if you use this script step on a relationship that has four matching records in Table B for the current record in Table A, this option replaces any current found set in Table B with a new found set of just these four records. If the relationship has a sort order applied in the table occurrence to which you're navigating, this option causes the found set to be sorted by the relationship's sort criteria. If the Show Related Records Only option is not selected, the resulting found set is not sorted.

Match current record only will find only those records in the related table that are a match for the current record in the current table. This corresponds to the behavior of the Go To Related Records script step in previous versions of FileMaker.

Match all records in the current found set will find records in the related table that are a match for *any* record in the current found set in the current table. This capability is new in FileMaker 8.

Examples:
#The following example goes to a related record in the table "LineItems" and
shows a found set of related records only.
Go to Related Record [Show only related records;
From table: "LineItems"; Using layout: "List View"]

Description:

This script step goes to the table designated by the relationship selected in the script step, bringing its window to the foreground and selecting the first related record in the process. This step also works with portals. If a portal row is selected and the Go to Related Record step—specifying the portal's relationship—is executed, then the related table is brought to the forefront and the row that was selected in the portal corresponds to the record that is selected in the related table. This step may also use relationships to external files so that when the step is executed, the selected external file is opened and brought to the forefront, with its found set consisting of related records only. Further, if a layout was selected, then the records are displayed in that layout.

Comments:

This script step goes to one or more records in a related table (that is, a table that is related to the currently active table by one or more relationships in the Relationships Graph). There are a number of options to this script step, and they relate in somewhat complex ways. If more than one record in the target table is related to the current record in the table where the script is being called, FileMaker selects the first related record in the target table. If the relationship has a sort order on the target table, that sort order is used to determine which is the first of several related records. For example, if you have a table of Customers and a table of Orders, and a relationship between the two that is sorted on the Order side by OrderDate ascending, then the "first" related record when navigating from a specific customer to related orders is a given customer's earliest order. If the relationship has no sort order specified on the target table, then the first record is determined based on the creation order of the related records.

As part of this script step, you need to determine the layout that should be used to display the related records. Most likely, you'll want it to be a layout tied to a table occurrence that's based on the target table. If the target table is part of an externally referenced file, you may choose to display the records on a layout in the external file. If you choose to do so, that file comes to the forefront. You may also choose to display the related record set in a new window. If you choose to do so, you can specify a set of new window options, such as the window name, height, width, and screen position. One unfortunate limitation is that you can't direct the related records to appear in an existing window other than the currently active one. If you had to have that effect, you could select the desired target window, capture its name, dimensions, and positions into global fields, and then close that window and create a new window with exactly the same dimensions and use that as the target of this script step.

If the option to Show Related Records Only is checked, FileMaker creates a found set in the target table that contains only those records that are related to the current record or the current found set in the table in which the script is executing. For example, given a table of Salespeople and a table of Orders related to Salespeople by a SalespersonID field, if you issue a Go to Related Record[From table:"Orders"; Using layout "<Current Layout>"][Show only related records] while on a record in Salespeople, you end up with a found set of only those Orders related to the current Salesperson by the SalespersonID. If the option to Show Only Related Records is unchecked, the behavior is more complex: If there's a found set on the target layout and the first related record is within that found set, the found set is unchanged. If there's a found set on the target layout and the first related record is outside that found set, all records in the target table are found (though only the first related record is selected). If there is no found set on the target layout (that is, all records are currently found), that remains the case. No matter whether Show Related Records Only is checked or not, and no matter what the state of any found set on the target layout is, the first related record is always selected. If there are no related records, no navigation takes place, and a FileMaker Error of 101 is generated.

→ *For further discussion of the* Go To Related Records *script step,* **see** *Special Edition Using FileMaker 8, Chapter 15, "Advanced Scripting Techniques."*

Halt Script

Compatibility:

Menu Equivalent: None

Syntax: **Halt Script**

Options:

None

> *Examples:*
> # Example of using 'Halt Script' to return control immediately back to the user.
> Show Custom Dialog ["Print Report?"]
> If [Get (LastMessageChoice) = 2]
>   Halt Script
> End If
> Print[]

Description:

This script step causes all script activity to stop immediately. All scripts, subscripts, and external scripts are canceled and the system is left in whatever state it was in when the Halt step was executed. Halt Script is different from Exit Script in that the latter merely aborts the current subscript and allows the script that called the subscript to continue running, whereas the former stops all script activity, whether it is run from a subscript, a sub-subscript, and so on.

If

Compatibility: ⬤ ▯ ⊕

Menu Equivalent: None

Syntax: **If [<Boolean calculation>]**

Options:

Specify allows the definition of the Boolean calculation by which the If step determines its branching.

> *Examples:*
> If [gUsername = "Tom"]
>   Show Custom Dialog ["Hello Tom"]
> Else if [gUsername = "Raul"]
>   Show Custom Dialog ["Hola Raul"]
> Else If [gUsername = "Guido"]
>   Show Custom Dialog ["Ciao Guido"]
> Else
>   Show Custom Dialog ["I don't know who you are!"]
> End If

Description:

The If step introduces a block of conditional logic. It needs to be used with an End If statement and, optionally, one or more Else and Else If statements. This script step contains a calculation, which should perform a logical true/false test. If the specified Boolean calculation results in a 1 (or any number greater than 1), the specified action(s) will be performed. If the specified Boolean calculation results in a 0 (or nothing or any

non-number), then the specified action(s) will be skipped and control passed to the next
Else If or Else clause. If there are no more such clauses, then control passes to the End If
step and proceeds to any subsequent steps. Else If and Else clauses are optional. End If is
required when If is used.

Comments:

If you don't provide a Boolean test in the If step, it defaults to a result of False.

Import Records

Compatibility:  ▦

Menu Equivalent: File, Import Records

Syntax: **Import Records [No dialog; "<source or filename>";**
Add/Update existing/Update matching; <platform and character set>]

Options:

Perform Without Dialog prevents the display of FileMaker Pro's Import Records dialog box, which enables the user to select a file from which to import, to set new import
criteria, to map fields from import to target fields, and to see a summary of facts about
the import after it has been successfully completed.

Specify Data Source allows for the selection of the source for the data to be imported.
Data can be imported into FileMaker Pro from a file, a folder of files, a digital camera
(Mac OS), an XML data source, or an ODBC data source.

Specify Import Order allows the order in which FileMaker imports records to be set.
The last import order is used as the default for the subsequent import. This option allows
control of how FileMaker is to handle repeating field data, either by splitting it among
new records or keeping it together as a repeating field in the destination table. Also, the
import can be made to add new records with the imported data, to replace the records in
the found set with the imported data, or to attempt to reconcile data by matching keys
(ID fields).

Examples:
Import Records [Restore; No dialog; "Contacts"; Mac Helvetica]

Description:

This script step imports records from another file or data source specified either dynamically through the Import Records dialog or within the script step configuration itself.
Import order can be specified as either manually defined or based on matching field
names. (It is important to note that when import source fields and target fields are
mapped with matching names, field name matching is performed dynamically each time
the script step is performed.)

NEW FileMaker Pro 8 has the capability to create a new table in the target database when importing data. When this option is selected, the imported data will be used to create a new table. The field names in the new table will depend on the data source—if it's a data source, such as an XML file or an Excel file with headers, that contains field name information, FileMaker will use the provided field names. Otherwise, FileMaker will name the fields f1, f2, f3, and so on.

Note that this capability is different from the one in FileMaker Pro 8 Advanced to import table definitions from another file. That technique will import only the table definition, not any data within the table, whereas specifying a new table as an import target will always populate the new table with the imported data.

→ *For a full description of FileMaker's importing options,* **see** Special Edition Using FileMaker 8, Chapter 19, "Importing Data into FileMaker."

Insert Calculated Result

Compatibility: 🍎 📱 🌐

Menu Equivalent: None

Syntax: **Insert Calculated Result [Select; <table::field>; <formula>]**

Options:

Select Entire Contents replaces the contents of a field. If this option is not selected, Insert Calculated Result replaces only the selected portion of the current field, or inserts the result at the insertion point. The default insertion point is at the end of the field's data.

Go to Target Field allows the selection of the field into which the result of the specified calculation is to be inserted. The specified field must be available and modifiable on the current layout for this script step to operate properly.

Calculated Result allows the definition of a calculation whose result is inserted into the specified target field by this script step.

Examples:
Insert Calculated Result [Books::Author; Get(AccountName)]

Description:

This script step pastes the result of a calculation into the current (or specified) field on the current layout.

Comments:

In a web-published database, use a Commit Record/Request script step after an Insert Calculated Result script step to update the record in the browser window. All of the Insert... functions depend on the presence of fields on the current layout. If the correct field is not present, FileMaker will generate an internal error of 102.

Insert Current Date

Compatibility: ⚫ 📕 ⊕

Menu Equivalent: Insert, Current Date

Syntax: **Insert Current Date [Select; <table::field>]**

Options:

Select Entire Contents replaces the contents of the selected field with the current date. If this option is not selected, then the current date is appended to the end of the current contents of the field.

Go to Target Field allows for the selection of the field into which the current date will be inserted.

> *Examples:*
> New Record/Request
> Go To Layout ["Invoice"]
> Insert Current Date [Select; Invoices::Invoice Date]

Description:

This script step pastes the current system date into the specified field on the current layout.

Comments:

In a web-published database, use a Commit Record/Request script step after an Insert Current Date script step to update the record in the browser window. All the Insert... functions depend on the presence of fields on the current layout. If the correct field is not present, FileMaker generates an internal error of 102.

Insert Current Time

Compatibility: ⚫ 📕 ⊕

Menu Equivalent: Insert, Current Time

Syntax: **Insert Current Time [Select; <table::field>]**

Options:

Select Entire Contents replaces the contents of the selected field with the current time. If this option is not selected, then the current time is appended to the end of the current contents of the field.

Go to Target Field allows for the selection of the field into which the current time is to be inserted.

> *Examples:*
> New Record/Request
> Go To Layout ["Invoice"]
> Insert Current Date [Select; Invoices::Invoice Date]
> Insert Current Time [Select; Invoices::Invoice Time]

Description:

This script step pastes the current system time into the specified field on the current layout.

Comments:

In a web-published database, use a Commit Record/Request script step after an Insert Current Time script step to update the record in the browser window. All the Insert... functions depend on the presence of fields on the current layout. If the correct field is not present, FileMaker generates an internal error of 102.

Insert Current User Name

Compatibility: 🍎 🖥 ⊕

Menu Equivalent: Insert, Current User Name

Syntax: **Insert Current User Name [Select; <table::field>]**

Options:

Select Entire Contents replaces the contents of the selected field with the current username. If this option is not selected, then the current username is appended to the end of the current contents of the field.

Go to Target Field allows for the selection of the field into which the current user name is to be inserted.

> *Examples:*
> New Record/Request
> Go To Layout ["Invoice"]
> Insert Current Date [Select; Invoices::Invoice Date]
> Insert Current Time [Select; Invoices::Invoice Time]
> Insert Current User Name [Select; Invoices::Entered_By]

Description:

This script step pastes the current username into the specified field on the current layout.

Comments:

In a web-published database, use a Commit Record/Request script step after an Insert Current User Name script step to update the record in the browser window. All the Insert... functions depend on the presence of fields on the current layout. If the correct field is not present, FileMaker generates an internal error of 102.

Insert File

Compatibility: ♣ 🛒

Menu Equivalent: Insert, File

Syntax: **Insert File [Reference; <table::field>; "<filename>"]**

Options:

Store Only a Reference instructs FileMaker Pro to store only a link to a file in the container field, rather than the entire file. This option may reduce the size of your FileMaker Pro file, but if you move or delete the file being referenced, FileMaker Pro can't display it.

Select Go to Target Field or click Specify to specify the container field into which to insert the selected file.

Select Specify Source File or click Specify to designate the file to be inserted.

Examples:
Go To Field [Photos::Thumbnail]
Insert File ["house_thumb. jpg"]

Description:

This script step inserts a file into a selected container field on the current layout. Files may be stored in their entirety within FileMaker Pro, or you may choose to store only a file reference. File references certainly take up much less space within the database but they remove an element of control over a database's behavior. Files stored by reference can be moved or deleted, whereas this is much more difficult to achieve within FileMaker itself.

➔ *For more information on container fields, **see** Special Edition Using FileMaker 8, Chapter 3, "Defining and Working with Fields."*

Comments:

All the Insert... functions depend on the presence of fields on the current layout. If the correct field is not present, FileMaker generates an internal error of 102.

Insert from Index

Compatibility: ♣ 🛒

Menu Equivalent: Insert, From Index

Syntax: **Insert From Index [Select; <table::field>]**

Options:

Select Entire Contents replaces the contents of the selected field. If this option is not selected, then the selected index value is appended to the end of the current contents of the field if the field does not contain the cursor, or at the current cursor position if it does.

Go to Target Field allows for the selection of the field into which the selected index value is to be inserted.

Examples:
Enter Find Mode [ ]
Insert From Index [Users::User_Name]
Perform Find [ ]

Description:

This script step displays the index (if one exists) of the designated field in a dialog box and allows one of its values to be inserted into the field. If the Select Entire Contents option is selected, the contents of the field will be replaced with the selected value. If this option is not selected, then the value is inserted either at the position of the cursor in the field or appended to the end of the field's contents, depending on whether or not the field has the cursor in it. Note: If the specified field does not exist on the layout where the script is being performed or indexing has been disabled for the selected field, Insert from Index returns an error code, which can be captured with the Get(LastError) function.

Comments:

All the Insert... functions depend on the presence of fields on the current layout. If the correct field is not present, FileMaker generates an internal error of 102.

Insert from Last Visited

Compatibility: 🍎 🖥 🌐

Menu Equivalent: Insert, From Last Visited Record

Syntax: **Insert From Last Visited [Select; <table::field>]**

Options:

Select Entire Contents replaces the contents of the selected field. If this option is not selected, then the value from the last visited field is appended to the end of the current contents of the field if the field does not contain the cursor, or at the current cursor position if it does.

Go to Target Field allows for the selection of the field into which the last visited field value is to be inserted.

Examples:
Go to Record/Request/Page [Next]
Go to Field [Vendor Name]
Insert From Last Visited []
#Will use vendor from previous record

Description:

This script step pastes the value of the specified field from the same field in the last active record. This step is compatible with both Find and Browse mode. A record is considered as having been active if it has been operated upon by FileMaker Pro in some way.

Comments:

In a web-published database, use a Commit Record/Request script step after an Insert From Last Visited script step to update the record in the browser window. All the Insert... functions depend on the presence of fields on the current layout. If the correct field is not present, FileMaker generates an internal error of 102.

Insert Object

Compatibility: 🖩

Menu Equivalent: Insert, Object

Syntax: **Insert Object ["<object type>"]**

Options:

Specify displays the Insert Object dialog box.

Object Type allows the selection of the type of object to embed or link from the list of available file and application types.

Create New embeds a blank object of the specified object type.

Create from File allows the specification of the name of an existing file as the object to be embedded or linked.

When **Create from File** has been selected, **Link** can be selected to indicate that the object should be a linked object. When Link is not selected, the object is embedded instead.

Display As Icon tells FileMaker Pro not to display the embedded or linked object completely, but to display an icon that represents the object. The Change Icon button can be used to select a different icon for display. When **Display As Icon** is not selected, the complete object is displayed in the container field.

Examples:
Go to Field [Profile::Greeting]
Insert Object ["Video Clip"]

Description:

This Windows-specific script step allows the user, through the Insert Object dialog box, to select an OLE object and insert it into the current container field. If the specified object/file does not exist on the computer on which the script is being run, Insert Object returns an error code that can be captured with the Get(LastError) function.

Comments:

All of the Insert... functions depend on the presence of fields on the current layout. If the correct field is not present, FileMaker generates an internal error of 102. Insert Object works only on the Windows platform. Insert Object returns an error code if run on the Mac OS.

Insert Picture

Compatibility: 🍎 🪟

Menu Equivalent: Insert, Picture

Syntax: **Insert Picture [Select; <table::field>]**

Options:

Store Only a Reference to the File allows graphics to be stored by file system reference, thereby alleviating the need to store the actual image in the database. However, if the file is moved from the designated file path, FileMaker Pro can no longer display it.

Specify Source File or **Specify** allow the designation of the file path to the desired image file.

> *Examples:*
> Go to Field [Profile::Greeting]
> Insert Picture ["headshot.jpg"]

Description:

This script step imports an image file into the current container field. The desired field must be selected before this script is run. If the desired image file has not been specified, the user is given the Insert Picture dialog box.

Comments:

All the Insert... functions depend on the presence of fields on the current layout. If the correct field is not present, FileMaker generates an internal error of 102.

Insert QuickTime

Compatibility: 🍎 🪟

Menu Equivalent: Insert, QuickTime

Syntax: **Insert QuickTime ["<filename>"]**

Options:

Specify Source File or **Specify** allow the designation of the file path to the desired QuickTime file.

> *Examples:*
> Go to Field [Profile::Interview]
> Insert Picture ["Interview_Video"]

Description:

This step imports a QuickTime movie or sound file into the current container field. A container field must be selected before this step can function. If an appropriate QuickTime file has not been designated, a dialog box is presented to the user, through which she may select and preview the file to be imported. This step requires that QuickTime be installed on the system being used to import the desired file.

Comments:

All the Insert... functions depend on the presence of fields on the current layout. If the correct field is not present, FileMaker generates an internal error of 102.

Insert Text

Compatibility:

Menu Equivalent: None

Syntax: **Insert Text [Select; <table::field>; "<text>"]**

Options:

Select Entire Contents replaces the contents of a field. If this option is not selected, Insert Text inserts the specified value at the end of the field's data.

Use **Go to Target Field** or click **Specify** to specify the field to receive the pasted information. If no field is selected, the Insert Text command places the specified text after the insertion point. If no field is active at the time the command executes, it has no effect. If the selected field is not present on the current layout, the Insert Text command has no effect.

Specify displays the Specify dialog box where you can enter the text to be pasted.

Examples:
Insert Text [Select; Profile::Favorite_Color; "Red"]

Description:

This script step inserts text into the selected text field in the current record. If the Select Entire Contents option has not been selected, then the designated text is inserted at the cursor position or at the end of the field's contents, depending on whether or not there is a cursor in the field. The text to be inserted needs to be specified explicitly. If you want to insert variable text data, use the Insert Calculated Result script step or the Set Field script step.

Comments:

In a web-published database, use a Commit Record/Request script step after an Insert Text script step to update the record in the browser window. All the Insert... functions depend on the presence of fields on the current layout. If the correct field is not present, FileMaker generates an internal error of 102.

NEW Install Menu Set

Compatibility: ‍🍎 ▦

Menu Equivalent: None

Syntax: **Install Menu Set [specified menu set name]**

Options:

Use As File Default will cause the specified menu set to be used as the default menu set for the current file, for the duration of the current user session. The default menu set will be displayed in all circumstances where it is not overridden by a more specific menu set. Examples of "more specific" settings include menu sets that are specified at the individual layout level, and menu sets installed by later invocations of the Install Menu Set script step.

Examples:
```
# Install a user-specific menu set
If [$userRole = "Sales"]
   Install Menu Set["SalesMenus"]
Else
   Install Menu Set["RegularMenus"]
End If
```

Description:

This script step will install a new menu set based on the specified menu set name. This may be a custom menu set (defined by a developer using FileMaker Pro Advanced) or it may be the default FileMaker menu set.

Comments:

This script step affects only the current user. Others who may be using the file simultaneously will not see a change of menu sets, unless they too invoke a script containing this step. Likewise, when the current user closes the file, the effects of this step will be terminated.

Loop

Compatibility: 🍎 ▦ ⊕

Menu Equivalent: None

Syntax: **Loop**

Options:

None

```
Examples:
# Create 10 new blank records
Set Field [Table1::gCounter; "0"]
Loop
  New Record/Request
  Set Field [Table1::gCounter; Table1::gCounter + 1]
  Exit Loop If [gCounter > 10]
End
```

Description:

This script step marks the beginning of a Loop structure. The end of the Loop structure is defined by a matching End Loop step. Script control passes from the Loop step through all intervening steps to the End Loop step and back again until an Exit Loop directive is encountered or until a Halt Script or Exit Script step is encountered. The Exit Loop directive is available as an option with the Exit Loop If step, the Go To Record/Request/Page step, and the Go To Portal Row step. Loops are often used to perform an action over a group of records or portal rows.

Modify Last Find

Compatibility: 🍎 🖥 ⊕

Menu Equivalent: Records, Modify Last Find

Syntax: **Modify Last Find**

Options:

None

```
Examples:
Modify Last Find
Set Field [Contacts::Birthdate; "1/1/1974. . 1/1/1985"]
Perform Find[]
```

Description:

This script step activates Find mode and then recalls the last find request(s) used. The find request(s) may then be modified and executed with the Perform Find script step.

Move/Resize Window

Compatibility: 🍎 🖥

Menu Equivalent: None

Syntax: **Move/Resize Window [Current Window or Name: <name of window>; Height: <n>; Width: <n>; Top: <n>; Left: <n>]**

Options:

Specify allows the setting of the move/resize options.

Current Window causes the changes to be performed on the current window.

Window Name causes the changes to be performed on an open window, specified by name. Literal text may be entered or Specify clicked to create a window name from a calculation.

NEW **Current File Only** causes FileMaker to search only within windows based on table occurrences from within the current file.

Height is the height of the adjusted window in pixels. A number may be entered or Specify can be clicked to generate a number from a calculation.

Width is the width of the adjusted window in pixels. A number may be entered or Specify can be clicked to generate a number from a calculation.

Distance from Top is the adjusted window's distance in pixels from the top of the screen (Mac OS) or top of the FileMaker Pro window (Windows). A number may be entered or Specify clicked to generate a number from a calculation.

Distance from Left is the adjusted window's distance in pixels from the left of the screen (Mac OS) or left of the FileMaker Pro window (Windows). A number may be entered or Specify clicked to generate a number from a calculation.

Examples:
Move/Resize Window [Name:Invoices ; Height: 400; Width: 600; Top: 16; Left: 16]

Description:

This script step adjusts the size and location of the selected window. Every other aspect of the window, including found set, current table, and current record remain unchanged. Where an option is left without a value, the current value of that option is used. If position or size options exceed or fall below allowable minimums or maximums for a machine's particular operating system and configuration, the allowed minimums or maximums are used instead of the chosen values. In multiple-monitor environments, the use of negative position values makes it possible to position a window on monitors other than the main monitor. Note for Windows: FileMaker Pro orients the moved window to the top-left corner of the visible part of the application window. Note that this may not be the (0, 0) point of the window, depending on how the current file window is positioned (for example, if half of the file window extends past the left border of the application window, you would need to scroll to the left to see the [0, 0] point of the application window).

NEW **Current File Only** is a window management option that's new to FileMaker 8. In FileMaker 7, window management script steps could sometimes be "fooled" by the presence of windows from other files with the same name as the desired script step target, causing the script step to act on a window different from the desired one. In

FileMaker 8, the developer can restrict the scope of window management script steps to consider only windows based on the current file.

New File

Compatibility:

Menu Equivalent: File, New Database

Syntax: **New File**

Options:

None

Examples:
New File

Description:

This script step enables the user to create a new database file in FileMaker Pro's usual Create New File dialog box. If the Show Templates in New Database Dialog Box preference is selected, then the script step shows the New Database dialog box.

Comments:

The user is taken to the Define Database dialog. When he's finished defining the new database, and has closed the Define Database dialog, the script that invoked the New File command continues. The new database stays open, but it is not activated.

New Record/Request

Compatibility:

Menu Equivalent: Records, New Record

Syntax: **New Record/Request**

Options:

None

Examples:
```
# Create 10 new blank records
Set Variable [$counter; "0"]
Loop
  New Record/Request
  Set Variable [$counter; $counter + 1]
  Exit Loop If [$counter > 10]
End
```

Description:

This script step creates a new, blank record if the system is in Browse mode, and a new find request if the system is in Find mode.

Comments:

Note that this script step is context-dependent. The current layout determines which table is active, which determines in which table the record is created.

New Window

Compatibility: 🍎 🖥 ⊕

Menu Equivalent: Window, New Window

Syntax: **New Window [Name: <name of window>; Height: n; Width: n; Top: n; Left: n]**

Options:

Specify allows the setting of options for the new window.

Window Name is the name specified for the new window. Literal text may be entered or Specify clicked to create a window name from a calculation.

Height is the height of the new window in pixels. A number may be entered or Specify clicked to generate a number from a calculation.

Width is the width of the new window in pixels. A number may be entered or Specify clicked to generate a number from a calculation.

Distance from Top is the new window's distance in pixels from the top of the screen (Mac OS) or top of the FileMaker Pro window (Windows). A number may be entered or Specify clicked to generate a number from a calculation.

Distance from Left is the new window's distance in pixels from the left of the screen (Mac OS) or left of the FileMaker Pro window (Windows). A number may be entered or Specify clicked to generate a number from a calculation.

Examples:
New Window [Name: "Profile"; Height: 500; Width: 700; Top: 25; Left: 25]

Description:

This script step creates a new window based on the current window. The new window is the same as the current window except in the specified options. In the case where an option is left without a value, the default value (as specified in the Window menu, New Window command) for that option is used. If position or size options exceed or fall below allowable minimums or maximums for a machine's particular operating system and configuration, the allowed minimums or maximums are used instead of the chosen values. In multiple monitor environments, the use of negative position values makes it possible to position a window on alternate monitors. Note for Windows: FileMaker Pro orients the moved window to the top-left corner of the visible part of the application window. Note that this may not be the (0, 0) point of the window, depending on how the current file window is positioned. (For example, if half of the file window extends past the left border of the application window, you would need to scroll to the left to see the [0, 0] point of the application window.)

Omit Multiple Records

Compatibility: 🍎 🛒 🌐*

Menu Equivalent: Records, Omit Multiple

Syntax: **Omit Multiple Records [No dialog; <number of records>]**

Options:

Perform Without Dialog prevents a dialog box from displaying when the script step executes. Without this option selected, the user sees a dialog that allows the user to enter the number of records to be omitted.

When Perform Without Dialog is selected, if a number of records to omit is not specified, only the current record is omitted.

Selecting **Specify Records** or clicking **Specify** allows the entry of the exact number of records to omit. The Specify button may also be clicked in the Options dialog box to allow for the entry of a calculation. The calculation result must be a number.

Examples:
Perform Find [Restore]
Omit only the current record
Omit Multiple Records [No Dialog]

Description:

This script step omits the specified number of records from the found set, leaving the next available record as the current record. Omitted records are not deleted; they are just excluded from the found set. They remain in the database, as can be easily verified if you re-execute the Find Request that generated the found set in the first place.

Comments:

When programming for the Web, be sure to select Perform Without Dialog. Leaving the box unchecked is not web compatible and does not work on the Web.

Omit Record

Compatibility: 🍎 🛒 🌐

Menu Equivalent: Records, Omit Record

Syntax: **Omit Record**

Options:

None

Examples:
Omit records marked for omission
Go To Record/Request/Page [First]
Loop
 If [Contacts::Omit]
   Omit Record
 End If
 Go To Record/Request/Page [Next; Exit After Last]
End Loop

Description:

This script step omits the current record from the current found set when executed in Browse mode. The next available record becomes the new current record. Omitted records are not deleted. They are merely removed from the current found set. If this script step is executed while in Find mode, the current find request's Omit check box is toggled. (If it was checked, it will be unchecked and if it is unchecked it will be checked.) A find request that has the omit checkbox checked becomes an omit request that subtracts from rather than adds to the found set.

Open Define Database

Compatibility: ★ 🛒

Menu Equivalent: File, Define, Database

Syntax: **Open Define Database**

Options:

None

Examples:
If [Get (LastMessageChoice) = 1]
  #1=Yes, 2=No
   Open Define Database
End If

Description:

This script step opens the Define Database dialog box, where the user can create or edit tables, fields, and relationships. This script step is not performed if the user's account does not have the Full Access privilege set. (The script may be set to Run Script With Full Access Privileges in the ScriptMaker menu.) When the user closes the dialog box, the remaining steps in the script, if any, are executed.

Open Define File References

Compatibility: 🍎 🪟

Menu Equivalent: File, Define, File References

Syntax: **Open Define File References**

Options:

None

Examples:
Show Custom Dialog ["Do you want to create or edit a file reference?"]
If [Get (LastMessageChoice) = 1]
  #1=Yes, 2=No
  Open Define File References
End If

Description:

This script step opens the Define File References dialog box, where the user can create or edit references to files used throughout the database. This script step is not performed if the user's account does not have the Full Access privilege set. (The script may be set to Run Script With Full Access Privileges in the ScriptMaker menu.) When the user closes the dialog box, the remaining steps in the script, if any, are executed.

Open Define Value Lists

Compatibility: 🍎 🪟

Menu Equivalent: File, Define, Value Lists

Syntax: **Open Define Value Lists**

Options:

None

Examples:
Show Custom Dialog ["Do you want to create or edit a value list?"]
If [Get (LastMessageChoice) = 1]
  #1=Yes, 2=No
  Open Define Value Lists
End If

Description:

This script step opens the Define Value Lists dialog box, where the user can define new or edit existing value lists. This script step is not performed if the user's account does not have the Full Access privilege set. (The script may be set to Run Script With Full Access Privileges in the ScriptMaker menu.) When the user closes the dialog box, the remaining steps in the script, if any, are executed.

Open File

Compatibility: ⬤ ▥

Menu Equivalent: File, Open

Syntax: **Open File [Open hidden; "<filename>"]**

Options:

Open Hidden causes FileMaker Pro to open the specified database hidden (that is, with its window minimized).

Specify allows the selection of a FileMaker Pro database to be opened. Within the Specify menu, Add File Reference provides a dialog box to assist in the location and selection of a filename. After a file is selected, it is added to the Specify list. In the same menu, Define File References allows one to modify or delete a file reference already added to the list.

Examples:
Open File [Open Hidden; "Tempfile. fp7"]

Description:

This script step opens the specified file or allows the user to select a file to open in the Open File dialog box. The Open File dialog box is invoked when no file is specified in the script step or if the specified file cannot be found. The active file before the Open File step is executed remains active after it has completed.

Open File Options

Compatibility: ⬤ ▥

Menu Equivalent: File, File Options

Syntax: **Open File Options**

Options:

None

Examples:
Show Custom Dialog ["Open File Options dialog box?"]
If [Get (LastMessageChoice) = 1]
  #1=Yes, 2=No
  Open File Options
End If

Description:

This script step opens the File Options dialog box to the General Preferences area. This script step is not performed if the user's account does not have the Full Access privilege set. (The script may be set to Run Script With Full Access Privileges in the ScriptMaker menu.)

Open Find/Replace

Compatibility:

Menu Equivalent: Edit, Find/Replace, Find/Replace

Syntax: **Open Find/Replace**

Options:

None

```
Examples:
Show Custom Dialog ["Open the Find/Replace dialog box?"]
If [Get (LastMessageChoice) = 1]
  #1=Yes, 2=No
  Open Find/Replace
End If
```

Description:

This script step opens the Find/Replace dialog box. The remaining steps in the script, if any, are executed after the user closes the dialog box or completes a search.

Open Help

Compatibility:

Menu Equivalent: Help, FileMaker Pro Help

Syntax: **Open Help**

Options:

None

```
Examples:
Show Custom Dialog ["Do you want to open onscreen Help?"]
If [Get (LastMessageChoice) = 1]
  #1=Yes, 2=No
  Open Help
End If
```

Description:

This script step opens the FileMaker Pro Help system. By default, the user is placed in the Help System Contents screen.

Comments:

The Help dialog is non-modal, so any additional script steps after the Open Help step execute right away, possibly pushing the help window into the background.

Open Preferences

Compatibility: 🍎 🪟

Menu Equivalent: Edit, Preferences (Windows) or FileMaker Pro, Preferences (Mac OS)

Syntax: **Open Preferences**

Options:

None

```
Examples:
Show Custom Dialog ["Open Preferences dialog box?"]
If [Get (LastMessageChoice) = 1]
  #1=Yes, 2=No
  Open Preferences
End If
```

Description:

This script step opens the Preferences dialog box. The General Preferences area is selected by default.

Comments:

When the user closes the dialog box, the remaining steps in the script, if any, are executed.

Open Record/Request

Compatibility: 🍎 🪟 🌐

Menu Equivalent: None

Syntax: **Open Record/Request**

Options:

None

```
Examples:
Perform Find [Restore]
Go to Record/Request/Page [First]
Open Record/Request
If [ Get(LastError) = 200 or Get(LastError) = 300]
  Show Custom Dialog ["An error has ocurred. This record is locked or you do
  not have sufficient permission to access it."]
End If
```

Description:

This script step attempts to acquire exclusive access to the current record. Exclusive access prevents other users from editing the record. It has the same effect as a user selecting a data field on a layout (by clicking or tabbing) and then beginning to enter or edit field data. These actions either give exclusive access to that user or, if another user has already acquired exclusive access (otherwise known as a "lock"), the user attempting to gain control of the record sees an error message with a warning that another user has control of the record. It can be useful to try to gain exclusive access to a record in the course of a script. If you are looping over records and need to change each one, if a user is editing one of the records, your script may be prevented from changing it. Open Record/Request cannot override another user's access, but if the script step fails it generates an error that your script can inspect with the Get(LastError) statement.

Open Remote

Compatibility: 🍎 🪟

Menu Equivalent: File, Open Remote

Syntax: **Open Remote**

Options:

None

Examples:
Show Custom Dialog ["Do you want to look for a networked database?"]
If [Get (LastMessageChoice) = 1]
  #1=Yes, 2=No
  Open Remote
End If

Description:

This script step opens the Open Remote dialog box to allow the opening of a shared FileMaker Pro database over a network connection.

Comments:

When the user closes the dialog box, the remaining steps in the script, if any, are executed.

Open ScriptMaker

Compatibility: 🍎 🪟

Menu Equivalent: Scripts, ScriptMaker

Syntax: **Open ScriptMaker**

Options:

None

> *Examples:*
> Show Custom Dialog ["Open ScriptMaker?"]
> If [Get (LastMessageChoice) = 1]
>   #1=Yes, 2=No
>   Open ScriptMaker
> End If

Description:

This script step opens the ScriptMaker dialog box, which enables a user to create, edit, rename, and duplicate scripts. When this script step is performed, FileMaker halts the current script because if any currently executing scripts were to be edited, the resulting behavior could be unpredictable.

Open Sharing

Compatibility:

Menu Equivalent: Edit, Sharing, FileMaker Network (Windows) or FileMaker Pro, Sharing, FileMaker Network (Mac OS)

Syntax: **Open Sharing**

Options:

None

> *Examples:*
> Show Custom Dialog ["Do you want to open the sharing dialog?"]
> If [Get (LastMessageChoice) = 1]
>   #1=Yes, 2=No
>   Open Sharing
> End If

Description:

This script step opens the FileMaker Network Settings dialog box where users can configure network database sharing.

Open URL

Compatibility:

Menu Equivalent: None

Syntax: **Open URL [No dialog; <URL>]**

Options:

Perform Without Dialog prevents the Open URL Options dialog box from displaying when the script step executes.

Specify may be selected to display the Open URL Options dialog box, where the URL can be typed directly into the text entry area or created by a calculation.

> *Examples:*
> Open URL [No dialog; "http://www. apple. com/"]
> Open URL [No dialog; "file://c:/addresses. txt"]
> Open URL [No dialog; "mailto:no-one@name. net"]
> Open URL [No dialog; "fmp7://system:password@192. 168. 10. 46:591/WebDB"]
> #Note about the last example: "system" is the FileMaker Pro account name,
> "password" is that account's password, and "WebDB" is
> the FileMaker Pro filename.

Description:

This script step allows an URL to be opened in the appropriate application. Supported schemes include HTTP, FTP, file, mailto, HTTPS, and fmp7 for opening FileMaker files. FileMaker consults the operating system preferences to help decide which application to use to service a particular URL scheme.

Comments:

This could be one effective means to an asset management solution. If the solution stores only references to the files, and the files are stored in a web server directory, FileMaker can construct a full URL to the file based on the reference in the database, and bring the file up in the user's browser with an Open URL command.

When programming for the Web, be sure to select Perform Without Dialog. Leaving the box unchecked is not web compatible and does not work on the Web.

Paste

Compatibility: ⬛ 📖 ⊕

Menu Equivalent: Edit, Paste

Syntax: **Paste [Select; No style; <table::field>]**

Options:

Select Entire Contents replaces the contents of a field with the contents of the Clipboard. If Select Entire Contents is not used, Paste copies the contents of the Clipboard to the currently selected portion of the field.

Paste Without Style tells FileMaker Pro to ignore all text style and formatting associated with the Clipboard contents.

Select **Go to Target Field** or click **Specify** to specify the field into which to paste.

Link If Available (Windows only) tells FileMaker Pro to choose a link over other formats on the clipboard. If both a link and an embedded object are present on the clipboard, the link is selected. If a link is available, it is selected over other formats.

Examples:
Go to Record/Request/Page [First]
Copy [Select; Customer::ZipCode]
Loop
  Go to Record/Request/Page [Next; Exit after last]
  Paste [Select; No style; Customer::ZipCode]
End Loop

Description:

This script step pastes the contents of the clipboard into the specified field in the current record. If the data type of the data being pasted does not match the type of the field being pasted into, FileMaker Pro displays the customary validation alert when the record is committed. (It's also possible that the script that calls the Paste step may leave the record in an uncommitted state, in which case the error dialog appears later, when the record is committed.) If the field is not on the current layout, FileMaker Pro returns an error code, which can be captured with the Get(LastError) function. In a web-published database, use a Commit Record/Request script step after a Paste script step to update the record in the browser window.

Comments:

Paste is one of a number of script steps that depend on the presence of specific fields on the current layout. Other script steps with the same limitations include Cut, Copy, Paste, and Set Selection.

Pause/Resume Script

Compatibility: ◆ ▦ ⊕

Menu Equivalent: None

Syntax: **Pause/Resume Script [Duration (seconds) <n>]**

Options:

Specify displays the Pause/Resume Options dialog box, where the following options can be set.

Select Indefinitely to pause the script until the user clicks the Continue button in the Status Area.

Select For Duration to enter the number of seconds to pause the script.

Select For Duration and click Specify to create a calculation that determines the number of seconds to pause.

Examples:
Perform Find [Restore]
Pause/Resume Script [Indefinitely]
Set Field [Contacts::Status; "Ready for Review"]

Description:

This script step pauses a script for a specified period of time or indefinitely. This enables the user to perform data entry or other tasks before continuing the script. This step brings the active window of the file in which the script step is running to the foreground if it is not already there. The duration of a pause must be a number and represents the number of seconds that the pause will last before resuming execution for the script. Most FileMaker Pro menu options are not available to users while in a paused script. While paused, a script displays a Continue button in the status bar. The pause is terminated when a user clicks this button. There is also a Cancel button, which appears only if the Allow User Abort option is set to On. This button exits the currently running script. In the case where the status bar is hidden, the Enter key performs the same function as the Continue button. Buttons that run other scripts function while the current script is paused. A script run in this way is run as a subscript of the paused script.

Perform AppleScript

Compatibility: 

Menu Equivalent: None

Syntax: **Perform AppleScript ["<applescript text>"]**

Options:

Specify to display the Perform AppleScript Options dialog box, where the following options can be set:

Calculated AppleScript lets you draw the AppleScript code from the result of a calculation.

Native AppleScript allows you to enter an AppleScript by hand (up to 30,000 characters long).

Examples:
#This example sets the primary monitor to its minimum bit depth.
Perform AppleScript ["tell application "Finder" to set bounds of window "My Files" to {100, 100, 100, 100}"]

Description:

This script step sends AppleScript commands to an AppleScript-aware application. The AppleScript may be typed in manually or generated as the result of a specified calculation. Calculated scripts are compiled every time the script is run, whereas typed-in scripts are compiled only when the script is edited. Obviously, the latter is a faster process, but creating AppleScript code via a calculation provides much greater flexibility.

Comments:

Perform AppleScript is supported only on the Mac OS. The script step generates an error on Windows. For more information on AppleScript and AppleEvents, see the "Apple Events Reference" included with FileMaker Pro.

Perform Find

Compatibility:

Menu Equivalent: None

Syntax: **Perform Find [Restore]**

Options:

Select **Specify Find Requests** or click **Specify** to create or edit one or more find requests that will be stored with the script steps.

New opens a dialog box that enables you to create and specify a new find request to be stored with the script step.

Edit opens a selected find request from the existing list for editing.

Duplicate duplicates one or more selected find requests from the list and adds them to the stored set.

Delete deletes one or more selected find requests from the list.

Use the **Edit Find Request** dialog box to work with find request criteria.

Use **Find Records** or **Omit Records** to specify the behavior of the request. Selecting Omit Records is equivalent to checking the Omit check box in a find request in Find mode. Finding records adds them to the current found set. Omitting records excludes them. As in Find mode, use multiple requests if it's necessary to both find and omit records in the course of a single stored search.

Find Records When (or **Omit Records When**) shows a list of the fields in your current table. To construct a find request, begin by selecting a field from this list.

To select a field from a related table, click the name of the current table at the top of the list and select the related table you want. Select a related field from this new list.

Change the value in Repetition to specify a particular cell of a repeating field.

Type the search criteria for the selected field in the Criteria area.

Click Add to add criteria to the find request.

To change existing criteria, select the line containing the field and criteria from the top of the dialog box, and make the changes to the field and/or criteria. Click Change to store changes.

To delete existing criteria, select the line containing the field and criteria from the top of the dialog box and click Remove.

Examples:
```
Set Error Capture [On]
Perform Find [Restore]
#check for a "no records" error
If [Get (LastError) = 401]
   Show Custom Dialog ["Sorry, no records were found. "]
End If
```

Description:

This script step places the system in Find mode and performs the search request(s) that have been designated for this step. If no find requests have been designated, then the last find request(s) that the system performed is performed. If the system is in Find mode when Perform Find is executed, then the currently entered find request is performed. This behavior is often used in conjunction with the Enter Find Mode step with the Pause option selected to allow a user to define a search request or group of search requests and then perform them. If FileMaker Pro doesn't find any records that match the find criteria when a script is performed, the script can be stopped, execution of the script can be resumed with zero records in the current found set, and the find criteria can be changed. With the Set Error Capture script step and the Get(LastError) function, a script to handle such situations can be written.

Perform Find/Replace

Compatibility: 🍎 🖥

Menu Equivalent: None

Syntax: **Perform Find/Replace [No dialog; "\<text to be found>";
"\<replacement text>"; Find Next/Replace & Find/Replace/Replace All]**

Options:

Perform Without Dialog inhibits the display of the Find/Replace Summary dialog box at the end of the Find/Replace operation. This option also prevents display of the confirmation dialog box when a Replace All operation is executed.

If it is desired that the user be able to enter find or replace criteria, use the Open Find/Replace script step.

Specify displays the Specify Find/Replace dialog box, where search options, as well as the type of find/replace operation to be performed, can be set.

Examples:
Perform Find/Replace ["hte"; "the"; Replace All]

Description:

This script step looks for the specified text in one or more fields and records of the current found set and, if directed, replaces it with either literal text or the result of a calculation. The scope of the operation can be defined to be the current record or the entire found set. The Find/Replace can span all fields in a layout or just the current field. The operation can be defined to proceed forward or backward in the current found set (as sorted). Finally, options are available for the matching of whole words only instead of parts of words, and for the matching of case.

Perform Script

Compatibility: 🍎 🗔 ⊕

Menu Equivalent: None

Syntax: **Perform Script ["<script name>"; Parameter: <parameter>]**

Options:

To select a script, click Specify and choose the script from the list.

Specify a script parameter using the optional script parameter choice. You can specify the parameter as text, or click Edit and specify the parameter by means of a calculation formula.

Examples:
Go to Layout ["Detail"]
Perform Script ["Find Contact"; Parameter: Contact::ContactID]

Description:

This script step performs a script either in the current file or in another FileMaker Pro file. Scripts can be as simple or as complex as is required, but it is often more efficient to break larger scripts into smaller subscripts for ease of re-use, testing, and debugging. Script parameters allow scripts to communicate with one another without having to use database fields or globals. The script parameter may be accessed with the Get(ScriptParameter) function. It is important to note that script parameters exist only within a script into which they have been explicitly passed. For a subscript to have access to the parameter of the script that called it, it must, in turn, be passed into the subscript. Script parameters exist for only as long as the script to which they are passed exists. Parameter strings can contain many pieces of information as long as they are properly separated. Carriage returns and separator characters are common ways to pass many pieces of information in a parameter string.

→ *For more information about using script parameters and subscripts in programming,* **see** Special Edition Using FileMaker 8, *Chapter 15, "Advanced Scripting Techniques."*

NEW In FileMaker Pro 8, you can also return a value from a script when exiting the script. For more information, see the Exit Script step.

Print

Compatibility: 🍎 🗔

Menu Equivalent: File, Print

Syntax: **Print [Restore; No dialog]**

Options:

Perform Without Dialog prevents a dialog box from displaying when the script step executes. Ordinarily, users would see a dialog box permitting them to use their own settings. When this option is selected, FileMaker Pro uses the print settings that are stored with the script step.

Select **Specify Print Options** or click **Specify** to open the Print dialog box and set generic printing options, including the printer, number of copies, and the pages to print. FileMaker Pro can also set printing options such as printing the current record, printing records being browsed, or printing a blank record.

Examples:
Go To Layout ["Detail View"]
Show All Records
Sort Records [Restore; No dialog]
Print Setup [Restore; No dialog]
Print []

Description:

This script step prints selected information from a FileMaker Pro file. This information can include field contents, reports based on database data, and field or script definitions. Print setup settings are stored with the script step, but may be changed with the Print Setup script step. Multiple Print Setup steps may be used in a single script.

Comments:

Printer settings generally do not transfer well between platforms. Unless your settings are very generic, you may need to separate Print or Print Setup steps for each platform you intend to support. You may need to check the current user's platform with Get(SystemPlatform) and use separate print setups for each different platform.

Print Setup

Compatibility:

Menu Equivalent: File, Print Setup (Windows); File, Page Setup (Mac OS)

Syntax: **Print Setup [Restore; No dialog]**

Options:

Perform Without Dialog prevents a dialog box from displaying when the script step that lets the user enter new printing options executes. When this option is selected, FileMaker Pro uses the print settings that are stored with the script step.

Select **Specify Print Options** or click **Specify** to open the Print dialog box and set generic printing options, including the printer, number of copies, and the pages to print. FileMaker Pro can also set printing options such as printing the current record, printing records being browsed, or printing a blank record.

Examples:
Go To Layout ["Detail View"]
Show All Records
Sort Records [Restore; No dialog]
Print Setup [Restore; No dialog]
Print []

Description:

This script step sets printing options such as the printer, print layout, number of copies, and so on, all of which can be saved within the script step. There is the option to allow the user to modify the print setup by presenting him or her with the Print Setup dialog box. Multiple Print Setup steps may be used in a single script.

Comments:

Printer settings generally do not transfer well between platforms. Unless your settings are very generic, you may need separate Print or Print Setup steps for each platform you intend to support. You may need to use Get(SystemPlatform) to check the current user's platform and use separate print setups for each different platform.

Re-Login

Compatibility: 🍎 🖥 ⊕

Menu Equivalent: None

Syntax: **Re-Login [Account Name: <account name>; Password: <password>; No dialog]**

Options:

Perform Without Dialog prevents the Open File dialog box from displaying when the script step executes. When this option is unchecked, users see a normal FileMaker authentication dialog. When this option is checked, FileMaker Pro uses the account and password information that is stored with the script step, or derives the information from calculations.

Click **Specify** to display the Re-Login Options dialog box, where you can set the following options:

Account Name is the name of the account to be authenticated. This may be entered as literal text, or Specify can be clicked to create a new account name from a calculation.

Password is the password for this account. Literal text may be entered or Specify clicked to create a new password from a calculation.

Examples:
Re-Login [Account Name:"User"; Password:"Password"; Nodialog]

Description:

This script step allows a user to log in to the current database with a different account name and password. This does not require the database file to be closed or reopened. Privileges assigned to the new account take effect immediately, including access to tables, records, layouts, scripts, and value lists. Users get five attempts to enter an account and password, unless the Set Error Capture script step is enabled. If the Set Error Capture script step is enabled, users get a single attempt to enter an account and password. If a user fails the allotted number of times, she must close and reopen the database file before she can try to access the database again.

Comments:

This script step can be a very handy development aid. When developing a system with several privilege levels, you'll want to test the system's functions at each privilege level. It can be very beneficial to create Re-login scripts to allow you to instantly switch privilege levels without actually logging out of the file(s).

When programming for the Web, be sure to select Perform Without Dialog. Leaving the box unchecked is not web compatible and does not work on the Web.

Recover File

Compatibility: 🍎 🖥

Menu Equivalent: File, Recover

Syntax: **Recover File [No dialog; "<filename>"]**

Options:

Perform Without Dialog prevents a dialog box from displaying after the script step completes. Ordinarily, users would see a dialog box that shows how many bytes of data were recovered, the number of records and field values skipped, and the number of field definitions recovered.

Select **Specify Source File** or click **Specify** to display a dialog box where you can select the file to be recovered. If you don't select a source file, the Open Damaged File dialog box displays when the script is run.

> *Examples:*
> Recover File [No Dialog; "DataFile.fp7"]

Description:

This script step recovers damaged FileMaker Pro files. In the recovery process, FileMaker Pro attempts to repair and recover as much of the information in a damaged file as is possible. It then creates a new file and saves it to the selected directory. The original file is not deleted or replaced. The new recovered file is named exactly as the damaged file except "Recovered" is appended to its filename, before any extenders. For example, the recovery of DataFile.fp7 would produce the file DataFile Recovered.fp7.

Comments:

Recover File is intended only to recover data from a corrupted file. It does not remove any corruption that may be present in the file, nor does it necessarily render the file fit for production use again. You should try to avoid reusing a file that has been recovered. Import the extracted data into the most recent clean backup of the file and discard the recovered version.

NEW FileMaker Server 8 includes a new "aggressive" consistency check routine that is able to detect many forms of file corruption. Accordingly, FileMaker, Inc. has somewhat softened their longstanding advice against ever reusing a recovered file. If a file successfully passes FileMaker Server 8's consistency check, the file may be deemed fit for production use.

We find this new capability exciting, but the reader should note that this capability is not yet extensively field-tested.

Refresh Window

Compatibility:

Menu Equivalent: None

Syntax: **Refresh Window**

Options:

NEW **Flush cached join results** will cause data for related records displayed in the current window to be refreshed. Choose this option if your script may have changed related data and you want to make sure the new data are visible after the screen refresh. If your script won't change related data, you may avoid a performance hit by leaving the option unchecked.

Examples:
Freeze Window
Go to Record/Request/Page [First]
Give everyone a 10% raise.
Loop
  Set Field [Employee::Salary; Employee::Salary * 1.1]
  Go to Record/Request/Page [Next; Exit after last]
End Loop
Refresh Window

Description:

This script step updates the active FileMaker Pro document window. Use Refresh Window after Freeze Window to update a window.

Comments:

This step may also be used to force a portal to refresh after match fields (such as keys or other IDs) have been modified. It may also happen that complex related data is slow to refresh in a window, or user interaction—such as a mouse click—may be required to show the changed data. If you find such behavior, you may be able to cure it with an explicit Refresh Window step. (Note that for this application you must make sure to select the **Flush cached join results** option.)

Relookup Field Contents

Compatibility:

Menu Equivalent: Records, Relookup Field Contents

Syntax: **Relookup Field Contents [No dialog; <table::field>]**

Options:

Perform Without Dialog prevents the display of a dialog box that lets the user confirm field information from displaying when the script step executes.

Select **Go to Target Field** or click **Specify** to specify the field that is the match field of the relookup operation. FileMaker Pro moves the cursor to the field you specify. This must be the match field for the relationship upon which the lookup is based, not the lookup source or target field. If no field is selected, Relookup Field Contents returns an error code.

> *Examples:*
> Relookup Field Contents [No dialog, Invoice::Customer ID]

Description:

Use Relookup to "refresh" values that are copied from one place to another via the Lookup field option. It's important to realize that you must specify the field that's the *match field* for the lookup operation, rather than any of the fields that will receive the newly copied data. As an example, imagine you have a system with a Customer table and an Invoice table. The two tables are related by a shared CustomerID. The Invoice table also has fields for Customer Name and Customer Address, which are defined to look up the corresponding fields from the related Customer record. To "refresh" the customer name and address information on one or more invoices, it would be necessary to specify the Customer ID field in Invoices, which is the match field that links the two tables, rather than specify either of the two fields intended to receive the refreshed data. Note that the relookup operates only on records in the current found set.

Comments:

When programming for the Web, be sure to select Perform Without Dialog. Leaving the box unchecked is not web compatible and does not work on the Web.

→ *For further discussion of lookups and other auto-entry options,* **see** Special Edition Using FileMaker 8, *Chapter 3, "Defining and Working with Fields."*

Replace Field Contents

Compatibility: ⌘ ▓ ⊕*

Menu Equivalent: Records, Replace Field Contents

Syntax: **Replace Field Contents [No Dialog; <table::field>; Current contents/ Serial numbers/Calculation results]**

Options:

Perform Without Dialog prevents display of the Replace Field Contents dialog box when the script step executes.

Select **Go to Target Field** or click **Specify** to specify the target field for the replace operation.

Click **Specify** to display the Replace Contents dialog box, where you can determine the settings required for the Replace Field Contents command so that they'll be stored in the script.

Replace with Current Contents uses the current value in the specified field as the replacement value to place in that field in every other record in the current found set.

Replace with Serial Numbers updates the field with new serial numbers in every record in the current found set.

Entry Options causes FileMaker to consult the underlying database structure to determine how to serialize records. In particular, it causes the Replace step to use the database field settings for Next Value and Increment by, as stored in the field options for that field.

Custom Values lets you enter a value to be used as a starting point for the serialization, as well as a value by which to increment each serialized field in the current found set.

Update Serial Number in Entry Options resets the serial number value in the entry options for the field, so that the next serial number that is automatically entered follows the records you have reserialized with this script step. If this option is not used, the serial value in Entry Options is not changed, and may not be in sequence with the newly reserialized records. This may lead to duplicated serial numbers or data validation errors.

If the field to be replaced was set up for auto-entry of a serial number and Prohibit Modification of Value is not selected, FileMaker Pro still puts sequential numbers in the selected field, but does so starting with the next number to be automatically entered.

Replace with Calculated Result displays the Specify Calculation dialog box, where you can enter a calculation to be used as the replacement value.

Examples:
\# Fill in full names
Replace Field Contents [No Dialog; Contacts::FullName; FirstName & " " &LastName]

Description:

This script step replaces the contents of a selected field in the current record or every record in the found set with some value—the value of the field on the current record, a set of serial numbers, or a calculated result. This step can also be used to reserialize a field in every record in the found set. Note that if the specified field does not exist on the layout where the script is being performed, Replace Field Contents returns an error code which can be captured with the Get(LastError) function.

Comments:

It may be helpful to think of this step as being akin to filling in multiple cells in a spreadsheet column. Replace is particularly powerful when used in conjunction with a calculation (a technique often known as a *calculated replace*). The calculation can reference fields, which refer to the field values in whichever is the current record. So in a database with fields for FirstName and LastName, you could create an additional text field called FullName, and use a calculated replace to insert the results of a formula concatenating first and last names together with a space in between.

Reset Account Password

Compatibility:  ⊞ ⊕

Menu Equivalent: None

Syntax: **Reset Account Password [Account Name: <account name>; New Password: <password>; Expire password]**

Options:

Click **Specify** to display the Reset Account Password Options dialog box.

Account Name is the name of the account with the password to be reset. You can enter literal text or click Specify to create a new account name from a calculation.

New Password is the new password for this account. Literal text may be entered or Specify clicked to create a new password from a calculation.

When **User Must Change Password on Next Login** is selected, this option forces users to change their password the next time they log in to the database.

Examples:
Reset Account Password [Account Name:"Guest User"; New Password:"guestpassword"; Expire password]

Description:

This script step resets the account password for the selected account. The selected account must be existing. The Full Access privilege set is needed to perform this script step. The Run with Full Access Privileges option may be selected in the ScriptMaker dialog box to circumvent this restriction for all users.

Comments:

Be aware that using **User Must Change Password on Next Login** does not work correctly when users log in to a solution via the Web. It's also important to make sure that any user with that restriction can modify his password (so take care, for example, when using this option with accounts that are externally authenticated).

→ *For further discussion, **see** Special Edition Using FileMaker 8, Chapter 12, "Implementing Security."*

Revert Record/Request

Compatibility: ♣ ▥ ⊕*

Menu Equivalent: Records, Revert Record

Syntax: **Revert Record/Request [No dialog]**

Options:

Perform Without Dialog inhibits the display of a confirmation dialog when the script step executes.

Examples:
Show Custom Dialog ["Do you want to save your changes?";
"Click 'Save' to save your changes, or 'Revert' to
return the record to its original state."]
#1 = Save, 2 = Revert
If [Get(LastMessageChoice) = 1]
Commit Records/Requests
Else
    Revert Record/Request [No dialog]
End If

Description:

This script step discards changes made to a record and its fields, assuming the record has not been saved. After changes have been committed, such as through use of the Commit Records/Requests script step, they can no longer be reverted. This is also true if a user has clicked outside of any field.

Comments:

Note that record reversion applies not only to the current record on whatever layout is being viewed, but also to any records in related tables that are displayed in a portal on the current layout. If a user has edited one or more records in a portal, the Revert Record/Request script step, if carried out, undoes all uncommitted changes to portal records, as well as any uncommitted changes to the current record.

When programming for the Web, be sure to select Perform Without Dialog. Leaving the box unchecked is not web compatible and does not work on the Web.

Save a Copy As

Compatibility: ⬤ 🖳

Menu Equivalent: File, Save a Copy As

Syntax: **Save a Copy as ["<filename>"; copy/compacted/clone]**

Options:

Specify Output File displays the Specify Output File dialog box, which allows specification of the name and location of the resulting copy. If a save location is not specified in the script, FileMaker Pro displays a regular Save As dialog box so the user can specify copying options.

Use **Specify** to choose a save format: copy of current file, compacted copy (smaller), or clone (no records).

> *Examples:*
> Save a Copy as ["Customers. bak"]

Description:

This script step saves a copy of the current file to the designated location. If no location is designated, a dialog box is presented to the user. Three types of copies are available. **Copy** creates an exact replica of the current file. **Compressed** also creates a copy of the current file, but the copy will be compressed to utilize space more efficiently. This sort of copy takes longer to create but is generally smaller than the original. **Clone** creates a file that's structurally identical to the current database but contains no data. This is useful for backup purposes because clones are very compact.

🔷 Save Records As Excel

Compatibility: ⬤ 🖳

Menu Equivalent: File, Save/Send Records As Excel

Syntax: **Save Records As Excel [No dialog; "<output filename>"; Automatically open; Create email; Current records]**

Options:

Perform Without Dialog will prevent certain dialog boxes from appearing as the script step executes. If you have specified a file and stored that information with the script step, no dialog boxes will display. If you have not saved output file information with the script step, the Save Records as Excel dialog box will display (but the Excel options dialog still will not).

Specify Output File will allow you to save a file path with the script step. This file path will be used to determine where the new file should be saved. When specifying the output file you can also choose to **Automatically Open File**, in which case the file will be opened once created, or choose **Create Email with File As Attachment** to create a new blank email, with the Excel file as an attachment, using the local machine's default email software.

Specify Options will allow you to set a number of useful properties of the output file, such as which database records should be included, whether the first row should contain field names, and worksheet properties such as title and author.

Examples:
Go To Layout ["Customer List"]
Show All Records
Save Records as Excel [No dialog; "Customer_List.xls"]

Description:

This script step allows you to save a set of records directly to an Excel spreadsheet. With appropriate selections of options, you can also automatically open the file or attach it to an email.

Comments:

This and similar script steps are even more powerful when combined with FileMaker 8's new capability to specify output file paths dynamically using script variables.

→ *For further discussion of the new document publishing features in FileMaker 8,* **see** *Special Edition Using FileMaker 8, Chapter 10, "Getting Started with Reporting."*

→ *For further discussion of dynamically specified file paths,* **see** *Special Edition Using FileMaker 8, Chapter 15, "Advanced Scripting Techniques."*

🌟 Save Records as PDF

Compatibility: 🍎 🪟

Menu Equivalent: File, Save/Send Records As PDF

Syntax: **Save Records As PDF [No dialog; "<output filename>"; Automatically open; Create email; Current records]**

Options:

Perform Without Dialog will prevent certain dialog boxes from appearing as the script step executes. If you have specified a file and stored that information with the script step, no dialog boxes will display. If you have not saved output file information with the script step, the Save Records As PDF dialog box will display (but the PDF options dialog still will not).

Specify Output File will allow you to save a file path with the script step. This file path will be used to determine where the new file should be saved. When specifying the output file you can also choose to **Automatically Open File**, in which case the file will be opened once created, or choose **Create Email with File As Attachment** to create a new blank email, with the PDF file as an attachment, using the local machine's default email software.

Specify Options will allow you to set a number of useful properties of the output file, such as which database records should be included, and a variety of properties such as document author and PDF security settings.

→ *For further discussion of the new document publishing features in FileMaker 8,* **see** *Special Edition Using FileMaker 8, Chapter 10, "Getting Started with Reporting."*

Examples:
Go To Layout ["Customer List"]
Show All Records
Save Records as PDF [No dialog; "Customer_List.xls"]

Description:

This script step allows you to save a set of records directly to a PDF document. With appropriate selections of options, you can also automatically open the file or attach it to an email.

Comments:

This and similar script steps are even more powerful when combined with FileMaker 8's new capability to specify output file paths dynamically using script variables.

Scroll Window

Compatibility:

Menu Equivalent: None

Syntax: **Scroll Window [Home/End/Page Up/Page Down/To Selection]**

Options:

Use **Specify** to choose a scrolling option.

Home, **End**, **Page Up**, or **Page Down** scrolls the window to the beginning, to the end, up a page, or down a page.

To Selection brings the current field into view (similar to tabbing into a field).

Examples:
Go to Field["Scroll Right"]
Scroll Window [To Selection]
#The next step just makes sure we leave the "scroll to" field
Commit Records/Requests

Description:

This script step scrolls a window to its top or bottom, up or down, or to a specified field.

Comments:

You may want to use this script step for rapid, easy scrolling within a window. For example, if you've had to design a layout that's wider than some users' screens, you can put dummy "scroll left/scroll right" fields at the far left and right sides of the layout. If you make the field small and forbid entry, the user will not notice them. Then a script like the preceding example scrolls quickly to the right side of the window (assuming the field is placed somewhere to the right).

Select All

Compatibility: 🍎 🗔 ⊕

Menu Equivalent: Edit, Select All

Syntax: **Select All**

Options:

None

Examples:
Go To Field [Contacts::Statement]
Select All
Copy []
Go To Field [Contacts::PreviousStatement]
Paste[]

Description:

This script step selects the entire contents of the current field.

Select Dictionaries

Compatibility: 🍎 🗔

Menu Equivalent: Edit, Spelling, Select Dictionaries

Syntax: **Select Dictionaries**

Options:

None

Examples:
Select Dictionaries
Check Record

Description:

This script step opens the Select Dictionaries dialog box. This is often used to give users access to the Select Dictionaries dialog box when access to the FileMaker Pro menus has been restricted.

Select Window

Compatibility: ● ▥ ⊕

Menu Equivalent: None

Syntax: **Select Window [Current window or Name:<name of window>; Current file]**

Options:

Current Window brings the active window of the file that contains the script to the foreground.

Otherwise, click **Specify** to select the window FileMaker Pro should bring to the foreground. The name may be typed as literal text, or derived from a calculation.

NEW **Current File Only** is a window management option that's new to FileMaker 8. In FileMaker 7, window management script steps could sometimes be "fooled" by the presence of windows from other files with the same name as the desired script step target, causing the script step to act on a window different from the desired one. In FileMaker 8, the developer can restrict the scope of window management script steps to consider only windows based on the current file.

Examples:
Select Window [Name: "Contract Players"]

Description:

This script step specifies a window by name and makes it the current window. FileMaker Pro script steps are always performed in the foreground table. It is, therefore, sometimes necessary to bring a specific window to the front. Use this script step when working with scripts in multitable files to make certain that a script step is performed in the intended table. (You may also need to use a Go to Layout step to establish context correctly.) The Select Window script step does not open a window of a related file when the related file is open in a hidden state, such as when a file is opened, because it is the source file of a related field. The related file must be explicitly opened with the Open File script step before its windows are allowable targets for the Select Window step.

Send DDE Execute

Compatibility: 🀫

Menu Equivalent: None

Syntax: **Send DDE Execute [<topic text or filename>; <service name>]**

Options:

Click **Specify** to display the Send DDE Execute Options dialog box.

Service Name is the name of the application that will execute any specified commands. Refer to the documentation for the specified application to find the valid service name. The service name may be entered directly as text, or Specify can be clicked to create the service name from a calculation.

Topic is a filename or text string that describes the topic on which the application executes the commands. Refer to the documentation for the application specified in the Service Name to determine valid topics. Enter the topic name directly as text, or click Specify to create the topic name from a calculation.

Commands are calculated values or text strings that specify what the application does. Refer to the documentation for the application specified in the Service Name to determine valid commands and formats. Enter the commands directly as text or click Specify to create the commands from a calculation.

Examples:
Send DDE Execute [Service Name: "iexplore"; Topic: "WWW_OpenURL"; Commands: "www.soliantconsulting.com"]

Description:

This script step sends a DDE (Dynamic Data Exchange) command to another DDE-aware application. FileMaker can send DDE commands but cannot receive them. When a FileMaker Pro script first establishes a DDE connection, the connection stays open to execute subsequent script steps for the same service name and topic. If the script includes another DDE Execute script step that specifies a different service name or topic, FileMaker Pro closes the current connection and opens another with the new service name and topic. All open connections close when the script is completed.

Send Event (Windows)

Compatibility: 🀫

Menu Equivalent: None

Syntax: **Send Event ["<aevt>"; "<event name>"; "<filename>"]**

Options:

Click **Specify** to display the Send Event Options dialog box.

For **Send the <*Event Name*> Message**, select

- **Open Document/Application** to tell FileMaker Pro to open a document file or application. The application that Windows has associated with the document's file type is used to open it.
- **Print Document** to tell FileMaker Pro to print a document in another application.

Select **File** or click **Specify** to specify a document/application to open or a document to print.

Select **Calculation** or click **Specify** to create a message from a calculation.

Select **Text** to manually enter text for the message to be sent.

Select **Bring Target Application to Foreground** to activate the target application and display it on the screen. Displaying the target application can slow down the performance of a script. If Bring Target Application to Foreground is not selected, the event is performed in the background.

Examples:
#To launch the Notepad application, select the open document/application message, click File, and specify notepad.exe. The following script step appears in the Script Definition dialog box:
Send Message ["NOTEPAD. EXE ", "aevt", "odoc"]

Description:

This script step communicates with other Windows applications. It can instruct them to either open or print a document in its associated application. Custom code written in a language such as C or BASIC can be executed this way.

Send Event (Mac OS)

Compatibility:

Menu Equivalent: None

Syntax: **Send Event ["<Target Application>"; "<Event Class>"; "<Event ID>", "<Document or Calculation or Script Text>"]**

Options:

Click **Specify** to display the Send Event Options dialog box.

Send The <*Value*> Event With offers a choice between the following:

- **Open Application** tells FileMaker Pro to open an application. Click Specify Application to select the application.
- **Open Document** tells FileMaker Pro to open a document in the target application. You can also specify a calculated value or script.

- **Do Script** tells FileMaker Pro to perform a script in the language of the target application. Click Specify Application to select an application, and use Document to select the document to use with the target application. Or select Script Text and enter script text or type in the name of the script. (Make sure it is one that will be recognized by the target program.)

- **Other** displays the Specify Event dialog box, where you can manually enter the Apple Event class and Event ID.

Select **Document** or click **Specify** to select the document you want used with the target application.

Select **Calculation** or click **Specify** to create a calculation that generates a value you want to send with the event.

Bring Target Application to Foreground activates the target application and displays it on the screen. Displaying the target application can slow down the performance of a script. If Bring Target Application to Foreground is not selected, the event is performed in the background.

Wait for Event Completion Before Continuing tells FileMaker Pro to wait until the event is finished before continuing. If you don't want to wait until the event is completed, deselect this option.

Copy Event Result to the Clipboard copies the resulting events data to the Clipboard, from which it can later be retrieved. This option is disabled if Bring Target Application to Foreground is selected.

Click **Specify Application** to display a dialog box where you can select the target application.

Examples:
Send Event ["TextEdit", "aevt", "oapp"]

Description:

This script step sends an Apple Event to another Apple Event–aware application. The desired event is selected in the Send Event Options dialog box. When FileMaker Pro sends an Apple Event, it sends text (not compiled) data. You must know what information the target application expects to receive with an event. Each Send Event script step sends one event. You can include more than one Send Event in a script.

Send Mail

Compatibility: 🍎 🪟

Menu Equivalent: None

Syntax: **Send Mail [No dialog; To: <to>; CC: <CC>; BCC: <BCC>; Subject: <subject>; Message: <message>; "<attachment>"]**

Options:

Perform Without Dialog instructs FileMaker Pro to put the composed email message in the email application's Out box, ready to be sent. If this option is not selected, the composed message is left open in the email application so that it can be reviewed. In Microsoft Outlook Express or Microsoft Entourage on the Macintosh operating system, the new message is left in the Drafts folder.

Click **Specify** to display the Specify Mail dialog box, where options for mail can be set. For each of the following options, one can enter text directly, or click > to enter values from an address book, field, or calculation.

- Select **Specify Email Addresses** to select an email address from the email application's address book.
- Select **Specify Calculation** to create an address (or subject or message text) from a calculation.
- Select **Specify Field Name** to choose a single field that contains the desired value.
- If the **Specify Field Name** option is used to specify a value for the To:, CC:, or BCC: entries, one can also select Get Values from Every Record in Found Set to specify that all the values from this field in the current found set be used (to address a message to multiple recipients).

To stores the address(es) of the recipient(s).

CC stores the address(es) of the carbon copy recipient(s).

BCC stores the address(es) of the blind carbon copy recipient(s).

Subject indicates the title for the email message.

Message indicates the text of the email message. The message may be typed as text, designated as a field value, or created by a calculation.

Select **Attach File** to select a file to send as an attachment to the mail message.

Examples:
Perform Find [Restore]
Send the same email to everyone in the found set.
Send Mail [To: sContacts::email; Subject: "This is a test email"; Message: "Testing..."]

Description:

The Send Mail script steps allow you to send email to one or more recipients via a client-side email application. The following things are necessary to send mail from FileMaker:

- Windows: A [Mail] section in the Win.ini file, and Microsoft Exchange or another email application that is MAPI-compliant, installed, and configured to work with an existing email account.
- Mac OS: Mac OS X Mail or Microsoft Entourage installed and configured as the default email application.

Comments:

To send mail, you must have an Internet connection and a correctly configured email client (see the previous Description section for configurations). It's not possible to use the Send Mail step to send email directly via an SMTP server.

Set Error Capture

Compatibility: 🍎 🗔 ⊕

Menu Equivalent: None

Syntax: **Set Error Capture [<on or off>]**

Options:

Setting Error Capture to **On** suppresses most FileMaker Pro alert messages and some dialog boxes. If the error result is 100 or 803, then certain standard file dialog boxes are suppressed, such as the Open dialog box.

Setting Error Capture to **Off** re-enables the alert messages.

```
Examples:
Perform Find [Restore]
Go to Record/Request/Page [First]
Open Record/Request
if [ Get(LastError) = 200 or Get(LastError) = 300]
   Show Custom Dialog ["An error has ocurred. This record is locked or you do
not have sufficient permission to access it."]
End If
```

Description:

This script step suppresses or enables the FileMaker Pro error dialogs and messages. This provides the developer with the opportunity to write scripts to handle errors in a manner that is customizable and appropriate to the functions being performed. The Get(LastError) function, when used immediately after a script step is executed, gives the code of the error that was encountered, if an error was encountered.

Set Field

Compatibility: 🍎 🗔 ⊕

Menu Equivalent: None

Syntax: **Set Field [<table::field>; <value or formula>]**

Options:

Select **Specify Target Field** or click **Specify** to specify the field whose contents you want to replace. If no field is specified and a field is already selected in Browse mode or Find mode, that field is used.

Click **Specify** to define a calculation, the results of which will replace the current contents of the target field.

Examples:
Freeze Window
Go to Record/Request/Page [First]
Give everyone a 10% raise.
Loop
  Set Field [Employee::Salary; Employee::Salary * 1. 1]
  Go to Record/Request/Page [Next; Exit after last]
End Loop
Refresh Window

Description:

This script step replaces the contents of the designated field on the current record with the result of the specified calculation. The result of the calculation must match the field type of the target field, or the results may be unexpected. If the result of the calculation doesn't match the target field type, and the Validate option for the field is set to Always, the field is not set and an error code is returned (which can be captured with the Get(LastError) function).

Comments:

When possible, the Set Field script step makes the record active and leaves it active until the record is exited or committed. Scripts that use a series of Set Field script steps should thus group these steps together if possible so that subsequent Set Field script steps can act on the record without having to lock the record, synchronize data with the server, index the field, and so on, after each individual Set Field script step. Synchronization, indexing, and record-level validation are performed after the record has been exited or committed.

Unlike many other script steps that deal with field contents, Set Field does not require that the field being targeted be on the active layout.

Be sure to commit record data as appropriate after using the Set Field step in order to avoid leaving the record open and encountering a record lock error later.

Set Multi-User

Compatibility: 🍎 🪟

Menu Equivalent: None

Syntax: **Set Multi-User [On/On (Hidden)/Off]**

Options:

Select **On** to allow network access via FileMaker Network Sharing. This is the same as enabling Network Sharing and selecting All Users in the FileMaker Network Settings dialog box.

Select **On (Hidden)** to allow network access but prevent the name of the shared database from appearing in the Open Remote File dialog box. This is the same as enabling Network Sharing and selecting the All Users and Don't Display in Open Remote File dialog options in the FileMaker Network Settings dialog box.

Select **Off** to disallow network access. This is the same as selecting No Users in the FileMaker Network Settings dialog box.

```
Examples:
If [Get (MultiUserState) = 0]
  Show Custom Dialog ["Would you like to enable network sharing?"]
  If [Get (LastMessageChoice) = 1]
    Set Multi-User [On]
  End If
End
```

Description:

This script step allows or disallows network access to the current database. The Hidden option allows a file to be accessed by other files and in dialogs but not through the Open Remote dialog.

Comments:

If FileMaker's Network Sharing is currently set to Off, both of this script step's On options will also enable network sharing. This could possibly enable sharing access to other files than just the one in which this script step is run. The converse is not true: The Off option to this script step does not also turn off FileMaker Network Sharing. It's sometimes helpful to have Set Multi-User On/Off script steps in all the files of a multi-file solution. By means of a single master script in one of the files, all these individual files can execute their Set Multi-User On/Off scripts. This makes it possible to fully enable or fully disable multi-user access to a set of files with just a single script.

Set Next Serial Value

Compatibility: 🍎 🖥 ⊕

Menu Equivalent: None

Syntax: **Set Next Serial Value [<table::field>; <value or formula>]**

Options:

Select **Specify Target Field** or click **Specify** to specify the serial number field on which the script step is to operate. The field specified must be defined as an auto-entry serial number field.

Calculated Result: Click **Specify** to enter the next serial value by hand or create a calculation to determine the next serial value.

Examples:
Find All
Set Next Serial Value [Contacts::ContactID;Contacts::MaxContactID + 1]
Note: MaxContactID would be a summary field defined as the max of the serial field ContactID

Description:

This script step resets the next serial value for an auto-enter serial number field. This is especially useful to ensure that there are no duplicate serial numbers when a large number of records have been imported into a backup clone of a system. It is also useful for importing records when it is not desirable to allow auto-enter calculations. The calculated result always evaluates to a text result. Note this script step can operate on multiple files. If a field in another file is specified, then FileMaker Pro attempts to update the serial number for the specified field in the other file. To specify a field in another file, define a relationship to that file and use **Specify Target Field** to select a field from that file. Also, if a serial number is not strictly a number, special care must be taken to ensure that the newly set serial number matches the format of the existing serial numbers.

Comments:

This script step does not change any field data. Instead, it changes the definition of the target field. Specifically, it changes the Next Serial Number you see in the Field Options dialog for that field.

Set Selection

Compatibility: ⬤ ▥ ⊕

Menu Equivalent: None

Syntax: **Set Selection [Start Position: <n>; End Position: <n>]**

Options:

Select **Go to Target Field** or click the **Specify** button by the check box to specify the field whose contents you want to select.

The second **Specify** option lets you set the starting and ending positions of a selection, either by entering the start and end numbers directly or by using a calculation to determine them.

Examples:
Set Selection [Shipper::CompanyName; Start Position: 1; End Position: Length(Shipper::Company Name)]

Description:

This script step makes it possible to "select" some or all of a field's contents without direct user intervention. It's possible to specify the start and end positions (in terms of numbers of characters) for the new selection. These values may be entered literally or generated as the result of a specified calculation. This step does not operate on container fields. Data that is out of the visible portion of a layout or field is scrolled into view to show the newly selected contents. The start and end values must be integers between 1 and the number of characters in the target field. If the start position number is valid and the end position number is invalid, then the selection goes from the start position number to the end of the field contents. If the start position number is invalid and the end position is valid, the cursor (or insertion point) is placed at the specified end position with no characters selected. If neither the start nor the end numbers are valid, then the cursor is placed at the end of the fields' contents.

Comments:

You might use this script step to "set up" additional operations that act on the current selection, such as cut or copy. You might also choose to transform the selection (for example, by removing it and substituting a styled version of the same text).

Set Selection is one of a number of script steps that depend on the presence of specific fields on the current layout. Other script steps with the same limitations include Cut, Copy, and Paste.

Set Use System Formats

Compatibility:

Menu Equivalent: None

Syntax: **Set Use System Formats [On/Off]**

Options:

Use System Formats may be set to **On** or **Off**.

Examples:
If [Get (SystemLanguage) <> "English"]
    Set Use System Formats [On]
End If

Description:

FileMaker Pro databases store date, time, and number format preferences. These are taken from the computer on which the database was created. These creation settings may differ from those in use on other machines on which the database may later be opened. This script step can be used to determine whether a file draws its time display settings from those stored in the file, or those in effect on the local machine.

Comments:

If a FileMaker file is opened on a computer with different locale settings than those stored in the file, the user will see an alert showing the difference. This script step can be used to automatically intruct the system to use the current locale settings when it starts up.

This script step does not change the locale settings stored in the file. It simply instructs FileMaker whether or not to use the locale settings on the current computer.

NEW Set Variable

Compatibility: ■ ▣ ◌

Menu Equivalent: None

Syntax: **Set Variable [<variable name> ([<Repetition number>]);**
      Value: <value or formula>]

Options:

Clicking **Specify** will give you access to a dialog where you can set the variable options:

- **Name** is the name you wish to assign to the variable. Variables names are prefixed with $ (for local variables) or $$ (for global variables). With no prefix, $ is assumed.
- **Value** is the value to which the variable will be set. You can specify some text manually, or enter a calculation.
- **Repetition** is the repetition index you wish to set within the variable. The default is 1.

Examples:
```
# use a local variable
Set Variable [$loopCounter; Value: $loopCounter + 1]


# use a global variable
Set Variable [$$lastLoginTime; Value: Status(CurrentTime)]


 # use a repetition index
Set Variable [$myArray[3]; Value: "Fred Smith"]


# use a dynamic repetition index
Set Variable [$$array; Value: ""]
Set Variable [$index; Value: 20]
Loop
     Set Variable[$$array[$index]; Value: $index]
     Set Variable [$index; Value: $index – 1]
     Exit Loop If[$index = 0]
End Loop
```

Description:

Set a variable, or a repetition of a variable, with a specific value. If the variable is a local variable, the value will persist within that script and that script only; the variable is not directly available to subscripts, and ceases to exist when the script that created it stops executing. A global variable exists across all scripts and calculations, and continues to retain its value even when the script that created it stops executing.

Comments:

NEW Variables are one of the most powerful new features of FileMaker 8. For a full discussion, see *Special Edition Using FileMaker 8*. We'll stick to pertinent comments here.

A variable can hold data of any type, including text, number, date, time, timestamp, and container.

It's possible to set discontiguous variable repetitions. You can set $var[3] and $var[33] without defining or setting the other slots from 1 to 33.

Variables don't need to be declared or initialized, as in other languages. They are created implicitly the first time they are referred to.

Variables can be set from within a Let statement:

    Let ([$$counter = $$counter + 1; result = "success]; result)

This technique is generally only useful for global variables, and should be used with considerable caution.

Use local variables to replace global fields used for "bookeeping" purposes within single scripts—for example, a loop counter. Use global variables to replace global fields used for user session data, such as user preferences, last layout visited, and the like. But note that global fields are still necessary for things like accepting user input and "driving" certain kinds of relationships.

Variables also have an important use for creating "dynamic file paths" from scripts, allowing a developer to determine on the fly where files will be created or read from.

→ *For more information on dynamic file paths, and on variables in scripting,* **see** Special Edition Using FileMaker 8, *Chapter 15, "Advanced Scripting Techniques."*

Set Window Title

Compatibility: 🍎 🖥 🌐

Menu Equivalent: None

Syntax: **Set Window Title [Current Window or Name: <name of window>; New Title: <new window name>]**

Options:

Click **Specify** to set any of the options for this script.

Window to Rename tells FileMaker Pro which window to rename. Current Window renames the current window. You may also specify a different window, either by typing the window name in plain text or deriving the window name from a calculation.

Rename Window To is the new title for the window. Here again, you can enter literal text or click **Specify** to derive a name from the result of a calculation.

Current File Only causes FileMaker to search only within windows based on table occurrences from within the current file.

Examples:
Set Error Capture [On]
Allow User Abort [Off]
Perform Find [Restore]
Set Window Title [Get(FoundCount) &" Contacts Found"]

Description:
Set Window Title sets the name of the current window or the window specified by name.

Comments:

 Current File Only is a window management option that's new to FileMaker 8. In FileMaker 7, window management script steps could sometimes be "fooled" by the presence of windows from other files with the same name as the desired script step target, causing the script step to act on a window different from the desired one. In FileMaker 8, the developer can restrict the scope of window management script steps to consider only windows based on the current file.

Window names aren't case sensitive when you select them in this way, so be sure not to rely on case sensitivity in window names.

Set Zoom Level

Compatibility: 🍎 🪟

Menu Equivalent: None

Syntax: **Set Zoom Level [Lock; 25%. . . 400%/Zoom In/Zoom Out]**

Options:

Lock prohibits users from making changes to the zoom level.

Specify lets you select a zoom level:
- Specific reduction values: 100%, 75%, 50%, or 25%.
- Specific enlargement values: 150%, 200%, 300%, or 400%.
- Zoom In: reduces the screen image by one zoom level.
- Zoom Out: enlarges the screen image by one zoom level.

Examples:
Allow User Abort [Off]
Set Error Capture [On]
If[// the screen resolution is too low// Get (ScreenHeight) < 600]
  Set Zoom Level [Lock; 100%]
Else
  Set Zoom Level [100%]
End

Description:

Set Zoom Level enlarges or reduces the image on the screen and optionally locks screen scaling. It is equivalent to using the magnification icons beneath the status area.

Show All Records

Compatibility: 🍎 🗔 ⊕

Menu Equivalent: Records, Show All Records

Syntax: **Show All Records**

Options:

None

Examples:
Allow User Abort [Off]
Set Error Capture [On]
Enter Find Mode [Pause]
Perform Find []
If[Get(CurrentFoundCount) = 0] // no records were found
   Show Message ["No Records Found"; "Sorry, no records that match your find criteria were found."]
   Show All Records [ ] // don't leave the user on an empty found set

---

Description:

Displays all the records in the current table and leaves the user on the current record. Show All Records is used in Browse mode or Preview mode. If you perform this step in Find mode or Layout mode, FileMaker Pro switches to Browse mode after the records have been found.

Show Custom Dialog

Compatibility: 🍎 🗔

Menu Equivalent: None

Syntax: **Show Custom Dialog [<title>; <message text>; Table1::input field 1;. . .]**

Options:

Click **Specify** to display a dialog box where you can set the custom dialog box title, message text, and buttons, and specify up to three fields to use for input or display.

Title lets you specify the title of the custom dialog box. You can enter literal text or click Specify to create the dialog box title from a calculation.

Message lets you specify the message of the dialog box. You can enter literal text or click Specify to create the message text from a calculation.

Button Labels let you specify how many buttons (up to three) to display in the custom dialog box, and labels for these buttons. If you leave a button label blank, the button does not appear in the custom dialog box. If you leave all button titles blank, an OK button displays in the lower-right corner of the custom dialog box.

Input Field options:

Select **Show Input Field <n>** to activate an input field.

Select **Specify** to choose the field for input. Each input area maps to one field.

Select **Use Password Character** (*) to mask text as it is entered, or as it is displayed from the database. This option obscures data being input into the custom dialog box or being displayed, but does not alter the actual data as it is stored in the database.

Use **Label** to specify a field label (the text that will identify this input to the user). You can enter literal text or create the label from a calculation.

```
Examples:
Allow User Abort [ Off ]
Set Error Capture [ On ]
#
Show Custom Dialog [ Title: "Password Change"; Buttons: "OK", "Cancel";
Input #1: zgPassword_Old. t, "Old Password:";
Input #2: zgPassword_New. t, "New Password:" ]
#
If [ /* user did not cancel the dialog */ Get(LastMessageChoice)=1 ]
  Change Password [ Old Password: zgPassword_Old. t;
  New Password: zgPassword_New. t ]
  # send password change onto other files
  Perform Script [ "Change Password"; from file "Contacts" Parameter:
  zgPassword_Old. t&"¶"&zgPassword_New. t ]
  Perform Script [ "Change Password"; from file "Invoices" Parameter:
  zgPassword_Old. t&"¶"&zgPassword_New. t ]
End If
# be sure to clear the globals for security reasons
Set Field [zgPassword_Old.t; ""]
Set Field [zgPassword_New.t; ""]
```

Description:

Show Custom Dialog enables you to display a custom message dialog box. The dialog box is modal, with from one to three buttons, each with a custom title. The custom message window can also display up to three input fields, each with a custom label. Each of these input fields corresponds to a FileMaker data field. When the window is opened, each input area displays the most recent contents of the corresponding field. When the user closes the window, the button clicked can be determined by the Get(LastMessageChoice) function. A result of 1 represents the first button on the right, whereas 2 and 3 would represent the middle and leftmost buttons if they were used. Button 1, the rightmost, is the default. It's also the only button that, when clicked, causes the data from any input fields to be written back to the corresponding FileMaker fields.

Comments:

If values entered into any input fields don't match the field type of the underlying FileMaker field, a validation error message displays. The user must resolve validation errors before the dialog box can be closed. The fields you specify don't need to appear on the current layout. Show Custom Dialog input fields are independent of layouts, similar to the Set Field script step. And as with the Set Field script step, Show Custom Dialog bypasses the Allow Entry Into Field field formatting option. Data entry via the Show Custom Dialog script step is limited by any access privilege rules that may be in place. In other words, users can't use a custom dialog to edit data in fields that they can't normally change because of access restriction. If you select Run Script With Full Access Privileges, this restriction is lifted. In Windows, you can create a keyboard shortcut for a custom dialog box button by placing an ampersand before the shortcut key letter in the button label. For example, to create a keyboard shortcut D (Alt+D) for a button labeled Done, type the label **&Done**.

Show Omitted Only

Compatibility: 🍎 🪟 🌐

Menu Equivalent: Records, Show Omitted Only

Syntax: **Show Omitted Only**

Options:

None

Examples:
// reduce found set to zero
Show All Records
Show Omitted Only

Description:

Show Omitted Only "inverts" the found set to show records that are currently not displayed, and omits records that are currently displayed.

Show/Hide Status Area

Compatibility: 🍎 🪟 🌐

Menu Equivalent: None

Syntax: **Show/Hide Status Area [Lock; Show/Hide/Toggle]**

Options:

Lock prohibits the user from using the status area control button to manually show or hide the status area.

Show tells FileMaker Pro to show the status area.

Hide tells FileMaker Pro to hide the status area.

Toggle switches between showing and hiding the status area (equivalent to clicking the status area control button).

```
Examples:
Allow User Abort [Off]
Set Error Capture [On]
Go to Layout ["Invoice"]
Show/Hide Status Area [Lock; Show] // show status area so the user can click
'Continue'
Enter Preview Mode [Pause]
Show/Hide Status Area [Lock; Hide] // shut the status area back down
Enter Browse Mode [ ]
Go To Layout [Original Layout]
```

Description:

Show/Hide Status Area allows for control of the display of status area from scripts.

Comments:

In databases where it's important to tightly control the user's navigation, it may be desirable to prevent users from using the status area either to page through records or to change layouts. Hiding and locking the status area may well be the right thing to do in such a case.

Show/Hide Text Ruler

Compatibility: 🍎 🪟

Menu Equivalent: View, Text Ruler

Syntax: **Show/Hide Text Ruler [Show/Hide/Toggle]**

Options:

Show tells FileMaker Pro to show the text ruler.

Hide tells FileMaker Pro to hide the text ruler.

Toggle switches between showing and hiding the text ruler.

```
Examples:
Allow User Abort [Off]
Set Error Capture [On]
If[ // the screen resolution to too low// Get (ScreenHeight) < 600]
   Show/Hide Text Ruler [Hide]
End
```

Description:

Hides or shows the text ruler. Choosing the Toggle option switches the current state of the ruler. The Text Ruler is used with text fields, and also to aid in design in Layout mode.

It can be used to set tabs and indents for a text area. Hiding the text ruler is sometimes required to save screen space. Unless you have disabled access to menus, users can generally enable the text rulers by choosing View, Text Ruler, and it may later be desirable to disable the rulers again to save room.

Sort Records

Compatibility: 🍎 ▦ ⊕

Menu Equivalent: Records, Sort Records

Syntax: **Sort Records [Restore; No dialog]**

Options:

Perform Without Dialog prevents display of a dialog box that lets the user enter a different set of sort instructions.

Select **Specify Sort Order** or click **Specify** to create a sort order and store it with the script step. When Specify Sort Order is not selected, FileMaker Pro uses the most recently executed sort instructions.

Examples:
Allow User Abort [Off]
Set Error Capture [On]
Perform Find [Restore] // find overdue invoices
Sort [Restore] // sort by due date and customer
Go to Layout ["Invoice"]
Enter Preview Mode [Pause]
Enter Browse Mode [ ]
Go To Layout [Original Layout]
Unsort

Description:

Sort Records sorts the records in the current found set according to specified criteria. Be sure to perform any operations that might change the found set before calling Sort Records. If you sort a repeating field, FileMaker Pro sorts on only the first entry in that field. Note that in previous versions of FileMaker Pro, only one sort order could be saved with a script. However, in the current version, sort criteria are saved with individual Sort Record script steps, so any number of sorts can be saved with a single script.

Comments:

Note that saved sort criteria are relative to the current table context. If the table Contact was the active table when the sort criteria were entered, and fields from Contacts are used in the sort order, then that table must be active when the sort is executed. If your sort step makes field references that are not valid at the time the step is executed, the invalid field references are ignored. Table context is controlled by the current layout; to change table context, navigate to a layout that is used by the table in question.

Speak

Compatibility:

Menu Equivalent: None

Syntax: **Speak [<text to be spoken>]**

Options:

Click **Specify** to display the Speak Options dialog box, where you can set the following options.

You can enter the text to be spoken directly by hand, or draw the text from a calculation.

Use Voice lets you select from the various voices available on your computer.

Wait for Speech Completion Before Continuing tells FileMaker Pro to wait until the speech is completed before continuing with the next script step. If you leave this option unchecked, the script continues while the text is being spoken.

Examples:
Speak ["Hello"]
Speak[Get(CurrentDate)]

Description:

Speaks the specified text. You can specify which voice synthesizer to use and whether or not FileMaker Pro is to wait for the speech to be completed before continuing with the next script step. On a computer without speech capabilities, the script can still be edited, but only the default voice synthesizer is available. Speak script steps are not executed when the script is run on a computer without speech capability.

Spelling Options

Compatibility:

Menu Equivalent: File, File Options, Spelling

Syntax: **Spelling Options**

Options:

None

Examples:
a button on a layout calls this script step directly:
Spelling Options

Description:

Opens the Spelling tab of the File Options dialog box. Use this script step to open the File Options dialog box for users if you have restricted their access to FileMaker Pro menus.

Undo

Compatibility: ⬛ 🍎 ⊕

Menu Equivalent: Edit, Undo

Syntax: **Undo**

Options:

None

> *Examples:*
> Undo

Description:

Undo acts the same as choosing Undo from the edit menu: The most recent edits to the record are reversed.

Unsort Records

Compatibility: 🍎 ⬛ ⊕

Menu Equivalent: None

Syntax: **Unsort Records**

Options:

None

> *Examples:*
> Allow User Abort [Off]
> Set Error Capture [On]
> Enter Browse Mode []
> Unsort Records
> Go to Record/Request/Page [First]

Description:

Unsort Records restores the found set to its natural order (order in which records were created).

Update Link

Compatibility: ⬛

Menu Equivalent: None

Syntax: **Update Link [<table::field>]**

Options:

Select **Go to Target Field** or click **Specify** to specify the field to be updated.

Examples:
Set Error Capture [On]
Allow User Abort [Off]
Update Link [Contact::Resume]
If [//an error occured// Get(LastError)]
  Show Message ["An error occurred updating the resume link"]
End If

Description:

Update Link updates the OLE link in the specified container field. If the field does not contain an OLE link, then Update Link returns an error. Both manual and automatic links are updated.

View As

Compatibility: 🍎 🖥 ⊕

Menu Equivalent: View, View As Form/List/Table

Syntax: **View As [Form/List/Table/Cycle]**

Options:

View As Form tells FileMaker Pro to display records page by page on the current layout, so that only one record at a time is shown.

View As List tells FileMaker Pro to display records as records in a list so that the user can see multiple records at once in a list.

View As Table tells FileMaker Pro to display the records onscreen in a spreadsheet-like grid.

Cycle switches from the current view type to the next type.

Examples:
Set Error Capture [On]
Allow User Abort [Off]
Go to Layout ["Contact List"]
View As [View As List

Description:

View As sets the view mode for the current layout. Note that Layout Setup can be used to limit which views are accessible via the View menu, but the View As script step can override those settings and enable you to view a layout in any of the three styles.

PART 5

Quick Reference

FileMaker Error Codes

Error Codes in FileMaker

FileMaker can generate quite a number of possible errors in the course of a script. FileMaker generates errors at various times, such as during normal use of the application—but in general these errors are reported directly to the user, via a dialog box. It's only during scripting, or during certain interactions with the Web Publishing Engine, that developers are in a position to trap and examine the error codes FileMaker generates. To do so requires that Error Capture be set to On during the script, and that the script developer use the Get(LastError) function to inspect any possible errors.

The error list in the tables that follow is broken into two groups: those that can arise during normal operation of FileMaker or during ODBC access, which have numbers up to 1408, and those that are generated by the Web Publishing Engine, which have codes of 10000 or above.

Remember that the FileMaker error results that occur during scripts are transient. You must check for an error immediately after a script step. If script step A produces an error, and a subsequent script step B executes with no error, the error from script step A will be "forgotten" after script step B executes. Hence the name of the Get(LastError) function: It reports only the last error code, even if that error code is 0 (no error). (Note, though, that the error code from the last script step will be retained even after the script has stopped executing, until replaced by another script. Further, the script steps Exit Script and Halt Script do *not* clear the previous error code.)

FileMaker Error Codes

The following error codes may be encountered in the normal operation of the FileMaker Pro or Pro Advanced clients. These errors appear and are reported strictly within the client. FileMaker Server has its own error codes, which are not accessible from within a FileMaker database. Also note that error codes 951 through 958 are returned only by databases that are being accessed via the Web.

Table 11.1 FileMaker Error Codes

Code	Error Description
-1	Unknown error
0	No error
1	User canceled action
2	Memory error
3	Command is unavailable (for example, wrong operating system, wrong mode, and so on)
4	Command is unknown
5	Command is invalid (for example, a Set Field script step does not have a calculation specified)
6	File is read-only
7	Running out of memory
8	Empty result
9	Insufficient privileges
10	Requested data is missing
11	Name is not valid
12	Name already exists
13	File or object is in use
14	Out of range
15	Can't divide by zero
16	Operation failed, request retry (for example, a user query)
17	Attempt to convert foreign character set to UTF-16 failed
18	Client must provide account information to proceed
19	String contains characters other than A-Z, a-z, 0-9 (ASCII)
100	File is missing
101	Record is missing
102	Field is missing
103	Relationship is missing
104	Script is missing
105	Layout is missing
106	Table is missing
107	Index is missing
108	Value list is missing
109	Privilege set is missing
110	Related tables are missing
111	Field repetition is invalid
112	Window is missing
113	Function is missing
114	File reference is missing

Table 11.1   FileMaker Error Codes (continued)

Code	Error Description
115	Specified menu set is not present
130	Files are damaged or missing and must be reinstalled
131	Language pack files are missing (such as template files)
200	Record access is denied
201	Field cannot be modified
202	Field access is denied
203	No records in file to print, or password doesn't allow print access
204	No access to field(s) in sort order
205	User does not have access privileges to create new records; import will overwrite existing data
206	User does not have password change privileges, or file is not modifiable
207	User does not have sufficient privileges to change database schema, or file is not modifiable
208	Password does not contain enough characters
209	New password must be different from existing one
210	User account is inactive
211	Password has expired
212	Invalid user account and/or password. Please try again
213	User account and/or password does not exist
214	Too many login attempts
215	Administrator privileges cannot be duplicated
216	Guest account cannot be duplicated
217	User does not have sufficient privileges to modify administrator account
300	File is locked or in use
301	Record is in use by another user
302	Table is in use by another user
303	Database schema is in use by another user
304	Layout is in use by another user
306	Record modification ID does not match
400	Find criteria are empty
401	No records match the request
402	Selected field is not a match field for a lookup
403	Exceeding maximum record limit for trial version of FileMaker Pro
404	Sort order is invalid
405	Number of records specified exceeds number of records that can be omitted
406	Replace/Reserialize criteria are invalid
407	One or both match fields are missing (invalid relationship)
408	Specified field has inappropriate data type for this operation

Table 11.1   FileMaker Error Codes (continued)

Code	Error Description
409	Import order is invalid
410	Export order is invalid
412	Wrong version of FileMaker Pro used to recover file
413	Specified field has inappropriate field type
414	Layout cannot display the result
415	One or more required related records are not available
500	Date value does not meet validation entry options
501	Time value does not meet validation entry options
502	Number value does not meet validation entry options
503	Value in field is not within the range specified in validation entry options
504	Value in field is not unique as required in validation entry options
505	Value in field is not an existing value in the database file as required in validation entry options
506	Value in field is not listed on the value list specified in validation entry option
507	Value in field failed calculation test of validation entry option
508	Invalid value entered in Find mode
509	Field requires a valid value
510	Related value is empty or unavailable
511	Value in field exceeds maximum number of allowed characters
600	Print error has occurred
601	Combined header and footer exceed one page
602	Body doesn't fit on a page for current column setup
603	Print connection lost
700	File is of the wrong file type for import
706	EPSF file has no preview image
707	Graphic translator cannot be found
708	Can't import the file or need color monitor support to import file
709	QuickTime movie import failed
710	Unable to update QuickTime file reference because the database file is read-only
711	Import translator cannot be found
714	Password privileges do not allow the operation
715	Specified Excel worksheet or named range is missing
716	A SQL query using DELETE, INSERT, or UPDATE is not allowed for ODBC import
717	There is not enough XML/XSL information to proceed with the import or export
718	Error in parsing XML file (from Xerces)
719	Error in transforming XML using XSL (from Xalan)
720	Error when exporting; intended format does not support repeating fields
721	Unknown error occurred in the parser or the transformer

Table 11.1   FileMaker Error Codes (continued)

Code	Error Description
722	Cannot import data into a file that has no fields
723	You do not have permission to add records to or modify records in the target table
724	You do not have permission to add records to the target table
725	You do not have permission to modify records in the target table
726	There are more records in the import file than in the target table. Not all records were imported
727	There are more records in the target table than in the import file. Not all records were updated
729	Errors occurred during import. Records could not be imported
730	Unsupported Excel version. (Convert file to Excel 7.0 (Excel 95), Excel 97, 2000, or XP format and try again)
731	The file you are importing from contains no data
732	This file cannot be inserted because it contains other files
733	A table cannot be imported into itself
734	This file type cannot be displayed as a picture
735	This file type cannot be displayed as a picture. It will be inserted and displayed as a file
736	Too much data to export to this format. It will be truncated
800	Unable to create file on disk
801	Unable to create temporary file on System disk
802	Unable to open file
803	File is single user or host cannot be found
804	File cannot be opened as read-only in its current state
805	File is damaged; use Recover command
806	File cannot be opened with this version of FileMaker Pro
807	File is not a FileMaker Pro file or is severely damaged
808	Cannot open file because access privileges are damaged
809	Disk/volume is full
810	Disk/volume is locked
811	Temporary file cannot be opened as FileMaker Pro file
813	Record Synchronization error on network
814	File(s) cannot be opened because maximum number is open
815	Couldn't open lookup file
816	Unable to convert file
817	Unable to open file because it does not belong to this solution
819	Cannot save a local copy of a remote file
820	File is in the process of being closed
821	Host forced a disconnect

Table 11.1   FileMaker Error Codes (continued)

Code	Error Description
822	FMI files not found; reinstall missing files
823	Cannot set file to single-user, guests are connected
824	File is damaged or not a FileMaker file
900	General spelling engine error
901	Main spelling dictionary not installed
902	Could not launch the Help system
903	Command cannot be used in a shared file
905	No active field selected; command can only be used if there is an active field
920	Can't initialize the spelling engine
921	User dictionary cannot be loaded for editing
922	User dictionary cannot be found
923	User dictionary is read-only
951	An unexpected error occurred (web)
954	Unsupported XML grammar (web)
955	No database name (web)
956	Maximum number of database sessions exceeded (web)
957	Conflicting commands (web)
958	Parameter missing (web)
1200	Generic calculation error
1201	Too few parameters in the function
1202	Too many parameters in the function
1203	Unexpected end of calculation
1204	Number, text constant, field name or "(" expected
1205	Comment is not terminated with "*/"
1206	Text constant must end with a quotation mark
1207	Unbalanced parenthesis
1208	Operator missing, function not found or "(" not expected
1209	Name (such as field name or layout name) is missing
1210	Plug-in function has already been registered
1211	List usage is not allowed in this function
1212	An operator (for example, +, -, *) is expected here
1213	This variable has already been defined in the Let function
1214	AVERAGE, COUNT, EXTEND, GETREPETITION, MAX, MIN, NPV, STDEV, SUM, and GETSUMMARY: Expression found where a field alone is needed
1215	This parameter is an invalid Get function parameter
1216	Only Summary fields allowed as first argument in GETSUMMARY
1217	Break field is invalid
1218	Cannot evaluate the number

Table 11.1   FileMaker Error Codes (continued)

Code	Error Description
1219	A field cannot be used in its own formula
1220	Field type must be normal or calculated
1221	Data type must be number, date, time, or timestamp
1222	Calculation cannot be stored
1223	The function is not implemented
1224	The function is not defined
1300	The specified name can't be used
1400	ODBC driver initialization failed; make sure the ODBC drivers are properly installed
1401	Failed to allocate environment (ODBC)
1402	Failed to free environment (ODBC)
1403	Failed to disconnect (ODBC)
1404	Failed to allocate connection (ODBC)
1405	Failed to free connection (ODBC)
1406	Failed check for SQL API (ODBC)
1407	Failed to allocate statement (ODBC)
1408	Extended error (ODBC)

Web Publishing Engine Error Codes

These errors are reported by FileMaker Server Advanced's Web Publishing Engine (WPE), and will only appear in XML data generated by the WPE.

Table 11.2   Publishing Engine Error Codes

Code	Error Description
10000	Invalid header name
10001	Invalid HTTP status code
10100	Unknown session error
10101	Requested session name is already used
10102	Session could not be accessed—maybe it does not exist
10103	Session has timed out
10104	Specified session object does not exist
10200	Unknown messaging error
10201	Message formatting error
10202	Message SMTP fields error
10203	Message "To Field" error
10204	Message "From Field" error
10205	Message "CC Field" error

Table 11.2 Publishing Engine Error Codes (continued)

Code	Error Description
10206	Message "BCC Field" error
10207	Message "Subject Field" error
10208	Message "Reply-To Field" error
10209	Message body error
10210	Recursive mail error—attempted to call send_email() inside an email XSLT stylesheet
10211	SMTP authentication error—either login failed or wrong type of authentication provided
10212	Invalid function usage—attempted to call set_header(), set_status_code(), or set_cookie() inside an email XSLT stylesheet
10213	SMTP server is invalid or is not working

FileMaker Keyboard Shortcuts

Working Quickly, Saving Time

FileMaker is a rapid application development (RAD) tool. As with any tool, how "rapid" it really is depends to a great degree on a developer's mastery of the tool. It's one thing to know how to get something done—another to know how to get it done quickly. There are many aspects to knowing how to work quickly in FileMaker, from using the new Copy Table/Field/Script step commands in FileMaker 8 Advanced, to using custom functions and script parameters to abstract and automate frequently used logic. But we have also observed over the years that the fastest users of the tool tend to be those who also make fairly heavy use of keyboard shortcuts.

Like any modern software application, FileMaker has many keyboard shortcuts hidden under the hood—probably about 400 by our count, though that number is not exact. Of those, we'd list a couple dozen or so as being critical to working quickly in FileMaker, and perhaps another dozen as very desirable to master.

This chapter is divided into two broad areas. In the first, we examine a number of important areas of FileMaker development and discuss the shortcuts we feel are most important in each area. The second section is a comprehensive listing of keyboard shortcuts for menu items.

Note

NEW With the arrival of FileMaker Pro 8 Advanced and its Custom Menus feature, it's possible to alter the landscape of FileMaker keyboard shortcuts almost beyond recognition. It's for this reason that the About FileMaker dialog box now includes the words Custom Menus Active in the Info section if you're working in a file that has a custom menu set active. (If you're trying to provide phone help to someone, and their copy of FileMaker doesn't respond to "normal" commands, you can have them check this dialog to see whether custom menus may be in effect.) So just be advised that all information in this chapter assumes the standard FileMaker menu set is in effect.

Essential Shortcuts by Group

In this section we'll call out shortcuts we believe are essential in each of a number of areas. We'll also delve into some more specialized or lesser-known shortcuts in each area as well.

Keyboard Essentials

Shortcuts in this section should be required knowledge for all FileMaker developers. If you haven't mastered these, you need to spend more time with FileMaker!

Working with Modes

Function	Mac Key	Windows Key
Browse Mode	⌘-B	Ctrl+B
Layout Mode	⌘-L	Ctrl+L
Find Mode	⌘-F	Ctrl+F
Preview Mode	⌘-U	Ctrl+U

Working with Files

Function	Mac Key	Windows Key
Open (File)	⌘-O	Ctrl+O
Open Remote (File)	Shift-⌘-O	Ctrl+Shift+O
Force a password dialog to display when opening a file.	Hold down the Option key while opening the file.	Hold down the Shift key while opening the file.

Working with Records

Function	Mac Key	Windows Key
New Record/Request/Layout	⌘-N	Ctrl+N
Delete Record/Request/Layout	⌘+E	Ctrl+E
Duplicate Record/Request	⌘-D	Ctrl+D
Omit Record	⌘-T	Ctrl+T
Show All Records	⌘-J	Ctrl+J
Sort Records	⌘-S	Ctrl-S

Developer Essentials

Function	Mac Key	Windows Key
Define Fields	Shift-⌘-D	Shift+Ctrl+D
Define Custom Functions		Alt+F+D+C
Define Value Lists		Alt+F+D+V
ScriptMaker	Shift-⌘-S	Shift+Ctrl+S

When using keyboard shortcuts, keep the following in mind:

- It's possible to hold down the Option key (Mac) or Shift key (Windows) to skip a confirmation dialog when deleting an item, be it a record, a field, a script step, or the like. The sole exception concerns deleting a layout: FileMaker will always prompt you before deleting a layout.

- The only available shortcuts for Define Custom Functions and Define Value Lists are Windows Alt-key combinations. This is unfortunate because these tools form an integral part of at least our own development processes, so we'd love to see a single shortcut working on both Mac and PC for each of these items.

Navigation

The shortcuts in this section are not only concerned with moving around between records, but also between layouts and among found sets of records.

Function	Mac Key	Windows Key
Next/Previous Record	Ctrl-up/down arrow	Ctrl+up/down arrow
Next/Previous Layout		
Next/Previous Request		
Next/Previous Page		
Hide/Unhide Status Area	⌘-Option-S	Ctrl+Shift+S
Zoom/Unzoom Window	⌘-Option-Z	Ctrl+Shift+Z
Omit Multiple Records	⌘-Shift-M	Ctrl+Shift+M

When using shortcuts for navigation, keep the following in mind:

- The Ctrl+up/down arrow shortcut has a different meaning in each mode; in Browse mode it moves between records, in Layout mode between layouts, in Find mode between find requests, and in Preview mode between different pages of the output.

- In order to omit all records from the current record to the end of the found set, perform the Omit Multiple Records command and choose a very large number of records to omit. FileMaker will respond that it can only omit a certain number of records, and fill in the correct number of remaining records. You can then go ahead and omit these without needing to calculate the exact number yourself.

Data Entry and Formatting

The shortcuts in this section have to do with the mechanics of putting data into fields, and with formatting data after it's been entered into a field.

Function	Mac Key	Windows Key
Select All	⌘-A	Ctrl+A
Cut, Copy, Paste	⌘-X, C, V	Ctrl+X, C, V
Copy Current Record (When Not In A Field)	⌘-C	Ctrl+C

Function (continued)	Mac Key	Windows Key
Copy All Records	⌘-Opt-C	Ctrl+Shift+C
Paste Without Text Styles	⌘-Opt-V	Ctrl+Alt+V
Plain Text	Shift-⌘-P	Ctrl+Shift+P
Bold Text	Shift-⌘-B	Ctrl+Shift+B
Italic Text	Shift-⌘-I	Ctrl+Shift+I
Underline Text	Shift-⌘-U	Ctrl+Shift+U
Left-Justify Selected Text	⌘-[	Ctrl+[
Center Selected Text	⌘-\	Ctrl+\
Right-Justify Selected Text	⌘-]	Ctrl+]
Increase/Decrease Font Size	Shift-⌘->/<	Ctrl+Shift+>/<
Insert Current Date	⌘-<hyphen>	Ctrl+<hyphen>
Insert Current Time/Timestamp	⌘-;	Ctrl+;
Insert Non-breaking Space Into Text	Opt-space	Ctrl+space
Insert Tab Character Into Text	Opt-tab	Ctrl+tab

Be aware of the following when using keyboard shortcuts for data entry and formatting:

- Using Ctrl+C or ⌘-C in Browse mode when you're not in any field of the current record will copy the entire record as tab-delimited text. Using ⌘-Opt-C or Ctrl+Shift+C will copy all records in the found set, again as a tab-delimited text block.

- Using Shift-⌘->/< or Ctrl+Shift+>/< to increase or decrease font sizes will normally move the font size up or down through the list of "standard" font sizes. If you hold down Shift (Windows) or Option (Mac), the changes will occur in one-point increments instead.

- The ⌘/Ctrl+; shortcut will insert the current time if the selected field is of type text, time, or number, but will insert the current timestamp if the current field is of type timestamp.

Defining Fields

The shortcuts in this section work only within the Fields tab of the Define Database dialog.

Function	Mac Key	Windows Key
Define Database	Shift-⌘-D	Ctrl+Shift+D
Text Data Type	⌘-T	Ctrl+T
Number Data Type	⌘-N	Ctrl+N
Date Data Type	⌘-D	Ctrl+D
Time Data Type	⌘-I	Ctrl+I
Timestamp Data Type	⌘-M	Ctrl+M

Function (continued)	Mac Key	Windows Key
Container Data Type	⌘-R	Ctrl+R
Calculation Data Type	⌘-L	Ctrl+L
Summary Data Type	⌘-S	Ctrl+S
Field Options	Shift-⌘-O	Alt+N
Reorder Tables or Fields in a List	⌘-<up/down arrow>	Ctrl+<up/down arrow>

Working with the Relationships Graph

There are quite a large number of keyboard shortcuts and techniques that apply to the Relationships Graph. The following is a selection of the most useful: Consult the online help for a full listing.

Function	Mac Key	Windows Key
New Table Occurrence	Shift-⌘-T	Ctrl+Shift+T
New Relationship	Shift-⌘-R	Ctrl+Shift+R, Insert
New Text Note	Shift-⌘-N	Ctrl+Shift+N
Duplicate Selected Items	⌘-D	Ctrl+D
Select All Table Occurences Directly Related to the Current Table Occurrence	⌘-R	Ctrl+R
Select All Table Occurences with the Same Source Table As the Current Table Occurrence	⌘-S	Ctrl+S
Toggle the Display Mode of Selected Table Occurrences (Toggles Among Fully Expanded, Fields, and Table Name Table and Related Name Alone)	⌘-T	Ctrl+T

Following are some additional shortcuts to be aware of:

- The Up, Down, Left, and Right arrows can be used to cycle through the elements of the Graph (table occurrences, relationships, notes), selecting each one in turn. Once an item has been selected, other keyboard shortcuts can open the item for editing.
- Typing on the keyboard will select objects containing text that matches what is being typed.
- Using the Option/Shift key in conjunction with the arrow keys will move any selected table occurrences.
- Using Ctrl+Shift in combination with the arrow keys will resize any selected table occurrences.

Working with Layouts

Layout mode is where FileMaker's famously quick-to-develop GUIs (graphical user interfaces) get built. A thorough knowledge of important layout shortcuts is a must-have for a FileMaker developer.

Function	Mac Key	Windows Key
Group	⌘-R	Ctrl+R
Ungroup	Shift-⌘-R	Ctrl+Shift+R
Lock	Opt-⌘-L	Ctrl+Alt+L
Unlock	Shift-Opt-⌘-L	Ctrl+Alt+Shift+L
Bring Forward	Shift-⌘-[	Ctrl+Shift+[
Bring to Front	Opt-⌘-[	Ctrl+Alt+[
Send Backward	Shift-⌘-]	Ctrl+Shift+]
Send to Back	Opt-⌘-]	Ctrl+Alt+]
Align Left, Right, Top, Bottom	Opt-⌘-<left, right, up, down arrow>	Ctrl+Alt+<left, right, up, down arrow>
Field Control Setup	Shift-⌘-F	Ctrl+Shift+F
Field Control Behavior	Shift-⌘-K	Ctrl+Shift+K
Field Control Borders	Shift-⌘-B	Ctrl+Shift+B
Insert Merge Field	Shift-⌘-M	Ctrl=Shift+M
View Object Sizes		Alt+V+Z
Select Similar Objects	Opt-⌘-A	Ctrl+Shift+A

When working with layouts, the following may also be of some value:

- In Layout mode, ⌘-dragging or Ctrl+dragging will cause all objects touched by the selection rectangle to be selected. This can be easier than dragging a selection rectangle that fully encloses the desired objects.

- Use Opt-⌘-A/Ctrl+Shift+A to select all objects of the same type as the currently selected objects. You can use this technique to select all text labels, for example.

- As in many graphical layout applications, the arrow keys can be used to move selected layout objects a pixel at a time in any direction.

- The Object Size window is extremely useful for exact positioning of objects. We usually set the measurement units to pixels. Unfortunately, the only shortcut to this feature at present is an Alt-key combination on Windows.

- Shift-dragging restricts the movement of selected objects to a horizontal or vertical direction.

- Ctrl+/⌘-dragging will create a duplicate of the selected objects.

- Shift-dragging, combined with the ⌘ or Ctrl key, will drag a duplicate of selected objects along a horizontal or vertical axis.

- Double-clicking a layout tool in the status area will "lock" the tool, causing it to remain selected through multiple uses. Pressing Esc or Enter will "unlock" and deselect the tool, selecting the Pointer tool instead (the default). Pressing Enter when the Pointer tool is selected will reselect the most recently used layout tool.

- Any object formatting options chosen while no layout object is selected will become the defaults for any new objects. If you ⌘-click (Mac) or Ctrl+click (Windows) an existing object, its attributes will become the default.

Scripting

There are a number of useful shortcuts that pertain to ScriptMaker.

Function	Mac Key	Windows Key
Open ScriptMaker	⌘-Shift-S	Ctrl+Shift+S
Scroll Through Script List	Up/Down arrows	Up/Down arrows
Move Selected Script Up or Down in the List	Ctrl-Up/Down arrows	Ctrl+Up/Down arrows
Toggle Checkbox to Include Selected Script in Scripts Menu	Space	Space
Select a Script by Name (When Scripts List Is Active)	Begin typing script name	Begin typing script name
Select All Scripts	⌘-A	Ctrl+A
Copy Selected Scripts (A)	⌘-C	Ctrl+C
Paste Copied Script(s) (A)	⌘-V	Ctrl+V
Navigate Up or Down Through Available Script Steps	Up/Down arrows	Up/Down arrows
Select a Script Step by Name (When Script Steps List Is Active)	Begin typing script name	Begin typing script name
Insert Selected Script Step into Script	Return/Enter or Space	Enter
Select All Script Steps	⌘-A	Ctrl+A
Copy Selected Script Steps (A)	⌘-C	Ctrl+C
Paste Copied Script Steps (A)	⌘-V	Ctrl+V
Move Selected Script Steps Up or Down in the List	Ctrl-Up/Down arrows	Ctrl+Up/Down arrows
Delete Selected Script Steps	Delete	Backspace/Delete

Note that functions marked with an (A) are only available in FileMaker Pro Advanced.

When editing a script step that has options accessible via a Specify button, pressing the spacebar on the Mac is generally equivalent to clicking the Specify button. On Windows, Alt+F accomplishes the same thing.

Navigating the FileMaker Interface

A number of shortcuts can help you navigate through the FileMaker interface itself. Using keyboard commands, you can trigger buttons, move between elements of a dialog box, and scroll quickly though pop-up lists and menus.

Function	Mac Key	Windows Key
Move Between Tabs in a Dialog Box		Ctrl+Tab
Move Backward and Forward Between Items Within a Dialog	Shift-Tab/Tab	Shift+Tab/Tab
Move Up and Down Within a Pop-up List or Menu	Up/Down arrow	Up/Down arrow
Move to Beginning or End of a Pop-up List or Menu	Home/End	Home/End
Cancel a Dialog	Esc	Esc
Submit a Dialog (Choose the Default Button)	Enter	Enter

The Mac OS has weaker support for tabbing through and activating elements in a dialog box. For those dialogs where it's possible to do this on the Mac OS, only a few of the elements are accessible via the keyboard. In Windows, by contrast, virtually every aspect of a dialog can be selected and triggered via the keyboard.

Menu Reference

The following table presents a list of all of the menu items in FileMaker Pro and FileMaker Pro Advanced. We list the Mac and Windows keyboard shortcuts, as well as the Windows Alt-key equivalents.

There are certain commands we consider essential knowledge for FileMaker developers. We've marked these with an asterisk (*).

File Menu

	Menu Item or Submenu	Mac OS Key	Windows Key	Windows Alt
	New Database			Alt+F+N
*	Open	⌘-O	Ctrl+O	Alt+F+O
*	Open Remote	Shift-⌘-O	Ctrl+Shift+O	Alt+F+M
	Open Recent			Alt+F+T + item number
*	Close	⌘-W	Ctrl+W	Alt+F+C
	Define			
*	Database	Shift-⌘-D	Ctrl+Shift+D	Alt+F+D+D
	Value Lists			Alt+F+D+V
	File References			Alt+F+D+F
	Accounts and Privileges			Alt+F+D+A
*	Custom Functions			Alt+F+D+C
	Custom Menus			Alt+F+D+M
	File Options			Alt+F+F
	Change Password			Alt+F+W
	Print Setup			Alt+F+S
	Print	⌘-P	Ctrl+P	Alt+F+P

File Menu (continued)

Menu Item or Submenu	Mac OS Key	Windows Key	Windows Alt
Import Records			
File			Alt+F+I+F
Folder			Alt+F+I+D
XML Data Source			Alt+F+I+X
ODBC Data Source			Alt+F+I+O
Export Records			Alt+F+E
Save/Send Records As			
Excel			Alt+F+R+E
PDF			Alt+F+R+P
Send Mail			Alt+F+I
Save a Copy As			Alt+F+Y
Recover			Alt+F+V
* Exit (Windows only)		Ctrl+Q	Alt+F+X

FileMaker Pro/Advanced Menu (Mac OS Only)

Menu Item or Submenu	Mac OS Key	Windows Key	Windows Alt
Preferences	⌘-,		
* Quit	⌘-Q		
Sharing			
FileMaker Network			
Instant Web Publishing			
ODBC/JDBC			

Edit Menu

Menu Item or Submenu	Mac OS Key	Windows Key	Windows Alt
* Undo	⌘-Z	Ctrl+Z	Alt+E+U
* Cut	⌘-X	Ctrl+X	Alt+E+T
* Copy	⌘-C	Ctrl+C	Alt+E+C
* Paste	⌘-V	Ctrl+V	Alt+E+P
Paste Special			Alt+E+S
* Clear	Del		Alt+E+E
* Select All	⌘-A	Ctrl+A	Alt+E+A
Find/Replace			
Find/Replace	Shift-⌘-F	Ctrl+Shift+F	Alt+E+L+F
Find Again	⌘-G	Ctrl+G	Alt+E+L+A
Replace and Find Again	Shift-⌘-G	Ctrl+Alt+G	Alt+E+L+R

Edit Menu (continued)

Menu Item or Submenu	Mac OS Key	Windows Key	Windows Alt
Find Selected	Shift-⌘-H	Ctrl+Alt+H	Alt+E+L+S
Spelling			
Check Selection			Alt+E+N+S
Check Record			Alt+E+N+R
Check All			Alt+E+N+A
Correct Word	Shift-⌘-Y	Ctrl+Shift+Y	Alt+E+N+W
Select Dictionaries			Alt+E+N+D
Edit User Dictionary			Alt+E+N+U
Object (Windows Only)			
Links			Alt+E+O+L
Show Object			Alt+E+O+S
Convert			Alt+E+O+C
Export Field Contents			Alt+E+X
Sharing (Windows Only; Located in the FileMaker Pro/Advanced Menu on the Mac OS)			
FileMaker Network			Alt+E+H+N
ODBC/JDBC			Alt+E+H+O
Instant Web Publishing			Alt+E+H+W
Preferences (Windows Only)			Alt+E+F

View Menu

	Menu Item or Submenu	Mac OS Key	Windows Key	Windows Alt
*	Browse Mode	⌘-B	Ctrl+B	Alt+V+N
*	Find Mode	⌘-F	Ctrl+F	Alt+V+F
*	Layout Mode	⌘-L	Ctrl+L	Alt+V+L
*	Preview Mode	⌘-U	Ctrl+U	Alt+V+P
	Go to Layout			Alt+V+Y
	View As Form			Alt+V+M
	View As List			Alt+V+S
	View As Table			Alt+V+E
	Toolbars			
	Standard			Alt+V+T+S
	Text Formatting			Alt+V+T+F
	Arrange			Alt+V+T+A
	Tools			Alt+V+T+T
	Status Bar			Alt+V+U
	Status Area	Opt-⌘-S	Ctrl+Alt+S	Alt+V+A
	Text Ruler			Alt+V+X
	Zoom In			Alt+V+I

View Menu (continued)

Menu Item or Submenu	Mac OS Key	Windows Key	Windows Alt
Zoom Out			Alt+V+O
Page Margins			Alt+V+M
Graphic Rulers			Alt+V+G
Text Ruler			Alt+V+X
Ruler Lines			Alt+V+R
TSquares	⌘-T	Ctrl+T	Alt+V+Q
Object Size			Alt+V+Z
Show			
Buttons			Alt+V+S+B
Sample Data			Alt+V+S+S
Text Boundaries			Alt+V+S+T
Field Boundaries			Alt+V+S+F
Sliding Objects			Alt+V+S+O
Nonprinting Objects			Alt+V+S+N
Tooltips			Alt+V+S+P

Insert Menu

Note that items marked with (L) are only available in Layout mode.

Menu Item or Submenu	Mac OS Key	Windows Key	Windows Alt
Picture			Alt+I+P
QuickTime			Alt+I+Q
Sound			Alt+I+S
File			Alt+I+F
Object (Windows Only)			Alt+I+O
* Current Date	⌘-<minus>	Ctrl+<minus>	Alt+I+D
* Current Time	⌘-;	Ctrl+;	Alt+I+T
Current User Name	Shift-⌘-N	Ctrl+Shift+N	Alt+I+U
(Insert) from Index	⌘-I	Ctrl+I	Alt+I+I
(Insert) from Last Visited Record	⌘-'	Ctrl+'	Alt+I+L
Field (L)			Alt+I+F
Part (L)			Alt+I+A
Graphic Object (L)			
Text (L)			Alt+I+G+T
Line (L)			Alt+I+G+L
Rectangle (L)			Alt+I+G+R
Rounded Rectangle (L)			Alt+I+G+U
Oval (L)			Alt+I+G+O

Insert Menu (continued)

Note that items marked with (L) are only available in Layout mode.

Menu Item or Submenu	Mac OS Key	Windows Key	Windows Alt
Button (L)			Alt+I+N
Field/Control (L)			Alt+I+O
Tab Control (L)			Alt+I+B
Portal (L)			Alt+I+P
Object (L, Windows Only)			Alt+I+J
Picture (L)			Alt+I+C
Date Symbol (L)			Alt+I+E
Time Symbol (L)			Alt+I+I
User Name Symbol (L)			Alt+I+S
Page Number Symbol (L)			Alt+I+Y
Record Number Symbol (L)			Alt+I+R
* (Insert) Merge Field (L)	Shift-⌘-M	Ctrl+Shift+M	Alt+I+M

Format Menu

Note that items marked with (L) are only available in Layout mode.

Menu Item or Submenu	Mac OS Key	Windows Key	Windows Alt
Font			
Configure/More Fonts (Windows Only)			Alt+M+F+F
Size			
Custom			Alt+M+Z+C
Style			
* Plain Text	Shift-⌘-P	Ctrl+Shift+P	Alt+M+S+P
* Bold	Shift-⌘-B	Ctrl+Shift+B	Alt+M+S+B
* Italic	Shift-⌘-I	Ctrl+Shift+I	Alt+M+S+I
* Underline	Shift-⌘-U	Ctrl+Shift+U	Alt+M+S+U
Word Underline			Alt+M+S+W
Double Underline			Alt+M+S+D
Condense			Alt+M+S+C
Extend			Alt+M+S+E
Strikeout			Alt+M+S+K
Small Caps			Alt+M+S+M
Uppercase			Alt+M+S+A
Lowercase			Alt+M+S+L

Format Menu (continued)

Note that items marked with (L) are only available in Layout mode.

	Menu Item or Submenu	Mac OS Key	Windows Key	Windows Alt
	Title Case			Alt+M+S+T
	Superscript	Shift-⌘-<plus>		Alt+M+S+S
	Subscript	Shift-⌘-<minus>		Alt+M+S+R
	Align Text			
*	Left	⌘-[	Ctrl+[	Alt+M+A+L
*	Center	⌘-\	Ctrl+\	Alt+M+A+C
*	Right	⌘-]	Ctrl+]	Alt+M+A+R
	Full	Shift-⌘-\	Ctrl+Shift+\	Alt+M+A+F
	Top			Alt+M+A+T
	Center			Alt+M+A+E
	Bottom			Alt+M+A+B
	Line Spacing			
	Single			Alt+M+L+S
	Double			Alt+M+L+D
	Custom			Alt+M+L+C
	Orientation			
	Horizontal			Alt+M+E+H
	Sideways (Asian Only)			Alt+M+E+S
	Text Color			Alt+M+R
	Text (L)			Alt+M+X
	Number (L)			Alt+M+N
	Date (L)			Alt+M+D
	Time (L)			Alt+M+M
	Graphic (L)			Alt+M+G
	Field/Control (L)			
*	Setup (L)	Shift-⌘-F	Ctrl+Shift+F	Alt+M+C+S
*	Behavior (L)	Shift-⌘-K	Ctrl+Shift+K	Alt+M+C+H
*	Borders (L)	Shift-⌘-B	Ctrl+Shift+B	Alt+M+C+B
	Portal Setup (L)			Alt+M+P
	Tab Control Setup (L)			Alt+M+B
	Button Setup (L)			Alt+M+U
	Format Painter (L)			Alt+M+O
	Set Sliding/Printing (L)			Alt+M+I
	Set Tooltip (L)			Alt+M+T

Layouts Menu (Layout Mode Only)

	Menu Item or Submenu	Mac OS Key	Windows Key	Windows Alt
*	New Layout/Report	⌘-N	Ctrl+N	Alt+L+N
	Duplicate Layout			Alt+L+U
*	Delete Layout	⌘-E	Ctrl+E	Alt+L+D
	Go to Layout			
	Next (Layout)	Ctrl-<up arrow>	Ctrl+<up arrow>	Alt+L+G+N
	Previous (Layout)	Ctrl-<down arrow>	Ctrl+<down arrow>	Alt+L+G+P
	Specify			Alt+L+G+S
	Layout Setup			Alt+L+Y
	Part Setup			Alt+L+A
	Set Layout Order			Alt+L+O
	Set Tab Order			Alt+L+T
	Set Rulers			Alt+L+R
	Save Layout	⌘-S	Ctrl+S	Alt+L+S
	Revert Layout			Alt+L+E

Arrange Menu (Layout Mode Only)

	Menu Item or Submenu	Mac OS Key	Windows Key	Windows Alt
*	Group	⌘-R	Ctrl+R	Alt+A+G
*	Ungroup	Shift-⌘-R	Ctrl+Shift+R	Alt+A+U
*	Lock	Opt-⌘-L	Ctrl+Alt+L	Alt+A+L
*	Unlock	Shift-Opt-⌘-L	Ctrl+Alt+Shift+L	Alt+A+K
	Bring to Front	Opt-⌘-[	Ctrl+Alt+[	Alt+A+F
	Bring Forward	Shift-⌘-[	Ctrl+Shift+[	Alt+A+W
	Send to Back	Opt-⌘-]	Ctrl+Alt+]	Alt+A+B
	Send Backward	Shift-⌘-]	Ctrl+Shift+]	Alt+A+C
	Rotate	Opt-⌘-R	Ctrl+Alt+R	Alt+A+R
	Align			
*	Left Edges	Opt-⌘-<left arrow>	Ctrl+Alt+<left arrow>	Alt+A+N+L
	Centers			Alt+A+N+C
*	Right Edges	Opt-⌘-<right arrow>	Ctrl+Alt+<right arrow>	Alt+A+N+R
*	Top Edges	Opt-⌘-<up arrow>	Ctrl+Alt+<up arrow>	Alt+A+N+T
	Middles			Alt+A+N+M
*	Bottom Edges	Opt-⌘-<down arrow>	Ctrl+Alt+<down arrow>	Alt+A+N+B

Arrange Menu (Layout Mode only) (continued)

Menu Item or Submenu	Mac OS Key	Windows Key	Windows Alt
Distribute			
Horizontally			Alt+A+D+H
Vertically			Alt+A+D+V
Resize To			
Smallest Width			Alt+A+S+S
Smallest Height			Alt+A+S+M
Smallest Width and Height			Alt+A+S+A
Largest Width			Alt+A+S+L
Largest Height			Alt+A+S+H
Largest Width and Height			Alt+A+S+W
Object Grids	⌘-Y	Ctrl+Y	Alt+A+O

Records Menu

Menu Item or Submenu	Mac OS Key	Windows Key	Windows Alt
* New Record	⌘-N	Ctrl+N	Alt+R+N
* Duplicate Record	⌘-D	Ctrl+D	Alt+R+A
* Delete Record	⌘-E	Ctrl+E	Alt+R+D
Delete Found/All Records			Alt+R+T
Go to Record			
Next (Record)	Ctrl-<down arrow>	Ctrl+<down arrow>	Alt+R+G+N
Previous (Record)	Ctrl-<up arrow>	Ctrl+<up arrow>	Alt+R+G+P
Specify			Alt+R+G+S
* Show All Records	⌘-J	Ctrl+J	Alt+R+W
Show Omitted Only			Alt+R+I
* Omit Record	⌘-T	Ctrl+T	Alt+R+O
Omit Multiple	Shift-⌘-T	Ctrl+Shift+T	Alt+R+M
* Modify Last Find	⌘-R	Ctrl+R	Alt+R+F
* Sort Records	⌘-S	Ctrl+S	Alt+R+S
Unsort			Alt+R+U
* Replace Field Contents	⌘-=	Ctrl+=	Alt+R+E
Relookup Field Contents			Alt+R+K
Revert Record			Alt+R+R

Requests Menu (Find Mode Only)

Menu Item or Submenu	Mac OS Key	Windows Key	Windows Alt
* Add New Request	⌘-N	Ctrl+N	Alt+R+N
* Duplicate Request	⌘-D	Ctrl+D	Alt+R+U
* Delete Request	⌘-E	Ctrl+E	Alt+R+D
Go to Request			
Next Request	Ctrl-<up arrow>	Ctrl+<up arrow>	Alt+R+G+N
Previous Request	Ctrl-<down arrow>	Ctrl+<down arrow>	Alt+R+G+P
Specify			Alt+R+G+S
Show All Records	⌘-J	Ctrl+J	Alt+R+W
Perform Find	Enter	Enter	Alt+R+P
Constrain Found Set			Alt+R+C
Extend Found Set			Alt+R+E
Revert Request			Alt+R+R

Scripts Menu

Menu Item or Submenu	Mac OS Key	Windows Key	Windows Alt
* ScriptMaker	Shift-⌘-S	Ctrl+Shift+S	Alt+S+S

Tools (FileMaker Pro Advanced Only)

Menu Item or Submenu	Mac OS Key	Windows Key	Windows Alt
Debug Scripts			Alt+T+D
Debugging Controls			
Step	F5	F5	Alt+T+E+S
Step Into	F6	F6	Alt+T+E+T
Step Out	F7	F7	Alt+T+E+O
Run	F8	F8	Alt+T+E+R
Halt Script	⌘-F8	Ctrl+F8	Alt+T+E+H
Set Next Step	⌘-Shift-F5	Ctrl+Shift+F5	Alt+T+E+N
Set Breakpoint	⌘-F9	Ctrl+F9	Alt+T+E+B
Remove Breakpoints	⌘-Shift-F9	Ctrl+Shift+F9	Alt+T+E+M
(Enter) ScriptMaker	⌘-F10	Ctrl+F10	Alt+T+E+P
Data Viewer			Alt+T+V
Custom Menus			
Define Custom Menus			Alt+T+C+M
Database Design Report			Alt+F+G
Developer Utilities			Alt+T+U
File Maintenance			Alt+T+A

Window Menu

Menu Item or Submenu	Mac OS Key	Windows Key	Windows Alt
New Window			Alt+W+N
Show Window			Alt+W+S
Hide Window			Alt+W+H
Minimize Window	⌘-H	Ctrl+H	Alt+W+M
Tile Horizontally		Shift+F4	Alt+W+T
Tile Vertically			Alt+W+V
Cascade Windows		Shift+F5	Alt+W+C
Arrange Icons			Alt+W+I

Help Menu

Menu Item or Submenu	Mac OS Key	Windows Key	Windows Alt
FileMaker Help	⌘-?	Ctrl+?	Alt+H+H

FileMaker Network Ports

About Network Ports

A network "port" may sound like a physical connection of some kind, like the USB ports on the back (or front or side) of your computer. In network terminology, though, a port is most often a logical or virtual concept, part of a network transport protocol (TCP/IP, for example, or UDP). In this sense, a port is a logical destination on a specific host that is identified with some particular service or listener. Port 21, for example, is often used for FTP servers.

Ports are most often significant to FileMaker administrators who administer or otherwise encounter firewalls. Many firewalls do port-based blocking or filtering of traffic. If traffic to or from a particular port is not permitted across a firewall, services may be disrupted or blocked. For example, if port 21 is blocked on a firewall, an FTP server behind that firewall will be unreachable. If port 5003 is blocked on a firewall, a FileMaker server behind the firewall will be unreachable.

For an extensive listing of port numbers, see the list maintained by IANA at http://www.iana.org/assignments/port-numbers. Some of the FileMaker network ports are registered whereas others are not, though this has little practical significance for FileMaker administrators.

FileMaker Network Ports

The bulk of these port numbers are set internally by the FileMaker products in question and cannot be changed or overridden. Exceptions are noted in Table 13.1.

Table 13.1 FileMaker Network Ports

Port	Service
80	The default port for HTTP (that is, for web traffic). This may be the default port for any web server being used to serve FileMaker data to the Web. This port is controlled in the settings for the web server and can be freely altered.

Table 13.1   FileMaker Network Ports (continued)

Port	Service
591	FileMaker, Inc. reserved port 591 for traffic to the FileMaker Web Companion, which was the web publishing technology available in FileMaker 4-6. Despite the fact that this is a reserved port, it was always possible to use a port other than 591 for Web Companion traffic, though administrators often found it convenient to use this one. (The port was settable in the plug-ins preference for the Web Companion, within the FileMaker client in FileMaker 6 and before.) The port is still reserved to FileMaker, Inc. and so makes a good second choice as a web port when the default web port of 80 is in use.
2399	Port used for ODBC and JDBC access to FileMaker Server Advanced. In addition to enabling ODBC/JDBC on the server and in the privilege sets of individual files, traffic must be able to flow to port 2399 on the server from any ODBC/JDBC clients.
5003	Port used for network access to hosted FileMaker databases. In order to open hosted FileMaker databases, traffic must be able to flow to port 5003 on the server from any FileMaker clients on the network.
16008-16018	These ports are used by the Web Publishing Engine. When configuring FileMaker Server Advanced on multiple machines, if the Web Publishing Engine and the web server are installed on different machines, then at a minimum traffic must be able to flow between the two machines on ports 16016 and 16018.
50003	FileMaker Server port for remote administration. In addition to enabling remote administration in the server configuration, traffic must be able to flow to port 50003 on the server from any remote instances of the Server Administration tool.
50006	FileMaker Server Helper port for remote administration. In addition to enabling remote administration in the server configuration, traffic must be able to flow to port 50006 on the server from any remote instances of the Server Administration tool.

FileMaker Server Command Line Reference

Administering FileMaker Server from the Command Line

In addition to administering FileMaker Server using the graphical Server Administration Tool (SAT), it's also possible to administer the server using a command-line tool called fmsadmin. The fmsadmin tool is installed along with FileMaker Server itself, and can be used to administer instances of FileMaker Server running on the same machine, or on a remote machine with remote administration enabled—much as the SAT can be used.

The fmsadmin tool behaves like any other command-line utility or tool in the Mac OS X or Windows operating systems. It can be invoked directly from the command line (Mac OS X Terminal, Windows Command Prompt). It can also be invoked from within any command-line script, and as such can form part of a variety of automated administrative processes.

In order to invoke fmsadmin from the command line, you'll need to know where the tool is located. If the install location is in your system path, simply issuing the command fmsadmin (plus necessary options) is sufficient. By default, though, the tool is installed outside the regular system paths. To address this problem, either add the tool's install location to the system path, or create a shortcut or symbolic link to the tool from one of the system path directories (/usr/bin on Mac OS X or C:\WINDOWS on Windows, for example). Alternatively, you can invoke the tool by referring to it by its full installed path.

The installed path can vary, but these are the default locations:

Mac OS X:

/Library/FileMaker\ Server\ 8/Tools/fmsadmin

Windows:

C:\Program Files\FileMaker Server 8\fmsadmin

Command Line Reference

To invoke fmsadmin from the command line, you'll need to supply three pieces of information. You'll need the name of the tool itself (fmsadmin, assuming it is accessible by an existing path; otherwise, the full path to the tool must be specified). You'll need the name of a particular *command* to invoke (such as "backup" to back up files or "close" to close files). And you may need one or more *options* that give further specificity to the command. An example would be

fmsadmin close –m "All files closing" –t 120

This command would close all files on the server after a two-minute (120-second) grace period, and send all connected clients a warning saying "All files closing."

FileMaker Server Command Line Reference

In the reference that follows, we list the name of each command, along with a description, a general usage template, one or more examples, and explanations of any applicable options. Some of the options are specific to only one or two commands, but most are applicable across several commands.

backup

fmsadmin backup [file...] [path...] [-diopuwy]

Description:

The backup command can be used to back up a single file, all the files in a directory, or all the files hosted by a single instance of FileMaker Server. The backup command can be used alone, in which case it performs a "live" or "hot" backup of the specified files. It can also be used in conjunction with the pause and resume commands. Though this method will interfere with user access to the files, it will also allow the backup to complete more quickly. The pause-backup-resume usage mimics the backup behavior of FileMaker Server 5.5.

Examples:

fmsadmin backup Products.fp7

fmsadmin backup /Products -d E:\FileMaker_Backups

Options:

-d PATH, --dest PATH	Specify a destination path for a backup.
-i address, --ip address	Specify the IP address of a remote server.
-o, --offline	Perform an offline backup.
-p pass, --password pass	Password to use to authenticate with the server.
-u user, --user user	Username to use to authenticate with the server.
-w seconds, --wait seconds	Specify time in seconds for command to time out.
-y, --yes	Automatically answer "yes" to all prompts.

close

fmsadmin close [file...] [path...] [-imptuwy]

Description:

This command closes one or more database files. It can be used to close a specific file, all the files in a directory, or all files on the server.

Examples:

    fmsadmin close

    fmsadmin close -y

    fmsadmin close -y Products.fp7

    fmsadmin close -y "Invoice Items.fp7"

Options:

-i address, --ip address	Specify the IP address of a remote server.
-m message, --message message	Specify a text message to send to clients.
-p pass, --password pass	Password to use to authenticate with the server.
-t, --grace-time	Specify time in seconds before clients will be forcibly disconnected.
-u user, --user user	Username to use to authenticate with the server.
-w seconds, --wait seconds	Specify time in seconds for command to time out.
-y, --yes	Automatically answer "yes" to all prompts.

delete

fmsadmin delete schedule [schedule #] [-ipuwy]

Description:

This command deletes a specific schedule, referenced by its schedule number. Schedule numbers can be determined using the list schedules command.

Examples:

    fmsadmin delete schedule 1

    fmsadmin delete schedule 3 --wait 5 -y

Options:

-i address, --ip address	Specify the IP address of a remote server.
-p pass, --password pass	Password to use to authenticate with the server.
-u user, --user user	Username to use to authenticate with the server.
-w seconds, --wait seconds	Specify time in seconds for command to time out.
-y, --yes	Automatically answer "yes" to all prompts.

disable

fmsadmin disable type [plug-in #] [schedule #] [-ipuwy]

Description:

This command is used to disable server-side plug-ins or schedules. Plug-ins and schedules are referenced by number. The numbers can be determined by using the list schedules or list plugins commands.

Examples:

    fmsadmin disable plugin 3 -y

    fmsadmin disable schedule 1 -y

Options:

-i address, --ip address	Specify the IP address of a remote server.
-p pass, --password pass	Password to use to authenticate with the server.
-u user, --user user	Username to use to authenticate with the server.
-w seconds, --wait seconds	Specify time in seconds for command to time out.
-y, --yes	Automatically answer "yes" to all prompts.

disconnect

fmsadmin disconnect client [client #] [-impuwy]

Description:

This command is used to disconnect a specific client. Clients are referenced by client number. Client numbers can be determined by using the list clients command. A specific message can be sent to the client(s) as well.

Examples:

fmsadmin disconnect client 13 -y

fmsadmin disconnect client 12 -m "It's time for lunch, Sarah" -y

Options:

-i address, --ip address	Specify the IP address of a remote server.
-m message, --message message	Specify a text message to send to clients.
-p pass, --password pass	Password to use to authenticate with the server.
-u user, --user user	Username to use to authenticate with the server.
-w seconds, --wait seconds	Specify time in seconds for command to time out.
-y, --yes	Automatically answer "yes" to all prompts.

enable

fmsadmin enable type [plug-in #] [schedule #][-ipuwy]

Description:

This command is used to enable plug-ins or schedules. Plug-ins and schedules are referenced by number. The numbers can be determined by using the list schedules or list plugins commands.

Examples:

fmsadmin enable schedule 3

fmasdmin enable plugin 1

Options:

-i address, --ip address	Specify the IP address of a remote server.
-p pass, --password pass	Password to use to authenticate with the server.
-u user, --user user	Username to use to authenticate with the server.

-w seconds, --wait seconds	Specify time in seconds for command to time out.
-y, --yes	Automatically answer "yes" to all prompts.

Help

fmsadmin help [command]

Description:

This command will display help information on the command line commands and syntax.

Examples:

fmsadmin help options

fmsadmin help commands

fmsadmin help resume

Options:

None

list

fmsadmin list type [-ipsuwy]

Description:

This command can be used to obtain a list of clients, files, plug-ins, or schedules from the server. Among other things, this command will return item numbers that are necessary for other commands such as enable schedule and similar commands.

Examples:

fmsadmin list clients

fmsadmin list plugins

Options:

-i address, --ip address	Specify the IP address of a remote server.
-p pass, --password pass	Password to use to authenticate with the server.
-s, --stats	Return additional detail about clients or files.
-u user, --user user	Username to use to authenticate with the server.
-w seconds, --wait seconds	Specify time in seconds for command to time out.
-y, --yes	Automatically answer "yes" to all prompts.

open

fmsadmin open [file...] [path...] [-ipuwy]

Description:

This command is used to open databases. Like the close command, it can be used to open all files on the server, all files within a single directory, or a single named file.

Examples:

fmsadmin open Clinic.fp7

fmsadmin open -y

fmsadmin open /ClinicFiles

Options:

-i address, --ip address	Specify the IP address of a remote server.
-p pass, --password pass	Password to use to authenticate with the server.
-u user, --user user	Username to use to authenticate with the server.
-w seconds, --wait seconds	Specify time in seconds for command to time out.
-y, --yes	Automatically answer "yes" to all prompts.

pause

fmsadmin pause [file...] [path...] [-ipuwy]

Description:

This command is used to pause databases. Like the open and close commands, it can be used to affect all files on the server, all files within a single directory, or a single named file.

Examples:

fmsadmin pause -y

fmsadmin pause --wait 30 -y

Options:

-i address, --ip address	Specify the IP address of a remote server.
-p pass, --password pass	Password to use to authenticate with the server.
-u user, --user user	Username to use to authenticate with the server.
-w seconds, --wait seconds	Specify time in seconds for command to time out.
-y, --yes	Automatically answer "yes" to all prompts.

reload

fmsadmin reload [-ipuvwy]

Description:

This command reloads the server configuration. Any unsaved properties will be replaced with the most recently stored values for those properties.

Examples:

   fmsadmin reload

Options:

-i address, --ip address	Specify the IP address of a remote server.
-p pass, --password pass	Password to use to authenticate with the server.
-u user, --user user	Username to use to authenticate with the server.
-w seconds, --wait seconds	Specify time in seconds for command to time out.
-y, --yes	Automatically answer "yes" to all prompts.

resume

fmsadmin resume [file...][path...] [-ipuwy]

Description:

This command is used to resume databases that have been paused. Like the open and close commands, it can be used to affect all files on the server, all files within a single directory, or a single named file.

Examples:

   fmsadmin resume -y

   fmsadmin resume "Clinic.fp7"

Options:

-i address, --ip address	Specify the IP address of a remote server.
-p pass, --password pass	Password to use to authenticate with the server.
-u user, --user user	Username to use to authenticate with the server.
-w seconds, --wait seconds	Specify time in seconds for command to time out.
-y, --yes	Automatically answer "yes" to all prompts.

run

fmsadmin run schedule [schedule #] [-ipuwy]

Description:

This command is used to run a schedule, specified by number. Schedule numbers can be obtained by using the list schedules command.

Examples:

fms admin run schedule 3

Options:

-i address, --ip address	Specify the IP address of a remote server.
-p pass, --password pass	Password to use to authenticate with the server.
-u user, --user user	Username to use to authenticate with the server.
-w seconds, --wait seconds	Specify time in seconds for command to time out.
-y, --yes	Automatically answer "yes" to all prompts.

send

fmsadmin send [-cimpuwy] [client #] [file...] [path...]

Description:

This command can be used to send a text message to all clients. The command can be used to affect all clients connected to the server, or limited to just those clients connected to files in a specific path, or to a single specific file, or to a single client specified by number. Unlike other commands, with send you must use the -c option when specifying a client number.

Examples:

fmsadmin send -m "The server will shut down for maintenance in 15 minutes."

fmsadmin send -c 17 -m "Fred, it's time to go home."

fmsadmin send "Clinics.fp7" -m "The Clinics file will shut down in 5 minutes."

Options:

-c, --client	Used to specify a client number.
-i address, --ip address	Specify the IP address of a remote server.
-m message, --message message	Specify a text message to send to clients.

-p pass, --password pass	Password to use to authenticate with the server.
-u user, --user user	Username to use to authenticate with the server.
-w seconds, --wait seconds	Specify time in seconds for command to time out.
-y, --yes	Automatically answer "yes" to all prompts.

status

fmsadmin status type [-ipuwy] [id #] [file]

Description:

This command is used to determine the status of a client or a file.

Examples:

    fmsadmin status file "Clinics.fp7"

    fmsadmin status client 30

Options:

-i address, --ip address	Specify the IP address of a remote server.
-p pass, --password pass	Password to use to authenticate with the server.
-u user, --user user	Username to use to authenticate with the server.
-w seconds, --wait seconds	Specify time in seconds for command to time out.
-y, --yes	Automatically answer "yes" to all prompts.

stop

fmsadmin stop [-fimptuwy]

Description:

This command will stop the server process. All connected users will have 30 seconds to close their open files. This grace period can be changed using the -t option.

Examples:

    fmsadmin stop

    fmsadmin stop -f

    fmsadmin stop -t 120 -m "The server will shut down in two minutes."

Options:

-f, --force	Close databases or shut down the server forcefully, without waiting for clients to disconnect gracefully.
-i address, --ip address	Specify the IP address of a remote server.
-m message, --message message	Specify a text message to send to clients.
-p pass, --password pass	Password to use to authenticate with the server.
-t, --grace-time	Specify time in seconds before clients will be forcibly disconnected.
-u user, --user user	Username to use to authenticate with the server.
-w seconds, --wait seconds	Specify time in seconds for command to time out.
-y, --yes	Automatically answer "yes" to all prompts.

FileMaker XML Reference

About FileMaker and XML

XML (along with its companion technology, XSLT), is the driving technology behind FileMaker's Custom Web Publishing (CWP). FileMaker Server Advanced can serve out FileMaker data as XML, for use in applications that require XML data. It can also transform the XML data extracted using XSLT stylesheets, to create a variety of output formats, including, of course, an HTML presentation layer.

This section is a reference guide to FileMaker XML syntax. We cover the following areas:

- URL syntax for accessing FileMaker data over the Web
- Syntax of the various FileMaker XML grammars
- FileMaker URL query commands and query string parameters
- Important XML namespaces for use with Custom Web Publishing

We do not cover in detail all of the XSLT extension functions available in Custom Web Publishing.

URL Syntax for Web Access to FileMaker Data

FileMaker can provide data in XML format in two ways: via the Export As XML feature in the regular FileMaker client, and via URL-based access requests sent directly to databases hosted via FileMaker Server Advanced.

A URL designed to extract data from FileMaker Server Advanced has two components: a resource name, and a query string. This section demonstrates the correct syntax for resource names within a URL. The query string is made up of potentially many commands and parameters: later sections of this chapter discuss those in more detail.

→ For more information on the structure of query requests, see "Query Parameters for XML/XSLT URL Requests," later in this chapter.

URL Syntax for XML Access

In order to extract data from FileMaker Server Advanced in XML format, a URL of the following form is used:

<protocol>://<host>[:<port>]/fmi/xml/<grammar>.xml?<query string>

- <protocol> is either http (for regular HTTP access) or https (for secure HTTP access).
- <host> is the hostname or the IP address of the web server that's been configured with FileMaker Server Advanced. (Note that if the web server is on a machine other than the FileMaker Server, it's the address of the web server that must be used here, not that of the FileMaker Server machine.)
- <port> need only be specified if the web server has been configured to run on a port other than the default for the specified protocol (80 for HTTP, 443 for HTTPS).
- <grammar> is the name of one of the four valid FileMaker XML grammars, discussed in the next section.
- <query string> is a query string composed of some number of query parameters in combination with a query command. Specifics are discussed in upcoming sections.

Example:

http://my.filemakerserver.net:8080/fmi/xml/fmresultset.xml?-dbnames

This query will access a server running on port 8080 on the machine my.filemakerserver.net, and will request a list of all databases available for XML access on that server, with the results returned in the fmresultset grammar.

URL Syntax for Access to Container Objects

FileMaker Server Advanced has a special URL syntax for accessing data in container fields. Such a request will cause the container data to be returned directly (much like clicking on a PDF link in a web page). The exact mechanism depends on whether the container data is stored directly in the database, or stored by reference. In order to extract container data stored directly in a FileMaker database, a URL of the following form is used:

<protocol>://<host>[:<port>]/fmi/xml/cnt/data.<extension>?<query string>

- <protocol>, <host>, <port>, and <query string> are as described in the previous section.
- <extension> is the file type extension for the container data being fetched (.jpg, .txt, and the like). This extension allows the web server to set the MIME type of the data correctly.

The query string must contain a –field query parameter with a fully qualified field name, meaning it must contain a repetition index number reference even if the field is not a repeating field.

Example:

http://my.filemakerserver.net:8080/fmi/xml/cnt/data.tiffgif?-db=
Customers&-lay=web_search&-field=photo[1]&-recid=303

This URL will extract container data from a specific field (called photo) from the record with recid=303. Even though photo is not a repeating field, the syntax photo[1] is still necessary. The web server will return this container data as GIF data, assuming the .gif suffix is correctly mapped to the TIFF MIME type on the server.

For information on how to manage container data when the container data is stored only by reference, please see the FileMaker Server Custom Web Publishing Documentation.

URL Syntax for XSLT Access

When extracting XML data from FileMaker Server Advanced, it's also possible to apply an XSLT stylesheet in order to transform the XML into something else, such as an HTML page. The syntax for XSLT access is as follows:

<protocol>://<host>[:<port>]/fmi/xsl/<path>/<stylesheet>.xsl?<query string>

- <protocol>, <host>, <port>, and <query string> are as described in the previous sections.
- The <path> element is optional. Without it, the Web Publishing engine will look for the specified stylesheet within the xslt-template-files directory on the web server. If you wish to create additional directory structures within the xslt-template-files folder, the relative path to the stylesheet must be specified here.
- <stylesheet> is the name of the stylesheet that will be applied to the XML data.

Example:

http://my.filemakerserver.net/fmi/xsl/customer-files/customer_list.xsl?-db=Customer&-lay=list&-max=50&-findall

FileMaker XML Grammars

FileMaker can publish data in any of four XML "grammars." Note that the grammar names are case sensitive.

- **FMPXMLRESULT**—This grammar is available either via Custom Web Publishing or via Export As XML. It's a complete data export grammar, but can be a bit difficult to parse or read.
- **FMPDSORESULT**—Also a complete data export grammar, available via either CWP or export, but this grammar has been deprecated and we recommend that you do not use it.
- **fmresultset**—This grammar was introduced with FileMaker Server 7 Advanced and is in some sense the "best" data export grammar, being rather easier to parse and read than FMPXMLRESULT. We recommend you use it where possible. It is available only via CWP using FileMaker Server Advanced, not via Export As XML.
- **FMPXMLLAYOUT**—A specialized grammar used for extracting information about a FileMaker layout. Only available via CWP.

Following is a sample of each grammar.

FMPXMLRESULT

```xml
<?xml version="1.0" encoding="UTF-8" standalone="no"?>
<!DOCTYPE FMPXMLRESULT PUBLIC "-//FMI//DTD FMPXMLRESULT//EN"
"/fmi/xml/FMPXMLRESULT.dtd">
<FMPXMLRESULT xmlns="http://www.filemaker.com/fmpxmlresult">
 <ERRORCODE>0</ERRORCODE>
 <PRODUCT BUILD="08/12/2004" NAME="FileMaker Web Publishing Engine"
VERSION="7.0v3"/>
 <DATABASE DATEFORMAT="MM/dd/yyyy" LAYOUT="house_web" NAME="House" RECORDS="14"
TIMEFORMAT="HH:mm:ss"/>
 <METADATA>
  <FIELD EMPTYOK="YES" MAXREPEAT="1" NAME="Address" TYPE="TEXT"/>
  <FIELD EMPTYOK="YES" MAXREPEAT="1" NAME="City" TYPE="TEXT"/>
  <FIELD EMPTYOK="YES" MAXREPEAT="1" NAME="State" TYPE="TEXT"/>
  <FIELD EMPTYOK="YES" MAXREPEAT="1" NAME="PostalCode" TYPE="TEXT"/>
  <FIELD EMPTYOK="YES" MAXREPEAT="1" NAME="LotSizeAcres" TYPE="NUMBER"/>
  <FIELD EMPTYOK="YES" MAXREPEAT="1" NAME="CountBedrooms" TYPE="NUMBER"/>
  <FIELD EMPTYOK="YES" MAXREPEAT="1" NAME="AskingPrice" TYPE="NUMBER"/>
 </METADATA>
 <RESULTSET FOUND="14">
  <ROW MODID="1" RECORDID="1">
   <COL>
    <DATA>12 Oak Lane</DATA>
   </COL>
   <COL>
    <DATA>Morten</DATA>
   </COL>
   <COL>
    <DATA>MO</DATA>
   </COL>
   <COL>
    <DATA>14231</DATA>
   </COL>
   <COL>
    <DATA>.65</DATA>
   </COL>
   <COL>
    <DATA>3</DATA>
   </COL>
   <COL>
    <DATA>265000</DATA>
   </COL>
  </ROW>
 </RESULTSET>
</FMPXMLRESULT>
```

FMPDSORESULT

```
<?xml version="1.0" encoding="UTF-8" standalone="no"?>
<!--This grammar has been deprecated - use fmresultset or FMPXMLRESULT
instead-->
<!--DOCTYPE FMPDSORESULT SYSTEM "/fmi/xml/FMPDSORESULT.dtd?-db=House&-lay=house_web"-
->
<FMPDSORESULT xmlns="http://www.filemaker.com/fmpdsoresult">
 <ERRORCODE>0</ERRORCODE>
 <DATABASE>House</DATABASE>
 <LAYOUT>house_web</LAYOUT>
 <ROW MODID="1" RECORDID="1">
  <Address>12 Oak Lane</Address>
  <City>Morten</City>
  <State>MO</State>
  <PostalCode>14231</PostalCode>
  <LotSizeAcres>.65</LotSizeAcres>
  <CountBedrooms>3</CountBedrooms>
  <AskingPrice>265000</AskingPrice>
 </ROW>
</FMPDSORESULT>
```

fmresultset

```
<?xml version="1.0" encoding="UTF-8" standalone="no"?>
<!DOCTYPE fmresultset PUBLIC "-//FMI//DTD fmresultset//EN"
"/fmi/xml/fmresultset.dtd">
<fmresultset xmlns="http://www.filemaker.com/xml/fmresultset" version="1.0">
 <error code="0"/>
 <product build="08/12/2004" name="FileMaker Web Publishing Engine"
version="7.0v3"/>
 <datasource database="House" date-format="MM/dd/yyyy" layout="house_web"
table="House"
  time-format="HH:mm:ss" timestamp-format="MM/dd/yyyy HH:mm:ss"
total-count="14"/>
 <metadata>
  <field-definition auto-enter="no" global="no" max-repeat="1" name="Address"
not-empty="no"
    result="text" type="normal"/>
  <field-definition auto-enter="no" global="no" max-repeat="1" name="City"
not-empty="no"
    result="text" type="normal"/>
  <field-definition auto-enter="no" global="no" max-repeat="1" name="State"
not-empty="no"
    result="text" type="normal"/>
  <field-definition auto-enter="no" global="no" max-repeat="1"
```

```
name="PostalCode" not-empty="no"
  result="text" type="normal"/>
 <field-definition auto-enter="no" global="no" max-repeat="1"
name="LotSizeAcres" not-empty="no"
  result="number" type="normal"/>
 <field-definition auto-enter="no" global="no" max-repeat="1"
name="CountBedrooms" not-empty="no"
  result="number" type="normal"/>
 <field-definition auto-enter="no" global="no" max-repeat="1"
name="AskingPrice" not-empty="no"
  result="number" type="normal"/>
</metadata>
<resultset count="14" fetch-size="1">
 <record mod-id="1" record-id="1">
  <field name="Address">
   <data>12 Oak Lane</data>
  </field>
  <field name="City">
   <data>Morten</data>
  </field>
  <field name="State">
   <data>MO</data>
  </field>
  <field name="PostalCode">
   <data>14231</data>
  </field>
  <field name="LotSizeAcres">
   <data>.65</data>
  </field>
  <field name="CountBedrooms">
   <data>3</data>
  </field>
  <field name="AskingPrice">
   <data>265000</data>
  </field>
 </record>
</resultset>
</fmresultset>
```

FMPXMLLAYOUT

```
<?xml version="1.0" encoding="UTF-8" standalone="no"?>
<!DOCTYPE FMPXMLLAYOUT PUBLIC "-//FMI//DTD FMPXMLLAYOUT//EN" "/fmi/xml/FMPXMLLAY-
OUT.dtd">
<FMPXMLLAYOUT xmlns="http://www.filemaker.com/fmpxmllayout">
 <ERRORCODE>0</ERRORCODE>
```

```
<PRODUCT BUILD="08/12/2004" NAME="FileMaker Web Publishing Engine" VERSION="7.0v3"/>
<LAYOUT DATABASE="House" NAME="house_web">
 <FIELD NAME="Address">
  <STYLE TYPE="EDITTEXT" VALUELIST=""/>
 </FIELD>
 <FIELD NAME="City">
  <STYLE TYPE="EDITTEXT" VALUELIST=""/>
 </FIELD>
 <FIELD NAME="State">
  <STYLE TYPE="EDITTEXT" VALUELIST=""/>
 </FIELD>
 <FIELD NAME="PostalCode">
  <STYLE TYPE="EDITTEXT" VALUELIST=""/>
 </FIELD>
 <FIELD NAME="LotSizeAcres">
  <STYLE TYPE="EDITTEXT" VALUELIST=""/>
 </FIELD>
 <FIELD NAME="CountBedrooms">
  <STYLE TYPE="EDITTEXT" VALUELIST=""/>
 </FIELD>
 <FIELD NAME="AskingPrice">
  <STYLE TYPE="EDITTEXT" VALUELIST=""/>
 </FIELD>
</LAYOUT>
<VALUELISTS/>
</FMPXMLLAYOUT>
```

Query Parameters for XML/XSLT URL Requests

The FileMaker Web Publishing Engine delivers XML data in response to specially format-ted URLs. The specific details of the request are contained in the *query string*, which is a specific portion of the URL. For example, the query string is highlighted in the following URL:

http://my.filemakerserver.net/fmi/xsl/customer-files/customer_list.xsl?**-db=Customer&-lay=list&-max=50&-findall**

The query string consists of a series of *name-value pairs*, of the form name=value, sepa-rated by ampersands, and following a question mark within the URL.

Generally, a query string intended for the Web Publishing Engine consists of a single *query command*, representing the type of request being made, supported by additional query parameters that add specificity to the request. In the preceding example, the request is –findall (find all records). Additional query parameters specify the database, the layout, and the maximum number of records to be returned.

Please note the following important points about URL queries.

- Each URL query string must contain one and only one query command (though it may contain many additional query parameters).
- Query commands and query parameters begin with a hyphen (-). Omitting the hyphen will cause an error.
- A query command is expressed as a plain name, not as a name-value pair. Any supplied value will be ignored. (So you can say ...&-findall=somevalue, but the =somevalue will be ignored.)
- The names of FileMaker fields, when included in the URL for purposes of searching, or creating or editing records, do *not* require a hyphen.
- Most query commands have a minimum set of query parameters that *must* also be provided in the URL. These are noted in the tables below.

Query Commands

This section lists the possible query commands. If the command requires certain specific additional parameters, those are listed.

Command	Parameters Required	Description
-dbnames	None	Returns a list of all databases on the given server that are enabled for XML or XSLT publishing.

http://my.server.com/fmi/xml/fmresultset.xml?-dbnames

-delete	-db, -lay, -recid	Delete the record with the specified recid from the specified database. (The affected table is determined by the specified layout.)

http://my.server.com/fmi/xml/fmresultset.xml?-db=Customer&-lay=web&-recid=303&-delete

-dup	-db, -lay, -recid	Duplicate the record with the specified record ID from the specified database. (The affected table is determined by the specified layout.)

http://my.server.com/fmi/xml/fmresultset.xml?-db=Customer&-lay=web&-recid=303&-dup

-edit	-db, -lay, -recid, field name(s)	Edit the record with the specified recid from the specified database. (The affected table is determined by the specified layout.) Field names and associated field values determine what data gets written into the record.

http://my.server.com/fmi/xml/fmresultset.xml?-db=Customer&-lay=web&-recid=303&name_first=Sarah&-edit

Command	Parameters Required	Description
-find	-db, -lay, field name(s)	Find a record in the specified database and table, with search criteria determined by the supplied field data.

http://my.server.com/fmi/xml/fmresultset.xml?-db=Customer&-lay=web&name_last=Smith&-find

Command	Parameters Required	Description
-findall	-db, –lay	Find all records in the specified database and table.

http://my.server.com/fmi/xml/fmresultset.xml?-db=Customer&-lay=web&-findall

Command	Parameters Required	Description
-findany	-db, -lay	Find a random record in the specified database and table.

http://my.server.com/fmi/xml/fmresultset.xml?-db=Customer&-lay=web&-findany

Command	Parameters Required	Description
-layoutnames	-db	Returns a list of all layout names from the specified database.

http://my.server.com/fmi/xml/fmresultset.xml?-db=Customer&-layoutnames

Command	Parameters Required	Description
-new	-db, -lay	Create a new record in the specified database and table. If field names and field values are also supplied, these will create specific data values in the new record.

http://my.server.com/fmi/xml/fmresultset.xml?-db=Customer&-lay=web&name_first=Kai&name_last=Love&-new

Command	Parameters Required	Description
-process	-grammar	**XSLT only**. This command instructs the Web Publishing Engine to process a stylesheet without performing any database transactions.

http://my.server.com/fmi/xsl/stylesheet.xsl?-grammar=fmresultset&-process

Command	Parameters Required	Description
-scriptnames	-db	Returns a list of the names of all scripts in the specified database.

http://my.server.com/fmi/xml/fmresultset.xml?-db=Customer&-scriptnames

Command	Parameters Required	Description
-view	-db, -lay	Used with the FMPXMLLAYOUT grammar, -view retrieves layout information in the FMPXMLLAYOUT format. Used with the other grammars, it retrieves the database metadata and an empty result set.

http://my.server.com/fmi/xml/FMPXMLLAYOUT.xml?-db=Customer&-lay=web&-view

Query Parameters

Parameter Name	Required Value(s)	Description
-db	Name of a database (without file extension)	Specify a database as a target of the URL command. Most commands require this parameter.

http://my.server.com/fmi/xml/fmresultset.xml?-db=Customer&-lay=web&name_first=Kai&name_last=Love&-new

-encoding	US-ASCII, ISO-8859-1, ISO-8859-15, ISO-2022-JP, Shift_JIS, UTF-8	**XSLT only**. Specify the text encoding for an XSLT request. This governs only the encoding of the request, not of the output page. Encoding for the output page is set within an XSL stylesheet using the "encoding" attribute of an <xml:output> element.

http://my.server.com/fmi/xsl/stylesheet.xsl?-grammar=fmresultset&-db=Company&-lay=detail&-encoding=ISO-8859-1&name=Beech%20Street&-new

-field	Name of a container field	Specify a container field from which to extract data.

http://my.filemakerserver.net:8080/fmi/xml/cnt/data.tiff?-db=Customers&-lay=web_search&-field=photo[1]&-recid=303

<fieldname>	Name of a non-container field	Used to specify search parameters (with a –find command) or data values to be inserted (with the –edit and –new commands).

http://my.server.com/fmi/xml/fmresultset.xml?-db=Customer&-lay=web&name_first=Kai&name_last=Love&-new

<fieldname>.op	eq	(equals)	Specify a search comparison operator to use when searching on <fieldname>. Used with the –find command.
	cn	(contains)	
	bw	(begins with)	
	ew	(ends with)	
	gt	(greater than)	
	gte	(greater than or equal)	
	lt	(less than)	
	lte	(less than or equal)	
	neq	(not equal)	

http://my.server.com/fmi/xml/fmresultset.xml?-db=Agent&-lay=web&commission=.3&commission.op=gte&-find

-grammar	One of the four FileMaker XMLgrammars	**XSLT only**. Specify the grammar in which the XML data should be passed to the XSL stylesheet.

http://my.server.com/fmi/xsl/stylesheet.xsl?-grammar=fmresultset&-process

Parameter Name	Required Value(s)	Description
-lay	Name of a layout in the database specified by the –db parameter	Required by many commands. Note that the choice of layout also governs which table the command is performed against.

http://my.server.com/fmi/xml/fmresultset.xml?-db=Customer&-lay=web&name_first=Kai&name_last=Love&-new

-lay.response	Name of a layout in the database specified by the –db parameter	You may wish to return data from an alternate layout. For example, you may wish to search on a particular field (in which case that field must be present on the layout specified by –lay), but not return that field in the result set (in which case you would return XML from the layout named in –lay.response, which would not contain the field in question).

http://my.server.com/fmi/xml/fmresultset.xml?-db=Customer&-lay=web&-lay.response=web_response&-findall

-lop	and or or	Specifies whether the criteria in a –find request represent an "and" search or an "or" search. (The default is "and".)

http://my.server.com/fmi/xml/fmresultset.xml?-db=Customer&-lay=web&name_last=Smythe&hair_color=red&-lop=or&-find

-max	A positive number, or the value "all"	For a –find or –findall request, specifies how many records to return.

http://my.server.com/fmi/xml/fmresultset.xml?-db=Customer&-lay=web&name_last=Smythe&hair_color=red&-max=25&-find

-modid	A FileMaker modification ID	Use with the –edit command to specify a valid modification ID for the record being updated. If the –modid value does not match the target record's modification ID, the edit will be rejected. This is to ensure that the record has not been modified by someone else since the time it was fetched for a web user.

http://my.server.com/fmi/xml/fmresultset.xml?-db=Customer&-lay=web&name_last=Smythe&recid=10003&-modid=13&-edit

Parameter Name	Required Value(s)	Description (continued)
-recid	A FileMaker record ID	The –edit, -dup and –delete commands need to know the ID of a specific record on which to operate. Generally this record ID will be extracted from the result of a previous request. The –recid parameter can also be used with the –find command.

http://my.server.com/fmi/xml/fmresultset.xml?-db=Customer&-lay=web&name_last=Smythe&recid=10003&-modid=13&-edit

| -script | The name of a script in the database specified by the –db parameter | Specifies a script to be run *after* the query and any sorting are performed. Make sure you understand the issue of web compatibility for scripts when using this parameter. |

http://my.server.com/fmi/xml/fmresultset.xml?-db=Customer&-lay=web&-lay.response=web_response&-script=OmitDuplicates&-findall

| -script.param | Value of a script parameter to be passed to the script named in –script | The script named in –script may be passed a script parameter. |

http://my.server.com/fmi/xml/fmresultset.xml?-db=Customer&-lay=web&-lay.response=web_response&-script=Omit&-script.param=3&-find

| -script.prefind | The name of a script in the database specified by the –db parameter | Specifies a script to be run *before* the specified query is run and sorted. |

http://my.server.com/fmi/xml/fmresultset.xml?-db=Customer&-lay=web&-lay.response=web_response&-script.prefind=Omit&-script.prefind.param=3&-find

| -script.prefind.param | Value of a script parameter to be passed to the script named in –script.prefind | The script named in –script.prefind may be passed a script parameter. |

http://my.server.com/fmi/xml/fmresultset.xml?-db=Customer&-lay=web&-lay.response=web_response&-script.prefind=Omit&-script.prefind.param=3&-find

| -script.presort | The name of a script in the database specified by the –db parameter | Specifies a script to be run *after* the specified query is run and *before* the results are sorted. |

http://my.server.com/fmi/xml/fmresultset.xml?-db=Customer&-lay=web&-lay.response=web_response&-script.presort=Omit&-script.presort.param=3&-find

Parameter Name	Required Value(s)	Description
-script.presort.param	Value of a script parameter to be passed to the script named in –script.presort	The script named in –script.presort may be passed a script parameter.

http://my.server.com/fmi/xml/fmresultset.xml?-db=Customer&-lay=web&-lay.response=web_response&-script.presort=Omit&-script.presort.param=3&-find

-skip	A number of records to skip	Based on this value, the Web Publishing Engine will skip some of the records normally returned by a query and begin returning records from later in the result set.

http://my.server.com/fmi/xml/fmresultset.xml?-db=Customer&-lay=web&-lay.response=web_response&-skip=20&-max=25&-find

-sortfield.precedence	Name of a field to sort on, along with a sort precedence from 1 to 9	Using the values –sortfield.1 through –sortfield.9, it's possible to specify up to nine fields on which to sort. The precedence value is mandatory, even for a single sort criterion.

http://my.server.com/fmi/xml/fmresultset.xml?-db=Customer&-lay=web&-lay.response=web_response&-skip=20&-max=25&sortfield.1=name&-find

-sortorder.precedence	ascend, descend, or a value list name	Specify a sort order for a specific sort field.

http://my.server.com/fmi/xml/fmresultset.xml?-db=Customer&-lay=web&-lay.response=web_response&-skip=20&-max=25&sortfield.1=name&-sortorder.1=descend&-find

-stylehref	Path to a client-side stylesheet	This will cause the output document to contain XML processing instructions that link to a CSS or XSLT stylesheet. The stylesheet name must end in .css or .xsl. Used in conjunction with –styletype.

http://my.server.com/fmi/xsl/stylesheet.xsl?-grammar=fmresultset&-stylehref=/stylesheets/display.css&-styletype=text/css&-process

-styletype	text/css or text/xsl	Used in conjunction with –stylehref, specifies the MIME type of an associated client-side stylesheet.

http://my.server.com/fmi/xsl/stylesheet.xsl?-grammar=fmresultset&-stylehref=/stylesheets/display.css&-styletype=text/css&-process

-token.<token-name	Any name for a token, plus the specific value to be assigned to the token of that name	XSLT only. Tokens provide a means to pass information from one stylesheet to the next without using other session mechanisms.

http://my.server.com/fmi/xsl/stylesheet.xsl?-grammar=fmresultset&-token.name=Fred&-process

FileMaker XML and XSLT Namespaces

FileMaker's XML and XSLT publishing technologies use a number of XML namespaces. Each of the four XML grammars has its own namespace. In addition, a number of the XSLT features of Custom Web Publishing have their own namespaces as well. You generally only need to concern yourself with namespaces if you are writing XSLT stylesheets that transform FileMaker XML data.

Table 15.1 lists each namespace, along with its significance, and the conventional namespace prefix used to abbreviate it. The prefix is "conventional" in the sense that, in creating a stylesheet, you may choose any prefix you want for a namespace, but the ones listed below are those used by FileMaker, Inc., in the official documentation.

Table 15.1 Namespace Usage and Prefixes

Usage	Namespace	Prefix
FMPXMLRESULT grammar	http://www.filemaker.com/fmpxmlresult	fmp
FMPDSORESULT grammar	http://www.filemaker.com/fmpdsoresult	(*)
fmresultset grammar	http://www.filemaker.com/xml/fmresultset	fmrs
FMPXMLLAYOUT grammar	http://www.filemaker.com/fmpxmllayout	fml
Request query grammar	http://www.filemaker.com/xml/query	fmq
FileMaker XSLT extension functions	xalan://com.fmi.xslt.ExtensionFunctions	fmxslt

(*) Since the FMPDSORESULT grammar is deprecated, FileMaker makes no recommendation for a default prefix.

Other Resources

Where to Go for More Information

FileMaker

Special Edition Using FileMaker 8 (ISBN: 0-7897-3512-1) is our companion book and covers in-depth topics on the FileMaker 8 suite of products. While not dependent on each other, our intent was that these two books work well in concert. Turn to *Special Edition Using FileMaker 8* for explanations of concepts, in-depth examples, and a comprehensive overview of features.

General Information on Relational Databases

"A Relational Model of Data for Large Shared Data Banks," by E. F. Codd shows that the relational model was first conceived by E. F. Codd. This is the paper that started the entire relational database industry. Originally published in 1970 in CACM 13, No. 6, this paper is now available online as a PDF file through the ACM Digital Library:

http://doi.acm.org/10.1145/362384.362685

If you'd like to read up on the roots of the relational model (set theory and predicate logic), a pretty readable math book is *Discrete Mathematics* by Richard Johnsonbaugh (ISBN: 0-13-089008-1). We have found it to be succinct on the topics of set theory and predicate logic.

An Introduction to Database Systems by C.J. Date (ISBN: 0-32-119784-4) is a classic overview of database systems with an emphasis on relational database systems. You should consider it essential reading if you want to know your craft well.

Data Modeling and Database Design

Data Modeling for Information Professionals by Bob Schmidt (ISBN: 0-13-080450-9) gets into much more than just data modeling, but the content is great.

The Data Modeling Handbook by Michael Reingruber and William Gregory (ISBN: 0-471-05290-6) gets a lot more into the data modeling design process.

Handbook of Relational Database Design by Candace Fleming and Barbara von Halle (ISBN: 0-201-11434-8) has full coverage of design methodologies.

Project Management, Programming, and Software Development

Software Project Survival Guide by Steve McConnell (ISBN: 1-57231-621-7) is a great place to start with project management methodologies if your work still has a bit of the Wild West flavor to it. McConnell's work is all-around excellent...you can't go wrong with anything he writes.

The Rational Unified Process, An Introduction by Philippe Kruchten (ISBN: 0-201-70710-1) or *The Unified Modeling Language User Guide* by Grady Booch, James Rumbaugh, and Ivar Jacobson (ISBN: 0-201-57168-4) talks about the Rational Unified Process, or RUP, an end-to-end methodology for software design. It's overkill for most FileMaker projects, but it can be mined for many useful insights that apply to smaller projects.

Extreme Programming Explained by Kent Beck (ISBN: 0-201-61641-6) and *Extreme Programming in Practice* by James Newkirk and Robert C. Martin (ISBN: 0-201-70937-6) contain many useful ideas to be had here, especially in the area of estimating time required to complete tasks, although FileMaker Pro database development isn't completely compatible with extreme programming.

Code Complete by Steve McConnell (second edition) (ISBN: 0-73561-967-0), while the original book is over 10 years old, still is an extremely solid, fundamental book on good programming practices. This new edition is thoroughly updated. It's oriented toward structured languages like C and Java, but includes plenty of useful information for developers in any language. You might also try his more recent *Rapid Development* (ISBN: 1-55615-900-5) or *Professional Software Development* (ISBN: 0-32119-367-9).

Practical Software Requirements by Benjamin L. Kovitz (ISBN: 1-884777-59-7) is an extremely useful and readable book about developing requirements for software, including plenty of information useful to database developers. It contains some nice discussions of data modeling, among many other topics.

The Pragmatic Programmer: From Journeyman to Master by Andrew Hunt (ISBN: 0-20161-622-X) is a masterful selection of compact, easy-to-digest precepts about the craft of programming, and will benefit any software developer, regardless of the tools he uses.

Joel on Software by Joel Spolsky (ISBN: 1-59059-389-8) is a very assorted collection of incisive and often irreverent essays on various topics in software development. If you don't feel like buying the book, the essays can be read from the archives of Spolsky's website, www.joelonsoftware.com.

Running a FileMaker Consulting Practice

Managing the Professional Service Firm by David H. Maister (ISBN: 0-684-83431-6) is an essential book that will open your eyes, if you run or work in a consulting company. It explores every aspect of the running of a service firm.

The Trusted Advisor by David H. Maister, Charles H. Green, and Robert M. Galford (ISBN: 0-743-21234-7) offers plenty of food for thought for database consultants, but is more conceptual than the other book.

General Resources for Tips and Tricks

Soliant Consulting: http://www.soliantconsulting.com/

Soliant Consulting, the company the authors founded and manage, offers some materials on its site.

FileMaker Pro Advisor: http://filemakeradvisor.com/

For years, FileMaker Advisor has been the place to look for product announcements, news about upcoming FileMaker conferences, product reviews, and tips and tricks.

ISO FileMaker Magazine: http://www.filemakermagazine.com/

ISO Productions has been publishing tips and tricks longer than just about anyone. This site has two levels of content: one for the general public and one for subscribers only.

Database Pros: http://www.databasepros.com/index.html

Database Pros has the largest collection of FileMaker templates and technique examples on the Internet. Especially if you're still learning FileMaker Pro, you should bookmark this site.

FileMaker TechInfo database: http://www.filemaker.com/support/techinfo.html

FileMaker, Inc. publishes its own technical support database online. It contains thousands of articles to help you troubleshoot problems and to help you learn the important details about seldom-visited corners of FileMaker Pro's feature set.

Data Concepts Tips: http://www.dwdataconcepts.com/dwdctips.htm

Don Wieland has created dozens of tips in the form of free downloadable example files. He has separate versions for Windows and Mac.

FileMaker World Web Ring: http://l.webring.com/hub?ring=fmpring

This web ring links together more than 150 websites with FileMaker-themed content.

FileMaker Developers: http://www.filemaker.com/solutions/find/consultants.html

Trying to find a FileMaker developer or trainer in your part of the world? This site has a list of consultants and trainers in more than 20 different countries.

Hosting FileMaker Databases on the Web

FileMaker ISPs: http://www.filemaker.com/support/isp.html

After you've created a FileMaker-based web solution, you need to host it on a server that's connected to the Internet. If you or your client don't have such a server, you can find a FileMaker Pro Web Hosting provider at this link.

FileMaker News Sources

FileMaker Now: http://www.filemaker.com/news/newsletter.html

FileMaker Now is a web-based newsletter published by FileMaker, Inc. It contains news about product announcements and upcoming events, as well as a tech support Q&A.

FM NewsWire: http://www.fmnewswire.com/

Another service provided by ISO Productions, the FM Newswire is exactly what it sounds like. It lists training announcements, product update announcements, and other FileMaker-related news stories.

FMPro.org;FMPro.org: http://www.fmpro.org/

The Hot FileMaker Pro News section lists FileMaker-related product announcements and user group meetings.

Plug-ins

FileMaker Plug-in Directory: http://solutions.filemaker.com/solutions/index.jsp

or

http://solutions.filemaker.com/solutions/search_results.jsp?developer=plug-in&status=Plug-In

FileMaker's own site has the most complete listing of available plug-ins. If you need to find out whether a specialized plug-in even exists, this is the place to start. Although there are many plug-in developers, the following publishers have some of the largest selections. Note that some may or may not be compatible with the latest version of FileMaker.

New Millenium Communications: http://www.nmci.com

Some of New Millenium's more popular plug-ins include

   DialogMagic: Allows for enhanced control of standard FileMaker Pro dialogs.

   ExportFM: Enables developers to export images, sound, and movie files in their native formats. (This tool is due to be replaced by a new product known as Media Manager.)

   SecureFM: This tool allows extensive customization of the FileMaker menu and command system.

Troi Automatisering: http://www.troi.com/

Troi Activator Plug-in: Controls scripts on different computers; includes scheduling capabilities.

Troi Coding Plug-in: Adds capability to use DES encryption to encrypt and decrypt fields.

Troi Dialog Plug-in: Allows use of dynamic dialogs, including calculation-based progress bars and up to nine input fields.

Troi File Plug-in: Works with files from within a database. Enables saving and reading of files and the capability to use file and folder information.

Troi Serial Plug-in: Adds the capability to read and write to serial ports.

Troi Text Plug-in: Includes XML parsing and a variety of powerful text manipulation tools.

Troi URL Plug-in: Fills in web forms and retrieves raw data from any HTTP URL.

Troi ClipSave Plug-in: Saves and restores the clipboard.

Troi Grabber Plug-in: Records images and video from a video camera and puts them in container fields.

Troi Graphic Plug-in: Adds color container creation, screenshot capture, and thumbnail creation.

Troi Number Plug-in: Adds Dynamic Balance Functions.

Troi Ranges Plug-in: Generates date and number ranges between endpoints.

Waves in Motion: http://www.wmotion.com

eAuthorize: Allows users to authorize credit cards securely from within FileMaker. The current version supports U.S. protocols; the FMNext version will support credit card processing in England and Australia as well.

Events: Triggers scripts based on specified scheduling. Re-engineering for FMNext will ensure additional reliability.

24U Software: www.24usoftware.com

24U SimpleTalk Plug-in: SimpleTalk enables FileMaker to communicate with other FileMaker Pro clients and other applications across TCP/IP. The range of uses for this is quite impressive: trigger scripts or evaluate calculations in remote FileMaker Pro clients, or seamlessly integrate FileMaker Pro with other TCP/IP-capable applications, such as those created with Real Basic. You can also control a FileMaker solution via Telnet.

24U SimpleFile Plug-in: From within FileMaker Pro, control folder and file structures on your operating system by creating, deleting, copying, and moving files.

24U FM Template: This template file assists in developing plug-ins for FileMaker and is a great starting point for learning how to build plug-ins.

24U SimpleHighlight Plug-in: SimpleHighlight is a sample plug-in based on 24U's FM Template. It implements two functions for highlighting text and rectangular areas with a user-defined color.

24U Plug-in AutoInstaller: 24U Plug-in AutoInstaller is a utility for simplifying the installation, registration, and update of plug-ins in multiuser FileMaker solutions.

Developer Tools

Chaparral Software: http://www.chapsoft.com/

Chaparral Software publishes two tools that assist developers with the analysis of existing database solutions as well as the migration of data:

Brushfire: Creates an easy-to-read HTML document illustrating script relationships, designed to aid in refactoring. Aids in migration from FileMaker 6 to FileMaker 7.

EZxslt: Produces perfectly formatted Microsoft Word documents by generating XSLT stylesheets based on templates. Allows for a better way to do mail merges, contracts, and more.

ERwin: http://www3.ca.com/Solutions/Product.asp?ID=260

ERWIN is a Windows-only data modeling tool published by Computer Associates.

Visio: http://www.microsoft.com/office/visio/prodinfo/default.mspx

Visio, published by Microsoft, is a Windows-only technical diagramming tool that does a great job on entity-relationship (ER) diagrams.

OmniGraffle: http://www.omnigroup.com/applications/omnigraffle/

OmniGraffle, published by The Omni Group, is a Mac OS X–based diagramming and charting tool that also does a great job on ER diagrams.

WinA&D & MacA&D: http://www.excelsoftware.com

WinA&D and MacA&D, published by Excel Software, are CASE tools, useful for generating ER diagrams.

MetadataMagic: http://www.nmci.com/

MetadataMagic, published by New Millenium, is an outstanding database analysis tool. The File Reference Fixer feature is an essential tool for assisting with migration of pre-FileMaker 7 databases to the FileMaker 7 format.

FMrobot, also published by New Millennium, this tool allows the easy moving of tables, fields, custom functions, value lists, and privilege sets among files.

Conversion Log Analysis Tool, published by New Millenium, this imports the conversion log that is generated when files are converted. It presents the important issues to the user, with appropriate ranking of significance, and provides an interface so that they can be grouped by category of problem, rather than only by file, as is the default.

Web Programming

If you're going to venture into web deployments of FileMaker, you'll find it beneficial to be well read on web programming technologies. Even if you're using only Instant Web Publishing, it helps to be very familiar with how the Web works. A good—though very exact and technical—discussion is *HTTP: The Definitive Guide* by David Gourley, Brian Totty, et al. (ISBN: 1-56592-509-2). You can also consult the *HTTP Developer's Handbook* by Chris Shiflett (ISBN: 0-672-32454-7).

If you're getting into Custom Web Publishing, you'll likely be well served by a solid reference library on the fundamental web technologies: HTML, JavaScript, and CSS. In general, we've found the books from O'Reilly Press (http://www.oreilly.com) to be impeccable. Sams also has a strong lineup in this area. You can also sign up for a nifty e-book subscription service, Safari (http://safari.informit.com) to take these and other hefty volumes for a test drive.

XML/XSL

FileMaker XSLT Library:
http://www.filemaker.com/products/technologies/xslt_library.html.

Here you'll find a range of useful XSLT examples that interact with FileMaker data. Note that these files were primarily for import and export functions and are starting to show their age, but they're a great place to start with XSLT and FileMaker.

XML.com: http://www.xml.com/. This site gives access to a wide range of XML resources.

Jeni Tennison's site: http://www.jenitennison.com/xslt/. Jeni Tennison is a very sharp XML author and consultant, and her personal pages contain many useful links, documents, and references.

We find a lot of the books from (the now defunct, but purchased by Wiley) Wrox Press to be quite good. You might want to look into *Beginning XML* by David Hunter, et al. (ISBN: 0764543946) as well as *Professional XML* by Mark Birbeck, et al. (ISBN: 1861003110), and *Beginning XSLT* by Jeni Tennison (ISBN: 1861005946).

After you get further into XSLT you might also look at *Professional XSL* by Kurt Cagle, et al. (ISBN: 1861003579) or *XSLT: Programmer's Reference* by Michael Kay (ISBN: 0764543814). These books, even the beginning ones, are meaty and do presume some hands-on experience with some form of web programming such as HTML, or similar experience and familiarity with web technology. Out of all of these, Jeni Tennison's XSLT book may be the best starting point. She's extremely knowledgeable about the subject and a very effective writer. A number of the Wrox books are out of print, but widely available on the used market. The other Wrox books, especially the multi-author ones, tend to mingle generally useful chapters with more specialized ones. As a reference work, though not a tutorial, you might consult *The XML Companion* by Neil Bradley (ISBN: 0-20177-059-8). The same goes for *Definitive XSLT and Xpath* by G. Ken Holman (ISBN: 0-13065-196-6). For a tour of the esoteric power of XSLT, check out *XSLT and XPath on the Edge* by Jeni Tennison (ISBN: 0-76454-776-3).

PHP

For complex web development, we make heavy use of PHP. There's an embarrassment of riches as far as PHP books and resources go.

http://www.php.net

This is the official PHP project website, home to tutorials, to the annotated online manual (a great resource), the PHP software itself, and links to many other useful sites and resources.

http://www.zend.com

Zend is a commercial entity, founded by some of the core authors and developers of PHP, that sells a number of tools for working with and enhancing PHP.

For books, you might look at *Learning PHP 5* by David Sklar (ISBN: 0-59600-560-1). As your learning progresses, you'll definitely want to look at *Advanced PHP Programming* by George Schlossnagle (ISBN: 0-67232-561-6).

ODBC/JDBC

http://demo.openlinksw.com/

If you don't already have the appropriate drivers, OpenLink Software is the place to go for ODBC drivers for both Windows and Mac platforms. They have 30-day trial downloads so you can try before you buy.

http://java.sun.com/products/jdbc/index.jsp

JDBC is Sun's Java-based cross-platform database access technology. Sun's main JDBC page gives a nice overview of the technology. You'll also find a link to Sun's driver database. It lists available drivers for dozens of different databases.

Index